Logic and its Applications

Prentice Hall International Series in Computer Science

C.A.R. Hoare, Series Editor

Logic and its Applications

Edmund Burke and Eric Foxley

PRENTICE HALL
London New York Toronto Sydney Tokyo Singapore
Madrid Mexico City Munich

First published 1996 by
Prentice Hall Europe
Campus 400, Maylands Avenue
Hemel Hempstead
Hertfordshire, HP2 7EZ
A division of
Simon & Schuster International Group

Typeset at the Pi-squared Press, Nottingham

Printed and bound in Great Britain by
Redwood Books, Trowbridge, Wiltshire

Library of Congress Cataloging-in-Publication Data

Burke, Edmund
    Logic and its applications / Burke and Foxley
      p. cm. – (Prentice Hall International series in computer science)
    Includes bibliographical references and index.
    ISBN 0-13-030263-5 (alk. paper)
    1. Logic programming. 2. Logic, Symbolic and mathematical.
I. Foxley, Eric. II. Title. III. Series
QA76.63.B87 1996
511.3–dc20   95-49896
                                                          CIP

British Library Cataloguing-in-Publication Data

A catalogue record for this book is available
from the British Library

ISBN 0-13-030263-5

2 3 4 5   00 99 98 97

Contents

Preface   **xiii**

1 Propositional logic   **1**
  1.1 Informal introduction   1
  1.2 Logical connectives   2
      1.2.1 *Negation (not)*   2
      1.2.2 *Conjunction (and)*   2
      1.2.3 *Disjunction (or)*   4
      1.2.4 *Implication*   5
      1.2.5 *Equivalence*   7
      1.2.6 *Sum and product notations*   7
      1.2.7 *Priorities of operators*   8
  1.3 Truth-tables of formulae   9
      1.3.1 *How to construct the truth-table of a formula*   9
      1.3.2 *Identical truth-tables*   11
      1.3.3 *Interpretations and models*   12
      1.3.4 *Tautologies, absurdities and mixed formulae*   12
  1.4 Other logical connectives   14
      1.4.1 *Truth functions*   14
      1.4.2 *Monadic operators*   15
      1.4.3 *Dyadic operators*   15
      1.4.4 *Triadic operators*   17
      1.4.5 *Representing truth functions in terms of dyadic
             and monadic operators*   19
  1.5 Manipulating propositional formulae   20
      1.5.1 *Standard identities*   20
      1.5.2 *Complete sets of connectives*   21
      1.5.3 *Other complete sets of connectives*   22
      1.5.4 *Sheffer functions*   23

      1.5.5 *Normal forms*   24
1.6   The negation of propositional formulae   26
      1.6.1 *Definition*   26
      1.6.2 *Generalized De Morgan's law*   27
      1.6.3 *Extended disjunction and conjunction*   29
      1.6.4 *Duality*   29
1.7   Arguments and argument forms   32
      1.7.1 *Some definitions associated with formulae*   32
      1.7.2 *Some rules for propositional formulae*   33
      1.7.3 *The validity of an argument*   34
      1.7.4 *Mathematical if-and-only-if proofs*   36
      1.7.5 *A theorem*   37
      1.7.6 *Another theorem*   38
1.8   Summary   39
1.9   Worked examples   39
1.10 Exercises   47

2 Formal approach to propositional logic   **52**
2.1   Introduction   52
      2.1.1 *Formal systems of propositional logic*   53
      2.1.2 *Proofs and deductions*   55
      2.1.3 *Constructing formal systems*   57
      2.1.4 *The relationship between formal systems and*
           interpretations   59
2.2   The formal propositional logic system L 59
      2.2.1 *The construction of system L*   60
      2.2.2 *Proofs in system L*   62
      2.2.3 *Deductions in system L*   63
      2.2.4 *Derived rules of inference in system L*   65
      2.2.5 *Examples*   69
      2.2.6 *Notation for rules*   70
2.3   The soundness and completeness theorems for system L 71
      2.3.1 *Introduction*   71
      2.3.2 *The soundness theorem for system L*   72
      2.3.3 *The completeness theorem for system L*   73
2.4   Independence of axioms and rules   76
2.5   Lemmon's system of propositional logic   78
      2.5.1 *An introduction to the system*   78
      2.5.2 *Proofs and deductions in Lemmon's system*   80
      2.5.3 *Examples of deductions in Lemmon's system*   80
2.6   Summary   85
2.7   Worked examples   86
2.8   Exercises   92

3   **Applications to logic design**   **95**
    3.1   Introduction   95
    3.2   Simplification techniques   98
          3.2.1 *A simple example*   98
          3.2.2 *Karnaugh maps*   101
          3.2.3 *Quine–McClusky minimization*   105
    3.3   Universal decision elements (UDEs)   110
          3.3.1 *Definition*   111
          3.3.2 *A few four-variable universal decision elements*   111
    3.4   Logic design   113
          3.4.1 *Binary arithmetic adders*   113
          3.4.2 *Sequential logic*   115
    3.5   Summary   122
    3.6   Worked examples   122
    3.7   Exercises   128

4   **Predicate logic**   **131**
    4.1   Informal introduction   131
          4.1.1 *Background*   131
          4.1.2 *Universal and existential quantifiers*   133
          4.1.3 *Translating between first-order languages and the*
                 English language   136
          4.1.4 *Hints for translating from English to logic*   139
          4.1.5 *Examples*   140
          4.1.6 *Summary*   141
          4.1.7 *Exercises*   142
    4.2   The semantics of predicate logic   143
          4.2.1 *First-order languages*   143
          4.2.2 *Interpretations*   148
          4.2.3 *Satisfaction*   151
          4.2.4 *Truth-tables of interpretations*   153
          4.2.5 *Herbrand interpretations*   155
          4.2.6 *Summary*   157
          4.2.7 *Worked examples*   157
          4.2.8 *Exercises*   159
    4.3   Syntactical systems of predicate logic   161
          4.3.1 *The system K of predicate logic*   162
          4.3.2 *Discussion of the system K*   163
          4.3.3 *First-order theories*   171
          4.3.4 *Summary*   173
          4.3.5 *Worked example*   173
          4.3.6 *Exercises*   174
    4.4   Soundness and completeness   175

4.4.1 *Introduction*   175
4.4.2 *The soundness of system K*   176
4.4.3 *Consistency*   180
4.4.4 *The completeness of system K*   180
4.4.5 *Summary*   185
4.4.6 *Worked examples*   185
4.4.7 *Exercises*   188

5   Logic programming   **190**
5.1   Introduction   190
5.2   Programming with propositional logic   190
      5.2.1 *Definitions for propositional logic*   190
      5.2.2 *Propositional resolution*   191
      5.2.3 *Refutation and deductions*   193
      5.2.4 *Negation in logic programming*   198
      5.2.5 *SLD-resolution*   199
5.3   Clausal form for predicate logic   202
      5.3.1 *Prenex form*   202
      5.3.2 *Clausal form*   204
      5.3.3 *Horn clauses*   206
5.4   The semantics of logic programming   207
      5.4.1 *Horn clauses and their Herbrand models*   209
      5.4.2 *Logic programs and their Herbrand models*   210
      5.4.3 *Least Herbrand models*   210
      5.4.4 *Construction of least Herbrand models*   211
5.5   Unification and answer substitutions   214
      5.5.1 *Substitutions*   214
      5.5.2 *Unification*   216
      5.5.3 *Practicalities*   218
5.6   Programming with predicate logic   219
      5.6.1 *The resolution rule*   219
      5.6.2 *The proof strategy of Prolog: SLD-resolution*   219
      5.6.3 *Negation in logic programming: the closed-world
            assumption*   222
5.7   Concluding remarks   223
5.8   Worked examples   224
5.9   Exercises   228

6   Formal system specification   **232**
6.1   Introduction   232
      6.1.1 *A simple example*   233
      6.1.2 *A state schema*   233
      6.1.3 *Operations or events and their schema*   235

	6.1.4 *Pre- and post-conditions*	241
6.2	Notational differences	241
6.3	The Z specification language	243
	6.3.1 *Basic type definitions*	244
	6.3.2 *Free type definitions*	244
	6.3.3 *Schema inclusion*	245
	6.3.4 *Schema types*	245
	6.3.5 *Example: a computer file system*	249
	6.3.6 *Axiom schema*	255
6.4	Schema algebra	256
	6.4.1 *Linear notation*	256
	6.4.2 *Schema extension*	256
	6.4.3 *Some other types of definition*	256
	6.4.4 *Schema inclusion*	257
	6.4.5 *The tuple and pred operators*	257
	6.4.6 *Ornamentation of schema names*	257
	6.4.7 *Logical operations on schema*	257
	6.4.8 *Schema quantification*	258
	6.4.9 *Identifier renaming*	259
	6.4.10 *Identifier hiding*	259
	6.4.11 *Schema pre-condition*	260
	6.4.12 *Schema composition*	260
	6.4.13 *Schema piping*	262
	6.4.14 *Axiomatic descriptions*	263
6.5	Summary	263
6.6	Worked examples	264
	6.6.1 *Some simple examples*	264
	6.6.2 *Case study: a video-rental shop*	271
	6.6.3 *Case study: a car-ferry terminal*	274
6.7	Exercises	282

Appendix A: Mathematical background		**284**
A1	Induction proofs	284
A2	Set theory	286
	A2.1 *Comprehensive specification of a set*	286
	A2.2 *Operations involving sets*	287
A3	Bags	288
A4	Relations	289
	A4.1 *Domain and range*	289
	A4.2 *Composition*	290
	A4.3 *Domain and range operations*	290
	A4.4 *Override operation*	292
	A4.5 *Set image*	292

x   Contents

       A4.6 *Equivalence relations*   293
  A5   Functions   294
  A6   Sequences   295

Appendix B: Other notations   **297**
  B1   Alternative notations   297
  B2   Polish notation   297
  B3   Worked examples   300
  B4   Exercises   300

Appendix C: Symbols used in the book   **302**

Index   **305**

To
our
parents

Preface

General

Even though the study of 'Logic' has been in existence since the earliest days of scientific thinking, the general view of mathematical logic has changed significantly over the last 50 years or so. Logic used to be a topic studied by pure mathematicians, and its objective was the ability to construct proofs about the foundations of mathematical theory. Logic was used to find the minimum number of assumptions which were necessary to produce all the mathematical theory in a given area. Most people would still consider logic as a part of 'Pure Mathematics' rather than 'Applied Mathematics'. However, the advent of the computer has led to some very important real-world applications. As with many such developments, this has in turn led to extensive new areas of theory, and the new developments associated with logic are essential to any modern logician.

One of the first applications to arise was in the use of propositional logic and Boolean algebra to assist in the digital design process, expressing the design of internal computer operations as models in Boolean algebra. More recently, and with much greater mathematical sophistication, predicate logic has been applied to artificial-intelligence theory, and to the development of automated theorem proving. This has resulted in its use as the basis of computer programming languages such as Prolog, which are aimed at the solution of problems with a mainly logical (rather than numeric) content. Another important application has been the use of predicate logic together with other mathematics to specify real-world systems formally; this book summarizes the Z specification language, developed at Oxford University. The provision of an exact specification of a real-world system becomes more essential as systems become more complicated, and financial contracts for software become bigger.

Features of the book

This book is aimed at both computer-science and mathematics undergraduates. Many of the fundamental proofs are included, and are thorough; a number of the exercises involve the proof of theorems. However, three of the chapters cover modern applications of logic. It is hoped that these chapters will be directly useful to computer-science students in other areas of their study, and will act as motivation to students in mathematics departments.

The main purpose of the book is to introduce logic in a readable way to novice students, starting with a gentle introduction, but (if the book is covered in its entirety) to leave the student with a complete grounding in modern logic methods, and an understanding of the theory needed for most current applications. To reduce the total workload, some of the detailed mathematics could be avoided (see below) if so required by computer-science departments, and some of the applications could be skipped over for a theoretical mathematics course. It is our opinion and practice (hence the content of this book) that both categories of student benefit from seeing as much of the picture as possible.

Using the book

The only background needed for the first five chapters is an understanding of the ideas of proof by induction, elementary set theory, and the notation for natural numbers. All of this is summarised in the first appendix so that the book is complete in itself. These chapters should therefore be accessible to all undergraduates.

The last chapter (Formal specification) needs a number of further ideas from discrete mathematics. These include relations and discrete functions. Again everything required is summarised in the first appendix.

Exercises

All chapters include a significant number of worked examples, and suggestions for student exercises. These are usually gathered together at the end of the chapter, or at the end of each major section within a chapter. The exercise suggestions include where possible some ideas for computer programming work, many of which could form the basis for project activities.

The authors would be delighted to receive suggestions for further examples and exercises.

Outline

Chapter 1. The first chapter forms a gentle introduction to propositional logic. We begin by introducing statements, the standard logical connectives and truth-tables. The chapter then goes on to give methods for the manipulation of formulae, and for the validation of simple propositional argument forms. The reader is encouraged to become familiar with the manipulation of formulae.

Chapter 2. In this chapter we present formal proof systems of propositional logic and discuss in some detail the generation of results from axiom/rule systems. The importance of the soundness and completeness theorems is discussed, and proofs outlined. Two completely different and contrasting proof systems are outlined in detail and compared.

Chapter 3. This chapter introduces some applications of propositional logic to digital design. The purpose of this chapter is not to teach the latest digital electronic techniques, but to show applications which will again enable the reader to become fluent in the manipulation of logic formulae.

Chapter 4. This chapter starts with a discussion of the needs for predicate logic, and how it overcomes the restrictions of propositional logic. It describes first-order predicate logic and then looks at the semantics of first-order predicate formulae. A particular formal syntactic system is developed, and linked through soundness and completeness to the early part of the chapter and to the results of chapter 2.

Chapter 5. In this chapter we discuss methods for automating systems of logic, both propositional and predicate. The reduction of formulae to prenex and clausal forms is described. The chapter then shows how predicate logic can be used to deduce theorems automatically. The significance of unification as part of the proof process is described in detail.

Chapter 6. The final chapter outlines one of the best-known current techniques for the formal specification of systems. The chosen system (Z, for references see chapter 6) makes extensive use of predicate logic in its specifications.

A computer-science course

Chapters 1 to 4 provide the basic logic concepts that any first-year computer-science course should cover. Parts of chapter 5 might be included, or could be delayed until the appropriate artificial-intelligence or Prolog course is taken.

In chapters 2 and 4, the proofs of soundness and completeness might be omitted for a computer-science course; you may consider an understanding of the result of these theorems to be sufficient. Chapter 5 could be used to provide the theoretical background to a logic programming or artificial-intelligence programming course. Chapter 6 provides enough information to introduce the reader to the formal specification language Z.

A mathematics course

For a more traditional logic course, such as a mathematics department would run, chapters 3, 5 and 6 might be omitted. In fact, chapter 5 includes perhaps the most high-powered mathematics of the three applications chapters, and the authors consider this theory to be vital to the background of any practising logician.

Chapter 6 is a good illustration of the coming together of a variety of mathematical areas in one single important modern application. Undergraduates are far too often given separate courses in each area of mathematics, and see too little of the interaction of the different areas.

Further reading

A few references are included in the text. In addition, we would recommend the following.

For general mathematical background, see A. Chetwynd and P. Diggle, *Discrete Mathematics*, 1995, Edward Arnold, J. K. Truss, *Discrete Mathematics for Computer Scientists*, 1991, Addison-Wesley, or A. Vince and C. Morris, *Discrete Mathematics for Computing*, 1990, Ellis Horwood.

Chapters 2 and 4. One of the best books here is A. G. Hamilton, *Logic for Mathematicians*, 1988, Cambridge University Press. Another excellent text is Elliot Mendelson, *Introduction to Mathematical Logic*, 3rd edition, 1987, Wadsworth and Brooks/Cole, a classic which has been updated, and is still available. Another popular book is E. J. Lemmon, *Beginning Logic*, 2nd edition, 1987, Chapman & Hall, which is an excellent text in its own small area of the subject.

Chapter 3. A comprehensive text covering modern developments in this area from a computer-engineering viewpoint is R. H. Katz, *Contemporary Logic Design*, 1994, Addison Wesley.

Chapter 5. An excellent text in this area is provided by Ulf Nilsson and Jan Matuszynski, *Logic, Programming and Prolog*, 2nd edition, 1955, Wiley.

Chapter 6. In addition to the book by D. C. Ince, (*An introduction to Discrete Mathematics, Formal System Specification and Z*, 2nd edition, 1992, Oxford University Press) another important text in this area is J. M. Spivey, *The Z Notation*, 2nd edition, 1992, Prentice Hall International Series in Computer Science. Yet another very readable one is Ben Potter, Jane Sinclair and David Till, *An Introduction to Formal Specification and Z*, 1991, Prentice Hall International Series in Computer Science.

Acknowledgements

Many people have provided us with a great deal of help to bring this book to completion.

We would like to thank in particular the following people for their detailed and very useful comments. They are named in alphabetical order, all their contributions have been very valuable: Maurice Clint, Les Neal, Peter Schofield, David Simpson, Colin Sterling, John Truss.

Valuable discussion and suggestions of examples on the early chapters have come from Dr Ram Mohan of MS University, Vadodora, India. Helpful examples and suggestions for chapter 6 were provided by Professor Abdullah Mohd Zin and Jim Newall.

Particularly grateful thanks go to Dr George Paechter. George is a professional typesetter of mathematical text, and a high-powered mathematician in his own right. His understanding of the content has resulted in a wonderfully laid-out text, which has encapsulated the qualities of both readability and beauty.

Thanks must also go to the Prentice Hall staff. At all stages, they have given us great support, co-operation and encouragement.

This book could not have arisen without the help of many students who have attended the various courses, offering constructive criticisms, and transforming the notes over the years during which they have developed.

We thank also our supervisors and lecturers in younger days; without their inspiration, neither of us would have entered the field of logic. We mention particularly John Derrick, John Frith, Alan Rose, Peter Schofield and John Truss. Inevitably, some of the content may have a style reminiscent of the way that they taught us. We hope all such sources have been acknowledged, and apologize for any omissions. We would be happy to include further acknowledgements in later editions.

Last but not least, thanks go to our wives Michelle and Joy, who have tolerated our long out-of-hours work on the manuscript with visible restraint.

The preceding paragraphs mention everyone who has helped with the book; we apologise profusely for any inadvertent omissions we have made. So many people have helped us both recently and over the years, it is difficult to remember them all.

Finally, any errors which still remain are entirely the responsibility of the authors, and not of any of our reviewers or sources. Suggestions for corrections, modifications, additional material and exercises would be welcome at any time.

We hope to produce in the near future a complete set of worked solutions to the exercises, and overhead slides to go with the teaching.

University of Nottingham   Edmund Burke and Eric Foxley
E-mail: ekb, ef @ cs.nott.ac.uk
WWW: http://www.cs.nott.ac.uk/Department/Staff/ef
February 19, 1996

CHAPTER 1

Propositional logic

1.1 Informal introduction

We will introduce the main concepts of propositional logic in a practical way, so that you will soon have a feel for these ideas. In this chapter we will not concern ourselves with mathematically precise arguments; they will be left to the next chapter.

Let *p* and *q* be *variables* representing logical propositions. They may represent statements such as

```
This box is red.
The moon is made of green cheese.
I have money.
I am hungry.
The block is dense.
The block will sink.
```

each of which takes one of the fixed *truth-value*s T (true) or F (false). These variables will be connected together using logical *connectives* (sometimes called *operators* or *functors*). For example, it is possible to build more complex statements from the above simple statements, such as

```
I have money and I am hungry.
If the block is dense it will sink.
```

Observe the problems caused by the use of natural language here. The last example can also be expressed

```
The block will sink if it is dense.
```

and the word 'it' has a meaning dependent on a relevant word earlier in the sentence.

We do not (in this book!) consider that the sentence

```
This sentence is false.
```

can be called a statement, since it cannot be either T or F. We will also refuse

1

to admit

```
The value of x lies between zero and one.
```

This type of sentence is acceptable only if x has a fixed value. If x is a variable, then this is a function whose value is either T or F but whose result depends on the value of x at the time we make the statement. This is known as a *predicate* and will be dealt with later on in the book.

1.2 Logical connectives

The common logical connectives are as follows.

1.2.1 Negation (not)

If p is any proposition, the statement 'not p' or 'the negation of p' takes the value F if p takes the value T and vice versa. It will be written

$\neg p$

and can be described by the *truth-table*

p	$\neg p$
T	F
F	T

If p represents the proposition 'the moon is made of green cheese', then $\neg p$ represents the proposition 'the moon is not made of green cheese'. If p represents the proposition 'Pauline is at home', then $\neg p$ represents the proposition 'Pauline is not at home', or 'Pauline is out'.

$\neg$ is a *unary* or *monadic* operator, taking one operand. The operator symbol appears before (to the left of) its operand in formulae.

1.2.2 Conjunction (and)

Conjunction is a *binary* or *dyadic* operator, taking two operands. If p and q are any two propositions, the statement 'p and q' takes the value T if and only if both p and q take the value T. It will be written

$p \wedge q$

with the operator appearing between the two operands, and has the truth-table

p	q	$p \wedge q$
T	T	T
T	F	F
F	T	F
F	F	F

The truth-table could also be written in a two-dimensional form as

$p \wedge q$	T	F	q
T	T	F	
F	F	F	
p			

but this form is applicable only to two-variable functions. The first form of truth-table generalizes more easily to larger numbers of variables, needing four lines to describe a two-variable function, eight lines for a three-variable function, and so on.

If p represents the statement 'I squeeze my accordion bellows' and q represents the statement 'I press a key on the keyboard', then to express the condition that the accordion will make a sound we need $p \wedge q$ to represent the statement 'I squeeze the bellows and (I) press a key'.

If p represents the statement 'this object is red' and q represents the statement 'this object is square' then $p \wedge q$ represents the statement 'this object is both red and square'.

If, when thinking about my car, p represents the statement 'reverse gear is selected' and q represents the statement 'the headlights are switched on', then the condition that the reversing lights will come on (for which both of these conditions must hold) is represented by the statement $p \wedge q$.

Notice that, in ordinary use of the English language, 'this object is red' implies that the object is wholly red, 'this object is green' implies that it is wholly green, but 'this object is red and green' implies that it is two-coloured, which is not the same as 'this object is red $\wedge$ this object is green'.

The following identities hold for the operator $\wedge$.

(a) For any values of the variables p and q (there are four possible combinations of the values T and F to two variables), $p \wedge q$ always has the same truth-value as $q \wedge p$. This can be seen either by observing that the formulae $F \wedge T$ and $T \wedge F$ both take the value F, or by seeing that the truth-table in the second form above is symmetrical about the top-left to bottom-right diagonal. This condition is called *commutativity*.

(b) For any values of the variables p, q and r (there are eight possible combinations of the values T and F to three variables), $p \wedge (q \wedge r)$ always has the same truth-value as $(p \wedge q) \wedge r$. Again, this can be proved by trying each of the eight possible combinations of the values of the variables in both of the formulae; the two formulae will be found to take the same truth-value. For example when p is T, q is F and r is F, we have

Formula 1 '$p \wedge (q \wedge r)$': $q \wedge r$ is F, so we have $p \wedge F$ which is F.
Formula 2 '$(p \wedge q) \wedge r$': $p \wedge q$ is F, so we have $F \wedge r$ which is F.

When p is T, q is T and r is F, we have

Formula 1: $q \wedge r$ is F, so we have $p \wedge F$ which is F.

Formula 2: $p \wedge q$ is T, so we have $T \wedge r$ which is F.

This condition is called *associativity*.

Hence formulae such as $p \wedge q \wedge r$ have no need of additional parentheses to avoid ambiguity. It is also the case that (again check by evaluating the truth-values) the order in which the variables are written has no effect on the resulting truth-value (by the commutativity conditions).

The operands of a conjunction are often referred to as its *conjuncts*.

1.2.3   Disjunction (or)

The term *disjunction* and the less-frequently used word *alternation* correspond to expressions of the form 'either ... or ...' in ordinary language. The statement '*p* or *q*' takes the value T if and only if either *p* or *q* (or both)* takes the value T. It will be written

   $p \vee q$

and has the truth-table

p	q	$p \vee q$
T	T	T
T	F	T
F	T	T
F	F	F

Using the same techniques as above, we can show by evaluating truth-values that this operator is again commutative

   $p \vee q$ has the same truth-value as $q \vee p$

and associative

   $p \vee (q \vee r)$ has the same truth-value as $(p \vee q) \vee r$.

The interior light on a car perhaps comes on if

   'the driver's door is open $\vee$ the passenger's door is open (or both)'.

I will buy an object if

   'it is cheap $\vee$ I need it (or both)'.

I will run if

   'I am late $\vee$ a big dog is chasing me (or both)'.

These are all examples of the $\vee$ operator which is known as the 'inclusive or'

---

*Because this includes either *p* or *q* **or both**, the operation is sometimes called 'inclusive or'. The term 'exclusive or' would then be used for *p* or *q* **but not both**, see later.

because both cases can be true at the same time. However, consider the example

'I am sitting down *OR* I am standing up (but not both)'.

This is an example of the 'exclusive or' operator. With this operator, both cases cannot be true at the same time. This is a different operator called 'not equivalent' which will be discussed separately later.

1.2.4   Implication

The meanings chosen for logical operators have been derived from the meanings of those terms in ordinary English usage. With the 'or' operator above, there were two possible English meanings, inclusive and exclusive; we chose the inclusive version. The meaning of the statements 'if p then q' or 'p implies q' or 'q if p' is open to various interpretations in ordinary conversation. We will choose the definition that the statement takes the value T if either p is T and q is T, or if p is F. Otherwise (p is T and q is F), it takes the value F. This choice can be justified by considering the following example.

If p represents the statement 'The car is not at home', and q represents the statement 'Pauline is out', consider the statement

'If the car is not at home then Pauline is out'.

If the car is not at home, I can make a positive deduction that Pauline is out; the complete statement is T if Pauline is out, and F if she is in. If, on the other hand, the car is at home, I can make no definite deduction; Pauline may be in, or may have gone out by some other means of transport. The complete statement is always T.

Thus if the *premise p* is F ('The car is at home'), then I cannot make any deductions about whether Pauline is in or not; she may have gone out using other means of transport. We have thus chosen a definition in which, if the premise p is F, the truth of what follows is immaterial, hence the result is T independent of the truth-value of q. If the premise is T, then the combined statement is T if and only if the following part is also T.

This operator will be written

$p \Rightarrow q$

and, from the above definition, will have the truth-table

p	q	$p \Rightarrow q$
T	T	T
T	F	F
F	T	T
F	F	T

It will be seen immediately that the implication operator is not commutative, because we can find values of p and q such that $p \Rightarrow q$ does not have the same truth-value as $q \Rightarrow p$. For example let p and q have truth-values T and F respectively. Now $p \Rightarrow q$ has the truth-value F and $q \Rightarrow p$ has the truth value T.

It will similarly be observed that the operator is not associative, since we can find values of p, q and r such that $p \Rightarrow (q \Rightarrow r)$ does not have the same truth-value as $(p \Rightarrow q) \Rightarrow r$. For example let p, q and r have truth-values F, F and F, respectively. In this case p has the truth-value F so $p \Rightarrow (q \Rightarrow r)$ has the truth-value T (F $\Rightarrow$ *anything* takes the value T). However, $p \Rightarrow q$ has truth-value T and so $(p \Rightarrow q) \Rightarrow r$ has truth-value F.

The implication operator is sometimes called the *conditional* operator.

The *contrapositive* statement of $p \Rightarrow q$ is defined to be $(\neg q) \Rightarrow (\neg p)$; we interchange and negate the arguments of the implication. For our above example, the contrapositive is then 'If Pauline is in then the car is at home', which is equivalent to the previous statement, and would be written as

$$(\neg q) \Rightarrow (\neg p)$$

and again note that, if the premise is F (in this case 'Pauline is out') we cannot make deductions about whether the car will be at home or not.

The statements 'If the car is on the road it must be licensed', 'If the microwave oven is switched on, its door must be shut' and 'If I go abroad I need a passport' are also of this form. Note that in colloquial English the word 'then' is often omitted.

Artificial intelligence users sometimes write implication the other way round as

$$q \Leftarrow p$$

and read it as 'q if p'. This is another typical way of representing the same meaning in English where we often say

'Pauline is out if the car is not there'

or

'The car is at home if Pauline is there'

or

'I need a passport if I go abroad'

with 'if' in the middle of the sentence, the two parts interchanged, and with no word 'then'. We could perhaps use the word *whenever* instead of *if*, and state

'The car is at home whenever Pauline is there'

with the same meaning as before.

Note that the statement $p \Rightarrow q$ always takes the same truth-value as $(\neg p) \vee q$ and as $\neg(p \wedge \neg q)$. We can check this by evaluating each of the formulae for each of the four combinations of truth-values to p and q. In this way we are constructing the truth-tables of each of these formulae; this is covered in the next section. You will see that the truth-tables are identical.

1.2.5 Equivalence

The statement 'p is equivalent to q' takes the value T if and only if p and q have the same truth-value. It will be written

$p \Leftrightarrow q$

and has the truth-table

p	q	$p \Leftrightarrow q$
T	T	T
T	F	F
F	T	F
F	F	T

It is both commutative and associative, these properties being provable as above. (The statement $\neg(p \Leftrightarrow q)$ has the same truth-table as the 'exclusive or' operator introduced earlier.) It can also be thought of as 'p if and only if q'. The statement $p \Leftrightarrow q$ is sometimes called the *biconditional* of p and q, since it always has the same truth-value as

$(p \Rightarrow q) \wedge (q \Rightarrow p)$

or

$(p \Rightarrow q) \wedge (p \Leftarrow q).$

Once again, this can be checked by evaluating the truth-value of the function for different combinations of truth-values of its variables.

If p represents the statement 'the light switch is turned on' and q the statement 'the lamp lights', then the statement

$p \Leftrightarrow q$

represents the normal situation that the switch will be on if and only if the light is alight. You could complicate the formula to include conditions that the power supply and the light bulb (or tube) are both functioning.

Another example can be given by the statement

'I will be a rich man if, and only if, I win the football pools or the national lottery'.

If p represents the statement 'I will be a rich man', q the statement 'I win the football pools' and r the statement 'I win the national lottery', then the above statement can be represented by $p \Leftrightarrow (q \vee r)$.

1.2.6 Sum and product notations

In ordinary algebra, we use the '+' operator for addition, and the $\sum$ operator for extended addition of a number of terms. In logic we can similarly relate disjunction to addition using the $\sum$ notation as in

$$\sum_{k=1}^{4} p_k,$$

which is short for the repeated disjunction

$$p_1 \vee p_2 \vee p_3 \vee p_4.$$

It is sometimes written with a large $\vee$-symbol as in

$$\bigvee_{k=1}^{4} p_k.$$

The $\prod$ notation is used similarly for a repeated conjunction.

1.2.7   Priorities of operators

As with ordinary arithmetic expressions, some parentheses can be omitted as long as there is an agreed priority associated with each operator. The rules for logical formulae start by defining that the monadic operator $\neg$ has the highest priority. For the dyadic operators, $\wedge$ has the highest priority, then comes $\vee$, then $\Rightarrow$, then all the others (including $\Leftrightarrow$ and several others we have not yet met). The highest priority operators are sometimes said to *bind more tightly*.

Thus the unbracketed formula

$$p \wedge q \Rightarrow r \vee s$$

will be interpreted as

$$(p \wedge q) \Rightarrow (r \vee s)$$

and

$$\neg p \wedge q$$

will be interpreted as

$$(\neg p) \wedge q.$$

The fact that $\wedge$ has a higher priority than $\vee$ gives the result you would expect in

'I am hungry' $\wedge$ 'I am sad' $\vee$ 'I am happy' $\wedge$ 'I have eaten too much',

which is interpreted as

('I am hungry' $\wedge$ 'I am sad') $\vee$ ('I am happy' $\wedge$ 'I have eaten too much').

Operators of equal priority are evaluated from left to right.

As we have seen earlier, the operators $\wedge$, $\vee$ and $\Leftrightarrow$ are associative, so we can omit the parentheses when one of these operators is repeated. However, implication is not associative, so we cannot omit the parentheses without mention. It is possible to adopt the practice of omitting the parentheses from implications (to simplify the notation) and assuming that the truth-value is evaluated from left to right. Thus the statement

$$p_1 \Rightarrow p_2 \Rightarrow p_3 \Rightarrow p_4 \Rightarrow p_5$$

would be interpreted as

$$(((p_1 \Rightarrow p_2) \Rightarrow p_3) \Rightarrow p_4) \Rightarrow p_5.$$

1.3 Truth-tables of formulae

1.3.1 How to construct the truth-table of a formula

In this section we look at systematic methods for constructing the truth-table of any formula.

A truth-table can be determined by taking each possible combination of truth-values for the variables, and evaluating the effect of each operator. For the formula

$$((\neg p) \vee q)$$

we would have

p	q	$((\neg p) \vee q)$
T	T	T
T	F	F
F	T	T
F	F	T

To work out the truth-table of a formula, fill in the columns as below in the order indicated. First write all possible combinations of truth-values under the variables, then fill in the values of the lowest level operators (those acting directly on variables), and so on. For the formula

$$((p \wedge q) \Rightarrow p)$$

we fill in first the columns headed 1 (the variables), then 2 (operators acting directly on variable values) and then 3.

$((p$	$\wedge$	$q)$	$\Rightarrow$	$p)$
1	2	1	3	1
T	T	T	T	T
T	F	F	T	T
F	F	T	T	F
F	F	F	T	F

If we are interested in writing just the final result, it could be written as

p	q	$((p \wedge q) \Rightarrow p)$
T	T	T
T	F	T
F	T	T
F	F	T

For the more complicated formula

$$(\neg(p \wedge q) \Leftrightarrow ((\neg p) \vee (\neg q)))$$

the order of evaluation would be

(¬	(p	∧	q)	⇔	((¬	p)	∨	(¬	q)))
3	1	2	1	4	2	1	3	2	1
F	T	T	T	T	F	T	F	F	T
T	T	F	F	T	F	T	T	T	F
T	F	F	T	T	T	F	T	F	T
T	F	F	F	T	T	F	T	T	F

The final result would be written

p	q	$(\neg(p \wedge q) \Leftrightarrow ((\neg p) \vee (\neg q)))$
T	T	T
T	F	T
F	T	T
F	F	T

There would be $8 = 2^3$ lines for three variables, $16 = 2^4$ for four variables, and so on. The process becomes very tedious for more than four variables.
    For the formula

$$(\neg(p \wedge q) \Leftrightarrow ((\neg p) \vee (\neg r)))$$

the order would be

(¬	(p	∧	q)	⇔	((¬	p)	∨	(¬	r)))
3	1	2	1	4	2	1	3	2	1
F	T	T	T	T	F	T	F	F	T
F	T	T	T	F	F	T	T	T	F
T	T	F	F	F	F	T	F	F	T
T	T	F	F	T	F	T	T	T	F
T	F	F	T	T	T	F	T	F	T
T	F	F	T	T	T	F	T	T	F
T	F	F	F	T	T	F	T	F	T
T	F	F	F	T	T	F	T	T	F

The table can be summarized as

p	q	r	$(\neg(p \wedge q) \Leftrightarrow ((\neg p) \vee (\neg r)))$
T	T	T	T
T	T	F	F
T	F	T	F
T	F	F	T
F	T	T	T
F	T	F	T
F	F	T	T
F	F	F	T

The order of the 2^n lines in the truth-table of an n-variable formula is (strictly speaking) immaterial, providing that all 2^n possible combinations of truth-value of the variables are covered. It is best, however, if they are ordered in a predictable way, so that the tables can be inspected easily. This is usually interpreted as a *binary* ordering such as that used above. The ordering can be increasing or decreasing, giving 'TTT', 'TTF', 'TFT', 'TFF', 'FTT', 'FTF', 'FFT', 'FFF', or its reverse.

1.3.2 Identical truth-tables

We use the metasymbol $=_T$ between two logical formulae to express the meaning that the truth-tables of the two formulae each side of the symbol are identical. Examples of such statements are

$$p =_T \neg(\neg p)$$

(to mean 'p has the same truth-table as $\neg(\neg p)$', or 'p always takes the same truth-value as $\neg(\neg p)$') or

$$p \vee q =_T q \vee p$$

(to mean '$p \vee q$ has the same truth-table as $q \vee p$' or '$p \vee q$ always takes the same truth-value as $q \vee p$'), or

$$\neg(p \vee q) =_T (\neg p) \wedge (\neg q).$$

If this is the case, then whenever the variables of the two formulae take the same truth-values, the truth-values of the two formulae will be the same. (Note that in the last example only the first two parenthesis are essential; our rules for the priority of operators make the last four redundant.) Algebraic identities (which will be looked at more closely in section 5) can be expressed using this symbol. For example we can express the fact that

$\neg(p \wedge q)$ always takes the same truth-value as $\neg p \vee \neg q$

using the notation

$$\neg(p \wedge q) =_T \neg p \vee \neg q.$$

Such results can be proved by inspection, by working out the truth-tables for the formulae on the two sides of the $=_T$ symbol, and verifying that they are identical.

Notice that $=_T$ is a metasymbol, *not* a logical operator. It is used to make statements about logical formulae, it is not part of such a formula. If you are asked for a logic formula, it should *never* contain this symbol.

We say that two propositional formulae, P and Q are *equivalent* if $P =_T Q$.

1.3.3   Interpretations and models

Let P be a propositional formula. (We will use upper-case [capital] letters to represent formulae and lower-case letters to represent propositional variables.) An *interpretation* of P is an assignment of truth-values to all the propositional variables occurring in P. An interpretation is, in fact, a single line of the truth-table. For each given interpretation (line of the truth-table) a formula P has a truth-value. If I is an interpretation we say that P is T (or F) for I.

Let S be a set of propositional formulae. An interpretation is called a *model* of S if every member of S is T for that interpretation.

Example   Let S be the set of propositional formulae

$$\{p \wedge q,\ q \vee \neg r,\ r \Rightarrow s\}.$$

Which of the following interpretations are models of S?

	p	q	r	s	$p \wedge q$	$q \vee \neg r$	$r \Rightarrow s$
I_1	T	F	T	T	F		
I_2	T	T	T	T	T	T	T
I_3	T	T	F	F	T	T	T
I_4	T	T	T	F	T	T	F

I_2 and I_3 are models of S.

Note: We did not need to work out the truth-values of $q \vee \neg r$ and $r \Rightarrow s$ for I_1 because the question could be answered immediately from the truth-value of $p \wedge q$.

1.3.4   Tautologies, absurdities and mixed formulae

Tautologies

Any formula which always takes the truth-value T (irrespective of the truth-values of its propositional variables) is called a *tautology*, and is said to be either *tautological* or *valid*. A tautology is a propositional formula which takes the value T for every possible interpretation. All entries in the column of the truth-table representing the formula's value are T. A simple example of a tautology is the formula

$\neg p \vee p$.

To indicate that a formula is a tautology, we will use the metasymbol $\vDash$ as in the example

$\vDash (p \vee \neg p)$.

Note again that $\vDash$ is a metasymbol, not a logical operator.

Notice also that there is a relationship between the metasymbol $\vDash$ and $=_T$. The examples of the previous section could be written using this notation as

Using $\vDash$	Using $=_T$
$\vDash p \Leftrightarrow \neg(\neg p)$	$p =_T \neg(\neg p)$
$\vDash (p \vee q) \Leftrightarrow (q \vee p)$	$p \vee q =_T q \vee p$
$\vDash \neg(p \vee q) \Leftrightarrow (\neg p) \wedge (\neg q)$	$\neg(p \vee q) =_T (\neg p) \wedge (\neg q)$
$\vDash (\neg(p \wedge q)) \Leftrightarrow ((\neg p) \vee (\neg q))$	$(\neg(p \wedge q)) =_T ((\neg p) \vee (\neg q))$

The first entry in the left-hand column is read '$p \Leftrightarrow \neg(\neg p)$ is a tautology'. The first entry in the right-hand column reads slightly differently, but with the same meaning 'The formula p has the same truth-table as the formula $\neg(\neg p)$'. These are assertions about logical formulae, not logical formulae in themselves.

We will say that two formulae P and Q are *logically equivalent* if their logical equivalence '$P \Leftrightarrow Q$' is a tautology (which is the same as saying that they have the same truth-table).

We will say that a formula P *logically implies* a formula Q if their logical implication '$P \Rightarrow Q$' is a tautology.

Absurdities

There is a corresponding concept for formulae which always take the truth-value F. Any formula which always takes the truth-value F (irrespective of the truth-values of its variables) is called an *absurdity* or a *contradiction*. An absurdity is a formula which takes the value F for every possible interpretation. All entries in the column of the truth-table representing the formula's value are F. The formulae $\neg(p \vee \neg p)$ and $p \wedge \neg p$ are both absurdities.

It should be obvious that if P is a propositional formula which is an absurdity, then the formula $\neg P$ is a tautology, and vice versa. If any formula P is an absurdity, we can write

$\vDash \neg P$.

Mixed formulae

Any formula which, depending on the truth-values of its variables, can take both the value T and the value F is called a *mixed formula*, or more classically a *contingent*.

Example   For each of the following, determine whether it is a tautology, an absurdity, or a mixed formula:

(a) $p \Leftrightarrow (\neg q \Rightarrow p)$;

(b) $p \Leftrightarrow (\neg p \vee (q \wedge \neg p))$.

(c) $\neg p \Leftrightarrow (\neg p \wedge (q \Rightarrow \neg p))$.

Solution

(a) The truth table is as follows:

p	$\Leftrightarrow$	$(\neg$	q	$\Rightarrow$	$p)$
1	4	2	1	3	1
T	T	F	T	T	T
T	T	T	F	T	T
F	F	F	T	T	F
F	T	T	F	F	F

The final truth value can be either T or F (depending on the interpretation), so the formula is mixed.

(b) The truth table is as follows:

p	$\Leftrightarrow$	$(\neg$	p	$\vee$	$(q$	$\wedge$	$\neg$	$p))$
1	5	2	1	4	1	3	2	1
T	F	F	T	F	T	F	F	T
T	F	F	T	F	F	F	F	T
F	F	T	F	T	T	T	T	F
F	F	T	F	T	F	F	T	F

The final truth value is always F, so the formula is an absurdity.

(c) The truth table is as follows:

$\neg$	p	$\Leftrightarrow$	$(\neg$	p	$\wedge$	$(q$	$\Rightarrow$	$\neg$	$p))$
2	1	5	2	1	4	1	3	2	1
F	T	T	F	T	F	T	F	F	T
F	T	T	F	T	F	F	T	F	T
T	F	T	T	F	T	T	T	T	F
T	F	T	T	F	T	F	T	T	F

The final truth value is always T, so the formula is a tautology.

1.4   Other logical connectives

1.4.1   Truth functions

A *truth function* (sometimes called a logical operator) is a function which takes truth-values as arguments and always returns either the value T or the value F. A truth function can have any number of operands (sometimes called arguments or places). A function with one operand is called a *monadic* truth function. We have already seen the monadic truth function $\neg$. If the function has two operands, it is called a *dyadic* truth function. Examples we have already seen are $\wedge$, $\vee$, $\Rightarrow$ and $\Leftrightarrow$. These examples are standard truth functions which are fundamental to the study of logic. In this section we will consider other less common truth functions.

1.4.2   Monadic operators

There are in all 4 ($= 2^2$) possible truth-tables for monadic operators (there are two entries in the truth-table, each of which can be T or F) which can be shown as follows:

p	f_0	f_1	f_2	f_3
T	F	F	T	T
F	F	T	F	T

These four columns correspond to*

f_0: a function whose result is always F irrespective of the value of its operand;

f_1: the negation operator $\neg p$ discussed earlier;

f_2: a function which simply delivers the value of its operand p;

f_3: a function whose result is always T irrespective of the truth-value of the operand.

Of these, only f_2 (which corresponds to $\neg$) is really of interest, and has already been discussed.

1.4.3   Dyadic operators

There are 16 ($= 2^4$) possible truth-tables for dyadic operators. The 16 possible truth-tables are

p q	g_0	g_1	g_2	g_3	g_4	g_5	g_6	g_7	g_8	g_9	g_{10}	g_{11}	g_{12}	g_{13}	g_{14}	g_{15}
T T	F	F	F	F	F	F	F	F	T	T	T	T	T	T	T	T
T F	F	F	F	F	T	T	T	T	F	F	F	F	T	T	T	T
F T	F	F	T	T	F	F	T	T	F	F	T	T	F	F	T	T
F F	F	T	F	T	F	T	F	T	F	T	F	T	F	T	F	T

We have numbered the functions g_0 to g_{15}. Of these, six represent the degenerate cases corresponding to *verum* (the dyadic function which always returns

*The classical name for f_3, the function of p which is always T, is *verum*; and for the function f_0 which is always F is *falsum*; and for the function f_2 which takes the same truth-value as p is *assertium*.

value T, a dyadic tautology, g_{15}), *falsum* (the dyadic function which always returns value F, a dyadic absurdity, g_0), p (always takes the value of p, g_{12}), q (always takes the value of q, g_{10}), $\neg p$ (always takes the value of $\neg p$, g_3), and $\neg q$ (g_5), leaving ten of interest. Of these, we have already seen $\vee$ (g_{14}), $\wedge$ (g_8), $\Leftrightarrow$ (g_9) and $\Rightarrow$ (this is not commutative, so occurs in two forms g_{11} and g_{13}), leaving five new truth-tables not yet explained. The remaining five truth-tables are as follows:

p	q	g_6	g_1	g_7	g_4	g_2
T	T	F	F	F	F	F
T	F	T	F	T	T	F
F	T	T	F	T	F	T
F	F	F	T	T	F	F

We will discuss these now in a little more detail.

g_6 This is the 'non-equivalence' or 'exclusive or' operator (written $\not\Leftrightarrow$ or in some books $\vee_e$), the negation of equivalence. It will be seen from the truth-table that it takes the value T if one of the arguments or the other (but not both) takes the value T; this can be expressed as

$$p \not\Leftrightarrow q =_T (p \vee q) \wedge \neg (p \wedge q).$$

Alternatively g_6 can be thought of as the function which takes the value T if the arguments have different values, and F if they are the same. This can be expressed by

$$p \not\Leftrightarrow q =_T (p \wedge \neg q) \vee (q \wedge \neg p)$$

(where the parentheses are unnecessary, but helpful). This is similar to the use of 'not equals' between numeric expressions in ordinary algebra.

g_1 This is the 'nor' or 'joint denial' or 'Pierce's arrow' operator, which we will write as $\downarrow$. It is T if neither p nor q are T, hence the name *nor* used in some books. You may think of it as the negation of disjunction, expressed by the statement

$$p \downarrow q =_T \neg (p \vee q),$$

or that it takes the value T if and only if both the arguments take the value F, expressed by

$$p \downarrow q =_T \neg p \wedge \neg q.$$

g_7 This is the 'nand' or 'incompatibility' or 'stroke' operator or the 'Sheffer stroke function' (written $/$), the negation of conjunction. It takes the value T if either (or both) of the arguments take the value F, and so we can state

$$p / q =_T \neg p \vee \neg q.$$

They must not both be T, so that we could state instead that

$$p \, / \, q \;=_T\; \neg(p \wedge q).$$

It is the negation of *and*, hence the name *nand* used in some books.

g_4, g_2 These two functions are 'non-implication' (written $\not\Rightarrow$), the negation of implication, in its two non-commutative forms. We can express this in two ways:

$$p \not\Rightarrow q \;=_T\; \neg(p \Rightarrow q); \qquad p \not\Rightarrow q \;=_T\; p \wedge (\neg q).$$

This is the least frequently encountered of all the dyadic operators.

All of the above dyadic operators are written (in infix form) between their operands. Their priorities (if we omit parentheses) are equal, and the same as that of equivalence.

1.4.4   Triadic operators

We could use the same exhaustive arguments to look at triadic operators, those which take three operands. Few of these (there will be $256 = 2^8$ of them) are of direct interest. Triadic operators are difficult to write as operators since they cannot be expressed by a single infix symbol. We will describe a few triadic operators which sometimes occur in logic.

Conditioned disjunction

This is written

$$[p, q, r]$$

and has the truth-table expressed by the statement

$$[p, q, r] \;=_T\; (q \wedge p) \vee (\neg q \wedge r).$$

The middle operand q acts as a kind of switch. If q is T the result is the value of p, if q is F the result is the value of r. It provides a simple notation for conditional or 'if ... then ... else ...' types of sentence, but note that the 'if' argument has been put in the middle.

Conditioned Incompatibility

This is related to the previous operator, and is written

$$[[p, q, r]].$$

Its truth-table is given by the statement

$$[[p, q, r]] \;=_T\; (q \wedge \neg p) \vee (\neg q \wedge \neg r).$$

In this case, if the middle operand q is T the result is $\neg p$, if q is F the result is $\neg r$, giving the negation of conditioned disjunction as in

$$[[p,q,r]] =_T \neg[p,q,r].$$

L_2 (majority)

This is written with the operands given in parentheses following the name of the function. We now more often refer to the operands as 'arguments' of the function. The formula

$$L_2(p,q,r)$$

takes the value T if and only if two or more of the arguments take the value T. The 'L_2' stands for 'at Least two'. There are many safety-conscious control systems in which decision mechanisms are triplicated, and a majority decision of the three results is used.

The truth-table can be expressed in terms of dyadic operators as follows:

$$L_2(p,q,r) =_T (p \wedge q) \vee (q \wedge r) \vee (r \wedge p).$$

Alternatively we could use conditioned disjunction and write

$$L_2(p,q,r) =_T [q \vee r, p, q \wedge r].$$

This function could also be defined as the function of three arguments which takes the value F if and only if two or more of the arguments take the value F.

L_1 (at least one)

The notation used for the function L_2 above can be extended to define L_1 in a similar way. Thus

$$L_1(p,q,r)$$

is defined to take the value T if at least one (one or more) of its arguments take the value T; it is thus a three-argument $\vee$ operator. It can be represented as

$$L_1(p,q,r) =_T p \vee q \vee r.$$

L_3 (at least three)

The formula

$$L_3(p,q,r)$$

which takes the value T if at least three (all three) of its arguments take the value T will be observed to be a three-argument $\wedge$ operator. It is equivalent to

$$L_3(p,q,r) =_T p \wedge q \wedge r.$$

The *M*-functions

There are similar operators using the letter M instead of L, typified by $M_1(p,q,r)$ which takes the truth-value T if at *M*ost one of its arguments takes the truth-value T. M_1 is the negation of the L_2 operator. The function M_0 is like a three-variable joint denial (to say that at most zero arguments must be T is equivalent to saying that all the arguments must be F), and M_2 is like a three-variable incompatibility operator (to say that at most two arguments are T is equivalent to saying that the only excluded case is when all three are T, so that the result is T unless all of the arguments are T).

1.4.5   Representing truth functions in terms of dyadic and monadic operators

In this section we will show how any truth function (in any number of variables) can be represented in terms of just dyadic and monadic operators (recall that the only useful monadic operator is $\neg$). To do this we will use a technique known as *induction**.

Theorem   Any truth function $f(p_1,p_2,...,p_n)$ of n propositional variables $p_1,p_2,...,p_n$ can always be expressed in terms of dyadic and monadic truth functions.

Proof   We use the technique of weak induction on the number of propositional variables.

We will use as our base case the value of $n = 2$.   This case trivially holds (see section 4.3). We also need to point out that the case $n = 1$ holds trivially.

For the induction step ($n \geqslant 3$) we assume that all truth functions of $n-1$ variables can be written in terms of dyadic and monadic truth functions. It can now be shown that $f(p_1,p_2,...,p_n)$ can always be defined in terms of truth functions in $n-1$ variables.

All we need to do is to fix the value of one of the variables (say p_1) at T, and this leaves an $(n-1)$-variable truth function representing the value when p_1 is T, say $f_1(p_2,...,p_n)$. There will similarly be a second $(n-1)$-variable truth function representing the value when p_1 is F, say $f_2(p_2,..., p_n)$.   These can then be combined with p_1 as in

$$f(p_1,p_2,...,p_n) =_T (p_1 \wedge f_1(p_2,...,p_n)) \vee (\neg p_1 \wedge f_2(p_2,...,p_n)),$$

where the functions f_1 and f_2 are the two halves of the truth-table corresponding to $p_1 = T$ and $p_1 = F$, respectively.   Thus we have shown that $f(p_1,p_2,...,p_n)$ can be defined in terms of truth functions with $n-1$ variables together with the operators $\neg$, $\wedge$ and $\vee$. Hence by induction, $f(p_1,p_2,...,p_n)$ can be expressed in terms of dyadic and monadic truth functions.

*Induction *must* be understood for other proofs later in this book. See Appendix 1 for a short discussion on induction.

The above could also be expressed using conditioned disjunction in the definition as in

$$f(p_1, p_2, \ldots, p_n) =_T [f_1(p_2, \ldots, p_n), p_1, f_2(p_2, \ldots, p_n)]$$

and we showed above that conditioned disjunction can be expressed in terms of conjunction, disjunction and negation.

It is possible to define f_1 and f_2 more specifically as follows:

$$f_1(p_2, \ldots, p_n) =_T f(T, p_2, \ldots, p_n); \qquad f_2(p_2, \ldots, p_n) =_T f(F, p_2, \ldots, p_n).$$

The result now follows for all values of n by weak induction.

1.5 Manipulating propositional formulae

We are often presented with propositional formulae which require manipulation or simplification. In this section we will see how formulae can be rewritten in different forms while retaining the same truth-table (and so remaining in some sense equivalent to the original formula).

1.5.1 Standard identities

Let p, q and r be variables representing any propositions. The following identities allow us to rewrite certain formulae as equivalent ones. Some of these have already been encountered, but they are repeated in order to provide a comprehensive list.

1	$p \vee p =_T p$	
2	$p \wedge p =_T p$	
3	$(p \vee q) \vee r =_T p \vee (q \vee r)$	Associativity of $\vee$
4	$(p \wedge q) \wedge r =_T p \wedge (q \wedge r)$	Associativity of $\wedge$
5	$p \vee q =_T q \vee p$	Commutativity of $\vee$
6	$p \wedge q =_T q \wedge p$	Commutativity of $\wedge$
7	$p \vee (q \wedge r) =_T (p \vee q) \wedge (p \vee r)$	Distributivity of $\vee$ over $\wedge$
8	$p \wedge (q \vee r) =_T (p \wedge q) \vee (p \wedge r)$	Distributivity of $\wedge$ over $\vee$
9	$p \vee T =_T T$	
10	$p \wedge F =_T F$	
11	$p \vee F =_T p$	
12	$p \wedge T =_T p$	
13	$p \vee \neg p =_T T$	
14	$p \wedge \neg p =_T F$	
15	$\neg(p \vee q) =_T \neg p \wedge \neg q$	De Morgan's law
16	$\neg(p \wedge q) =_T \neg p \vee \neg q$	De Morgan's law
17	$p \Rightarrow q =_T \neg p \vee q$	
18	$p \Leftrightarrow q =_T (p \Rightarrow q) \wedge (q \Rightarrow p)$	

19      $p \Rightarrow q =_T \neg q \Rightarrow \neg p$ Contrapositive
20          $\neg\neg p =_T p$

Each of 1–20 above can be verified using truth-tables. Formulae can be substituted for the variables using the substitution rule of section 3.5 above.

Example   Without using truth-tables show that

$\neg p \wedge ((r \wedge s) \vee (r \wedge \neg s)) \wedge (p \vee q) =_T \neg p \wedge q \wedge r.$

Solution

$\neg p \wedge ((r \wedge s) \vee (r \wedge \neg s)) \wedge (p \vee q)$

$\qquad =_T ((r \wedge s) \vee (r \wedge \neg s)) \wedge \neg p \wedge (p \vee q)$ (by rule 6)

$\qquad =_T (r \wedge (s \vee \neg s)) \wedge \neg p \wedge (p \vee q)$ (by rule 8)

$\qquad =_T (r \wedge T) \wedge \neg p \wedge (p \vee q)$ (by rule 13)

$\qquad =_T r \wedge \neg p \wedge (p \vee q)$ (by rule 12)

$\qquad =_T r \wedge ((\neg p \wedge p) \vee (\neg p \wedge q))$ (by rule 8)

$\qquad =_T r \wedge (F \vee (\neg p \wedge q))$ (by rule 14)

$\qquad =_T r \wedge \neg p \wedge q$ (by rule 11)

$\qquad =_T \neg p \wedge q \wedge r$ (by rule 6).

Throughout the proof we used the associativity of $\wedge$ (identity 4 above) without explicitly mentioning it. After some practice you will find yourself applying several of these identities at one step.

Example   Prove that

$p \wedge (p \vee q) =_T p.$

Solution

$p \wedge (p \vee q) =_T (p \vee F) \wedge (p \vee q)$ (by rule 11)

$\qquad =_T p \vee (F \wedge q)$ (by rule 7)

$\qquad =_T p \vee F$ (by rule 10)

$\qquad =_T p$ (by rule 11).

1.5.2   Complete sets of connectives

Definitions

(a) If a set of operators can be used to define all possible truth functions (propositional formulae) then it is said to be *complete* (the word 'adequate' is used in some textbooks).

(b) The metasymbol $=_{df}$ is read as 'is defined to be'*. We must distinguish here between $=_T$ and $=_{df}$. These two concepts are very similar. We could in fact, use $=_T$ instead of $=_{df}$. However, there is a difference in emphasis. $P =_T Q$ means that two propositional formulae, P and Q, have identical truth-tables. $P =_{df} Q$ means that we are *defining* the statement on the left P as the statement Q (when P is written, this is to be interpreted as Q). Of course, it would not be sensible to write $P =_{df} Q$ if P did not have exactly the same truth-table as Q. The $=_{df}$ symbol is used because, in this section, we wish to write formulae using only certain connectives.

It will be seen that, for example, all the dyadic operators can be defined in terms of $\neg$ and $\vee$ as follows:

$$p \Rightarrow q =_{df} \neg p \vee q;$$
$$p \nRightarrow q =_{df} \neg(\neg p \vee q);$$
$$p \wedge q =_{df} \neg(\neg p \vee \neg q);$$
$$p \,/\, q =_{df} \neg p \vee \neg q;$$
$$p \downarrow q =_{df} \neg(p \vee q);$$

$$p \Leftrightarrow q =_{df} (p \wedge q) \vee (p \downarrow q) \qquad \text{(using } \wedge \text{ and } \downarrow \text{)};$$
$$p \nLeftrightarrow q =_{df} \neg(p \Leftrightarrow q) \qquad \text{(using } \Leftrightarrow \text{)}.$$

Although the definition of $\Leftrightarrow$ is in terms of $\wedge$ and $\downarrow$, it is really in terms of $\vee$ and $\neg$ since $\wedge$ and $\downarrow$ have already been defined in terms of operators in our initial set.

Theorem The set $\{\vee, \neg\}$ is a complete set of connectives.

Proof In section 4.5 we showed that all propositional formulae can be represented in terms of dyadic and monadic functions and we have just seen that that all dyadic functions can be represented in terms of $\vee$ and $\neg$. Hence all propositional formulae can be represented in terms of $\vee$ and $\neg$.

1.5.3 Other complete sets of connectives

We may wish to know which other sets of operators are complete. To show that a set of operators is complete it is sufficient to show that $\neg$ and $\vee$ can be defined in terms of these operators since $\neg$ and $\vee$ form a complete set.

Example The set $\{\wedge, \neg\}$ is a complete set since $p \vee q =_{df} \neg (p \wedge \neg q)$. This means that whenever $p \vee q$ occurs in an expression we can replace it by $\neg p \wedge \neg q$. Now by the last theorem, all expressions can be written in terms of $\vee$ and $\neg$ and so by performing the replacement all expressions can be written in terms of $\wedge$ and $\neg$.

*Note again that $=_{df}$ is a metasymbol, not a logical operator. The operation we are defining is always on the left, and the formula defining it on the right.

The commonly used complete sets are

$\{\neg, \vee\}$,

$\{\neg, \wedge\}$,

$\{\neg, \Rightarrow\}$,

$\{\neg$, conditioned disjunction$\}$.

Any exercise in this book asking for proof of completeness of a set of operators will make it clear whether you are being expected to prove completeness *ab initio* by defining all dyadic operators, or whether you may merely define $\neg$ and $\vee$, and quote the result that these form a complete set.

An important practical application of this theory is that, if we possess mechanisms which can perform negation and disjunction functions, then they can be combined to construct mechanisms to represent absolutely any formula.

1.5.4   Sheffer functions

Joint denial and incompatibility have a special property, in that either of them forms a complete set on its own, so that each one can define all the other dyadic operators. Using incompatibility, for example, we can define $\neg$ using

$\neg p =_{\mathrm{df}} p\,/\,p$

and can use that definition of negation with incompatibility to define $\vee$ using

$p \vee q =_{\mathrm{df}} (\neg p)\,/\,(\neg q)$

Alternatively we could have written a full definition for $\vee$ in terms of $/$, as in

$p \vee q =_{\mathrm{df}} (p\,/\,p)\,/\,(q\,/\,q)$.

Since we can define both $\neg$ and $\vee$ in terms of $/$, we can define all operators, and so $/$ is complete on its own. Such functions (complete on their own) are called *Sheffer functions*, not to be confused with the Sheffer stroke function itself.

If we wish to construct a practical device to represent some logical formula and we have a basic unit which can represent a Sheffer function such as incompatibility, then a number of these units can be used to represent any formula we require.

There is another property which functions can have, and such functions are classed as *pseudo-Sheffer functions*. These are functions which are complete in themselves if use of the logical constants T and F is permitted. For example, with non-implication and the logical constants negation can be defined as

$\neg p =_{\mathrm{df}} \mathrm{T} \not\Rightarrow p$

and disjunction as

$$p \vee q =_{df} \neg(\neg p \Rightarrow q).$$

These results demonstrate that $\Rightarrow$ is a pseudo-Sheffer function. (Remember that $p \Rightarrow q$ has the same truth-table as $p \wedge \neg q$.)

Similarly, conditioned disjunction is a pseudo-Sheffer function since we can define negation by

$$\neg p =_{df} [F, p, T]$$

and disjunction by

$$p \vee q =_{df} [T, p, q].$$

1.5.5   Normal forms

In order to compare formulae, it is useful to have a standard form in which they can be expressed.

Disjunctive normal form and full disjunctive normal form

For any formula in the n propositional variables $p_1, p_2, \ldots, p_n$ which is not an absurdity (it must therefore take the truth-value T for at least one combination of truth-values of its variables, or we could say that it must have a model) there is a logically equivalent formula of the form

$$U \vee V \vee W \vee \cdots$$

(a disjunction of a number of terms) where the disjuncts $U, V, W, \ldots$ each take the form

$$P_1 \wedge P_2 \wedge \cdots \wedge P_n$$

(a conjunction of exactly n terms) where P_i is either p_i (the ith variable) or $\neg p_i$ (the negation of the ith variable). This is known as the *full disjunctive normal form* or *FDNF* of the original formula.

Note that in the formula

$$U \vee V \vee W \vee \cdots$$

we have not specified how many terms there are, whereas in the formula

$$P_1 \wedge P_2 \wedge \cdots \wedge P_n$$

there are exactly n (the number of variables) terms.

To write any formula in full disjunctive normal form, pick out each T entry in the truth-table, express that entry as a conjunction of all the variables or their negations, and then disjoin (form the disjunction of) the entries. For the formula

$$(\neg(p \wedge q) \Leftrightarrow ((\neg p) \vee (\neg r))),$$

work out the truth-table and use the following table:

p	q	r	$(\neg(p \wedge q) \Leftrightarrow ((\neg p) \vee (\neg r)))$	conjunct
T	T	T	T	$p \wedge q \wedge r$
T	T	F	F	
T	F	T	F	
T	F	F	T	$p \wedge \neg q \wedge \neg r$
F	T	T	T	$\neg p \wedge q \wedge r$
F	T	F	T	$\neg p \wedge q \wedge \neg r$
F	F	T	T	$\neg p \wedge \neg q \wedge r$
F	F	F	T	$\neg p \wedge \neg q \wedge \neg r$

The FDNF of this formula is thus

$$(p \wedge q \wedge r) \vee (p \wedge \neg q \wedge \neg r)$$

$$\vee (\neg p \wedge q \wedge r) \vee (\neg p \wedge q \wedge \neg r)$$

$$\vee (\neg p \wedge \neg q \wedge r) \vee (\neg p \wedge \neg q \wedge \neg r).$$

(The parentheses are strictly unnecessary, but make the meaning clearer.)

The number of disjuncts in a FDNF formula is thus the number of T entries in the truth-table. Each conjunction of variables or their negations takes the value T only at one point in the truth-table, so that the expression

$$\neg p \wedge \neg q \wedge r$$

for example takes the value T only on the line where p, q and r are F, F and T, respectively. When we combine several of these by disjunction, the resulting formula is T at each of these points in the truth-table, but will remain F elsewhere.

The reason for the restriction that the formula must not be an absurdity now becomes obvious; if it is an absurdity, there are no T entries on which to base the FDNF.

We will need to distinguish elsewhere in this book between *disjunctive normal form* as opposed to *full disjunctive normal form*. It will be apparent that the full disjunctive normal form is often open to simplification. The example used here can be expressed as

$$(p \wedge q \wedge r) \vee (p \wedge \neg q \wedge \neg r) \vee \neg p.$$

Similar terms (terms which differ only in whether a particular variable is negated or not) can be combined. The term *disjunctive normal form* (DNF) refers to any formula consisting of the disjunction of a number of conjunctions, where the conjunctions need not necessarily involve all of the variables.

Full conjunctive normal form and conjunctive normal form

There is also *full conjunctive normal form* or *FCNF*, a similar concept to FDNF, but this time applicable only to a function which is not a tautology. The full definition is as follows.

For any formula in the n variables $p_1, p_2, ..., p_n$ which is not a tautology (one which takes the truth-value F for at least one combination of truth-values of its variables) there is a logically equivalent formula of the form

$$U \wedge V \wedge W \wedge \cdots$$

(a conjunction of terms) where $U, V, W, ...$ each take the form

$$P_1 \vee P_2 \vee \cdots \vee P_n$$

(a disjunction of exactly n terms) where P_i is either p_i or $\neg p_i$. Thus the FCNF of a formula is a conjunction of a number of terms, each of which is a disjunction of exactly n terms, either variables or their negation.

Using the same formula as our FDNF example, its full conjunctive normal form is

$$(\neg p \vee \neg q \vee r) \wedge (\neg p \vee q \vee \neg r).$$

There is now one term for each F entry in the truth-table, and each entry is represented by the disjunction of the negations of the variable values for that entry. Each of the terms such as

$$\neg p \vee \neg q \vee r$$

(corresponding to the third line of the truth-table) is now T everywhere except at the chosen single position in the truth-table. This one is T everywhere except at the single position where p and q are T and r is F. The term

$$\neg p \vee q \vee \neg r$$

is T everywhere except where p and r are T and q is F. When we combine several such terms with conjunction, the result will be T everywhere except at the combination of the F points of each of the terms.

It will be seen that, in the example we have used, six of the eight entries in the truth-table were T, and two were F. The FDNF of the formula thus involved six terms disjuncted together, while the FCNF involved two terms conjuncted.

Again, we will use the term *conjunctive normal form* (CNF) as opposed to *full conjunctive normal form* to describe formulae in which not all of the variables need to appear in each of the conjuncts.

1.6   The negation of propositional formulae

1.6.1   Definition

Given a propositional formula P, the negation of P is simply $\neg P$. However, if a propositional formula is negated, we often need to use the methods of section 5 to simplify it.

Example   Convert the following English sentence into propositional logic, negate it and convert the negation back into English.

'If the creature has long ears and big teeth it is a rabbit.'

Solution

Let p stand for 'the creature has long ears'.
Let q stand for 'the creature has big teeth'.
Let r stand for 'the creature is a rabbit'.

The logical form of this sentence obtained directly from the English is

$(p \wedge q) \Rightarrow r.$

This can be transformed to

$\neg(p \wedge q) \vee r$

and then to

$\neg p \vee \neg q \vee r.$

The negation of this last formula is

$\neg(\neg p \vee \neg q \vee r),$

which we can rewrite as

$p \wedge q \wedge \neg r.$

The corresponding English statement is

'The creature has long ears, big teeth and is not a rabbit'.

1.6.2   Generalized De Morgan's law

Let P be a fully bracketed formula containing as operators only $\neg$, $\wedge$ and $\vee$. By fully bracketed we mean that, for every occurrence of an operator (we have one monadic and two dyadic) the operator and its corresponding operands are enclosed in brackets. We know by section 5 that any propositional formulae can be put in this form. Now we will define a new formula P^* as the formula obtained from P using the following two rules.

Rule 1: Replace every occurrence of $\wedge$ by $\vee$ and of $\vee$ by $\wedge$;
Rule 2: Replace each negated propositional variable $\neg p$ by p and each un-negated propositional variable p by $\neg p$.

Negations other than at the level of a propositional variable are not affected. The formula must be fully bracketed to ensure that the binding of operators (the operands on which they operate) does not change under the transformation.

Some examples of the transformation are

P	$P*$
$(\neg(p \wedge \neg q))$	$(\neg(\neg p \vee q))$
$(\neg p \vee q)$	$(p \wedge \neg q)$
$((\neg(p_1 \vee \neg p_2)) \wedge \neg p_3)$	$((\neg(\neg p_1 \wedge p_2)) \vee p_3)$

Theorem $P*$ is the negation of P.

Proof   We use strong induction on the *length* of the formula, which is defined for the purpose of this exercise only as the number of operators ($\neg$, $\wedge$, $\vee$) in the formula, excluding negations acting immediately on propositional variables. Note that the length of $P*$ (the above definition) will always be the same as the length of P.

What we are proving can be expressed using our metasymbols as

$$\models \neg P \Leftrightarrow P*$$

or

$$\neg P =_T P*.$$

These are equivalent statements using different metasymbols.

Base case.   The base case of our induction proof is to prove the theorem for formulae of length zero.

If the formula P has length zero it must be of the form p or $\neg p$ for some variable p, the formula consisting simply of a variable or its negation. Then $P*$ is $\neg p$ or p respectively, which has the same truth-table in both cases as $\neg P$. The base case of our induction proof is thus proved.

Induction step.   We now assume that the theorem holds for all lengths up to a given value. Note that the formula P must be either of the form $(\neg Q)$, or of the form $(Q \wedge R)$ or of the form $(Q \vee R)$ for some formulae Q and R.

Case 1.   Assume that P is of the form $(\neg Q)$. Since the length of Q is one less than the length of $(\neg Q)$, the induction hypothesis tells us that the theorem is true for the formula Q, so that we can assume

$$Q* =_T (\neg Q).$$

The transformation of the formula P is the formula $(\neg Q*)$, since the transformation will not affect the leading negation. So, by the induction hypothesis, $P*$ is equivalent to $(\neg\neg Q)$, which has the same truth-table as Q, and so is equivalent to the formula $(\neg P)$.

Case 2.   In this case we assume that P is of the form $(Q \wedge R)$. The induction hypothesis holds for both Q and R separately, since they must both have length less than that of P. (Note that this is why we use strong induction here, rather than weak induction.) Then $P*$ is the formula $(Q* \vee R*)$, and so, by the assumptions of the induction hypothesis, $Q*$ has the truth-table of $\neg Q$, and $R*$ has that of $\neg R$. Thus $P*$ is equivalent to $((\neg Q) \vee (\neg R))$, which by the methods of section 4 is equivalent to $(\neg (Q \wedge R))$ which itself is the formula $(\neg P)$.

Case 3.   We assume that P is of the form $(Q \vee R)$. The proof here follows exactly that of case 2 above, with the operators $\wedge$ and $\vee$ interchanged.

1.6.3   Extended disjunction and conjunction

Using a notation described in section 2.6 earlier, we can write the generalized De Morgan's laws as

$$\sum_{i=1}^{n} \neg p_i =_{\mathrm{T}} \neg \prod_{i=1}^{n} p_i, \qquad \prod_{i=1}^{n} \neg p_i =_{\mathrm{T}} \neg \sum_{i=1}^{n} p_i,$$

where Σ is interpreted as repeated disjunction, and Π as repeated conjunction.

1.6.4   Duality

There are at least two definitions of the concept of duality in logic. They can be shown to be exactly equivalent. We will write the dual of any formula P as P^{D}.

The Rose definition of duality

This is the definition due to Alan Rose; it applies to absolutely any formula or function, and is generally the most convenient to use. To find the dual of any formula or function, take its truth-table, and replace T by F and F by T everywhere. By everywhere, we mean everywhere, both the values inside (the function values) and outside (the variable values) the truth-table. The new truth-table defines the dual; this definition defines the dual in terms of a truth-table, we can then if required express that truth-table as a formula in any way if we wish.

We first give as a first simple example the truth-table of the conjunction operator.

p	q	$p \wedge q$	p	q	$(p \wedge q)^{\mathrm{D}}$	p	q	$(p \wedge q)^{\mathrm{D}}$
T	T	T	F	F	F	T	T	T
T	F	F	F	T	T	T	F	T
F	T	F	T	F	T	F	T	T
F	F	F	T	T	T	F	F	F

The first table represents the truth-table of the function $p \wedge q$. The second table is that obtained by interchanging T and F everywhere in the first. The third table is the second reordered into the conventional binary ordering of variable truth-values (by reversing the order of the lines). The dual by inspection has the same truth-table as $p \vee q$, so that we can write

$$(p \wedge q)^D =_T p \vee q.$$

Alternatively we can say that $\vee$ is the dual operator of $\wedge$.

For a more complicated function such as

$$(p \vee q) \Rightarrow r,$$

we have the following sequence of truth-tables. First, we write the truth-table of the original function.

p	q	r	$(p \vee q) \Rightarrow r$
T	T	T	T
T	T	F	F
T	F	T	T
T	F	F	F
F	T	T	T
F	T	F	F
F	F	T	T
F	F	F	T

The dual by Rose's definition is written by interchanging T and F entries everywhere.

p	q	r	$((p \vee q) \Rightarrow r)^D$
F	F	F	F
F	F	T	T
F	T	F	F
F	T	T	T
T	F	F	F
T	F	T	T
T	T	F	F
T	T	T	F

As the final operation, this table is reprinted in the conventional order, giving

p	q	r	$((p \vee q) \Rightarrow r)^D$
T	T	T	F
T	T	F	F
T	F	T	T
T	F	F	F
F	T	T	T
F	T	F	F
F	F	T	T
F	F	F	F

The truth-table of the dual function can now be expressed as a direct formula of its variables using any of the standard truth-table simplification techniques. One possible formula obtained by inspection is

$$(p/q) \wedge r$$

but there are many others. Note again that this definition of a dual gives a truth-table, not a specific formula.

We can thus write the dual relationship as

$$((p \vee q) \Rightarrow r)^D =_T (p/q) \wedge r.$$

In general, we can write for any function f

$$f(p,q,r)^D =_T \neg f(\neg p, \neg q, \neg r)$$

since the dual can be obtained by negating the variables and the result.

Using this definition of duality, we can now talk of the dual of a functor as well as the dual of a formula. You will find by using the above operations that the dual of the formula $p \wedge q$ is the formula $p \vee q$; we will now say that the dual of the operator $\wedge$ is the operator $\vee$; the dual of $\vee$ is $\wedge$.

You will also observe that, by this definition, the dual of a tautology is immediately and obviously an absurdity (since if the original truth-table contained only T entries, the dual will contain only F entries), and that the dual of the dual is the original function.

An alternative definition of duality

Most other books on logic give a different definition of duality. This alternative definition applies only to those formulae which consist only of propositional variables and the operators $\wedge$, $\vee$ and $\neg$. However, we have already seen that every propositional formula can be written in this form. The dual of such a formula is defined to be the formula obtained by replacing $\wedge$ by $\vee$ and $\vee$ by $\wedge$ everywhere. The formula must be fully bracketed to avoid problems associated with the priority of operators.

In our above example $p \wedge q$ under this duality transformation becomes immediately the formula $p \vee q$. The formula

$$(p \vee q) \Rightarrow r$$

must be rewritten for this approach using only the operators $\wedge$, $\vee$ and $\neg$, for example as either

$$(\neg(p \vee q)) \vee r$$

or

$$(\neg p \wedge \neg q) \vee r.$$

Under these duality transformation rules these two formulae become

$$(\neg(p \land q)) \land r$$

and

$$(\neg p \lor \neg q) \land r,$$

respectively. Do not confuse this definition of duality with De Morgan's laws presented in section 4, where we negated un-negated variables; in this case, variables are unaffected.

The two definitions of duality can be proved to be equivalent using arguments similar to those involved in the proof of the generalized De Morgan's law in the previous section.

Theorem   The dual of a formula is a tautology if and only if the formula is an absurdity.

This theorem can be expressed as

$$\vDash \neg A \quad \text{if and only if} \quad \vDash A^D.$$

The proof with the Rose definition is trivial for reasons explained above. The proof with the second definition of duality is a variation of the De Morgan proof in the previous section (Exercise 1.13 (b)).

1.7   Arguments and argument forms

1.7.1   Some definitions associated with formulae

Logical implication

If P and Q are propositional formulae, then we will say that 'P *logically implies* Q' if and only if $(P \Rightarrow Q)$ is a tautology. At this stage of the book, this is saying that for any combination of truth-values to the variables of P for which that formula takes the value T, the formula Q must also be T. Thus we can write that

$$p \text{ logically implies } (\neg p \Rightarrow q);$$
$$q \text{ logically implies } (p \Rightarrow q);$$
$$r \text{ logically implies } ((\neg p \Rightarrow q) \Rightarrow r);$$
$$\neg(p \Rightarrow q) \text{ logically implies } p;$$
$$\neg p \text{ logically implies } (p \Rightarrow q).$$

Logical equivalence

If P and Q are propositional formulae, then we say that 'P is *logically equivalent* to Q' if and only if $(P \Leftrightarrow Q)$ is a tautology. The function $\Leftrightarrow$ can, of course, be defined in terms of $\Rightarrow$ and $\neg$. The concept of logical equivalence at this point is saying that, for any combination of truth-values of its variables, 'P is T if and only if Q is T', but it is possible to express the concept as 'P logically implies Q and Q logically implies P'. Examples are:

$(q \Rightarrow p)$ is logically equivalent to $((\neg(p \Rightarrow q)) \Rightarrow \neg(q \Rightarrow p))$;
$(p \wedge q)$ is logically equivalent to $\neg((\neg p) \vee (\neg q))$.

In the next chapter, when we are formalizing our system to a greater extent, we will prove logical implication and equivalence between formulae by using algebraic manipulation of the formulae. At this stage of the course, logical implication and equivalence are proved by evaluating the truth-tables of the formulae.

1.7.2   Some rules for propositional formulae

The first rule relates to the rule of *modus ponens* (MP) discussed in the next chapter. It will appear in many guises at different points in future.

Let P and Q be propositional formulae. Modus ponens (informally) lets us make the following deduction.

'If P and $(P \Rightarrow Q)$ are T for an interpretation I, then Q is T for I.'

This rule makes sense because of the truth-table of $\Rightarrow$. If P is T then the only way that $P \Rightarrow Q$ can be T is if Q is T (because if P were T and Q were F then $P \Rightarrow Q$ would be F).

Another form of MP (which follows immediately from the above form) is:

'If P and $(P \Rightarrow Q)$ are tautologies, then Q is a tautology.'

More subtle than this is the substitution rule, which we use instinctively on many occasions, but should be quoted whenever it is used. Let P be a propositional formula containing the propositional variable p. The substitution rule states:

'If P is a tautology, the formula obtained by substituting another formula for p consistently throughout P is also a tautology.'

Since $(p \vee (\neg p))$ is a tautology, then $((p \Rightarrow q) \vee (\neg(p \Rightarrow q)))$ will also be a tautology (it can be obtained by substituting $(p \Rightarrow q)$ for p everywhere in $(p \vee (\neg p))$). The truth-values of the substituted formula, $(p \Rightarrow q)$ in this case, are immaterial.

From this rule it can be proved that, if P and Q are any propositional formulae,

$$(\neg(P \wedge Q)) =_{\mathrm{T}} ((\neg P) \vee (\neg Q)),$$

since the similar formula with the variables p and q instead of the more general propositions P and Q is a tautology (by the evaluation of truth-tables).

Similarly

$$(\neg(P \vee Q)) =_{\mathrm{T}} ((\neg P) \wedge (\neg Q)).$$

In this part of the book, we wish to be able to prove whether or not certain forms of argument are valid. Each argument will have one or more hypotheses, and one or more consequents. As an example, we may wish to test the validity of the argument form

$(p \Rightarrow q), (\neg q \Rightarrow r), r$ therefore p.

In English, this is interpreted as:

Is it true that, providing all of $p \Rightarrow q$ and $\neg q \Rightarrow r$ and r hold in a particular interpretation, we can guarantee that p will also hold?

We will show in the next section that this argument is not valid.

However, if we let p, q and r stand for 'I water my garden', 'the flowers will grow' and 'the weeds will grow', respectively, we can intuitively see that the following argument is not valid:

If I water my garden then the flowers will grow;
if the flowers do not grow then the weeds will grow;
we know that the weeds will actually grow in my garden;
therefore I water my garden.

Some books would express such an argument using the notation

$$\frac{(p \Rightarrow q); (\neg q \Rightarrow \neg r); r}{p} \; .$$

1.7.3 The validity of an argument

To test whether or not the argument is *valid*, we first construct the truth-table of all the functions involved (those to the left of the word *therefore* or above the line are called *hypotheses* and those to the right or below the line *consequents*) evaluated for all possible values of the variables. The size of the truth-table obviously depends on the total number of variables involved, eight entries for three variables, sixteen entries for four variables, and so on. We then mark each of the lines of the truth-table for which all the hypotheses are true; these lines represent models of the set of hypotheses. If the consequent is F on any of these lines, then the argument form is invalid; we have discovered a situation where all the hypotheses are true, but the consequent does not hold. If the consequent is T on all of these lines, then the argument is valid.

If we have a valid argument of the form

$P_1, P_2, \ldots, P_n$ therefore Q,

we write

$P_1, P_2, \ldots, P_n \vDash Q$.

(The *tautology* symbol is used but it is prefixed with the hypotheses; if the set of hypotheses is empty the formula on the right is a tautology.) We say that Q is a *semantic consequence* of $P_1, P_2, \ldots, P_n$.

To define formally the idea of a semantic consequence we have

$$P_1, P_2, \ldots, P_n \vDash Q \text{ if and only if } Q \text{ is T for every model of } \{P_1, P_2, \ldots, P_n\}.$$

Let us now return to our garden example. The argument form is

$(p \Rightarrow q)$, $(\neg q \Rightarrow r)$, r therefore p

quoted above. There are three variables involved, so an eight-line truth-table is required.

Variables	Hypotheses			Consequent	Hypotheses	Consequent
p q r	$p \Rightarrow q$	$\neg q \Rightarrow r$	r	p	all true?	true?
T T T	T	T	T	T	yes	yes, OK
T T F	T	T	F	T		
T F T	F	T	T	T		
T F F	F	F	F	T		
F T T	T	T	T	F	yes	no, fail
F T F	T	T	F	F		
F F T	T	T	T	F	yes	no, fail
F F F	T	F	F	F		

In this case there are two lines of the table on which the hypotheses all take the value T, but the consequent takes the value F. The above argument form is thus invalid. The following example shows a valid argument.

Example   Translate the following argument into symbolic form and determine whether or not it is valid.

    (a) If I sing a song then I am happy.
    (b) If I dance then I look silly.
    (c) If I am happy and look silly then I am smiling.
    (d) I am not smiling.
    (e) Therefore I am not singing a song or not dancing.

Solution   We will represent the basic propositions as follows:

p represents 'I sing a song'.
q represents 'I am happy'.
r represents 'I dance'.
s represents 'I look silly'.
t represents 'I am smiling'.

The symbolic form of the five statements is

    (a) $p \Rightarrow q$,   (b) $r \Rightarrow s$,   (c) $(q \wedge s) \Rightarrow t$,

(d) $\neg t$,   (e) $\neg p \vee \neg r$.

The argument form is valid if (a), (b), (c), (d) $\vDash$ (e).

Suppose we have a model of (a), (b), (c), (d). Since (d) is T, t must be F, so that $q \wedge s$ is F because (c) is T. Thus q is F or s is F.

(i) If q is F then p is F from (a), so that (e) is T.
(ii) If s is F then r is F from (b), so that (e) is T.

Thus (e) is true in all models, and so the argument is valid.

Note: If you are trying to prove that a given general argument form is valid, you may find that there is no situation in which all of the hypotheses are true together. In this case, although the argument form will always be technically valid, it is useless, since every proposition is now provable. An example is

$P, \neg P \vDash Q.$

This argument is always T, whatever P and Q are. It is always the case that every proposition can be proved from an inconsistent set of premises. Such proofs are not, however, of much use.

1.7.4   Mathematical if-and-only-if proofs

Typically in mathematics we often need to prove

P if and only if Q.

This is usually done in two stages, either by the two steps:

if P is true, then Q must be true,
if P is false, then Q must be false*;

or by the two steps:

if P is true, then Q must be true,
if Q is true, then P must be true**.

Notice that * is the contrapositive of **. These two statements are actually equivalent. As argument forms, these two techniques would be expressed as

$P \Rightarrow Q, \neg P \Rightarrow \neg Q \vDash P \Leftrightarrow Q$

and

$P \Rightarrow Q, Q \Rightarrow P \vDash P \Leftrightarrow Q.$

They can be shown to be valid argument forms using the above techniques.

We are often required to show that formulae of the form $P \Rightarrow Q$ follow from a set of hypotheses. A standard approach is to assume that the hypotheses and P are true and show that Q is true. The following theorem justifies this approach.

1.7.5   A theorem

Let $P_1,\ldots,P_{n-1},P_n,Q$ be propositional formulae. The theorem states:

$P_1,\ldots,P_{n-1},P_n \vDash Q$ if and only if $P_1,\ldots,P_{n-1} \vDash P_n \Rightarrow Q$.

Proof   We will prove the theorem in both directions.

LHS $\Rightarrow$ RHS:

Assume that

$P_1,P_2,\ldots,P_n \vDash Q$ and that we have a model M of
$P_1,P_2,\ldots,P_{n-1}$.

Now either P_n is F for M or it is T for M.

(i) If P_n is F for M then $P_n \Rightarrow Q$ is T for M (from the truth-table of $\Rightarrow$).

(ii) If P_n is T for M then Q is T for M (since $P_1,P_2,\ldots,P_n \vDash Q$).

Therefore $P_n \Rightarrow Q$ for M, and it follows that $P_1,P_2,\ldots,P_{n-1} \vDash P_n \Rightarrow Q$.

RHS $\Rightarrow$ LHS:

Conversely, assume that

$P_1,P_2,\ldots,P_{n-1} \vDash P_n \Rightarrow Q$

and that we have a model M of

$P_1,P_2,\ldots,P_{n-1},P_n$.

Since P_n is T for M and $P_n \Rightarrow Q$ is T for M we have that Q is T for M, so that

$P_1,P_2,\ldots,P_n \vDash Q$.

We have thus proved the required result and have a general technique for testing conditional argument forms.

Example   Show that

$p \Rightarrow q, \neg q \vee r \vDash p \Rightarrow r$.

Solution   We will show instead that

$p \Rightarrow q, \neg q \vee r, p \vDash r$

and then apply the above theorem.

1.	$p \Rightarrow q$	Assume that this is T.
2.	$\neg q \vee r$	Assume that this is T.
3.	p	Make an added assumption that this is T.
4.	q	This is T by MP applied to 1 and 3.
5.	$q \Rightarrow r$	This is T because $2 =_T 5$.
6.	r	This is T by MP applied to 4 and 5.

We have thus shown that

$$p \Rightarrow q, \neg q \vee r, p \models r.$$

The above theorem can now be used to give the required result.

Many proofs in logic use a method known as proof by contradiction. To prove a statement we assume its negation and derive a contradiction (this is actually a central idea in logic programming). The following theorem justifies this approach.

1.7.6   Another theorem

Let $P_1, \ldots, P_{n-1}, P_n, Q$ be propositional formulae. This theorem states:

> If $P_1, \ldots, P_{n-1}, P_n, \neg Q \models F$
> then $P_1, \ldots, P_{n-1}, P_n \models Q$.

Proof   Assume that

$$P_1, \ldots, P_{n-1}, P_n, \neg Q \models F.$$

We have (by the above theorem) that

$$P_1, \ldots, P_{n-1}, P_n \models \neg Q \Rightarrow F.$$

Let M be a model of $P_1, \ldots, P_{n-1}, P_n$. Then we have that $\neg Q \Rightarrow F$ is T for M, so that $\neg Q$ is F for M, giving us that Q is T for M.

Example   Show that $r \Rightarrow p, s \Rightarrow q, q \Rightarrow \neg p \models \neg r \vee \neg s$.

Solution   Using the above theorem we show instead

$$r \Rightarrow p, s \Rightarrow q, q \Rightarrow \neg p, \neg(\neg r \vee \neg s) \models F.$$

1.	$r \Rightarrow p$	Assume that this is T.
2.	$s \Rightarrow q$	Assume that this is T.
3.	$q \Rightarrow \neg p$	Assume that this is T.
4.	$\neg(\neg r \vee \neg s)$	Make an added assumption that this is T.
5.	$r \wedge s$	This is T because $4 =_T 5$.
6.	r	This is T because 5 is T.
7.	s	This is T because 5 is T.
8.	p	This is T by MP applied to 1 and 6.
9.	q	This is T by MP applied to 2 and 7.
10.	$\neg p$	This is T by MP applied to 3 and 9.
11.	$p \wedge \neg p$	This is T because both 8 and 10 are T.
12.	F	This is T because $11 =_T 12$ which is, of course, a contradiction.

1.8   Summary

In this chapter we have given an informal introduction to propositional logic and introduced all the most frequently used logical connectives. You should now be capable of converting between English sentences and logical formulae. You will be familiar with all of the logical operators, and will be able to manipulate logical formulae, construct truth-tables and find out, for example, whether or not a formula is a tautology. You should also be familiar with the concepts of negation and duality. Finally, you should be able to determine whether or not a propositional argument is a valid one.

In the next chapter, we will formalize these ideas, and provide a more theoretical environment for activities related to proofs and tautologies. The emphasis will be on the algebraic manipulation of the formulae rather than the evaluation of their truth-tables.

1.9   Worked examples

Example 1.1   Evaluate the truth-table of the formula

$$p \wedge (p \vee q \Rightarrow (q \Rightarrow r \Rightarrow s)).$$

Solution   We will evaluate in the order

$$p \wedge ((p \vee q) \Rightarrow ((q \Rightarrow r) \Rightarrow s)).$$

p	$\wedge$	((p	$\vee$	q)	$\Rightarrow$	((q	$\Rightarrow$	r)	$\Rightarrow$	s))
1	5	1	2	1	4	1	2	1	3	1
T	T	T	T	T	T	T	T	T	T	T
T	F	T	T	T	F	T	T	T	F	F
T	T	T	T	T	T	T	F	F	T	T
T	T	T	T	T	T	T	F	F	T	F
T	T	T	T	F	T	F	T	T	T	T
T	F	T	T	F	F	F	T	T	F	F
T	T	T	T	F	T	F	T	F	T	T
T	F	T	T	F	F	F	T	F	F	F
F	F	F	T	T	T	T	T	T	T	T
F	F	F	T	T	F	T	T	T	F	F
F	F	F	T	T	T	T	F	F	T	T
F	F	F	T	T	T	T	F	F	T	F
F	F	F	F	F	T	F	T	T	T	T
F	F	F	F	F	T	F	T	T	F	F
F	F	F	F	F	T	F	T	F	T	T
F	F	F	F	F	T	F	T	F	F	F

Example 1.2   For the formula

$$p \Rightarrow q \wedge r \Rightarrow (q \Leftrightarrow \neg r \Leftrightarrow (r/p))$$

perform each of the following operations:

   (a) write out its truth-table;
   (b) state whether it is a tautology, absurdity or mixed formula;
   (c) express it in FDNF and FCNF.

Solution

(a)   Truth-table

(p	⇒	(q	∧	r))	⇒	(((q	⇔	(¬	r))	⇔	(r	/	p)))
1	3	1	2	1	5	1	3	2	1	4	1	2	1
T	T	T	T	T	T	T	F	F	T	T	T	F	T
T	F	T	F	F	T	T	T	T	F	T	F	T	T
T	F	F	F	T	T	F	T	F	T	F	T	F	T
T	F	F	F	F	T	F	F	T	F	F	F	T	T
F	T	T	T	T	F	T	F	F	T	F	T	T	F
F	T	T	F	F	T	T	T	T	F	T	F	T	F
F	T	F	F	T	T	F	T	F	T	T	T	T	F
F	T	F	F	F	F	F	F	T	F	F	F	T	F

(b)   The formula is a mixed formula.
(c)   The FDNF is

$$(p \wedge q \wedge r) \vee (p \wedge q \wedge \neg r) \vee$$

$$(p \wedge \neg q \wedge r) \vee (p \wedge \neg q \wedge \neg r) \vee$$

$$(\neg p \wedge q \wedge \neg r) \vee (\neg p \wedge \neg q \wedge r).$$

The FCNF is

$$(p \vee \neg q \vee \neg r) \wedge (p \vee q \vee r).$$

Example 1.3   For the formula

$$(p \Rightarrow q \wedge r) \Rightarrow (q \Leftrightarrow \neg s \Leftrightarrow (r/p))$$

perform the following operations:

   (a) write out its truth-table;
   (b) state whether it is a tautology, absurdity or mixed formula;
   (c) express it in FDNF and FCNF.

Solution

(a)   Truth-table

(p	⇒	q	∧	r)	⇒	(q	⇔	¬	s	⇔	(r	/	p))
1	3	1	2	1	5	1	3	2	1	4	1	2	1
T	T	T	T	T	T	T	F	F	T	T	T	F	T
T	T	T	T	T	F	T	T	T	F	F	T	F	T
T	F	T	F	F	T	T	F	F	T	F	F	T	T
T	F	T	F	F	T	T	T	T	F	T	F	T	T
T	F	F	F	T	T	F	T	F	T	F	T	F	T
T	F	F	F	T	T	F	F	T	F	T	T	F	T
T	F	F	F	F	T	F	T	F	T	T	F	T	T
T	F	F	F	F	T	F	F	T	F	F	F	T	T
F	T	T	T	T	F	T	F	F	T	F	T	T	F
F	T	T	T	T	T	T	T	T	F	T	T	T	F
F	T	T	F	F	F	T	F	F	T	F	F	T	F
F	T	T	F	F	T	T	T	T	F	T	F	T	F
F	T	F	F	T	T	F	T	F	T	T	T	T	F
F	T	F	F	T	F	F	F	T	F	F	T	T	F
F	T	F	F	F	T	F	T	F	T	T	F	T	F
F	T	F	F	F	F	F	F	T	F	F	F	T	F

(b) The formula is a mixed formula.

(c) The FDNF is

$$(p \wedge q \wedge r \wedge s) \wedge (p \wedge q \wedge \neg r \wedge s) \wedge (p \wedge q \wedge \neg r \wedge \neg s) \wedge$$

$$(p \wedge \neg q \wedge r \wedge s) \wedge (p \wedge \neg q \wedge r \wedge \neg s) \wedge (p \wedge \neg q \wedge \neg r \wedge s) \wedge$$

$$(p \wedge \neg q \wedge \neg r \wedge \neg s) \wedge (\neg p \wedge q \wedge r \wedge \neg s) \wedge (\neg p \wedge q \wedge \neg r \wedge \neg s) \wedge$$

$$(\neg p \wedge \neg q \wedge r \wedge s) \wedge (\neg p \wedge \neg q \wedge \neg r \wedge s).$$

The FCNF is

$$(\neg p \wedge \neg q \wedge \neg r \wedge s) \wedge (p \wedge \neg q \wedge \neg r \wedge \neg s) \wedge$$

$$(p \wedge \neg q \wedge r \wedge \neg s) \wedge (p \wedge q \wedge \neg r \wedge s) \wedge (p \wedge q \wedge r \wedge s).$$

Example 1.4   Construct the truth-tables of each of the following four formulae:

(a) $((p \vee q) \Leftrightarrow (r \wedge s)) \downarrow (p / (q \Rightarrow r))$;

(b) $((p \Leftrightarrow (q \Rightarrow r)) \vee q) \wedge (p \Rightarrow r) \wedge (q / (p \wedge q))$;

(c) $(p \vee (p \downarrow q) \wedge (r \Rightarrow p)) \Rightarrow ((p \Leftrightarrow q) \Leftrightarrow \neg (p \wedge r))$;

(d) $(((p \Rightarrow q) \Rightarrow r) \Rightarrow s) \Rrightarrow (p / \neg q) \wedge (p \Rightarrow r)$.

Express the formula (d) above in FDNF and in FCNF.

Solution   The truth-tables are as follows.

(a) Formula: $((p \vee q) \Leftrightarrow (r \wedge s)) \downarrow (p/(q \Rightarrow r))$.

		F	F	T	T	r
		F	T	F	T	s
F	F	F	F	F	F	
F	T	F	F	F	F	
T	F	T	T	T	F	
T	T	F	F	T	F	
p	q					

(b) Formula: $((p \Leftrightarrow (q \Rightarrow r)) \vee q) \wedge (p \Rightarrow r) \wedge (q/(p \wedge q))$

		F	T	r
F	F	T	T	
F	T	T	T	
T	F	F	F	
T	T	F	F	
p	q			

(c) Formula: $(p \vee (p \downarrow q) \wedge (r \Rightarrow p)) \Rightarrow ((p \Leftrightarrow q) \Leftrightarrow \neg(p \wedge r))$

		F	T	r
F	F	F	T	
F	T	T	T	
T	F	T	F	
T	T	F	T	
p	q			

(d) Formula: $(((p \Rightarrow q) \Rightarrow r) \Rightarrow s) \Leftrightarrow (p/\neg q) \wedge (p \Rightarrow r)$

		F	F	T	T	r
		F	T	F	T	s
F	F	F	F	F	F	
F	T	F	F	F	F	
T	F	F	T	F	T	
T	T	T	T	F	F	
p	q					

The last formula in FDNF is

$$(p \wedge q \wedge \neg r \wedge s) \vee (p \wedge q \wedge \neg r \wedge \neg s) \vee (p \wedge \neg q \wedge r \wedge s) \vee (p \wedge \neg q \wedge \neg r \wedge s).$$

The last formula in FCNF is

$$(\neg p \vee \neg q \vee \neg r \vee \neg s) \wedge (\neg p \vee \neg q \vee \neg r \vee s) \wedge (\neg p \vee q \vee \neg r \vee s) \wedge$$

$$(\neg p \vee q \vee r \vee s) \wedge (p \vee \neg q \vee \neg r \vee \neg s) \wedge (p \vee \neg q \vee \neg r \vee s) \wedge$$

$$(p \vee \neg q \vee r \vee \neg s) \wedge (p \vee \neg q \vee r \vee s) \wedge (p \vee q \vee \neg r \vee \neg s) \wedge$$

$$(p \vee q \vee \neg r \vee s) \wedge (p \vee q \vee r \vee \neg s) \wedge (p \vee q \vee r \vee s).$$

Example 1.5

(a) Using the second definition given in the text, write the dual of the formula

$$p \wedge \neg q \vee q \wedge r \wedge \neg s \wedge (\neg p \vee q)$$

and express the dual in FDNF.

(b) Using Rose's definition, write the truth-table of the dual of

$$(p \Rightarrow (q \vee r)) \Rightarrow (r \Leftrightarrow s)$$

and express it in FCNF.

Solution

(a) The bracketed version is

$$(p \wedge \neg q) \vee (q \wedge r \wedge \neg s \wedge (\neg p \vee q)).$$

The dual of this formula is

$$(p \vee \neg q) \wedge (q \vee r \vee \neg s \vee \neg p \wedge q).$$

The truth-table of this dual is

p	q	r	s	
T	T	T	T	T
T	T	T	F	T
T	T	F	T	T
T	T	F	F	T
T	F	T	T	T
T	F	T	F	T
T	F	F	T	T
T	F	F	F	T
F	T	T	T	F
F	T	T	F	F
F	T	F	T	F
F	T	F	F	F
F	F	T	T	F
F	F	T	F	T
F	F	F	T	F
F	F	F	F	T

The FDNF is

$$(p \wedge q \wedge r \wedge s) \vee (p \wedge q \wedge r \wedge \neg s) \vee (p \wedge q \wedge \neg r \wedge s) \vee$$

$$(p \wedge q \wedge \neg r \wedge \neg s) \vee (p \wedge \neg q \wedge r \wedge s) \vee (p \wedge \neg q \wedge r \wedge \neg s) \vee$$

$$(p \wedge \neg q \wedge \neg r \wedge s) \vee (p \wedge \neg q \wedge \neg r \wedge \neg s) \vee (\neg p \wedge \neg q \wedge r \wedge \neg s) \vee$$

$$(\neg p \wedge \neg q \wedge \neg r \wedge \neg s).$$

(b) The truth-table of the dual (obtained directly in the Rose definition) is

p	q	r	s	
T	T	T	T	F
T	T	T	F	T
T	T	F	T	T
T	T	F	F	F
T	F	T	T	F
T	F	T	F	T
T	F	F	T	F
T	F	F	F	F
F	T	T	T	F
F	T	T	F	T
F	T	F	T	T
F	T	F	F	F
F	F	T	T	F
F	F	T	F	T
F	F	F	T	T
F	F	F	F	T

The FCNF is

$$(p \vee q \vee r \vee s) \wedge (p \vee q \vee \neg r \vee \neg s) \wedge (p \vee \neg q \vee r \vee s) \wedge$$

$$(p \vee \neg q \vee \neg r \vee \neg s) \wedge (\neg p \vee q \vee r \vee s) \wedge (\neg p \vee q \vee r \vee \neg s) \wedge$$

$$(\neg p \vee q \vee \neg r \vee \neg s) \wedge (\neg p \vee \neg q \vee r \vee s) \wedge (\neg p \vee \neg q \vee \neg r \vee \neg s).$$

Example 1.6 Let $P_1, \ldots, P_{n-1}, P_n, Q$ be propositional formulae. Show that

$$P_1, \ldots, P_{n-1}, P_n \vDash Q$$

if and only if

$$\vDash (P_1 \wedge \cdots \wedge P_n) \Rightarrow Q.$$

Proof We will prove the implication in both directions.

LHS $\Rightarrow$ RHS:

Assume that $P_1, \ldots, P_{n-1}, P_n \vDash Q$.

This means that whenever $P_1, \ldots, P_{n-1}, P_n$ are T then Q is T. In this case, whenever $P_1 \wedge \cdots \wedge P_{n-1} \wedge P_n$ is T then Q is T. It follows that $\vDash (P_1 \wedge \cdots \wedge P_n) \Rightarrow Q$ from the definition of implication.

RHS $\Rightarrow$ LHS:

Conversely, assume that $\vDash (P_1 \wedge \cdots \wedge P_n) \Rightarrow Q$

This means that whenever $P_1 \wedge \cdots \wedge P_{n-1} \wedge P_n$ is T then Q is also T. So, whenever $P_1, \ldots, P_{n-1}, P_n$ are T then Q is T. From this we obtain our result $P_1, \ldots, P_{n-1}, P_n \vDash Q$.

Example 1.7   Establish the truth, or otherwise, of the the following argument form:

$$r \downarrow p \downarrow p \wedge q,\, r \wedge \neg p,\, r \Rightarrow (p/q),\, \neg p \ \text{ therefore } \ \neg r \downarrow p \wedge q.$$

Solution   Using the result of the previous example we can simply check that

(conjunction of LHSs) implies (RHS) is a tautology.

This becomes

$$(r \downarrow p \downarrow p \wedge q) \wedge r \wedge \neg p \wedge (r \Rightarrow (p/q)) \wedge \neg p \Rightarrow (\neg r \downarrow p \wedge q).$$

We evaluate the truth-table.

(r	↓	p	↓	p	∧	q)	∧	r	∧	¬	p	∧	(r	⇒	(p	/	q))	∧	¬	p	⇒	(¬	r	↓	p	∧	q)
T	F	T	F	T	T	T	F	T	F	F	T	F	T	F	T	F	T	F	F	T	T	F	T	F	T	T	T
F	F	T	F	T	T	T	F	F	F	F	T	F	F	T	T	F	T	F	F	T	T	T	F	F	T	T	T
T	F	T	T	T	F	F	F	T	F	F	T	F	T	T	T	T	F	F	F	T	T	F	T	T	T	F	F
F	F	T	T	T	F	F	F	F	F	F	T	F	F	T	T	T	F	F	F	T	T	T	F	F	T	F	F
T	F	F	T	F	F	T	T	T	T	T	F	T	T	T	F	T	T	T	T	F	T	F	T	T	F	F	T
F	T	F	F	F	F	T	F	F	F	T	F	F	F	T	F	T	T	F	T	F	T	T	F	F	F	F	T
T	F	F	T	F	F	F	T	T	T	T	F	T	T	T	F	T	F	T	T	F	T	F	T	T	F	F	F
F	T	F	F	F	F	F	F	F	F	T	F	F	F	T	F	T	F	F	T	F	T	T	F	F	F	F	F

It is a tautology. The argument form is therefore valid.

Example 1.8   Test the validity of the argument forms:

(a) $p \Rightarrow q,\, p \Rightarrow (r \vee s),\, s \Rightarrow q$ therefore $q \vee r$;
(b) $p \Rightarrow (q \Rightarrow r),\, q$ therefore r;
(c) $p,\, p \downarrow (q \downarrow r)$ therefore r.

Solution

(a) To be a valid argument form, the formula

$$((p \Rightarrow q) \wedge (p \Rightarrow (r \vee s)) \wedge (s \Rightarrow q)) \Rightarrow (q \vee r)$$

must be a tautology. However, it is F when all the variables are F. The argument form is therefore invalid.
(b) For the argument to be valid the formula $((p \Rightarrow (q \Rightarrow r)) \wedge q) \Rightarrow r$ should be a tautology. However, this fails for $p = F$, $q = T$ and $r = F$. The argument form is therefore invalid.
(c) The formula $(p \wedge (p \downarrow (q \downarrow r))) \Rightarrow r$ is a tautology, so the argument is valid (but meaningless, since the two formulae on the left-hand side are never true together). The argument form is therefore only technically valid.

Example 1.9

(a) Show that joint denial is a Sheffer function.

(b) Prove that the formula

$$((p \wedge q) \wedge \neg(p \wedge r)) \wedge \neg(\neg r \wedge s)$$

takes the truth-value T if and only if p, q, r and s take the truth-values T, T, F and F, respectively.

Using the definition that the dual of a formula is obtained by replacing T by F and F by T everywhere in its truth-table,

(c) write down the truth-table of the dual of

$$(p \vee q \wedge r) \Leftrightarrow ((p/q) \Rightarrow \neg(s \vee r));$$

(d) prove that the functor L_2 is self-dual.

Solution

(a) We only need to define $\vee$ and $\neg$ in terms of joint denial by the theorem in section 1.5.2:

$$\neg p =_{\text{df}} p \downarrow p; \qquad p \vee q =_{\text{df}} \neg(p \downarrow q).$$

(b) The formula is a conjunction of three terms. All terms must therefore take the value T.

$p \wedge q$, so p and q are both true;
$\neg(p \wedge r)$, so $p \wedge r$ must be false, so r is false;
$\neg(\neg r \wedge s)$, so s must be false also.

(c) The truth-table of $(p \vee q \wedge r) \Leftrightarrow ((p/q) \Rightarrow \neg(s \vee r))$ is

		F	F	T	T	r
		F	T	F	T	s
F	F	F	T	T	T	
F	T	F	T	F	F	
T	F	T	F	F	F	
T	T	T	T	T	T	
p	q					

Therefore the truth-table of the dual is

		T	T	F	F	r
		T	F	T	F	s
T	T	T	F	F	F	
T	F	T	F	T	T	
F	T	F	T	T	T	
F	F	F	F	F	F	
p	q					

(d) The truth-table for L_2 is

	F	T	r
F	F	F	F
F	T	F	T
T	F	F	T
T	T	T	T
p	q		

The truth-table of the dual is

	T	F	r
T	T	T	T
T	F	T	F
F	T	T	F
F	F	F	F
p	q		

By inspection, the dual is identical.

Example 1.10   Given the following statements about a quadrilateral ABCD:

p	AB is parallel to CD;
q	BC is parallel to DA;
r	AB = CD;
s	BC = DA;
t	AB = BC,

express the following conditions in terms of them:

(a) ABCD is a parallelogram;
(b) ABCD is a rhombus.

Solution

(a) Any of the following will do:

p and q, p and r, q and s.

(b) p and q and t.

1.10   Exercises

Exercise 1.1   Convert the following statements into propositional logic, negate them and convert the negation back into the English language.

(a) Pickled onions are spherical and not very pleasant but Desmond likes them.
(b) My dog has got smelly breath, a withered ear and a missing fang but he has no problems with his fur or his skin.

(c) If there is a plum tree and an apple tree in my garden then in the autumn I can harvest plums or apples
(d) If I go to the casino, I either win some money or get very depressed (but not both).
(e) If the sun is shining I go out, otherwise I watch TV.
(f) I am happy if, and only if, I am lounging about or eating.

Exercise 1.2 For each of the formulae:

(a) $p \wedge (r/q) \vee r \wedge s$;
(b) $(p \downarrow q) \vee (r \downarrow s) \vee ((r \Leftrightarrow s) \wedge (p/q))$;
(c) $(q \Leftrightarrow r) \Rightarrow ((p \Leftrightarrow q) \Rightarrow (q \Leftrightarrow r))$,

perform all of the following operations:

(i) give its truth-table;
(ii) state whether it is a tautology, absurdity or mixed formula;
(iii) express in FCNF and FDNF.

Exercise 1.3 Show that the following hold without using truth-tables:

(a) $p \vee (p \wedge (\neg p \vee q)) \vee q =_T p \vee q$;
(b) $(p \wedge \neg q) \vee (\neg p \wedge q) =_T \neg (p \wedge q) \wedge (p \vee q)$;
(c) $p \Leftrightarrow q = \neg(\neg p \vee \neg q) \vee (\neg p \wedge \neg q)$;
(d) $\neg(p \Leftrightarrow q) =_T \neg p \Leftrightarrow q$;
(e) $(p \wedge q) \Rightarrow r =_T (p \wedge \neg r) \Rightarrow \neg q$.

Exercise 1.4 Construct an algorithm for writing any propositional formula in DNF and CNF without using truth-tables.

Exercise 1.5 Construct an algorithm for finding the FCNF and FDNF of formulae without using truth-tables.

Exercise 1.6 Write the FDNF of the formulae:

(a) $p \wedge q \vee r \Rightarrow p \wedge (q \vee r) \vee (q/(q \downarrow s))$;
(b) $(p \Rightarrow q) \Rightarrow ((q/r) \Rightarrow (p \Leftrightarrow r \vee s))$.

Exercise 1.7 Show the following:

(a) $(p \wedge q) \Rightarrow p$ is a tautology;
(b) $(p \vee q) \vee \neg(p \wedge q)$ is a tautology;
(c) $\neg((p \wedge q) \Rightarrow q)$ is an absurdity;
(d) $(p \vee q) \wedge (\neg q \vee p) \wedge (\neg p \vee q) \wedge \neg(p \wedge q)$ is an absurdity;
(e) $(p \vee q) \wedge (\neg p \wedge q) \wedge (q \vee r)$ is a mixed formula;
(f) $(p \Rightarrow q) \wedge (q \Rightarrow \neg p)$ is a mixed formula.

Exercise 1.8   For each of the following formulae:

  (a) $((q \vee \neg q) \Leftrightarrow (\neg q)) \vee q$;
  (b) $\neg((p \Rightarrow \neg p) \vee (p \vee \neg q))$;
  (c) $\neg((p \Rightarrow \neg q) \Rightarrow (\neg(q \Rightarrow \neg p)))$;
  (d) $((p) \wedge (\neg q)) \Rightarrow (\neg r \vee q)$;
  (e) $(p \wedge r) \Rightarrow (q \wedge p)$;
  (f) $\neg p \vee \neg r \vee \neg(\neg q \vee \neg p)$;
  (g) $(p \vee q \vee r) \Rightarrow ((\neg r \wedge p) \Rightarrow q)$;
  (h) $(p \Rightarrow (q \Rightarrow r)) \Rightarrow ((p \Rightarrow q) \Rightarrow (p \Rightarrow r))$;
  (i) $(\neg p \Rightarrow \neg q) \Rightarrow (q \Rightarrow p)$,

    (i) write out its truth-table;
    (ii) state whether it is a tautology, absurdity or mixed formula.

Are any of the given mixed formulae logically equivalent?

Exercise 1.9   For each of the following, state whether it is an absurdity, a tautology, or a mixed formula:

  (a) $p \wedge q \wedge (\neg p \vee \neg q)$;
  (b) $((p \wedge q) \wedge (r \wedge p)) \wedge (p \wedge \neg q)$;
  (c) $(p \wedge q) \wedge (\neg p \wedge r)$;
  (d) $(p \wedge q \wedge r) \wedge (\neg q \wedge p)$;
  (e) $(p \Rightarrow (r \wedge q)) \Rightarrow (\neg r \Rightarrow (p \vee r))$;
  (f) $(p \wedge q) \Rightarrow ((p \Rightarrow r) \Rightarrow ((r \Rightarrow p) \Rightarrow (p \Leftrightarrow q)))$;
  (g) $(r \Leftrightarrow q) \vee (p \Leftrightarrow q) \vee (p \Leftrightarrow r)$;
  (h) $((p \Rightarrow q) \Rightarrow (\neg q \Rightarrow \neg p))$.

Exercise 1.10   Verify that the pairs of formulae given in the table in section 1.5.1 are equivalent.

Exercise 1.11   Prove that the formula

$$((p \wedge \neg q) \wedge \neg(p \wedge \neg r)) \wedge (r \wedge s) \wedge (\neg p \vee \neg t)$$

takes the truth-value T if and only if p, q, r, s and t take the truth-values T, F, T, T and F, respectively.

Exercise 1.12   For each of the following sets of logical operators, prove whether or not they form a complete system:

  (a) $\{\wedge\}$;
  (b) $\{\wedge, \vee\}$;
  (c) $\{\neg, \Leftrightarrow\}$;
  (d) $\{\Rightarrow, \Leftrightarrow\}$;
  (e) $\{\Rightarrow, \Rightarrow\}$;

(f) $\{\Leftrightarrow, \nLeftrightarrow\}$;

(g) $\{M_1\}$, where $M_1(p, q, r)$ takes the truth-value T if and only if at most one of its arguments takes the truth-value T.

You may use any results established in the text.

Exercise 1.13   Using the definition that the dual of a formula involving only the operators $\neg$, $\wedge$ and $\vee$ is the formula obtained by replacing every $\wedge$ by $\vee$, and every $\vee$ by $\wedge$:

(a) write down the duals of the formulae

   (i) $p \wedge \neg q \wedge r \wedge s$;
   (ii) $((p \wedge \neg q) \wedge (q \Rightarrow r)) \wedge \neg (q \Leftrightarrow \neg p)$;
   (iii) $((p \downarrow q) \vee r) \wedge \neg (\neg p \Rightarrow r)$

   and compute their truth-tables;
(b) prove that the dual of a formula is a tautology if and only if the formula itself is an absurdity.

Exercise 1.14   Determine whether the functor M_1 is self-dual (see the definition in exercise 1.12 above).

Exercise 1.15   Prove that the functor $F_n(p_1, \ldots, p_{2n-1})$ which takes the truth-value T if and only if at least n of its $2n-1$ arguments takes the truth-value T is self-dual.

Exercise 1.16   Using the definition that the dual of a formula is obtained by replacing T by F and F by T everywhere in its truth-table, compute the duals of

(a) $(p \vee \neg q) \Rightarrow ((p \downarrow q) \Rightarrow \neg (s / r))$;
(b) $(p / q) \nRightarrow (p \downarrow \neg r)$.

Exercise 1.17   Test the validity of the argument forms:

(a) $p \Rightarrow q, r \Rightarrow q \vDash p \Rightarrow r$;
(b) $p \wedge q, q \wedge r \vDash p \Rightarrow r$;
(c) $p \Rightarrow q, p \Rightarrow r \vDash p \vee q \vee r$.

Exercise 1.18   Show that, for any propositional formulae P and Q,

$$P =_T Q \text{ if and only if } \vDash P \Leftrightarrow Q.$$

Exercise 1.19   Write programs to perform the following operations.

(a) Read in a logical formula, and print its truth-table.

(b) Extend the program of the previous question so that it will determine whether the formula was a tautology, absurdity or mixed formula.

(c) Extend the program of the first question so that it will read in a number of formulae, and will determine whether the last can be deduced as a valid argument from the others.

(d) Write a program to read in a logical formula, and print out the same function
 (i) in FDNF;
 (ii) as an equivalent formula using only the ↓ operator.

CHAPTER 2

Formal approach to propositional logic

2.1 Introduction

We will now develop formal logical systems corresponding to the ideas of propositional logic presented in the previous chapter. We showed there that a formula was a tautology by evaluating its truth-table. This can be tedious and perhaps impractical if the number of variables involved is large. The systems developed in this chapter will use purely algebraic means to *prove* that any particular *well-formed formula* is a *theorem*. By a well-formed formula we mean one which obeys certain conditions imposed by the system (for example, is syntactically correct in some sense). This will be defined more precisely in the following subsection. We will usually abbreviate the term well-formed formula to *wff* and the plural to *wffs**. The term *theorem* will also be formally defined below but it essentially means a well-formed formula which can be proved within the system.

The hidden agenda in our algebraic system is that the set of all the theorems that can possibly be derived will be exactly equivalent to the set of all possible tautologies of the previous chapter. However, during the development of proofs in this chapter, *we no longer evaluate or even consider truth-tables.*

Once a particular formal system is considered, we have the difficult task of proving that the new definition of a theorem agrees exactly with the old truth-table definition of a tautology. To show that this property holds for any particular formal system it first has to be shown that all theorems of the system correspond to formulae which are tautologies (this is known as the *soundness of the system*), and second (and harder to show), that all tautologies which are *wffs* of the system are theorems (this is known as the *completeness of the system*).

Part of the motivation for this work is that the construction of truth-tables with many variables is impossibly time-consuming. If we can find a way of proving which formulae are tautologies by some algebraic method, it should be a much faster process on a computer when many variables are involved.

---

*Perhaps the plural of *wff* should be *wff*e rather than *wff*s?

This chapter will begin by considering formal systems of propositional logic in general terms. Two particular formal systems will then be discussed in detail. Another type of formal system of propositional logic is considered in chapter 5. This is a computer-based logic system for solving real problems, known as a propositional logic program. There will usually be many variables in such a system, and algebraic means will be needed to generate the proofs.

2.1.1   Formal systems of propositional logic

To define a formal system four specific sets of objects are required.
    These sets of objects are as follows.

(a) An alphabet

This set consists of the *symbols* used by the system. This includes the following subsets.
   (i) A subset of propositional variables. Ordinarily, we will use the symbols p, q and r to represent propositional variables. To be really strict, the list would have to be infinite, using say the symbols $p_1, p_2, p_3, \ldots$, each of which is considered to be a single symbol. In practice, when working with a small number of variables we will just use symbols such as p, q and r.
  (ii) A subset of punctuation symbols. These will usually be the comma ',', and opening '(' and closing ')' parentheses.
 (iii) A subset of logical operators. In the system L (due to Łukasiewicz) that is discussed in the next section the subset of operators used is $\{\Rightarrow, \neg\}$. This means that only formulae using these operators can be used in the system. It was seen in the last chapter that all possible propositional formulae can be represented by these two operators anyway. It may be, as it is with the system L, that a requirement is to keep the number of operators to a minimum. In this case, $\{\Rightarrow, \neg\}$ is a good choice. If (as is the case with Lemmon's system that is presented later on in this chapter) we are not interested in restricting the number of operators to be as small as possible, then $\{\Rightarrow, \neg\}$ would not be a good choice. However it would at least be a *reasonable* choice in the sense that the operators can represent all possible truth functions. Whatever the *motivation* of the system, a choice of $\{\Rightarrow\}$ on its own as the set of operators would be very poor because some truth functions could not be represented.

(b) A set of *wffs*

The formulae being considered need to be syntactically correct. For example, if we were to write $p \Rightarrow$ it would have *no meaning* whatsoever. It would be syntactically incorrect because $\Rightarrow$ needs two arguments. A formula is syntactically correct if it has the correct number of arguments for each of the operators used. The truth-value of the formula has no relevance when considering whether or not a formula is syntactically correct. A formula such as $p \wedge \neg p$ is a syntactically correct formula even though its truth-value is always F. We are not saying anything about the truth-value, just that the sequence of symbols makes sense as a formula. If, in addition to being syntactically correct, the formulae use only the logical operators of the alphabet of the system then such formulae are referred to as *wffs*. Later on in this chapter we will see some examples of actual formal propositional logic systems. The concept of a *wff* is discussed below for system L in terms of formulae containing only the operators $\Rightarrow$ and $\neg$. For Lemmon's system, many more operators are allowed. It must be stressed that the set of *wffs* of a formal system depends entirely upon the alphabet of the system. The *wffs* of a particular system are *all* the syntactically correct formulae that can be constructed using the alphabet of the system.

(c) A set of axioms

These are basic formulae from which theorems are derived. Any axiom of the system is a theorem without further proof. Some logic systems have a specific finite set of axioms. Others, such as the system L that we will discuss later have an infinite set of axioms defined by *axiom schemes*. An axiom scheme involves variables which stand for *any wff* of the system. By substituting *wffs* consistently for a given variable throughout the scheme we can obtain an infinite number of axioms. In some systems such as Lemmon's (which is the other formal system that we look at in some detail) the set of axioms is empty.

   For example, suppose we had a system with the axiom scheme $\neg U \Rightarrow (U \Rightarrow V)$ where U and V stand for any *wff* of the system. Suppose also that the two propositional variables p and q and the connective $\wedge$ belong to the alphabet of the system, as well as the connectives appearing in the axiom scheme. Some axioms of the system are as follows:

$\neg p \Rightarrow (p \Rightarrow q)$ (obtained by substituting p for U and q for V);

$\neg(p \wedge q) \Rightarrow ((p \wedge q) \Rightarrow q)$ (obtained by substituting $p \wedge q$ for U and q for V).

The axioms can be thought of as formulae which are (in some sense) fundamental theorems of the system. Axioms do not have to be proved. We are simply given the fact that axioms are theorems of the system.

   Some authors define axioms in terms of propositional variables rather than *wffs*. In our example above, the axiom scheme could have been represented as the specific axiom $\neg p \Rightarrow (p \Rightarrow q)$, where p and q are propositional variables. In this case we need in addition a second rule, known as the *substitution rule*, which is:

   If P is a theorem involving the variable p, and Q is any *wff*, then the formula obtained by consistently substituting Q for p throughout P is also a theorem.

It will be apparent that the net effect of this system is the same as that of using axiom schemes.

(d) A set of rules of deduction*

These are rules which enable new *wff*s to be derived in the system from existing *wff*s.

Many systems (including the system L and Lemmon's system), use a rule known as *modus ponens* or one of its many variations. The rule can be expressed formally as:

> If P and $(P \Rightarrow Q)$ are both *provable* in the system, then Q is *provable* in the system (where P, Q are any *wff*s of the system).

In some systems (such as system L) this is the only rule. In other systems (such as Lemmon's) it is just one of many and in some systems it does not appear at all. A later chapter discusses logic programs which are essentially formal systems with a single rule of inference known as *resolution*. However, as we shall see in that chapter, resolution is similar to MP. This system is the basis of the modern computer programming language Prolog.

2.1.2 Proofs and deductions

A proof in a formal system

A *proof* in a given system is defined to be a sequence of *wff*s of that system such that each *wff* is either

(a) an instance of an axiom of the system, or
(b) derivable from earlier *wff*s in the sequence using one of the rules of the system.

If such a proof exists, then the sequence of *wff*s leading to a given *wff* W is said to be 'a proof of W in the system' and W is said to be 'a theorem of the system'.

A deduction in a formal system

We now have the idea of a *wff* which is a theorem in a particular system, and of a proof in general. These two concepts can be related to a system such as L or Lemmon's defined below. A *deduction* starts from certain additional *premises* or *hypotheses* in addition to the axioms. What is effectively being said is that we are working in a general formal system, but for a particular problem, certain additional assumptions or hypotheses can be made. Note that any result proved using these hypotheses is not a theorem of the system but is

---

*These are called *rules of procedure* in some texts.

deducible from the axioms taken together with the additional hypotheses. A *deduction* in a given system can formally be defined to be a sequence of *wff*s of that system such that each *wff* is either

   (a) an instance of an axiom of the system, or
   (b) one of the additional hypotheses, or
   (c) derivable from earlier *wff*s in the sequence using one of the rules of the system.

We employ the notation

$$\{P_1,\ldots,P_n\} \vdash Q$$

with a set of *wff*s on the left-hand side of the $\vdash$ symbol to mean that the *wff* Q *is deducible from* or *is a consequence of* the the set of *wff*s $\{P_1,\ldots,P_n\}$. The *wff*s $P_1,\ldots,P_n$ are the *hypotheses* or are called the *hypothesis set*, Q is the *consequence* or *consequent*. The variable n stands for a non-negative integer. This just indicates that there can be any number of hypotheses. If $n = 0$ (there are no hypotheses) then we have a *proof*, not a *deduction*. A proof could be defined to be a deduction with an empty hypothesis set.

We may out of laziness omit the set notation, and write simply

$$P_1,\ldots,P_n \vdash Q.$$

Where appropriate, the notation

$$\Gamma \vdash Q$$

will be used to mean that Q *is deducible from* the hypotheses in the set Γ, where Γ is a set of *wff*s. If Γ is equal to the empty set, then

$$\vdash Q$$

is written to indicate that Q is a theorem of the system, i.e. that Q can be *proved* in the system without any additional hypotheses.

In all the above, the symbol $\vdash$ is used in various ways. This indicates that we are deducing or proving some *wff* but the symbol does not indicate which system we are working in. For system L the symbol $\vdash_L$ should (strictly) be used and for Lemmon's system it should be $\vdash_{\text{Lemmon's}}$. However, a means of indicating the system is only required if there is some doubt over which system is being considered. Ordinarily, if we are working in a particular system and no other system is involved, then we just use the symbol $\vdash$.

Note 1:   The symbol $\vdash$ is *not* part of any particular formal system, it is used for talking about a formal system. The assertion

$$P,Q \vdash_L R$$

is a statement about particular formulae in L. It is not a statement in L, nor can it be part of an actual proof or deduction in L. It is part of what is called the *metalanguage*; this is the language used to make statements *about* the system, not statements *in* the system.

Note 2:   A deduction can be expressed either in terms of *wff*s with explicit (lower-case) propositional variables, or like our axiom schemes (upper-case letters representing any *wff*) representing patterns of *wff*s. Thus you may be required to show that

$$\{p, \neg p\} \vdash q$$

or, using the scheme notation, that

$$\{P, \neg P\} \vdash Q.$$

In the latter case any substitutions for P or Q must be performed consistently throughout the whole statement, not just in one hypothesis.

Note 3:   The *wff*s on the left may be expressed as a set of *wff*s in curly braces, or as a list of *wff*s simply separated by commas. To prove a deduction, the *wff*s on the left of the $\vdash$ act as additional axiom schemes.

Note 4:   Two *wff*s P, Q are said to be *interderivable* in a formal system if both $P \vdash Q$ and $Q \vdash P$. We write $P \dashv\vdash Q$.

2.1.3   Constructing formal systems

As we have indicated, there are many different formal systems of propositional logic in use. Indeed, a formal system could be just made up at random in any of an infinite number of ways. We could form an alphabet, a set of *wff*s, some axioms and some rules all at random without any thought at all. It would not be a very sensible system (unless we were very lucky!). All sensible systems are, hopefully, equivalent in the sense that, as mentioned at the beginning of this chapter, our hidden agenda is that the set of all possible tautologies of the previous chapter should be equivalent to the set of all possible theorems that can be derived in the system. In technical terms the system should be *sound* and *complete* (this is discussed more formally later). If that is the case, all sensible propositional formal systems (which have the same logical operators in their alphabet) will have the same set of *wff*s as theorems, namely all the tautologies which can be constructed using that set of operators. In this chapter we will be considering, in some detail, two very different systems. The first system, L (due to Łukasiewicz), uses only one rule of inference and three axiom schemes. The second system (due to Lemmon) has thirteen rules of inference and no axiom schemes. Now both of these systems are sound and complete, but Lemmon's system has a *larger* set of *wff*s because it uses more operators. If we were to restrict the alphabet of Lemmon's system to using just the operators $\neg$ and $\Rightarrow$, then the two systems would have the same set of formulae as theorems. This set would consist of all the tautologies that can be constructed from ¬ and ⇒. What would be essentially different about these systems is not the set of *wffs* that could be proved but *how* those *wffs* are proven.

The *motivation* behind system L is that there should be as few logical operators, axiom schemes and rules of inference as possible. It uses only the operators ¬ and ⇒ (recall from chapter 1 that all possible truth-values can be expressed in terms of these operators) and the single rule MP. This can make theorems difficult to prove and it will be seen that new rules of inference can be derived in L which make proofs easier to construct and understand. However, the derived rules are not additional rules for the system. They can be derived from the axioms and the single rule. They are actually *abbreviations* for a proof sequence using only MP and the axioms. Mechanized proof systems often require as few rules and operators as possible to reduce the choice a machine has available at each step in a proof. Numerous other systems exist which use only the operators ¬ and ⇒, and have only MP as their rule, but in which different sets of axioms have been chosen.

The *motivation* behind Lemmon's system is to make deductions and proofs easy to construct and read for humans. Consequently there are far fewer limitations on the number of operators and rules, and, because of the nature of the rules, there are no axioms. It is possible in Lemmon's system (as we mentioned above for system L) to derive new rules of inference from the old ones in order to make proofs and deductions even easier to construct. Systems such as Lemmon's are often called natural deduction systems.

Although we consider only two formal propositional systems in this chapter, the exercises at the end of this chapter describe other formal systems. One of these modifies the axiom schemes of L but does not change the class of theorems. It is designed so that the class of theorems is the same as the class of tautologies.

To summarize this section, many different formal systems of predicate logic can be constructed but the systems should be sound and complete (this is discussed in more detail later). Some use only the operators ¬ and ⇒, others are for different sets of operators, perhaps those involving the operators ¬, ∧ and ∨. Others have been designed to be perhaps simpler to use for creating proofs (such as Lemmon's), and have more operators and rules to help the user. Other systems are designed to provide a minimal base for proving the validity of certain mathematical systems.

Following the same minimalist route, a deduction system due to J. Nicod involves only the Sheffer stroke operator (introduced in chapter 1), with the single axiom

$$(X/(Y/Z))/((U/(U/U))/((V/Y)/((X/V)/(X/V))))$$

and the single rule

$$U, U/(V/W) \vdash W.$$

We emphasize again that at this point the symbols in these formulae have no meaning (in terms of truth-values); the formulae are simply strings of characters which can be manipulated according to certain rules. If one of our rules states that

$$U \wedge V \vdash U,$$

the property

$$U \wedge V \vdash V$$

cannot be used without first proving it.

2.1.4 The relationship between formal systems and interpretations

The systems of proofs and deductions described above are purely methods for performing manipulations on formulae, where the formulae are just strings of symbols satisfying certain rules. As far as this chapter goes, we have not ascribed any meaning to the operators involved in the formulae. Certain strings satisfy the rules for being a theorem, others do not. It has not been shown yet whether, given a particular *wff*, we can guarantee to show that it is a theorem.

For a system to be useful in application to the real world, it must be possible to give some meaning to the formulae. That is, we must have a mapping from symbols in our language to entities in the application domain. In this way, every formula has different interpretations (lines of the truth-table) each of which assigns a truth-value to the formula. We would wish to be able to have a particular property which is common to all the interpretations of all theorems of the system. This is the hidden agenda that has already been mentioned twice, that all the theorems of the system are tautologies and that all tautologies are theorems of the system. This means that

all the formulae that the system can prove should have truth-value T

and

all formulae which have truth-value T and are *wff*s of the system should be provable by the system.

These two concepts are known as *soundness* and *completeness*, respectively.

It will be shown later on in this chapter that system *L* is both sound and complete.

2.2 The formal propositional logic system *L*

It has already been seen what, in general, a formal system should look like. In this section we present perhaps the most famous propositional formal system of them all which was first developed by Łukasiewicz.

2.2.1   The construction of system *L*

As was seen in the previous section, every formal system must have the following sets of objects:

(a) an alphabet;
(b) a set of *wffs*;
(c) a set of axioms (which may be empty);
(d) a set of inference rules.

This section is started by presenting these sets for system *L*.

2.2.1.1   The alphabet of system *L*

This consists of the following sets.

(a) The infinite set of propositional variables $\{p_1, p_2, \ldots, \}$. When we are only using two or three variables at a time we will denote them by lower-case letters such as p, q and r.
(b) The set of punctuation symbols $\{',', '(', ')'\}$.
(c) The set of logical operators $\{\neg, \Rightarrow\}$.

2.2.1.2   The *wffs* of system *L*

General *wffs* will be denoted by upper-case letters such as P, Q and R, or, in a more general argument, by $P_1, P_2, P_3, \ldots, P_n$. A propositional statement P is a *wff* in system *L* if it conforms to one of the following conditions:

(a) P is a propositional variable; or
(b) P is of the form $(\neg Q)$, where Q is a *wff*; or
(c) P is of the form $(Q \Rightarrow R)$, where Q and R are *wffs*.

Other operators cannot be included because they do not belong to the alphabet of *L*. However, propositional formulae involving other operators can be represented because as we saw in chapter 1, all operators can be rewritten in terms of $\{\neg, \Rightarrow\}$. For example, $P \vee Q$ could be replaced by the *wff* $((\neg P) \Rightarrow Q)$. Recall that in system *L* (as in any formal system) when a particular *wff* is considered, we are saying nothing about its truth-value. The constant truth-values T or F are not allowed to appear in *wffs*. Such values do not lie in the alphabet of *L* and so have no place in the *wffs* of *L*. Only symbols which appear in the alphabet can be used. Of course, the truth-value T could perhaps be represented by the *wff* $(p \Rightarrow p)$ (or any other tautology involving only the operators $\neg$ and $\Rightarrow$). We could represent F by $(\neg(p \Rightarrow p))$.

Other examples of *wffs* in *L* are

$$(\neg p); \quad (((\neg p) \Rightarrow (\neg q)) \Rightarrow r); \quad (((\neg p) \Rightarrow (\neg(q \Rightarrow r))) \Rightarrow (\neg r)).$$

Essentially, the *wffs* of *L* are just the formulae involving $\neg$ and $\Rightarrow$.

2.2.1.3   The axioms of system *L*

Recall that the axioms of a formal system are the basic formulae from which all theorems are derived.

System *L* has the following three axiom schemes:

L1 $(U \Rightarrow (V \Rightarrow U))$;

L2 $((U \Rightarrow (V \Rightarrow W)) \Rightarrow ((U \Rightarrow V) \Rightarrow (U \Rightarrow W)))$;

L3 $(((\neg U) \Rightarrow (\neg V)) \Rightarrow (V \Rightarrow U))$,

where *U*, *V* and *W* are variables which stand for any *wff*. The first axiom scheme says that we can take as a basic axiom any of the doubly infinite set of formulae created by substituting any *wff* for *U* and any *wff* for *V* in the axiom scheme. There are infinitely many instances of any axiom scheme; any *wff* of the required form is an axiom. As has been mentioned before, the same *wff* must be substituted consistently for a given variable throughout the formula. Thus the formulae

$(p \Rightarrow (q \Rightarrow p))$ (substitute *p* for *U* and *q* for *V*);

$((q \Rightarrow p) \Rightarrow (r \Rightarrow (q \Rightarrow p)))$ (substitute $(q \Rightarrow p)$ for *U* and *r* for *V*);

$(r \Rightarrow (((p \Rightarrow q) \Rightarrow r) \Rightarrow r))$ (substitute *r* for *U* and $((p \Rightarrow q) \Rightarrow r)$ for *V*)

are all acceptable specific axioms obtained by performing various substitutions in the first of the axiom schemes. The exact substitution must always be specified.

Wffs expressed by applying the above rules strictly will generally have more parentheses than are necessary for non-ambiguous understanding. For example, L3 would normally be written as

$(\neg U \Rightarrow \neg V) \Rightarrow (V \Rightarrow U)$.

In the rest of the chapter we will omit superfluous parentheses.

2.2.1.4   The inference rule of system *L*

As we have already mentioned, system *L* has just one rule of inference, known as modus ponens, often abbreviated to MP. This can be defined formally as

If *V* and $(V \Rightarrow W)$ are *wffs* of *L* which are members of a proof (or deduction) sequence then the *wff* *W* can be added to the proof (or deduction sequence).

We could have, additionally, other similar rules which will be described later, but have chosen on this occasion to have a minimum number of rules. As has been indicated above, the *motivation* behind system *L* is that we use a minimum number of operators, axioms and rules.

2.2.2   Proofs in system *L*

A formal proof has already been defined in general terms. A proof in our specific system *L* is defined to be a sequence of *wff*s of *L* such that each *wff* is either

    (a) an instance of an axiom of *L*, or

    (b) derivable from two earlier *wff*s in the sequence using the rule MP. The two earlier *wff*s must therefore be of the form *P* and $(P \Rightarrow Q)$ (where *P* and *Q* are *wff*s of *L*) for the rule to be applied.

If such a proof exists, then the sequence of *wff*s leading to a given *wff* *R* is said to be a 'proof of *R* in *L*' and *R* is said to be 'a *theorem* of *L*'. Observe that all the *wff*s in the sequence are also theorems.

Examples of proofs in *L*

There are certain formalities to be observed in writing proofs. Every step must be justified clearly. To prove, for example, that

$$((\neg p \Rightarrow \neg q) \Rightarrow q) \Rightarrow ((\neg p \Rightarrow \neg q) \Rightarrow p)$$

is a theorem of *L*, we must give an appropriate sequence of *wff*s, each of which is either an instance of an axiom scheme (in which case it must be specified which axiom scheme is used, and what substitutions have been made) or is obtained by using the rule MP on two earlier *wff*s in the sequence (in which case we must specify which *wff*s have been used). To make references to earlier *wff*s easy, we number each *wff* in the sequence as shown below.

No.	*wff*	Derivation
1	$((\neg p \Rightarrow \neg q) \Rightarrow (q \Rightarrow p)) \Rightarrow$ $(((\neg p \Rightarrow \neg q) \Rightarrow q) \Rightarrow ((\neg p \Rightarrow \neg q) \Rightarrow p))$	L2 with $(\neg p \Rightarrow \neg q)$ for *U*, *q* for *V* and *p* for *W*;
2	$(\neg p \Rightarrow \neg q) \Rightarrow (q \Rightarrow p)$	L3 with *p* for *U* and *q* for *V*;
3	$((\neg p \Rightarrow \neg q) \Rightarrow q) \Rightarrow ((\neg p \Rightarrow \neg q) \Rightarrow p)$	MP on 2 and 1.

Observe the two lines referenced in the step applying the MP rule (step 3). The second line referenced (step 1) is an implication whose first part (whose premise, step 2 in this case) is identical to the first line quoted.

    All proofs must follow exactly the above format; the proof will consist of a sequence of *wff*s, each one numbered and justified.

    Another reminder: in this chapter, a system involves particular sets of symbols, of *wff*s, of axioms and of rules. Each line of the proof must be numbered, and will involve exactly the given rule, MP (or one of the derived rules that will be discussed shortly) or will actually be an instance of an axiom. The rule and the referenced *wff*s must be quoted or, in the case of an axiom instance, the axiom number and the substitutions used must be clearly stated. In these proofs it *cannot*, for example, simply be assumed that *p* and $\neg\neg p$ are in any way equivalent or interchangeable.

It can be very tricky to show that *wffs* which can trivially be shown to be tautologies using truth-tables are actually theorems of *L*, as will be seen in the next example.

Notice that in the above proof propositional variables were used. We could use, instead of propositional variables, variables which stand for any *wff* of *L*. This is the same idea as that used to differentiate between *axioms* and *axiom schemes*.

Consider the following proof of $\vdash P \Rightarrow P$ for any *wff P*.

No.	*wff*	Derivation
1	$P \Rightarrow (P \Rightarrow P)$	L1 with P for U and P for V;
2	$P \Rightarrow ((P \Rightarrow P) \Rightarrow P)$	L1 with P for U and $P \Rightarrow P$ for V;
3	$(P \Rightarrow ((P \Rightarrow P) \Rightarrow P)) \Rightarrow$ $((P \Rightarrow (P \Rightarrow P)) \Rightarrow (P \Rightarrow P))$	L2 with P for U, $P \Rightarrow P$ for V and P for W;
4	$(P \Rightarrow (P \Rightarrow P)) \Rightarrow (P \Rightarrow P)$	MP on 2 and 3;
5	$P \Rightarrow P$	MP on 1 and 4.

2.2.3   Deductions in system L

We have already defined deductions in general terms.

A *deduction* from the set of *wffs* Γ in the system *L* is defined to be a sequence of *wffs* such that each *wff* is either

(a) an instance of one of the axioms of *L*, or
(b) one of the hypotheses (either a member of the set Γ, or one of the formulae written explicitly on the left-hand side of the $\vdash$ symbol), or
(c) is derivable from two earlier *wffs* in the sequence using the rule MP.

What is effectively being done is that hypothesis set is added to the set of axioms.

If such a sequence exists, then the sequence of *wffs* leading to a given *wff P* is said to be a 'deduction of *P* from Γ in *L*', and *P* is said to be 'deducible from Γ in *L*'.

The MP rule itself could be expressed as a deduction

$$P, (P \Rightarrow Q) \vdash Q.$$

Remember that, because these statements refer to results which are yielded *in the system L*, they should strictly be written as

$$P, (P \Rightarrow Q) \vdash_L Q.$$

However, when there is no ambiguity over which system we are working in, it eases the notation to omit the subscript.

Examples of deductions in *L*

The deduction

$$(p \Rightarrow (q \Rightarrow r)) \Rightarrow (\neg\neg p \Rightarrow \neg(q \Rightarrow r)), p \Rightarrow (q \Rightarrow r), q \Rightarrow r \vdash \neg p,$$

where p, q and r are propositional variables, can be established by considering the following sequence of *wff*s.

1	$(p \Rightarrow (q \Rightarrow r) \Rightarrow ((\neg(\neg p)) \Rightarrow \neg(q \Rightarrow r))$	hypothesis;
2	$p \Rightarrow (q \Rightarrow r)$	hypothesis;
3	$q \Rightarrow r$	hypothesis;
4	$\neg\neg p \Rightarrow \neg(q \Rightarrow r)$	MP on 2 and 1;
5	$(\neg\neg p \Rightarrow \neg(q \Rightarrow r)) \Rightarrow ((q \Rightarrow r) \Rightarrow \neg p)$	L3 with $\neg p$ for U and $(q \Rightarrow r)$ for V;
6	$(q \Rightarrow r) \Rightarrow \neg p$	MP on 4 and 5;
7	$\neg p$	MP on 3 and 6.

Again, note that

$$(p \Rightarrow (q \Rightarrow r)) \Rightarrow ((\neg(\neg))p \Rightarrow \neg(q \Rightarrow r)), p \Rightarrow (q \Rightarrow r), q \Rightarrow r \vdash \neg p,$$

is a statement about *L*, not a theorem or *wff* of *L*. It does not appear as part of the deduction, only as a statement at the start of what you are aiming to achieve, or at the end of your formal deduction as a statement of what has been achieved. Remember that $\vdash$ is a metasymbol. It is used to make assertions about the system. It never appears in the proof or deduction itself.

In the next example we use variables standing for *wff*s of *L* instead of propositional variables.

We can establish the deduction

$$\neg R \Rightarrow (P \Rightarrow (P \Rightarrow Q)), \neg R \Rightarrow P \vdash \neg R \Rightarrow Q$$

(where P, Q and R are *wff*s of *L*) by presenting the following sequence of *wff*s.

1	$\neg R \Rightarrow (P \Rightarrow (P \Rightarrow Q))$	hypothesis;
2	$\neg R \Rightarrow P$	hypothesis;
3	$(\neg R \Rightarrow (P \Rightarrow (P \Rightarrow Q))) \Rightarrow$ $((\neg R \Rightarrow P) \Rightarrow (\neg R \Rightarrow (P \Rightarrow Q)))$	L2 with $\neg R$ for *U*, P for *V* and $P \Rightarrow Q$ for *W*;
4	$(\neg R \Rightarrow P) \Rightarrow (\neg R \Rightarrow (P \Rightarrow Q))$	MP on 1 and 3;
5	$\neg R \Rightarrow (P \Rightarrow Q)$	MP on 2 and 4;
6	$\neg R \Rightarrow (P \Rightarrow Q)$ $\Rightarrow ((\neg R \Rightarrow P) \Rightarrow (\neg R \Rightarrow Q))$	L2 with $\neg R$ for *U*, P for *V* and Q for *W*;
7	$(\neg R \Rightarrow P) \Rightarrow (\neg R \Rightarrow Q)$	MP on 5 and 6;
8	$\neg R \Rightarrow Q$	MP on 6 and 7.

2.2.4   Derived rules of inference in system *L*

As we have seen, the number of axiom schemes and rules in *L* is very small. This can make proofs and deductions very difficult to construct. In this section some *derived* rules of inference are introduced. These are not *new* rules. Nothing is being added to the system. The derived rules are not independent of MP. These rules can be *proved* using the axioms and single rule (MP) of *L*.

These derived rules are introduced to make proofs in system *L* easier to construct and read. Each derived rule is really an *abbreviation* for a longer proof involving just MP. If there is a proof that the new rule can be derived in *L* then, whenever it is used in a proof or deduction of *L*, we could (if we wish) replace each application of the new rule by the derivation of that rule. This would be very tedious and would make the proof long and cumbersome. However, the point is that any proof or deduction of *L* using derived rules can be turned into a proof or deduction using only MP.

We now consider perhaps the most useful of the derived rules in system *L*, known as the *deduction theorem*.

2.2.4.1   The deduction theorem

The use of this theorem can make the generation of proofs much simpler than they would otherwise be. If presented with a *wff* to prove in system *L*, we can often establish a related deduction instead and then apply the deduction theorem to complete the proof. The deduction theorem is stated as follows.

If

$$\Gamma \cup \{U\} \vdash V,$$

where *U* and *V* are *wff*s, and Γ is a set of *wff*s, then

$$\Gamma \vdash (U \Rightarrow V)$$

In English, 'If *V* is deducible from a set of hypothesis which includes *U*, then $U \Rightarrow V$ is deducible from that set with *U* removed'.

A proof of the deduction theorem in the system *L* is given below. It cannot be used in other formal systems unless it is proved first. The following proof of the deduction theorem may not be valid in other systems.

Proof   The proof of the deduction theorem is by strong induction on the number of *wff*s in the sequence which is the deduction of *V* from $\Gamma \cup \{U\}$.

Base case.   If there is only one step in the deduction, MP cannot be involved. Thus *V* is either an instance of an axiom, or a member of Γ, or is the *wff* *U*.

Suppose *V* is an axiom or member of Γ. If this is the case, we have no need of *U* (as a hypothesis) in the proof. The deduction of $(U \Rightarrow V)$ is given by:

   1   *V*   axiom or hypothesis (member of Γ);

2   $(V \Rightarrow (U \Rightarrow V))$ L1 with V for U and U for V;

3   $(U \Rightarrow V)$ MP on 1 and 2.

Suppose V is the *wff* U. If this is the case, then we have no need of any hypotheses. The proof of $\vdash P \Rightarrow P$ given in section 2.2.2 above with U substituted for P gives $\vdash U \Rightarrow U$.

Induction step.   Assume that the deduction $\Gamma \cup \{U\} \vdash V$ has k steps and that the deduction theorem holds at all the possible steps before the kth one. We must show that the deduction theorem also holds at the kth step.

Now the kth step in the proof sequence may have arisen as an instance of an axiom, as a hypothesis in Γ, as U, or by the application of MP to two earlier *wff*s.

The first three possibilities have already been dealt with in the base case.

Suppose the kth step was an application of MP. In this case V is obtained from two earlier *wff*s by an application of MP. Suppose these *wff*s are

W, $(W \Rightarrow V)$.

Since these *wff*s occur earlier in the proof, they themselves must be deducible from $\Gamma \cup \{U\}$, so that

$\Gamma \cup \{U\} \vdash W$, $\Gamma \cup \{U\} \vdash (W \Rightarrow V)$.

Since these deductions are shorter than that of V (they occur in the sequence leading up to V), the induction hypothesis will hold for both of them, so

$\Gamma \vdash (U \Rightarrow W)$, $\Gamma \vdash (U \Rightarrow (W \Rightarrow V))$.

A possible deduction of $(U \Rightarrow V)$ from Γ is now given as follows.

1   $(U \Rightarrow W)$ deduction given above;

2   $(U \Rightarrow (W \Rightarrow V))$ deduction given above;

3   $((U \Rightarrow (W \Rightarrow V))$ L2 with V for W

     $\Rightarrow ((U \Rightarrow W) \Rightarrow (U \Rightarrow V)))$ and W for V;

4   $((U \Rightarrow W) \Rightarrow (U \Rightarrow V))$ MP on 2 and 3;

5   $(U \Rightarrow V)$ MP on 1 and 4.

The deduction theorem follows by the principle of (strong) induction.

Note 1:   The set Γ could be empty which would give the following useful version of the theorem.

If

$U \vdash V$,

where U and V are *wff*s, then

$\vdash (U \Rightarrow V)$.

Our result $(U \Rightarrow V)$ is now a theorem of the system.

Note 2:   If asked to give, for example, a proof for

$$\vdash (p \Rightarrow q) \Rightarrow (((p \Rightarrow q) \Rightarrow r) \Rightarrow r),$$

it will usually (but not always) be easier to prove firstly that

$$(p \Rightarrow q) \vdash (((p \Rightarrow q) \Rightarrow r) \Rightarrow r)$$

and then apply the deduction theorem. In this case, we can go one stage further, and try first to show that

$$(p \Rightarrow q), (p \Rightarrow q) \Rightarrow r \vdash r,$$

which happens to be easy (use one application of MP on the hypotheses)! Having proved this deduction, two applications of the deduction theorem will give the required result.

You must always describe carefully exactly what you were asked to prove, what you have chosen to prove or deduce, and what you then do to obtain the exact required result. Do not confuse the sequence of *wffs* in the proof or deduction with your statements about what you are doing (for example *'Now apply the deduction theorem'* or some other English sentence). Such a solution might be presented in the form

> We are required to prove $\vdash U \Rightarrow V$.
> We will show instead that $U \vdash V$.
>   ... The deduction of V from U comes here ...
> The deduction theorem can now be applied, giving the result
> $\vdash U \Rightarrow V$
> as required.

Note 3:   The deduction theorem is not basic to the system L; it must be proved before use unless permission has been given to quote and use it directly.

Note 4:   The proof of the deduction theorem in other systems may be quite different from the proof given above (depending upon the rules and axioms of the other systems). Only the rules and axioms of system L have been used in the proof.

We now consider another useful derived rule of inference which is actually the converse of the deduction theorem.

2.2.4.2   The inverse deduction theorem

This reverses the argument of the deduction theorem, and states that if the deduction

$$\Gamma \vdash (U \Rightarrow V),$$

where U and V are *wffs*, can be established and Γ is a set of *wffs*, then the result

$\Gamma \cup \{U\} \vdash V$

holds.

Proof   Consider the following sequence of formulae:

   1 $(U \Rightarrow V)$ deduced from Γ, hence deducible from $\Gamma \cup \{U\}$;

   2 U member of $\Gamma \cup \{U\}$;

   3 V MP on 1 and 2.

The inverse deduction theorem is thus proved.

Again, if the set Γ is empty, we have the simplified theorem that if

   $\vdash (U \Rightarrow V)$,

where U and V are *wff*s, then

   $U \vdash V$

holds.

One more additional useful derived rule will be considered before this section is closed.

2.2.4.3   Hypothetical syllogism

The rule of *hypothetical syllogism* (HS) states that

   $(U \Rightarrow V), (V \Rightarrow W) \vdash (U \Rightarrow W)$.

Proof   We show instead

   $(U \Rightarrow V), (V \Rightarrow W), U \vdash W$.

The sequence is

   1 $(U \Rightarrow V)$ hypothesis;

   2 $(V \Rightarrow W)$ hypothesis;

   3 U hypothesis;

   4 V MP on 3 and 1;

   5 W MP on 4 and 2;

The deduction theorem can now be applied to obtain

   $(U \Rightarrow V), (V \Rightarrow W) \vdash (U \Rightarrow W)$.

Note: Remember that the derived rules of inference are rules which are additional to MP but which can be proved using it. The motivation for looking at these rules is that they can be very useful in certain circumstances. However, it must be stressed that they are not basic rules of the system L. They can be used in system L only if it is first proved that they hold in L (as we have done above). These rules may not hold in other systems. All we know, at the moment, is that they hold within system L.

2.2.5 Examples

Example 1 Suppose we are required to show that

(a) $\vdash (\neg P \Rightarrow Q) \Rightarrow ((Q \Rightarrow \neg R) \Rightarrow (R \Rightarrow P))$;
(b) $(\neg P \Rightarrow Q), (Q \Rightarrow \neg R), R \vdash P$,

where P, Q and R are *wff*s.

To prove both of these statements it can be shown instead that

$$(\neg P \Rightarrow Q), (Q \Rightarrow \neg R) \vdash (R \Rightarrow P).$$

The deduction is as follows:

1	$\neg P \Rightarrow Q$	hypothesis:
2	$Q \Rightarrow \neg R$	hypothesis;
3	$(\neg P \Rightarrow \neg R) \Rightarrow (R \Rightarrow P)$	L3 with P for U and R for V;
4	$\neg P \Rightarrow \neg R$	hypothetical syllogism on 1 and 2;
5	$R \Rightarrow P$	MP on 3 and 4.

Now from the statement $(\neg P \Rightarrow Q), (Q \Rightarrow \neg R) \vdash (R \Rightarrow P)$ the deduction theorem can be applied twice to obtain (a) and the inverse deduction theorem once to obtain (b). Of course, it would have been possible to show that (b) holds by making an extra hypothesis (namely R) and then using an extra application of MP at the end of the sequence. (a) could then be obtained by applying the deduction theorem three times.

Example 2 A proof in L of $\vdash \neg P \Rightarrow (P \Rightarrow Q)$ can be found by considering the following sequence of *wff*s.

1	$\neg P \Rightarrow (\neg Q \Rightarrow \neg P)$	L1 with $\neg Q$ for U and $\neg P$ for V;
2	$(\neg Q \Rightarrow \neg P) \Rightarrow (P \Rightarrow Q)$	L3 with P for U and Q for V;
3	$\neg P \Rightarrow (P \Rightarrow Q)$	hypothetical syllogism on 1 and 2.

Example 3 To show that $\neg\neg P \dashv\vdash P$ we have to show both

(a) $\neg\neg P \vdash P$

and

(b) $P \vdash \neg\neg P$.

(a)	1	$\neg\neg P$	hypothesis;
	2	$\neg\neg P \Rightarrow (\neg P \Rightarrow \neg\neg\neg P)$	example 2 above with $\neg P$ for P and $\neg\neg\neg P$ for Q;

3	$\neg P \Rightarrow \neg\neg\neg P$	MP on 1 and 2;
4	$(\neg P \Rightarrow \neg\neg\neg P) \Rightarrow (\neg\neg P \Rightarrow P)$	L3 with $\neg P$ for U and $\neg\neg P$ for V;
5	$\neg\neg P \Rightarrow P$	MP on 3 and 4;
6	P	MP on 1 and 5.

Notice that an application of the deduction theorem yields $\vdash \neg\neg P \Rightarrow P$.

(b) 1	P	hypothesis;
2	$\neg\neg\neg P \Rightarrow \neg P$	(a) with $\neg P$ for P;
3	$(\neg\neg\neg P \Rightarrow \neg P) \Rightarrow (P \Rightarrow \neg\neg P)$	L3 with $\neg\neg P$ for U and P for V;
4	$P \Rightarrow \neg\neg P$	MP on 2 and 3;
5	$\neg\neg P$	MP on 1 and 4.

Notice here that an application of the deduction theorem gives $\vdash P \Rightarrow \neg\neg P$.

More instances of these derived rules in action can be seen in the worked-examples section.

2.2.6   Notation for rules

Some authors write rules using a horizontal bar, with the hypotheses above the bar, and the consequents below the bar. Hypothetical syllogism would be written in this notation as

$$\frac{U \Rightarrow V, V \Rightarrow W}{U \Rightarrow W}.$$

The rule of MP can be written as

$$\frac{U, U \Rightarrow V}{V}.$$

The same notation can be used at a higher metalevel, writing the deduction theorem as

$$\frac{\Gamma \cup \{U\} \vdash V}{\Gamma \vdash (U \Rightarrow V)}.$$

In this notation, we have statements instead of *wffs* above and below the bar. As another example, a rule appearing in one of our later examples is

$$\frac{\vdash U \vee V; \; U \vdash W; \; V \vdash W}{\vdash W},$$

which states that, if the three deductions above the bar hold, then the deduction below the bar will also hold. The items above and below the bar are now statements about the system (metastatements), not simply *wffs*.

A double horizontal bar signifies interderivability. For example

$$\frac{U \vee V}{V \vee U}$$

states that $U \vee V \vdash V \vee U$ and vice versa.

Of course, these comments about notation for rules do not apply just to the system L. The horizontal bar can be used to denote a rule in other formal systems. However, just as with the $\vdash$ symbol, care must be taken to ensure that there is no ambiguity over which formal system is being used. We were considering system L in the above examples. As has already been mentioned, the rules may, or may not, hold in other systems.

2.3   The soundness and completeness theorems for system L

2.3.1   Introduction

We now proceed with the most important part of this chapter, to unite the above idea of proofs in system L with the idea of tautologies from the previous chapter. So far, the *wff*s of L have been considered to be merely strings of symbols without any *meaning*. The strings either satisfy the conditions of being a *wff* of L or they do not. We have not assigned truth-values to the propositional variables (and hence the *wff*s) but have simply considered the notions of *proof* and *deduction* within the system. As mentioned earlier, the motivation behind any useful formal system is that the concept of *proof* within the system should correspond in some way to *being true* or *holding* within real world applications. For system L we want to know that

(a) all formulae which are theorems of L are tautologies (the *soundness* theorem);

(b) all propositional formulae which are tautologies and are *wff*s of L are theorems of L (the *completeness* theorem).

Interpretations were introduced in the previous chapter. We now consider interpretations of *wff*s of L. Recall that an interpretation of a propositional formula is an assignment of truth-values (a line of the truth-table) to each propositional variable of the formula, and that a tautology is a propositional formula which has truth-value T for all possible interpretations. It is easy to decide whether or not a propositional formula is a tautology. We simply construct the truth-table of the formula and check each possible resulting truth-value. The truth-table may be very long and tedious to construct (if the formula has a large number of propositional variables) but there is nothing actually to stop us constructing it. The truth-table of any given propositional formula is always finite because any propositional formula has only a finite number of propositional variables.

Now given any *wff* of L, a truth-value can be assigned to that *wff* using the techniques of the previous chapter. What will be seen in this section is that the symbol for tautology (⊨) and the symbol for proof (or deduction) in L ($\vdash_L$) can be interchanged, so that that the concept of *proof* in system L has the same meaning as *truth* from the previous chapter. A theorem of system L is exactly the same thing as a tautology (using the operators ¬ and ⇒). Remember that any formula using ∧, ∨, ⇔, or any of the other operators discussed in chapter 1, can be represented by a formula using only the operators ¬ and ⇒ (a *wff* of L). A deduction of system L is exactly the same thing as a semantic consequence (or argument form) of the previous chapter.

The soundness theorem for L will be presented first. It is quite easy to prove. We then take a look at the completeness theorem.

2.3.2   The soundness theorem for system L

This states that

Every theorem of L is a tautology.

Proof   Let P be a theorem of L. We use strong induction on the length of the proof of P in L.

Base case.   P is an instance of an axiom. All the axioms are seen to be tautologies by considering the truth-tables of each of the axiom schemes.

Axiom L1:

U	⇒	(V	⇒	U)
T	T	T	T	T
T	T	F	T	T
F	T	T	F	F
F	T	F	T	F

Axiom L2:

(U	⇒	(V	⇒	W))	⇒	((U	⇒	V)	⇒	(U	⇒	W))
T	T	T	T	T	T	T	T	T	T	T	T	T
T	F	T	F	F	T	T	T	T	F	T	F	F
T	T	F	T	T	T	T	F	F	T	T	T	T
T	T	F	T	F	T	T	F	F	T	T	F	F
F	T	T	T	T	T	F	T	T	T	F	T	T
F	T	T	F	F	T	F	T	T	T	F	T	F
F	T	F	T	T	T	F	T	F	T	F	T	T
F	T	F	T	F	T	F	T	F	T	F	T	F

Axiom L3:

(¬	*U*	⇒	¬	*V*)	⇒	(*V*	⇒	*U*)
F	T	T	F	T	T	T	T	T
F	T	T	T	F	T	F	T	T
T	F	F	F	T	T	T	F	F
T	F	T	T	F	T	F	T	F

Induction step. There are two possible cases here. Either *P* is an instance of an axiom (and this has already been covered in the base case), or *P* follows by MP from two earlier *wff*s. The two earlier *wff*s to which the MP rule is applied must be tautologies by the induction hypothesis since their proof is shorter than that of *P*. Hence *P* is a tautology from the truth-table of implication.

The converse of this theorem is considered in the next section.

2.3.3   The completeness theorem for system *L*

2.3.3.1   Setting the scene

This theorem is mathematically a little more difficult to follow than the soundness theorem. The proof that is presented here was first published by Kalmar in 1935.

Before we go on to present the completeness theorem, some additional notation is required.

Notation

Let *P* be a *wff* of *L* and let $p_1, p_2, \ldots, p_n$ be the propositional variables occurring in *P*. Given a particular interpretation *I* of *P*, let

(a) $(p_i)^I$ denote p_i if *I* assigns truth-value T to p_i;
(b) $(p_i)^I$ denote $\neg p_i$ if *I* assigns truth-value F to p_i,

where $i = 1, 2, \ldots, n$.

P^I can be defined in a similar way depending upon whether the *wff* *P* is T or F for *I*.

The motivation behind this notation is that the completeness theorem can be established by first proving that, for any interpretation *I*,

$$(p_1)^I, (p_2)^I, \ldots, (p_n)^I \vdash P^I.$$

The formal proof of this is left as an exercise to the reader (see exercise 2.7).

This result allows us to write a distinct deduction for each interpretation (line of the truth-table). For example, suppose the formula $(\neg p \Rightarrow q) \Rightarrow p$ is given. The truth-table of the formula is:

	p	q	$(\neg p \Rightarrow q) \Rightarrow p$
I_1	T	T	T
I_2	T	F	T
I_3	F	T	F
I_4	F	F	T

By considering the first line of the truth-table (interpretation I_1) the result allows us to say

1    $p, q \vdash (\neg p \Rightarrow q) \Rightarrow p$.

By using the other three interpretations the following deductions can be obtained (respectively)

2    $p, \neg q \vdash (\neg p \Rightarrow q) \Rightarrow p$;

3    $\neg p, q \vdash \neg((\neg p \Rightarrow q) \Rightarrow p)$;

4    $\neg p, \neg q \vdash (\neg p \Rightarrow q) \Rightarrow p$.

It is important to note that, although truth-tables are used in the construction of the deductions, the result gives purely syntactical information. We start with a propositional formula and, by considering its truth-table, obtain a number of deductions in L (equivalent to the number of lines in the truth-table).

2.3.3.2   The completeness theorem for system L

This states that

If P is a *wff* of L and a tautology, then $\vdash_L P$.

Proof   Assume that P is a *wff* of L involving just the propositional variables $p_1, \ldots, p_n$ and that P is a tautology.

Let I be an interpretation of P that assigns the truth-value T to p_n. Notice that $P^I = P$ because P is a tautology; it follows that $(p_1)^I, \ldots, (p_n)^I \vdash P$ (by exercise 2.7) but because I assigns T to p_n we can see that

(a) $(p_1)^I, \ldots, (p_{n-1})^I, p_n \vdash P$.

Now, consider another interpretation J which is identical to I except that J assigns F to p_n. Notice, once again, that $P^J = P$ because P is a tautology.

Using exercise 2.7 (and noting that $(p_i)^J = (p_i)^I$ for $i = 1, \ldots, n-1$ and $(p_n)^J = \neg p_n$), we can obtain

(b) $(p_1)^I, \ldots, (p_{n-1})^I, \neg p_n \vdash P$.

Using the deduction theorem applied to both (a) and (b) we can now say that

$(p_1)^I, \ldots, (p_{n-1})^I \vdash p_n \Rightarrow P$

and

$(p_1)^I,\ldots,(p_{n-1})^I \vdash \neg p_n \Rightarrow P.$

However, an instance of exercise 2.1 (e) states that

$\vdash (p_n \Rightarrow P) \Rightarrow ((\neg p_n \Rightarrow P) \Rightarrow P).$

Two applications of MP to the above three formulae give us

$(p_1)^I,\ldots,(p_{n-1})^I \vdash P.$

Notice here that we started with

$(p_1)^I,\ldots,(p_n)^I \vdash P$

and have eliminated $(p_n)^I$ to obtain

$(p_1)^I,\ldots,(p_{n-1})^I \vdash P.$

This process can be repeated $n-1$ times to yield $\vdash P$ and prove the theorem.

This completeness result leads to the following conclusions.

2.3.3.3   Remarks

(a) The soundness and completeness results can be put together to obtain

   $\models P$ if and only if $\vdash_L P.$

(b) We have shown that in terms of *proof* and *tautology* we can interchange the symbols $\models$ and $\vdash_L$. It is quite easy to now show that these symbols can be interchanged in terms of *deduction* and *semantic consequence*, i.e. $\Gamma \models P$ if and only if $\Gamma \vdash_L P$. The proof of this is as follows.
   Assume $\Gamma = \{P_1,\ldots,P_n\}$. Then $\Gamma \models P$ if and only if

   $\models P_1 \Rightarrow (P_2 \Rightarrow (\cdots \Rightarrow (P_n \Rightarrow P)\ldots)$

   by n applications of theorem 1.7.5 in chapter 1. However, this is so if and only if

   $\vdash_L P_1 \Rightarrow (P_2 \Rightarrow (\ldots \Rightarrow (P_n \Rightarrow P)\ldots)$

   by (a), which is so if and only if

   $\Gamma \vdash_L P$

   by n applications of the deduction theorem (in one direction) and the inverse deduction theorem (in the other direction).
(c) The problem of deciding whether or not any *wff* of L is a theorem of L is a computable one. This means that there is an explicit constructive method (an algorithm or computer program) for deciding whether any particular *wff* is a theorem of L. Using the completeness theorem we can just evaluate the truth-table (which is a mechanical process). If all entries are T, then the *wff* is a theorem of L. This may not be a practical method

(because the truth-table may be huge and unwieldy), but nevertheless provides a (possibly very inefficient) algorithm for solving the problem.

(d) A given *wff* can now be shown not to be a theorem of *L* by showing that it is not a tautology, which requires that we show that the *wff* has the value F for a particular combination of truth-values to the propositional variables of the *wff*. We do not need to prove anything for all possible combinations of values to the variables.

2.4   Independence of axioms and rules

There are two approaches to the techniques developed for proving results in a system such as *L*. A pure mathematician may be interested in using logic to prove results about, for example, group theory or some other area of mathematics. He or she will be interested in using the minimum number of axioms (basic assumptions about the properties of groups) and rules to prove all the other properties required. The general idea is to show just what is the minimum set of assumptions which has to be made in order to generate all the required mathematical properties. Such a person would want for reasons of elegance to prove that none of the chosen axioms can be proved from the other axioms. If it could, that axiom would be redundant, and in general we are looking for a minimal set of axioms. Similarly, all the rules of deduction should be independent, so that each one is essential.

On the other hand, a person working in the production of computer systems for proving theorems would be happy to adopt any valid extra axioms and rules if they make the construction of proofs easier or more efficient. We are interested in whether a proof of the theorem exists, more than in the details of the actual proof. The extra axioms and rules involved must not, of course, make the system inconsistent or give any new theorems. The extra axioms and rules may be intended either to make the creation of proofs easier for a human whose activities are being mediated by the computer, or to make the computer generation of proofs easier.

To verify the independence of a particular axiom within a set of axioms, we usually look for some distinctive property which it has, rather than attempt to prove it from the other axioms. As an example, the third axiom of *L* is the only axiom including the negation operator, and the rules of *L* cannot introduce the negation operator; it follows that the third axiom could not possibly be proved from the other axioms.

Hilbert's method

Another recognized approach to proving the independence of axioms is due to Hilbert, and uses valuations with more than just the two values T and F as follows. We choose, for example, the three values $\{1, 2, 3\}$, and the valuations for negation and implication given by the following table:

p	$\neg p$	$p \Rightarrow q$		
		1	2	3 q
1	3	1	2	3
2	2	1	1	3
3	1	1	1	1

It can be shown that under these operations the first two axioms always take the value 1. For example, for axiom 1 we have two variables, so there are nine evaluations to be made as follows:

p	$\Rightarrow$	$(q$	$\Rightarrow$	$p)$
1	1	1	1	1
1	1	2	1	1
1	1	3	1	1
2	1	1	2	2
2	1	2	1	2
2	1	3	1	2
3	1	1	3	3
3	1	2	3	3
3	1	3	1	3

It is apparent from this that the formula always takes the value 1. A similar result can be shown for the second axiom.

Observe also that, if p and $p \Rightarrow q$ both take the value 1, examination of the implication operator's valuation table shows that q must also take the value 1. Thus any theorems proved from the first two axioms using the rule MP must take the value 1. But the third axiom can take the value 3 when $p = 3$ and $q = 2$, as is shown by the following evaluation:

$(\neg$	p	$\Rightarrow$	$\neg$	$q)$	$\Rightarrow$	$(q$	$\Rightarrow$	$p)$
3	1	1	3	1	1	1	1	1
3	1	1	2	2	1	2	1	1
3	1	1	1	3	1	3	1	1
2	2	3	3	1	1	1	2	2
2	2	1	2	2	1	2	1	2
2	2	1	1	3	1	3	1	2
1	3	3	3	1	1	1	3	3
1	3	2	2	2	3	2	3	3
1	3	1	1	3	1	3	1	3

It cannot therefore be deduced using MP from the first two axioms, so must be retained as one of the set of axioms.

Independence of rules

As well as showing that the axioms are independent and hence are all essential, we now need to show that all of the rules are independent and essential. We can easily show that the rule of MP is independent, since it is the only way of obtaining shorter formulae as theorems. There is no other way for example that the theorem

$$p \Rightarrow p$$

can be proved since it is shorter than any of the axioms, so cannot be an instance of one of them.

2.5 Lemmon's system of propositional logic

2.5.1 An introduction to the system

Any *proof* or *deduction* in a formal system of logic must consist of a series of *wff*s, each accompanied by a justification of its validity. Some systems, as we have seen, may use a minimum set of axioms, and a single rule such as MP. Other systems aimed at generating proofs and deductions more easily will probably also allow more rules (we look at such a system here). Other books use numerous rules of algebraic manipulation to prove equivalence between formulae in Boolean algebra (essentially a logic using the operators $\{\neg, \vee, \wedge\}$).

A well-known deduction system due to E. J. Lemmon [1] uses (as it must) sequences of *wff*s as deductions, but involves a different notation for specification of the hypotheses used at each stage in the deductions. Since this technique has now been adopted by some mechanized proof systems, we will describe its main principles here. The system has no axioms. Instead there is a rule of assumption. This rule is used to give hypotheses and then work from these to establish deductions. This can create some confusion over the difference between a deduction and a proof. Lemmon's system is aimed more at generating deductions than proofs, although it is possible to use some of the rules of the system to turn deductions into proofs in a similar way to the application of the deduction theorem for *L*. This is explained in more detail below. It has considerably more rules than system *L*. One major difference we wish to demonstrate is in the notation of the deductions (or proofs).

Now we know that every formal system must have the following sets of objects: (a) an alphabet, (b) a set of *wff*s, (c) a set of axioms (which may be empty) and (d) a set of inference rules. For Lemmon's system these sets are as follows.

The alphabet of Lemmon's system

This consists of the following sets:

(a) the infinite set of propositional variables $\{p_1, p_2, \ldots\}$: when we are only using two or three variables at a time they will be denoted by p, q and r;
(b) the set of punctuation symbols $\{',', '(', ')'\}$;
(c) the set of logical operators $\{\neg, \Rightarrow, \wedge, \vee\}$.

The *wffs* of Lemmon's system

A propositional statement P is a *wff* in the system if it conforms to one of the following conditions:

(a) P is a propositional variable; or
(b) P is of the form $(\neg Q)$, where Q is a *wff*; or
(c) P is of the form $(Q \Rightarrow R)$, $(Q \wedge R)$ or $(Q \vee R)$, where Q and R are *wffs*.

Note: Superfluous brackets can be omitted as in system L.

The axioms of Lemmon's system

There are no axioms in the system.

The inference rules of Lemmon's system

The first rule of this system that we will consider is the rule of assumption. It is denoted by the letter A. This rule allows the introduction of any assumptions that may be needed at any stage. Although it is stated as a rule in this system it is the same idea as introducing hypotheses to make deductions as we did with system L.

The complete list of all the other rules of the system is as follows:

Abbrev.	Full name	From	We obtain
DN	double negation	$\Gamma \vdash \neg\neg P$	$\Gamma \vdash P$
DN	double negation	$\Gamma \vdash P$	$\Gamma \vdash \neg\neg P$
MP	MP	$\Gamma_1 \vdash P, \Gamma_2 \vdash P \Rightarrow Q$	$\Gamma_1, \Gamma_2 \vdash Q$
MT	modus tollens	$\Gamma_1 \vdash P \Rightarrow Q, \Gamma_2 \vdash \neg Q$	$\Gamma_1, \Gamma_2 \vdash \neg P$
$\wedge$ I	$\wedge$ introduction	$\Gamma_1 \vdash P, \Gamma_2 \vdash Q$	$\Gamma_1, \Gamma_2 \vdash P \wedge Q$
$\wedge$ E	$\wedge$ elimination	$\Gamma \vdash P \wedge Q$	$\Gamma \vdash P$
$\wedge$ E	$\wedge$ elimination	$\Gamma \vdash P \wedge Q$	$\Gamma \vdash Q$
$\vee$ I	$\vee$ introduction	$\Gamma \vdash P$	$\Gamma \vdash P \vee Q$
$\vee$ I	$\vee$ introduction	$\Gamma \vdash Q$	$\Gamma \vdash P \vee Q$
$\vee$ E	$\vee$ elimination	$\Gamma_1 \vdash P \vee Q, \Gamma_2, P \vdash R,$ $\Gamma_3, Q \vdash R$	$\Gamma_1, \Gamma_2, \Gamma_3 \vdash R$
CP	conditional proof	$\Gamma, P \vdash Q$	$\Gamma \vdash P \Rightarrow Q$
RAA	reductio ad absurdum	$\Gamma_1, P \vdash Q, \Gamma_2, P \vdash \neg Q$	$\Gamma_1, \Gamma_2 \vdash \neg P$

where P, Q and R are *wffs* of Lemmon's system and Γ, Γ_1, Γ_2 and Γ_3 are sets of *wffs*. Note that it could well be the case that any of Γ, Γ_1, Γ_2 and Γ_3 in the above rules is empty.

The justifications for each of these rules are reasonably obvious. Each rule is based upon the truth-table of the appropriate operators. Note that the conditional-proof rule (CP) is the same rule for Lemmon's system as the deduction theorem is for L.

2.5.2   Proofs and deductions in Lemmon's system

Lemmon's system is a *deduction* system. By this we mean that it is aimed at generating deductions and consequents (rather than proofs and theorems). The assumption rule introduces the hypotheses of the deduction. However, applications of CP or RAA can turn deductions into proofs (where a proof is thought of as a deduction with no hypotheses) and a consequent of a proof is a *theorem* of the system. We have seen how this was done in system L by applying the deduction theorem.

Now in any written deduction (or proof), the Lemmon notation also keeps a record in the first column of the numbers of the assumptions (hypotheses) on which this line depends. This is a key part of deductions and proofs in this system.

Every line states in the first column the hypotheses involved, and in the third column the result which has been deduced from them. The last two rules *move* *wffs* from the left-hand side of the ⊢ symbol to the right-hand side. Whenever this is done, any reference to a relevant assumption is removed from the first column. If, when we have finished, there are no assumption references in the first column, then the sequence of *wffs* is a *proof* (a proof is a deduction with no hypotheses) in the system and a *theorem* of the system has been derived. If, however, there are some references left in the first column, then we have a *deduction* in the system. The references state the hypotheses of the deduction (applications of the rule of assumption).

2.5.3   Examples of deductions in Lemmon's system

We will briefly go through each of the rules and have a look at some simple examples.

Double negation

Double negations can be introduced and removed using the two variants of the double-negation rule. In both cases, the double negation must occur at the beginning of the formula; the rule does not permit us to introduce it in the interior of a formula. The set of assumptions in column 1 will be the same as the set in the single line referred to.

Modus ponens

This is the same rule as that used for system L. It is used in exactly the same way.

Modus tollens

This is a rule similar to MP, stating that

$$P \Rightarrow Q, \neg Q \vdash \neg P.$$

Now consider two examples of deductions in the system using the rules we have just introduced.

(a) To show that $R \Rightarrow Q, P \Rightarrow \neg Q, P \vdash \neg R$ consider the following sequence of *wff*s:

Assumptions	No.	wff	Rule	Refs.
1	1	$R \Rightarrow Q$	A	
2	2	$P \Rightarrow \neg Q$	A	
3	3	P	A	
2, 3	4	$\neg Q$	MP	2, 3
1, 2, 3	5	$\neg R$	MT	1, 4

The first three lines represent the three assumptions from which we start the deduction. The next line says that $\neg Q$ (column 3) was deduced from lines 2 and 3 using MP (column 4), and (in the first column) that this result depends on the assumptions on lines 2 and 3. On the last line we see that $\neg R$ follows from lines 1 and 4; we are using all the assumptions involved in lines 1 and 4. Hence, the assumptions used to derive $\neg R$ are those listed on lines 1, 2 and 3. The last line tells us that we have constructed a deduction of $\neg R$ from $R \Rightarrow Q, P \Rightarrow \neg Q$ and P.

(b) To show that $R \Rightarrow P, Q \Rightarrow \neg R, S \Rightarrow \neg Q, S \vdash P$ consider the following sequence of *wff*s:

Assumptions	No.	wff	Rule	Refs.
1	1	$R \Rightarrow P$	A	
2	2	$Q \Rightarrow \neg R$	A	
3	3	$S \Rightarrow \neg Q$	A	
4	4	S	A	
3, 4	5	$\neg Q$	MP	3, 4
2, 3, 4	6	$\neg\neg R$	MT	2, 5
2, 3, 4	7	R	DN	6
1, 2, 3, 4	8	P	MP	1, 7

Notice that whenever MP or MT are used, the list of assumptions in the first column will be the union of the assumptions involved in the two lines to which we refer.

∧ introduction and elimination

The rule for introducing the ∧ operator states that, given any two results earlier in the proof, their conjunction can be deduced. In the assumptions column we take the union of the assumptions of the earlier two referenced results.

For eliminating the ∧ operator, the rule states that if we have a conjunction, then either of its operands can be deduced. The references in the assumptions column will be the same as those on the single referenced line.

As an example involving both of these rules we give the following deduction:

$$P \Rightarrow (Q \Rightarrow U), P \wedge Q, \neg S \Rightarrow R, \neg R \vdash U \wedge S.$$

The deduction is:

Assumptions	No.	wff	Rule	Refs.
1	1	$P \Rightarrow (Q \Rightarrow U)$	A	
2	2	$P \wedge Q$	A	
3	3	$\neg S \Rightarrow R$	A	
4	4	$\neg R$	A	
3, 4	5	$\neg\neg S$	MT	3, 4
3, 4	6	S	DN	5
2	7	P	∧E	2
1, 2	8	$Q \Rightarrow U$	MP	1, 7
2	9	Q	∧E	2
1, 2	10	U	MP	8, 9
1, 2, 3, 4	11	$U \wedge S$	∧I	6, 10

Note the way that the assumptions involved in each line are listed in the first column. In the last column we must quote one earlier number for each application of the rule ∧E, and two for ∧I.

∨ introduction and elimination

The introduction of the ∨ operator is straightforward. If there is any result, we can refer to it, and disjunct it (on the left or the right) by any other operand of our choice. The first column will refer to the same line numbers as the line from which it was derived.

An example of a deduction using this rule is given by

$$S \wedge P, S \Rightarrow Q \vdash Q \vee R.$$

The deduction is:

Assumptions	No.	*wff*	Rule	Refs.
1	1	$S \wedge P$	A	
2	2	$S \Rightarrow Q$	A	
1	3	S	$\wedge E$	1
1, 2	4	Q	MP	2, 3
1, 2	5	$Q \vee R$	$\vee I$	4

Lemmon's rule for eliminating the $\vee$ operator is somewhat messy. It is stated in full as

if $\Gamma_1 \vdash P \vee Q$ and $\Gamma_2, P \vdash R$ and $\Gamma_3, Q \vdash R$ then $\Gamma_1, \Gamma_2, \Gamma_3 \vdash R$.

The first column of the new line will be the union of the references in Γ_1, Γ_2 and Γ_3. In most of our exercises the sets Γ_2 and Γ_3 will be empty. We will need to quote three numbers each time we use this rule.

Intuitively, the idea is as follows:

if   we can deduce P *or* Q
and we can deduce that R follows from P
and we can also deduce that R follows from Q
then (because we can deduce *either* P or Q) we must be able to deduce R.

As an example, consider

$P \vee \neg Q, P \Rightarrow R, S \Rightarrow Q, \neg S \Rightarrow R \vdash R$.

The deduction is:

Assumptions	No.	*wff*	Rule	Refs.
1	1	$P \vee \neg Q$	A	
2	2	$P \Rightarrow R$	A	
3	3	$S \Rightarrow Q$	A	
4	4	$\neg S \Rightarrow R$	A	
5	5	P	A	
2, 5	6	R	MP	2, 5
7	7	$\neg Q$	A	
3, 7	8	$\neg S$	MT	3, 7
3, 7, 4	9	R	MP	4, 8
1, 2, 3, 4	10	R	$\vee E$	1, 6, 9

Note in particular the $\vee$-elimination at step 10. The *strategy* of the deduction is as follows:

$P \vee \neg Q \vdash P \vee \neg Q$ an assumption on line 1 $\Gamma_1 = \{P \vee \neg Q\}$

$P \Rightarrow R, P \vdash R$ the deduction is given
                                     by lines 5 and 6 $\Gamma_2 = \{P \Rightarrow R\}$

$S \Rightarrow Q, \neg S \Rightarrow R,$ the deduction is given
$\dfrac{}{\neg Q \vdash R}$ by lines 7 to 9 $\Gamma_3 = \{S \Rightarrow Q, \neg S \Rightarrow R\}$

Therefore $P \vee \neg Q, P \Rightarrow R, S \Rightarrow Q, \neg S \Rightarrow R \vdash R$ at line 10 by $\vee$-elimination.

Notice also that at line 10 the assumptions made specifically to use the $\vee$-elimination rule (lines 5 and 7) are omitted from the assumptions column.

Conditional proof

The conditional rule *CP* is the same as the deduction theorem described earlier for system *L*. It can be expressed as

if $\Gamma, Q \vdash P,$ then $\Gamma \vdash Q \Rightarrow P.$

It reduces the set of assumptions in the first column by removing the reference for Q. As a simple example, we will prove that

$R \Rightarrow P, \neg R \Rightarrow Q \vdash \neg P \Rightarrow Q.$

The deduction is:

Assumptions	No.	*wff*	Rule	Refs.
1	1	$R \Rightarrow P$	A	
2	2	$\neg R \Rightarrow Q$	A	
3	3	$\neg P$	A	
1, 3	4	$\neg R$	MT	1, 3
1, 2, 3	5	Q	MP	2, 4
1, 2	6	$\neg P \Rightarrow Q$	CP	3, 5

Note that the CP line includes two reference numbers in the last column. One of these refers to the line to which CP was applied, and the other to the assumption on column 1 which has been moved across.

If what we are trying to deduce is an implication such as $P \Rightarrow Q$, we will normally introduce P as an assumption early on, and use the CP rule at the end to give the required result. This corresponds to the way the deduction theorem enabled deductions (and proofs) to be performed for system *L* earlier in this chapter. The deduction theorem is never quoted in this system, the conditional proof rule is used instead.

Reductio ad absurdum

This rule can be expressed as

if $\Gamma_1, P \vdash Q$ and $\Gamma_2, P \vdash \neg Q,$ then $\Gamma_1, \Gamma_2 \vdash \neg P.$

The rule corresponds to a proof by contradiction. P is taken as an assumption and both Q and $\neg Q$ are deduced; from this we infer $\neg P$. The following example uses RAA to show that

$R \wedge S, S \Rightarrow Q, Q \Rightarrow P \vdash P.$

Assumptions	No.	wff	Rule	Refs.
1	1	$R \wedge S$	A	
2	2	$S \Rightarrow Q$	A	
3	3	$Q \Rightarrow P$	A	
4	4	$\neg P$	A	
3, 4	5	$\neg Q$	MT	3, 4
1	6	S	$\wedge E$	1
1, 2	7	Q	MP	2, 6
1, 2, 3	8	$\neg\neg P$	RAA	5, 7
1, 2, 3	9	P	DN	8

In the RAA on line 8, we refer to line 5 ($\Gamma_1 = \{3,4\}$) and line 7 ($\Gamma_2 = \{1,2\}$). Notice that in the assumptions column when RAA is applied we do not include the assumption that was made in order to derive the contradiction (in this case line 4). Apart from this, all the assumptions that were required in the first column are included.

Note: CP and RAA are the only rules in Lemmon's system which *move wffs* from the left-hand side of the $\vdash$ symbol to the right-hand side. Thus proofs in Lemmon's system (recall that a proof is a deduction with no *wffs* on the left-hand side of $\vdash$) can be established only by using one of these two rules. See the worked-examples section of this chapter for more examples of deductions and proofs in Lemmon's system.

2.6 Summary

In this chapter we introduced the idea of a formal system of propositional logic and saw that these are essentially algebraic methods for proving the validity of certain propositional formulae. We have looked in some detail at both system L and Lemmon's system. Do not confuse proofs and deductions in L with proofs and deductions in Lemmon's system.

For work associated with this chapter, truth-tables cannot be used unless the soundness and completeness of the system under consideration are first established. The main features (and differences) of system L and Lemmon's system are summarized in the table at the top of the next page.

We showed that system L is sound and complete. To see that Lemmon's is also sound and complete look at exercises 2.9 and 2.10.

	L	Lemmon
Operators	$\neg, \Rightarrow$	$\neg, \wedge, \vee, \Rightarrow$
wff	Using above two operators	Using above four operators
Axioms	Arising from the three given schemes	No axioms
Rules	MP	10 rules
Proofs of theorems	Can be constructed using deduction, but need not be	Must be constructed by first creating a deduction

This chapter has presented algebraic ways of proving theorems in propositional logic, and has shown that these are equivalent to the empirical results obtained in the previous chapter. Similar idcas will be carried over to predicate logic in a later chapter.

2.7   Worked examples

Example 2.1   Find proofs in L for the following statements:

(a) $\vdash P \Rightarrow (\neg P \Rightarrow \neg(P \Rightarrow P))$;
(b) $\vdash (P \Rightarrow Q) \Rightarrow (\neg Q \Rightarrow \neg P)$;
(c) $\vdash P \Rightarrow (\neg Q \Rightarrow \neg(P \Rightarrow Q))$;
(d) $\vdash (\neg Q \Rightarrow \neg P) \Rightarrow ((\neg Q \Rightarrow P) \Rightarrow Q)$;
(e) $\vdash (\neg P \Rightarrow P) \Rightarrow P$;
(f) $\vdash \neg P \Rightarrow \neg(\neg P \Rightarrow P)$;
(g) $\vdash (\neg Q \Rightarrow \neg P) \Rightarrow ((\neg Q \Rightarrow P) \Rightarrow (\neg Q \Rightarrow \neg(Q \Rightarrow Q)))$,

where P and Q are any *wffs* of L.

Solution

(a) To show

$$\vdash P \Rightarrow (\neg P \Rightarrow \neg(P \Rightarrow P))$$

we show first that

$$P, \neg P \vdash \neg(P \Rightarrow P).$$

1	P	hypothesis;
2	$\neg P$	hypothesis;
3	$(\neg\neg(P \Rightarrow P) \Rightarrow \neg P))$ $\Rightarrow (P \Rightarrow \neg(P \Rightarrow P))$	L3 with $\neg(P \Rightarrow P)$ for U and P for V;
4	$\neg P \Rightarrow (\neg\neg(P \Rightarrow P) \Rightarrow \neg P)$	L1 with $\neg P$ for U and $\neg\neg(P \Rightarrow P)$ for V;
5	$\neg\neg(P \Rightarrow P) \Rightarrow \neg P)$	MP on 2 and 4;

6   $P \Rightarrow \neg(P \Rightarrow P)$ MP on 3 and 5;
7   $\neg(P \Rightarrow P)$ MP on 1 and 6.

Now two applications of the deduction theorem give the result in the form required.

(b) To show

$$\vdash (P \Rightarrow Q) \Rightarrow (\neg Q \Rightarrow \neg P),$$

we show first that

$$P \Rightarrow Q \vdash \neg Q \Rightarrow \neg P.$$

1   $P \Rightarrow Q$ hypothesis;
2   $(\neg\neg P \Rightarrow \neg\neg Q) \Rightarrow (\neg Q \Rightarrow \neg P)$ L3 with $\neg P$ for U and $\neg Q$ for V;
3   $Q \Rightarrow \neg\neg Q$ example 3 (b) in section 2.2.5
                                                   with Q for P;
4   $\neg\neg P \Rightarrow P$ example 3 (a) in section 2.2.5;
5   $P \Rightarrow \neg\neg Q$ HS on 1 and 3;
6   $\neg\neg P \Rightarrow \neg\neg Q$ HS on 4 and 5;
7   $\neg Q \Rightarrow \neg P$ MP on 2 and 6.

The result now follows by one application of the deduction theorem.

(c) To show that

$$\vdash P \Rightarrow (\neg Q \Rightarrow \neg(P \Rightarrow Q)),$$

we show first that

$$P, \neg Q \vdash \neg(P \Rightarrow Q).$$

1   P hypothesis;
2   $\neg Q$ hypothesis;
3   $P \Rightarrow ((P \Rightarrow Q) \Rightarrow Q))$ MP expressed as a theorem of L
                                                   (by using the deduction theorem twice);
4   $(P \Rightarrow Q) \Rightarrow Q$ MP on 1 and 3;
5   $((P \Rightarrow Q) \Rightarrow Q)$
        $\Rightarrow (\neg Q \Rightarrow \neg(P \Rightarrow Q))$ (b) with $P \Rightarrow Q$ for P and Q unchanged;
6   $\neg Q \Rightarrow \neg(P \Rightarrow Q)$ MP on 4 and 5.

The result now follows by two applications of the deduction theorem.

(d) To show

$$\vdash (\neg Q \Rightarrow \neg P) \Rightarrow ((\neg Q \Rightarrow P) \Rightarrow Q),$$

we show first that

$$\neg Q \Rightarrow \neg P, \neg Q \Rightarrow P \vdash Q.$$

1 $\neg Q \Rightarrow \neg P$	hypothesis;
2 $\neg Q \Rightarrow P$	hypothesis;
3 $\neg Q \Rightarrow (\neg P \Rightarrow \neg(\neg Q \Rightarrow P))$	(c) with $\neg Q$ for P and P for Q;
4 $(\neg Q \Rightarrow (\neg P \Rightarrow \neg(\neg Q \Rightarrow P))) \Rightarrow$ $((\neg Q \Rightarrow \neg P) \Rightarrow (\neg Q \Rightarrow \neg(\neg Q \Rightarrow P)))$	L2 with $\neg Q$ for U, $\neg P$ for V and $\neg(\neg Q \Rightarrow P)$ for W;
5 $(\neg Q \Rightarrow \neg P) \Rightarrow (\neg Q \Rightarrow \neg(\neg Q \Rightarrow P))$	MP on 3 and 4;
6 $\neg Q \Rightarrow \neg(\neg Q \Rightarrow P)$	MP on 1 and 5;
7 $(\neg Q \Rightarrow \neg(\neg Q \Rightarrow P))$ $\Rightarrow ((\neg Q \Rightarrow P) \Rightarrow Q))$	L3 with Q for U and $\neg Q \Rightarrow P$ for V;
8 $(\neg Q \Rightarrow P) \Rightarrow Q$	MP on 6 and 7;
9 Q	MP on 2 and 8.

Now two applications of the deduction theorem give the result.

(e) To show

$$\vdash (\neg P \Rightarrow P) \Rightarrow P,$$

we show first that

$$\neg P \Rightarrow P \vdash P.$$

1 $\neg P \Rightarrow P$	hypothesis;
2 $(\neg P \Rightarrow \neg P) \Rightarrow ((\neg P \Rightarrow P) \Rightarrow P)$	(d) with P for Q and P unchanged;
3 $\neg P \Rightarrow \neg P$	example in section 2.2.2 with $\neg P$ for P;
4 $(\neg P \Rightarrow P) \Rightarrow P$	MP on 2 and 3;
5 P	MP on 1 and 4.

Two applications of the deduction theorem give the result.

(f) To show

$$\vdash \neg P \Rightarrow \neg(\neg P \Rightarrow P),$$

consider the following proof sequence:

1 $((\neg P \Rightarrow P) \Rightarrow P)$ $\Rightarrow (\neg P \Rightarrow \neg(\neg P \Rightarrow P))$	(b) with $\neg P \Rightarrow P$ for P and P for Q;
2 $(\neg P \Rightarrow P) \Rightarrow P$	(e);
3 $\neg P \Rightarrow \neg(\neg P \Rightarrow P)$	MP on 1 and 2.

(g) To show

$$\vdash (\neg Q \Rightarrow \neg P) \Rightarrow ((\neg Q \Rightarrow P) \Rightarrow (\neg Q \Rightarrow \neg(Q \Rightarrow Q))),$$

we show first that

$$\neg Q \Rightarrow \neg P \vdash (\neg Q \Rightarrow P) \Rightarrow (\neg Q \Rightarrow \neg(Q \Rightarrow Q)):$$

1	$\neg Q \Rightarrow \neg P$	hypothesis;
2	$(\neg Q \Rightarrow \neg P) \Rightarrow ((\neg Q \Rightarrow P) \Rightarrow Q)$	(d);
3	$(\neg Q \Rightarrow P) \Rightarrow Q$	MP on 1 and 2;
4	$Q \Rightarrow (\neg Q \Rightarrow \neg(Q \Rightarrow Q))$	(a) (or (c) with Q for P);
5	$(\neg Q \Rightarrow P) \Rightarrow (\neg Q \Rightarrow \neg(Q \Rightarrow Q))$	HS on 3 and 4.

The result now follows by one application of MP.

Example 2.2   Establish the following deductions in Lemmon's system:

(a) $(P \wedge Q) \Rightarrow V, \neg S, \neg P \Rightarrow S, \neg S \Rightarrow R, R \Rightarrow Q \vdash V;$
(b) $V \Rightarrow P, (\neg V \wedge Q) \Rightarrow S \vdash \neg P \Rightarrow (Q \Rightarrow S);$
(c) $R \vee (V \wedge S), P \Rightarrow \neg R, V \Rightarrow Q, S \Rightarrow U, (Q \wedge U) \Rightarrow \neg P \vdash \neg P;$
(d) $P \Rightarrow R, R \Rightarrow S, S \Rightarrow \neg Q \vdash \neg(P \wedge Q),$

where P, Q, R, S, V and U are any *wffs* of the system.

Solution

(a) $(P \wedge Q) \Rightarrow V, \neg S, \neg P \Rightarrow S, \neg S \Rightarrow R, R \Rightarrow Q \vdash V:$

1	1	$(P \wedge Q) \Rightarrow V$	A
2	2	$\neg S$	A
3	3	$\neg P \Rightarrow S$	A
4	4	$\neg S \Rightarrow R$	A
5	5	$R \Rightarrow Q$	A
2, 3	6	$\neg \neg P$	2, 3 MT
2, 3	7	P	6 DN
2, 4	8	R	2, 4 MP
2, 4, 5	9	Q	8, 5 MP
2, 3, 4, 5	10	$P \wedge Q$	7, 9 $\wedge$I
1, 2, 3, 4, 5	11	V	1, 10 MP

(b) $V \Rightarrow P, (\neg V \wedge Q) \Rightarrow S \vdash \neg P \Rightarrow (Q \Rightarrow S):$

1	1	$V \Rightarrow P$	A
2	2	$(\neg V \wedge Q) \Rightarrow S$	A
3	3	$\neg P$	A
4	4	Q	A
1, 3	5	$\neg V$	1, 3 MT

1, 3, 4	6	$\neg V \wedge Q$	4, 5 $\wedge$ I
1, 2, 3, 4	7	S	2, 6 MP
1, 2, 3	8	$Q \Rightarrow S$	4, 7 CP
1, 2	9	$\neg P \Rightarrow (Q \Rightarrow S)$	3, 8 CP

(c) $R \vee (V \wedge S), P \Rightarrow \neg R, V \Rightarrow Q, S \Rightarrow U, (Q \wedge U) \Rightarrow \neg P \vdash \neg P$:

1	1	$R \vee (V \wedge S)$	A
2	2	$P \Rightarrow \neg R$	A
3	3	$V \Rightarrow Q$	A
4	4	$S \Rightarrow U$	A
5	5	$(Q \wedge U) \Rightarrow \neg P$	A
6	6	R	A
6	7	$\neg\neg R$	6 DN
2, 6	8	$\neg P$	2, 7 MT
9	9	$V \wedge S$	A
9	10	V	9 $\wedge$ E
3, 9	11	Q	3, 10 MP
9	12	S	9 $\wedge$ E
4, 9	13	U	4, 12 MP
3, 4, 9	14	$Q \wedge U$	11, 13 $\wedge$ I
3, 4, 5, 9	15	$\neg P$	5, 14 MP
1, 2, 3, 4, 5	16	$\neg P$	1, 8, 15 $\vee$ E

(d) $P \Rightarrow R, R \Rightarrow S, S \Rightarrow \neg Q \vdash \neg(P \wedge Q)$:

1	1	$P \Rightarrow R$	A
2	2	$R \Rightarrow S$	A
3	3	$S \Rightarrow \neg Q$	A
4	4	$P \wedge Q$	A
4	5	P	4 $\wedge$ E
1, 4	6	R	1, 5 MP
1, 2, 4	7	S	2, 6 MP
4	8	Q	4 $\wedge$ E
4	9	$\neg\neg Q$	9 DN
3, 4	10	$\neg S$	3, 9 MT
1, 2, 3	11	$\neg(P \wedge Q)$	4, 7, 10 RAA

Example 2.3   Show that every axiom of system L is a theorem of Lemmon's system.

Solution   We have to show that each axiom scheme of L can be proved in Lemmon's system and then apply the derived rule of inference SI given in exercise 2.6.

Axiom schema L1: $U \Rightarrow (V \Rightarrow U)$.

The proof in Lemmon's system is given by the following sequence of *wffs*:

Assumptions	No.	wff	Rule	Refs.
1	1	U	A	
2	2	V	A	
1	3	$V \Rightarrow U$	CP	1, 2
	4	$U \Rightarrow (V \Rightarrow U)$	CP	1, 3

Axiom schema L2: $(U \Rightarrow (V \Rightarrow W)) \Rightarrow ((U \Rightarrow V) \Rightarrow (U \Rightarrow W))$.

The proof in Lemmon's system is given by the following sequence of *wffs*:

Assumptions	No.	wff	Rule	Refs.
1	1	$U \Rightarrow (V \Rightarrow W)$	A	
2	2	$U \Rightarrow V$	A	
3	3	U	A	
1, 3	4	$V \Rightarrow W$	MP	1, 3
1, 2, 3	5	W	MP	2, 4
1, 2	6	$U \Rightarrow W$	CP	3, 5
1	7	$(U \Rightarrow V) \Rightarrow (U \Rightarrow W)$	CP	2, 6
	8	$(U \Rightarrow (V \Rightarrow W))$ $\Rightarrow ((U \Rightarrow V) \Rightarrow (U \Rightarrow W))$	CP	1, 7

Axiom schema L3: $(\neg U \Rightarrow \neg V) \Rightarrow (V \Rightarrow U)$.

The proof in Lemmon's system is given by the following sequence of *wffs*:

Assumptions	No.	wff	Rule	Refs.
1	1	$\neg U \Rightarrow \neg V$	A	
2	2	V	A	
2	3	$\neg\neg V$	DN	2
1, 2	4	$\neg\neg U$	MT	1, 3
1, 2	5	U	DN	4
1	6	$V \Rightarrow U$	CP	2, 5
	7	$(\neg U \Rightarrow \neg V) \Rightarrow (V \Rightarrow U)$	CP	1, 6

Example 2.4 Show that every theorem of system L is a theorem of Lemmon's system.

Solution Let P be a theorem of L. It is clear that P is a *wff* of Lemmon's system.

We show that P is a theorem of Lemmon's by induction on the number n of *wff*s in the sequence which forms the proof of P in L.

Base case $(n = 1)$. If this is the case, then P is an axiom of L and therefore a theorem of Lemmon's system by the previous question.

Induction step. We now assume that the result holds for all proofs in L of length k and assume we have a proof of length $k+1$. The only rule of system L is MP (remember that the other rules such as the deduction theorem are *derived* rules). We, therefore, know that either P is an axiom (which has already been dealt with in the base case) or P follows by MP from two *wff*s of L (and hence Lemmon's) of the form Q and $Q \Rightarrow P$.

We know (by the induction hypothesis) that Q and $Q \Rightarrow P$ are theorems of Lemmon's system therefore by the MP rule in Lemmon's system P is a theorem of Lemmon's.

2.8 Exercises

Exercise 2.1 Show that the following *wff*s are theorems of the system L:

    (a) $\neg(p \Rightarrow p) \Rightarrow \neg(p \Rightarrow q)$;
    (b) $(q \Rightarrow p) \Rightarrow (\neg q \Rightarrow \neg(\neg p \Rightarrow \neg q))$;
    (c) $p \Rightarrow (q \Rightarrow (p \Rightarrow q))$;
    (d) $(\neg\neg p \Rightarrow \neg\neg q) \Rightarrow (p \Rightarrow q)$;
    (e) $(p \Rightarrow q) \Rightarrow ((\neg p \Rightarrow q) \Rightarrow q)$.

Exercise 2.2 Show that the following deductions hold in the system L:

    (a) $p, \neg p \vdash q$;
    (b) $\neg p \vdash (\neg q \Rightarrow p) \Rightarrow q$;
    (c) $p \Rightarrow (q \Rightarrow r), q \Rightarrow p \vdash q \Rightarrow r$.

Exercise 2.3 A formal propositional system given by Mendelsohn [2] and used by Dowsing *et al.* [3] is the same as system L except that axiom scheme L3 is replaced by the axiom scheme

$$(\neg U \Rightarrow \neg V) \Rightarrow ((\neg U \Rightarrow V) \Rightarrow U).$$

Show that axiom scheme L3 of system L is a theorem of this system.

Show also that in this system:

(a) $\vdash (P \Rightarrow Q) \Rightarrow (\neg Q \Rightarrow \neg P)$;
(b) $\vdash P \Rightarrow (\neg Q \Rightarrow \neg(P \Rightarrow Q))$;
(c) $\neg\neg P \dashv\vdash P$.

Exercise 2.4   In section 5.3 we showed that $R \wedge S, S \Rightarrow Q, Q \Rightarrow P \vdash P$ in Lemmon's system. Establish this deduction without using RAA.

Exercise 2.5   Using Lemmon's system establish the following deductions:

(a) $P \wedge S, P \Rightarrow Q, Q \Rightarrow R, S \Rightarrow \neg T \vdash R \wedge \neg T$;
(b) $P, Q \Rightarrow R, P \Rightarrow Q, S \Rightarrow \neg R \vdash \neg S$;
(c) $\neg S \Rightarrow (P \vee Q), S \Rightarrow \neg T, T, P \Rightarrow R, \neg R \Rightarrow \neg Q \vdash R$;
(d) $\vdash P \Rightarrow (Q \Rightarrow (P \Rightarrow Q))$;
(e) $S, \neg P \Rightarrow Q, P \Rightarrow \neg S, Q \Rightarrow R \vdash R$;
(f) $\vdash (P \Rightarrow Q) \Rightarrow ((\neg Q \wedge \neg R) \Rightarrow \neg P)$;
(g) $P \vee Q \vdash (Q \Rightarrow R) \Rightarrow (\neg R \Rightarrow P)$.

Exercise 2.6   Show that the following rule of inference (called SI, for 'substitution instance') can be derived in Lemmon's system.

'Any substitution instance of a theorem of Lemmon's system is also a theorem.'

A substitution instance of a *wff* P is the consistent replacement of one or more propositional variables in P by other *wffs*.

Exercise 2.7   Let P be a *wff* of L, let I be any interpretation of P and let $p_1, p_2, \ldots, p_n$ be the propositional variables occurring in P. Using the notation presented in section 2.3.3.1, show that the following deduction holds in L:

$$(p_1)^I, (p_2^I), \ldots, (p_{n)}^I \vdash P^I.$$

Hint: To establish the result, use induction on the number of logical operators (occurrences of $\neg$ and $\Rightarrow$) in the formula P.

Exercise 2.8   You are given the following set of axioms due to Novikov:

A1.1 $p \Rightarrow (q \Rightarrow p)$;
A1.2 $(p \Rightarrow (q \Rightarrow r)) \Rightarrow ((p \Rightarrow q) \Rightarrow (p \Rightarrow r))$;
A2.1 $(p \wedge q) \Rightarrow p$;
A2.2 $(p \wedge q) \Rightarrow q$;
A2.3 $(p \Rightarrow q) \Rightarrow ((p \Rightarrow r) \Rightarrow (p \Rightarrow (q \wedge r)))$;
A3.1 $p \Rightarrow (p \vee q)$;

A3.2 $p \Rightarrow (q \vee p)$;

A3.3 $(p \Rightarrow r) \Rightarrow ((q \Rightarrow r) \Rightarrow ((p \vee q) \Rightarrow r))$;

A4.1 $(p \Rightarrow q) \Rightarrow (\neg q \Rightarrow \neg p)$;

A4.2 $p \Rightarrow \neg\neg p$;

A4.3 $\neg\neg p \Rightarrow p$.

Using the rules of substitution and MP prove

(a) $\vdash \neg q \Rightarrow \neg(p \wedge q)$;

(b) $\vdash (p \vee q) \Rightarrow (q \vee p)$;

(c) $\vdash (p \wedge q) \Rightarrow (q \wedge p)$;

(d) $\vdash ((p \wedge q) \vee \neg\neg p) \Rightarrow p$;

(e) $\vdash p \Rightarrow ((p \vee q) \wedge (q \Rightarrow p))$.

Exercise 2.9   Show that Lemmon's system is sound.

Exercise 2.10   Show that Lemmon's system is complete.

Hint: Use a similar method to the proof of the completeness of L outlined in section 2.3.3.

Exercise 2.11   Write programs to perform the following operations:

(a) Read in a proof in system L, and validate it. You may choose your own input conventions, and whether you permit the use of additional rules such as hypothetical syllogism. Validating a given proof is easy; to generate a proof would be much harder!

(b) Do the same for Lemmon's system.

(c) Read in a set of axioms, and using the method of section 2.4, try different three-valued truth-tables to prove the independence of each axiom.

References

1. R. D. Dowsing, V. J. Rayward-Smith and C. D. Walter, *A First Course in Formal Logic and its Applications in Computer Science*, 1986. Blackwell Scientific Publications.

2. E. J. Lemmon, *Beginning Logic*, 1965. Van Nostrand Reinhold.

3. E. Mendelson, *Introduction to Mathematical Logic* (3rd edn.), 1987. Wadsworth and Brooks/Cole.

CHAPTER 3

Applications to logic design

3.1 Introduction

Electronic and mechanical control devices can be classed as either *digital* or *analog* in operation. In analog devices, some internal quantity is proportional to a numeric value which it represents. Thus the needle of a mechanical car speedometer moves proportionally to the speed of the car; the opening of the throttle is proportional to the desired power output. In a digital system, quantities are represented by numeric registers which can move only in discrete steps. Telephone numbers, for example, are combinations of digits and perhaps letters, and there is no concept of a small quantitative change, only of a discrete change to another distinct number. Early mechanical industrial controllers used analog methods, so that, for example, a controller of the temperature of a kiln would have a lever which was moved proportionally by a cam to represent the temperature required.

A more modern device will store the information digitally in electronic form, and convert the numeric representation of, for example, the power output required, into actual power using a *digital to analog* or *d-to-a* converter on its output. To measure the temperature of the kiln (an input value needed for the calculation of the power output required) the controller may use the output of a thermocouple (which is a voltage representing the temperature) which will be converted for input to the controller using an *analog to digital* or *a-to-d* converter. All calculations internal to the controller are performed digitally, even though most interfaces to the real world are in an analog form. We talk of the controller consisting of a *model* of the real-world situation it is representing.

As another example of the analog versus digital concept, we can consider domestic audio equipment. The final output must be analog, creating vibrations in the air which are transmitted to the listener's ear. The means of generating these vibrations can be completely analog, using analog electronics to convert the strength of magnetic signals on a cassette tape or the movements of a needle in the groove of a record into the movement of the loudspeaker diaphragm. With more modern input, such as compact discs, the information is read from the disc in digital form, as a sequence of numbers representing the waveform to be generated, which has then to be converted to analog power to drive the loudspeaker.

Computers and other digital electronic equipment work with every internal point which represents a value in one of two states, for example 0 volts or +5 volts. Because this is the simplest electronic way to construct a mechanism, all numeric calculations are converted into two-state problems, the obvious representation technique being based on binary arithmetic. The exact technique for representing numeric quantities by binary patterns is beyond the scope of this text.

If we wish to construct a mathematical model of such a mechanism, all the variables in our model must take one of only two values. The principles of the operation can therefore be described and/or predicted using a model based on propositional logic. In such a model we may let one of the two internal states (say 0 volts) represent the value F, and the other (say 5 volts) represent the value T. Alternatively, we can talk in terms of modelling, and say that the value F will be represented by one particular state (say 0 volts) and T by the other (say 5 volts).

Note that if we choose to represent, for example, T by 0 volts, and F by +5 volts, a circuit with inputs and outputs will be modelled by a certain formula. If we reverse the convention, and represent T by +5 volts and F by 0 volts, then exactly the same circuit now represents the dual of the formula modelled in the previous case. We have effectively negated the input and output values of the formula. We must be consistent in whichever convention we choose.

Notation

Computer hardware texts tend to use the symbol 0 instead of F and 1 instead of T, '·' for '∧', '+' for '∨', and $\bar{p}$ or p' for $\neg p$. This convention was chosen since it can be seen for example that the ∧ operator is equivalent to numeric multiplication, since $1 \cdot 1 = 1$, $1 \cdot 0 = 0$, $0 \cdot 1 = 0$ and $0 \cdot 0 = 0$. This notation will be employed as far as possible in this chapter.

All functions of the electronic system can now be represented (modelled) by logical functions. Any logical formula can be constructed from black boxes which represent the components of the formula. The boxes may use any appropriate technology to represent their actions, and may be made of Meccano (purely mechanical), relays (switches controlled by electromagnets), transistors or valves (electronic components, but run in one of two states rather than in an analog form), or integrated circuits (many electronic components on a single silicon chip). Our concern now is to generate a mechanism using whatever technology is at our disposal to perform a given function. The function will usually be specified as a truth-table, not as a particular formula. The specification will define which outputs are to be set to 1 and which to 0 under which input conditions.

Different technologies perform different basic operations at the lowest level. Our mechanism must be designed to perform to the specified truth-table, but will have to be constructed from basic elements which depend on the technology chosen. Thus to generate a circuit for the formula $p \Rightarrow q$ is perfectly straightforward if we have $\Rightarrow$ boxes:

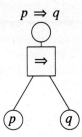

but may be harder if we have available only / boxes:

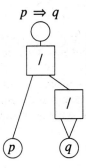

Typically only certain types of box are available. The types depend on the technology being used. The mechanical electro-magnetic relays used in some early computers essentially perform the conditioned disjunction function

$$[p, q \Leftrightarrow r, s]$$

with four inputs and one output. Transistors and integrated circuits can easily perform / and ↓ functions with two (or several) inputs and one output*, so any function we wish to construct must be described in terms of these basic boxes. Any function to be implemented is first defined by a truth-table; this definition must then be converted to a logic formula expressed in terms of basic operations which are available in the chosen technology.

---

*The multiple input equivalents of / and ↓ are the M_1 and M_0 functions of chapter 1.

It should be emphasized again that most problems here start from a truth-table, not from a function. The operation of the mechanism we are designing demands a certain truth-table; we must design a mechanism to emulate that truth-table. We must first convert the truth-table into a logical function (or model) which uses only the components at our disposal.

One of the skills is to minimize the cost or number of components required to model the required truth-table; this means more-or-less 'find the simplest formula'. There may well be other considerations affecting cost, perhaps the result of a subformula may be used in two places. We will not consider such specific complications in detail. We will require a formula expressed entirely in terms of the operators that we can construct. This may restrict us perhaps to / operators, and we know from earlier work that any function can be expressed in terms of the / operator. The formula $p \Rightarrow q$ now becomes $(q/q)/p$, requiring two boxes. Another complication is that certain entries in the truth-table defining the function may be empty; if that combination of inputs will never occur in practice, the entries can be filled in with either 1 or 0, the entries being chosen to give the simplest construction.

3.2   Simplification techniques

In the design of electronic machinery to perform given logical functions, we are anxious to find the cheapest/simplest formula to represent that function. Any truth-table can, of course, be expressed as a disjunctive-normal-form formula, but to implement this directly may involve an uneconomic number of components. The simplification of logical functions is therefore of great real commercial interest. We may be trying to simplify a given formula, or we may be trying to find the simplest formula to implement a given truth-table.

We will not define too closely the exact quantity which we are trying to minimize; in practice there are many complications. Maybe we could use one less and-box at the expense of two not-boxes. The relative cost of different basic mechanisms is obviously important. We may wish to share circuitry between two logical functions; there are physical upper limits to such sharing, and the cost of the necessary interconnections may be prohibitive. We may wish to simplify to use only $\downarrow$ functors, and the minimum number of them. A full study of reality here is more appropriate to the content of a VLSI book; we are concerned in this book to illustrate the applications of logic.

3.2.1   A simple example

We may be required to produce a mechanism to represent the following truth-table:

p	q	r	function
1	1	1	1
1	1	0	1
1	0	1	0
1	0	0	0
0	1	1	1
0	1	0	0
0	0	1	1
0	0	0	0

As a first step, the function could be represented (using full disjunctive normal form) as

$$F(p,q,r) =_{\text{df}} \bar{p}\cdot\bar{q}\cdot r + \bar{p}\cdot q\cdot r + p\cdot q\cdot\bar{r} + p\cdot q\cdot r.$$

The direct implementation of this as written would need four negation boxes, eight conjunction boxes and three disjunction boxes. The circuit in diagrammatic form would be as follows:

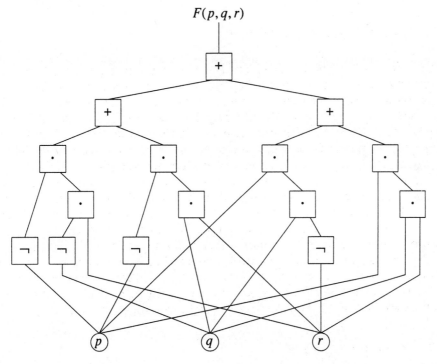

This could be simplified, since we really need only three negation boxes (the $\bar{p}$ needs generating only once), and the subformula $p\cdot q$ also appears twice. The diagram now becomes marginally simpler (it now contains fewer boxes).

$F(p,q,r)$

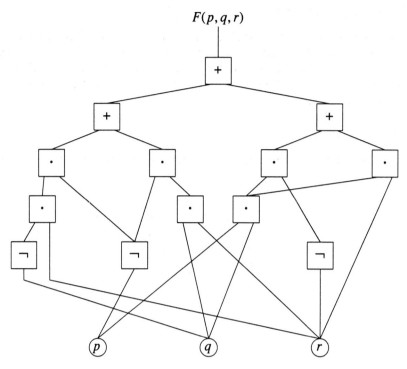

When expressed as

$$F(p,q,r) =_{\mathrm{df}} p \cdot q + \bar{p} \cdot r$$

(which you will find to be exactly equivalent) we have a very much cheaper construction with one negation box, two conjunction boxes and one disjunction box.

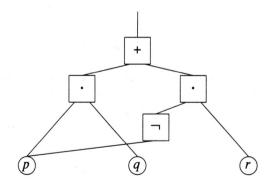

We will now look at two methods for producing simple logical formulae to represent given truth-tables.

3.2.2   Karnaugh maps

This is a simple graphical method for producing simplified formulae, suitable only for very simple functions (up to four variables). The truth-table is ordered to make it easy to pick out parts of a function, and ensures that only one variable changes truth-value when moving from one entry in the table to an adjacent entry.

A three-variable example

The Karnaugh map for the three-variable function defined by the truth-table

p	q	r	function
1	1	1	1
1	1	0	1
1	0	1	0
1	0	0	0
0	1	1	1
0	1	0	0
0	0	1	1
0	0	0	0

is first drawn as follows:

	1	1	0	0	p
	1	0	0	1	q
1	1	0	1	1	
0	1	0	0	0	
r					

Observe that, between any two adjacent squares, only one variable changes in value. The order of the columns is not what would be used in an ordinary truth-table. Thus if two adjacent squares contain 1 entries, they represent two disjuncts which differ in only one variable. The two 1 entries in the left-hand column represent the disjuncts $p \cdot q \cdot r$ and $p \cdot q \cdot \bar{r}$. Since these differ in only one variable, they can be combined into $p \cdot q$. We look for square or linear combinations containing four or two adjacent 1 entries. The groups of four can be either a square of four or a straight line of four. The groups of two can be either vertical or horizontal. The outer ends of the table must be considered to be joined. Each joined group represents a possible term. We look for boxes which will *cover* all of the 1 entries in the table with the minimum number of boxes.

The above diagram contains three possible pairs, indicated by the diagram

$$
\begin{array}{cccc}
1 & 1 & 0 & 0 \ \ p \\
1 & 0 & 0 & 1 \ \ q
\end{array}
$$

1	0	1	1
1	0	0	0

1

0

r

The final function for this table is

$$p \cdot q + \bar{p} \cdot r,$$

which covers all the 1 entries with two terms; the third possible term $q \cdot r$ is unnecessary. The term $p \cdot q$ is essential to cover the entry $p \cdot q \cdot \bar{r}$ (only one of the pairs covers it), and the term $\bar{p} \cdot r$ is essential to cover the entry $\bar{p} \cdot \bar{q} \cdot r$. All the 1 entries are now covered.

Another three-variable example

For a different function with five 1s in the truth-table we might have the definition

p	q	r	function
1	1	1	1
1	1	0	1
1	0	1	0
1	0	0	0
0	1	1	1
0	1	0	1
0	0	1	1
0	0	0	0

which is drawn for Karnaugh map purposes as

$$
\begin{array}{cccc}
1 & 1 & 0 & 0 \ \ p \\
1 & 0 & 0 & 1 \ \ q
\end{array}
$$

1	0	1	1
1	0	0	1

1

0

r

We have here a box of four entries overlapping the ends of the table. The available combinations are

1	1	0	0	p
1	0	0	1	q

This gives the final formula

$$q + \bar{p} \cdot r.$$

A four-variable example

We will now use a Karnaugh map to analyse the four-variable function defined by the truth-table

p	q	r	s	function
1	1	1	1	0
1	1	1	0	0
1	1	0	1	0
1	1	0	0	1
1	0	1	1	1
1	0	1	0	0
1	0	0	1	0
1	0	0	0	0
0	1	1	1	1
0	1	1	0	0
0	1	0	1	1
0	1	0	0	1
0	0	1	1	0
0	0	1	0	1
0	0	0	1	1
0	0	0	0	0

A four-variable table is again arranged so that only one variable changes between adjoining squares. This is given in (a) at the top of the next page.

We now look for adjacent groups of eight, four or two entries which are 1, and proceed as above. The possible combinations of entries in this case are given in (b) at the top of the next page.

The final simplified function is

$$q \cdot \bar{r} \cdot \bar{s} + \bar{p} \cdot \bar{r} \cdot s + \bar{p} \cdot q \cdot s + \bar{p} \cdot q \cdot r \cdot s + \bar{p} \cdot \bar{q} \cdot r \cdot \bar{s},$$

with no need for the term $\bar{p} \cdot q \cdot \bar{r}$.

	1	1	0	0	p
	1	0	0	1	q
1 1	0	1	0	1	
1 0	0	0	1	0	
0 0	1	0	0	1	
0 1	0	0	1	1	
r s					

(a)

	1	1	0	0	p
	1	0	0	1	q
1 1	0	1	0	1	
1 0	0	0	1	0	
0 0	1	0	0	1	
0 1	0	0	1	1	
r s					

(b)

Note: Never confuse ordinary truth-tables and Karnaugh map tables. Whenever you draw an ordinary truth-table, use the binary ordering 11, 10, 01, 00 for the columns and rows. Conversely, do not draw an ordinary truth-table and start looking for adjacent entries.

Don't care entries

Note that we may have *don't care* entries in the tables, usually indicated by an asterisk. These represent typically a combination of input truth-values which can never arise in practice, and for which the particular output truth-value is immaterial. We can fill these in with either 1 or 0 entries, whichever leads to the simplest formula. The following truth-table arises in the consideration of flip-flops later in this chapter; two of the input combinations ($p = 1, q = 1, r =$ either 1 or 0) are assumed never to arise in practice, so that the corresponding entries in the truth-table can take any values. The truth-table in standard form is:

	1	1	0	0	p
	1	0	1	0	q
1	*	1	0	1	
0	*	1	0	0	
r					

or in one-dimensional form:

p	q	r	function
1	1	1	*
1	1	0	*
1	0	1	1
1	0	0	1
0	1	1	0
0	1	0	0
0	0	1	1
0	0	0	0

In Karnaugh form this becomes

$$
\begin{array}{c|cccc}
 & 1 & 1 & 0 & 0 & p \\
 & 1 & 0 & 0 & 1 & q \\
\hline
1 & * & 1 & 1 & 0 \\
0 & * & 1 & 0 & 0 \\
r &
\end{array}
$$

There are four possible functions represented by this truth-table. If the *don't care* entries are both interpreted as 1, they can be combined with the column to their right to form a block of four 1s, which gives the formula

$p + \bar{q} \cdot r.$

If they are both interpreted as 0, we have the more complicated formula

$p \cdot \bar{q} + \bar{q} \cdot r.$

3.2.3   Quine–McClusky minimization

The Karnaugh map technique is applicable only to formulae of four or less variables. Quine–McClusky is a general-purpose algorithmic method based in the same principles, suitable for implementation by computer program, for use up to any number of variables.

The method operates in two distinct stages, first grouping terms together (effectively looking for all possible joining boxes in the Karnaugh technique), then choosing the essential terms, then eliminating redundant terms (choosing the minimum set of boxes to cover exactly the required set of 1 entries).

As an illustrative example, we will produce a minimal functional representation for the three-variable function specified by the truth-table

p	q	r	function
1	1	1	1
1	1	0	1
1	0	1	0
1	0	0	0
0	1	1	1
0	1	0	0
0	0	1	1
0	0	0	0

The full disjunctive normal form for this is

$\bar{p} \cdot \bar{q} \cdot r + \bar{p} \cdot q \cdot r + p \cdot q \cdot \bar{r} + p \cdot q \cdot r.$

We call the combinations of input values for which the output is required to be 1 as the *minterms* of the function. These form the basic components of the full DNF expression. We will effectively search for two of these terms which differ in only one variable; that variable must appear negated in one term and un-negated in the other. These two terms could be combined with this variable omitted altogether, since if g represents the remainder of the terms,

$$g \cdot p + g \cdot \bar{p} =_T g.$$

To differ in only one variable, one of the terms must have exactly one more negation operator than the other (although this is not a sufficient condition!). To find terms which differ from a given term in only one variable, we therefore compare each term which those with one more or one less negation operator.

3.2.3.1   Steps in Quine–McClusky minimization

Step 1.   We first write down the combinations of input values representing the minterms (those where the output value is to be 1).

p	q	r
1	1	1
1	1	0
0	1	1
0	0	1

Step 2.1.   We then enumerate the minterms in order of the numbers of 1s in the minterm. This will enable us to look for terms which can be combined to produce a simpler combination. We draw lines to separate the groups containing different numbers of 1s. Within each group the ordering is immaterial, but 'binary' ordering is normally maintained. The new table will not necessarily be in 'binary' order overall (see later examples).

row	p	q	r	
1	1	1	1	three 1s
2	1	1	0	two 1s
3	0	1	1	
4	0	0	1	one 1

Step 2.2.   Next we combine rows from adjacent sections of the above table, which differ in only one column; the two rows must be identical in every column except one if they are to be combined. We write a new row the same as the combined two where they agree, but replace the differing values (a combined 0 and 1) by a star. In an extra column we indicate the rows which have been combined.

row	p	q	r		
5	1	1	*	rows 1 and 2	two 1s
6	*	1	1	rows 1 and 3	
7	0	*	1	rows 3 and 4	one 1

We cannot combine rows 2 and 4.

Every new row will contain exactly one asterisk. Reorder this table by the number of 1s in the line. Delete from the first table all rows from which the new rows have been generated. In this case all rows of the first table are deleted. Any remaining rows would represent entries which cannot be combined with adjoining entries, so must occur in full in the final formula.

Step 2.3.   If there are now two new rows differing in only one variable, combine them in the same way. Rows to be combined must agree in the position of any asterisks, and differ in exactly one variable, taking the value 1 in one row and 0 in the other. The new table will consist of rows with exactly two asterisks. In this case there are no further simplifications possible. In more complex situations this operation (perform combinations replacing a variable value by an asterisk, order all the lines containing the extra asterisk in order of the number of 1s they contain, and look for more combinations) would be repeated until no more combinations are possible.

The three lines in the above table, each containing one asterisk, represent the two-variable terms

$$p \cdot q, \qquad q \cdot r, \qquad \bar{p} \cdot r,$$

respectively, each of which covers two minterms.

Step 3.   Eliminating unnecessary terms. We need to select a minimum number of terms to cover all the rows, each of which represents a 1 in the original truth-table. We have the minterms for each of the 1s across the top, and the reduced terms down the side. In each row, we indicate with an $\times$ the minterms covered by the reduced term shown on the left.

	111	110	011	001
11*	×	×		
*11	×		×	
0*1			×	×

Any row corresponding to a term with no stars will contain a single $\times$, any row corresponding to a term with one star will contain two $\times$s, any row corresponding to a term with two stars will contain four $\times$s, and so on.

If any column contains a single $\times$, then that reduced term must be included (the first and third here), since there is no other way of covering the minterm corresponding to that column. All the other columns which that reduced term covers can then be crossed off, including the column with the single $\times$, since all these minterms are now covered. In the above case we must therefore include the term 11* to cover the column 110, and this will also cover the 111 column. We also need the term 0*1 to include the column 001, and this also covers the 011 column. All of the columns (minterms) have now been covered, and no more reduced terms need to be included. The *11 term is unnecessary.

These two terms show us that the simplest formula to represent the truth-table from which we started can be constructed from two terms, $p \cdot q$ corresponding to the term 11*, and $\bar{p} \cdot r$ representing 0*1. The final formula we obtain is

$$p \cdot q + \bar{p} \cdot r.$$

The early steps af this method are explicit and straightforward. The final stage may not be so simple. There may perhaps be three columns, each with two × entries. The final solution must be arbitrary to that extent.

3.2.3.2   A four-variable Quine–McClusky example

We will now work through a four-variable example. We will produce a minimal functional representation for the four-variable truth-table

p	q	r	s	function
1	1	1	1	1
1	1	1	0	1
1	1	0	1	0
1	1	0	0	0
1	0	1	1	1
1	0	1	0	0
1	0	0	1	1
1	0	0	0	1
0	1	1	1	1
0	1	1	0	0
0	1	0	1	0
0	1	0	0	1
0	0	1	1	1
0	0	1	0	0
0	0	0	1	1
0	0	0	0	0

Step 1.   Write down the minterms.

p	q	r	s
1	1	1	1
1	1	1	0
1	0	1	1
1	0	0	1
1	0	0	0
0	1	1	1
0	1	0	0
0	0	1	1
0	0	0	1

Step 2.1. We enumerate the minterms in order of the number of 1s and number the resulting rows.

row	p	q	r	s	
1	1	1	1	1	four 1s
2	1	1	1	0	
3	1	0	1	1	three 1s
4	0	1	1	1	
5	0	0	1	1	two 1s
6	1	0	0	1	
7	1	0	0	0	
8	0	1	0	0	one 1
9	0	0	0	1	

Step 2.2. The next stage is to combine rows from adjacent sections which differ in only one position.

row	p	q	r	s	from rows	
10	1	1	1	*	rows 1 and 2	
11	1	*	1	1	rows 1 and 3	three 1s
12	*	1	1	1	rows 1 and 4	
13	*	0	1	1	rows 3 and 5	
14	1	0	*	1	rows 3 and 6	two 1s
15	0	*	1	1	rows 4 and 5	
16	0	0	*	1	rows 5 and 9	
17	1	0	0	*	rows 6 and 7	one 1
18	*	0	0	1	rows 6 and 9	

All rows except 8 of the previous table can now be eliminated. Row 8 (0100) must be retained for eventual inclusion as the four-variable term

$$\bar{p} \cdot q \cdot \bar{r} \cdot \bar{s}.$$

Step 2.3. Next we again combine rows from adjacent sections, where the asterisks must be in the same position, and the combined rows must differ in a single 0 and 1 entry.

row	p	q	r	s	from rows	
19	*	*	1	1	11 and 15; 12 and 13	two 1s
20	*	0	*	1	13 and 18; 14 and 16	one 1

Each of these will always be found in two separate ways, a useful double check when working by hand. All single-asterisk rows except numbers 10 and 17 of the preceding table can now be eliminated from our considerations.

In this particular case, we can proceed no further with simplification. None of the two-asterisk rows differ in a single entry. We are now left with the rows:

8 (no asterisks, four-variable term, one × below);
10, 17 (one asterisk, three-variable terms, two ×s below);
19, 20 (two asterisks, two-variable terms, four ×s below).

Step 3.   The next step is to eliminate unnecessary terms from these five.

	1111	1110	1011	1001	1000	0111	0100	0011	0001
**11	×		×			×		×	
*0*1			×	×				×	×
111*	×	×							
100*				×	×				
0100							×		

In this case it will be seen that we need all these five minterms, none can be
omitted; the first minterm is essential for column 6, the second for column 9, the
third for column 2, the fourth for column 5 and the fifth for column 7. This gives
us the simplified formula

$$r \cdot s + \bar{q} \cdot s + p \cdot q \cdot r + p \cdot \bar{q} \cdot \bar{r} + \bar{p} \cdot q \cdot \bar{r} \cdot \bar{s}.$$

The Quine–McClusky method can be programmed to work for any number of
variables. The method is mostly explicit, but there will be situations in the
determination of which terms to use in the coverage where arbitrary decisions will
have to be made. A good program would try all possible alternatives, and choose
the optimum; a simple program would choose the first option and proceed.

In the above discussions, we have described a method for producing simplified
formulae. We have not defined the term *simple* precisely, or proved that the
formulae produced are the most simple. In real-world applications, many other
considerations must be taken into account in producing circuits to implement a
given truth-table.

3.3   Universal decision elements (UDEs)

In the previous section, we studied the design of logic mechanisms using $\wedge$, $\vee$
and $\neg$ mechanisms to represent the required function. Another approach to
designing a logical machine which can perform a variety of logical functions is to
use universal decision elements. Consider the six-argument function

$$\Phi(p, q, r, s, t, u) =_{\mathrm{df}} [p, (q \vee r) \wedge (s / t), u].$$

(This example is based on a conditioned disjunction function, and corresponds to
a particular electromagnetic mechanism cheaply and easily available in early
research in this area.) We can use a single call of this function together with the
fixed truth-values 1 and 0 to define each of the two-argument functions as follows:

$$p \lor q =_{df} \Phi(1,p,q,0,0,0);$$
$$p \downarrow q =_{df} \Phi(0,p,q,0,0,1);$$
$$p \land q =_{df} \Phi(0,0,1,p,q,1);$$
$$p / q =_{df} \Phi(1,0,1,p,q,0);$$
$$p \Rightarrow q =_{df} \Phi(0,0,p,q,1,1);$$
$$p \nRightarrow q =_{df} \Phi(1,0,p,q,1,0);$$
$$p \Leftrightarrow q =_{df} \Phi(0,p,q,p,q,1);$$
$$p \nLeftrightarrow q =_{df} \Phi(1,p,q,p,q,0).$$

Notice that here we are using Φ only once in each definition, and, as appropriate, the truth-values 0 and 1. For some of the two-variable functions, there may be more than one possible definition in terms of Φ. The values 0 and 1 are, in practical computing terms, free, since they represent simple connections to the supply voltage or earth connections.

3.3.1 Definition

A logical functor Φ corresponds to a universal decision element if there exist substitutions of p, q, 1 and 0 to its arguments such that all the eight non-trivial two-variable functors can be defined. These are the eight functors $\land$, $\lor$, $\Rightarrow$, $\Leftrightarrow$, $\nLeftrightarrow$, $\nRightarrow$, $\downarrow$ and $/$. Note that, compared with Sheffer functions, we are allowing only one use of the function in the definition.

Theorem   A function of three variables cannot represent a universal decision element.

The proof of this is left as an exercise to the reader! Think about how many ways you can substitute at least one p and at least one q in the three variables, and the consequence of this.

The following two theorems should be obvious.

Theorem   The negation of a function representing a universal decision element also represents a universal decision element.

Theorem   The dual of a function representing a universal decision element also represents a universal decision element.

3.3.2 A few four-variable universal decision elements

We give below examples of output from a computer program which tests all possible four-variable truth-tables to see if they satisfy the conditions for a universal decision element. The program tests each truth-table in turn (there are 2^{16} of them), trying all possible substitutions of variables (how many of them are there?) looking for a definition of disjunction, then trying all the substitutions for a definition of conjunction, and so on. The results are in the form of truth-tables so that, if you require a formula representation, you must apply one of the simplification techniques to the truth-table.

The program found a total of 2880 solutions. These do not all represent distinct functions, since the number includes truth-tables representing, for example, reflections of symmetrical functions.

First example.   The first solution printed by the program represents a function with the truth-table:

		1	1	0	0	r
		1	0	1	0	s
1	1	0	0	0	0	
1	0	1	0	0	0	
0	1	1	0	0	1	
0	0	1	1	1	0	
p	q					

The definitions are:

$$p \vee q =_{df} f(0,0,p,q);$$
$$p \wedge q =_{df} f(1,0,p,q);$$
$$p \Leftrightarrow\!\!\!| \; q =_{df} f(0,p,0,q);$$
$$p \Leftrightarrow q =_{df} f(0,1,p,q);$$
$$p \downarrow q =_{df} f(p,1,0,q);$$
$$p / q =_{df} f(p,q,1,1);$$
$$p \Rightarrow q =_{df} f(0,p,1,q);$$
$$p \Rightarrow\!\!\!| \; q =_{df} f(1,p,1,q).$$

Second example.   Function truth-table:

		1	1	0	0	r
		1	0	1	0	s
1	1	0	0	0	0	
1	0	1	0	0	0	
0	1	1	1	1	0	
0	0	0	1	1	1	
p	q					

The definitions are:

$$p \vee q =_{df} f(0,1,p,q);$$
$$p \wedge q =_{df} f(1,0,p,q);$$

$$p \Leftrightarrow q =_{df} f(p,q,1,1);$$
$$p \Leftrightarrow q =_{df} f(p,0,1,q);$$
$$p \downarrow q =_{df} f(p,q,0,0);$$
$$p\,/\,q =_{df} f(0,0,p,q);$$
$$p \Rightarrow q =_{df} f(0,p,0,q);$$
$$p \Rrightarrow q =_{df} f(1,p,1,q).$$

Third example. Function truth-table:

		1	1	0	0	r
		1	0	1	0	s
1	1	0	0	0	0	
1	0	1	0	0	1	
0	1	1	0	0	0	
0	0	1	1	1	0	
p	q					

The definitions are:

$$p \vee q =_{df} f(0,0,p,q);$$
$$p \wedge q =_{df} f(0,1,p,q);$$
$$p \Leftrightarrow q =_{df} f(p,0,0,q);$$
$$p \Leftrightarrow q =_{df} f(1,0,p,q);$$
$$p \downarrow q =_{df} f(1,p,0,q);$$
$$p\,/\,q =_{df} f(p,q,1,1);$$
$$p \Rightarrow q =_{df} f(0,p,1,q);$$
$$p \Rrightarrow q =_{df} f(0,p,0,q).$$

To find a practical representation of such functions, we would need to use the Quine–McClusky method on its truth-table.

3.4 Logic design

3.4.1 Binary arithmetic adders

We now look at some of the basic elements of computers which are designed using logic techniques described above.

Binary arithmetic represents numeric values in terms of the digits zero (0) and one (1). We will represent these as logical values.

3.4.1.1   Half adder

A *half adder* is for the addition of two single binary digits. This will give a two-bit output representing the binary sum of the two input bits as follows:

p	q	carry	sum
0	0	0	0
0	1	0	1
1	0	0	1
1	1	1	0

We can write the outputs as logical functions of the inputs as follows:

$$carry =_T p \cdot q; \qquad sum =_T p \cdot \bar{q} + \bar{p} \cdot q.$$

In practice, to implement a computer system, these functions would have to be realized in different ways depending on the technology we are using, perhaps

in terms of $\cdot, +, \neg$;
in terms of $\downarrow$,

as appropriate.

3.4.1.2   Full adder

The half adder described above produces a carry bit. In binary arithmetic between large numbers, this bit would have to be added to the two input digits in the next more significant position in the numbers. The two-bit output now represents the sum of the three input bits; firstly, there are the two bits from the numbers being added together, and then there is the carry bit fed in from the addition of the previous bit.

p	q	carryin	carryout	sum
0	0	0	0	0
0	0	1	0	1
0	1	0	0	1
0	1	1	1	0
1	0	0	0	1
1	0	1	1	0
1	1	0	1	0
1	1	1	1	1

We can simply express the outputs as logical functions, in this case of three input variables:

$$sum =_T p \Leftrightarrow q \Leftrightarrow carryin; \qquad carry =_T L_2(p, q, carryin).$$

Again, these functions would need to be expressed in terms of the basic elements of the technology we are using.

3.4.1.3   Complete adders

In a working computer, we will need to add together a number of bits, say 16, representing a binary number. The number of bits chosen to represent a number is a fundamental aspect of the computer design. There will be other design decisions related to the representations of negative numbers, and of floating-point numbers, whose discussion is not appropriate here.

To construct a mechanism for adding such binary numbers, the usual approach is to use a number of full adders in parallel, one for each bit of the numbers, with each *carryout* connected to the *carryin* on the next more significant bit. The least significant adder adds the least significant bit of each number, has no *carryin* input, and can therefore be performed by a half adder. The other bits of the two numbers are combined by a full adder whose *carryin* input is connected to the *carryout* of the the adder for the adjacent less significant bit. The *carryout* from the most significant bit now represents an overall arithmetic overflow.

In the early days of computers, when circuitry was very expensive, the adding mechanism was made cheaper and simpler by using a single-bit full adder, and feeding the bits of the two numbers to it one after the other, least significant first. The bits were fed into the adder in order of increasing significance, and the *carryout* bit held for a short time at each stage and fed in as the next pair of bits were added. This technique made the overall addition much slower, since with 32-bit numbers, there would be 32 sequential steps in the addition. There can be problems here with real adders; they can run slowly if the carry is propagated through a large number of bits. The details of such design are more appropriate to hardware digital design courses.

3.4.2   Sequential logic

There are many occasions where a logic circuit is required to perform certain time-dependent operations. For example, we described above the possibility of constructing the serial adder in which we apply the least significant bits first, and store the carry bit until we then apply the next bits of the two numbers. The operation of this unit relies on the timing of its operations. Any circuit in which the output depends not just on the current inputs is called a sequential circuit.

Timing and synchronization always cause problems in real implementations. Certain elements may work faster than others; the inputs of a given mechanism may change their truth-values at slightly different times as the signals arrive. It may take a while for the output of a decision mechanism to *settle* to its eventual value. A *clock* pulse (a variable taking the value 1 then 0 at regular intervals at all points in the processor, typically changing at a frequency of a number of millions of times per second) is used for synchronization.

3.4.2.1   Flip-flops

This is a one-bit storage device, with a *trigger* input to set the stored value to 1, and a *reset* input to set it to 0. Once triggered by the *trigger* input, the output remains set to 1 indefinitely, even when the *trigger* input has returned to 0, until the *reset* input becomes 1. Once the unit has been triggered (stores the value 1), repeated changes of the trigger to 1 and back to 0 have no effect. Similarly, once it has been reset, repeated changes of the reset input to 1 and back to 0 will have no effect.

   Although this is essentially a two-input, one-output black box (the two inputs are the trigger and the reset variables, the one output is the stored one-bit value), it is not a straightforward two-variable functor. We could draw the diagram:

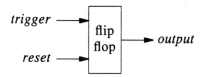

With both the inputs false, the output may be 1 or 0, depending on which of the two inputs was most recently 1. If the input most recently 1 was the *trigger* input, the output will be 1. If the input most recently 1 was the *reset* input, the output will be 0. To obtain the required functionality, we will use a three-variable functor, with the output fed back as a third input. The mechanism can be represented diagrammatically as follows:

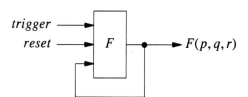

The sequence of operations which we require is as follows:

step	trigger	reset	feedback	output	event
1	0	0	0	0	quiescent off
2	1	0	0	1	triggered
3	1	0	1	1	feedback received
4	0	0	1	1	quiescent on
5	0	1	1	0	reset
6	0	1	0	0	feedback received
7	0	0	0	0	quiescent off

The significance of each of these steps is explained below.

(1) The mechanism is storing the value 0, with both inputs at 0, so that the stored value remains at 0 indefinitely. The value being fed back to the third input is 0. This is a stable configuration.

(2) The mechanism is now being triggered so that the stored value becomes 1. The *trigger* input now takes the value 1. We require the stored value (the output) to change from 0 to 1. However, at the instant following this change, the output fed back to the third input will still momentarily be at the value 0. We thus briefly have a situation with the three inputs to the mechanism taking the values 1, 0 and 0, and output being required to take the value 1.

(3) Within a very short time, the value fed back from the output to the third input will change to the value 1. We require the output to remain unchanged at 1. We now have inputs 1, 0 and 1, and output 1. This situation will pertain as long as the trigger input remains at 1.

(4) The trigger input then returns to the value 0, but we require the output to remain at the value 1. The inputs are now 0, 0 and 1, and the output 1. As long as both inputs remain at 0, this output value will be retained. If the trigger input comes on again, we return to the state of the previous step, step 3, the output remains at 1, and we return to this step when the trigger returns to 0.

(5) If the reset input comes on while the stored value is 1, we require the output to return to the value 0. The third input will still be 1 for a short period of time before the new value of the output is fed back to the input. The temporary state of the mechanism is thus input values 0, 1 and 1, and output value 0.

(6) A very short time later, the changed value of the output is received by the third input. The values of the inputs are now 0, 1 and 0, and the output is 0. This is stable as long as the reset input remains set to 1.

(7) When the reset input goes off (returns to the value 0), the stored value remains at 0. We are now in the same state as step 1 above. If the reset input comes on again, we return to the previous step, step 6, with the output remaining at 0.

We have assumed in all the above that the trigger and reset inputs are never both on simultaneously.

This sequence of operations of the mechanism gives us the truth-table

| | 1 | 1 | 0 | 0 | *trigger* |
	1	0	1	0	*reset*
1	*	1	0	1	
0	*	1	0	0	
feedback					

There are two *don't care* entries, corresponding to the cases when both the trigger and reset inputs are on, and the overall output either 0 or 1. Written in Karnaugh map ordering, the truth-table becomes

	1	1	0	0	trigger
	1	0	0	1	reset
1	*	1	1	0	
0	*	1	0	0	
feedback					

This gives us four possible truth-tables. The simplest result using Karnaugh map techniques is to set both of the *don't care* entries to 1, making a block of four 1s, giving the formula

$$trigger + \overline{reset} \cdot feedback.$$

There are two other substitutions $\begin{bmatrix} 0 \\ 1 \end{bmatrix}$ and $\begin{bmatrix} 0 \\ 0 \end{bmatrix}$ which each give two blocks of two 1s,

$$trigger \cdot \overline{feedback} + \overline{reset} \cdot feedback; \qquad trigger \cdot \overline{reset} + \overline{reset} \cdot feedback.$$

The remaining choice of $\begin{bmatrix} 1 \\ 0 \end{bmatrix}$ for the *don't care* entries gives the still more complicated function:

$$trigger \cdot \overline{reset} + \overline{reset} \cdot feedback + trigger \cdot feedback.$$

This shows how different choices of values for the *don't care* entries may produce very different results even in simple situations.

3.4.2.2　Scale-of-two circuits

A scale-of-two mechanism is basically a one-input, one-output box, whose output changes state at half the rate at which the input changes state. A schematic would be

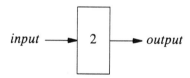

Each double reversal of the input state (from 0 to 1 and then back to 0, for example) causes a single reversal of the output state (either from 0 to 1 or from 1 to 0). The sequence wanted is

input	output
0	0
1	1
0	1
1	0
0	0

In this example every time the input changes to 1, the output changes state. The output changes on the *leading edge* (the start of) of the input pulses. The output thus changes state overall at half the frequency at which the input changes state.

Two of these mechanisms connected in series (with the output of the first connected as the input to the second) become a scale-of-four circuit and so on.

This function cannot be represented without a feedback of some sort; the output is obviously not a straightforward function of the input alone. Furthermore it cannot be implemented by a single feedback; the analysis used in the flip-flop example above produces inconsistencies. The diagram would be

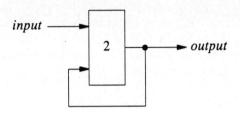

The sequence of operations would now be

row	input	feedback	output	event(s)
1	0	0	0	quiescent off
2	1	0	1	*input* becomes 1 *output* becomes 1
3	1	1	1	feedback arrives
4	0	1	1	*input* goes 0 *output* remains 1
5	1	1	0	*input* goes 1 *output* becomes 0
6	1	0	0	feedback arrives
7	0	0	0	*input* becomes 0 *output* remains 0

It can be seen that rows 2 and 6 conflict (both require the inputs at $(1,0)$ but with different outputs), as do rows 3 and 5. We must therefore seek another solution.

We choose instead to add a second output to feed back, independent of the first output. We now have an implementation consisting of two functions, each with three inputs. The three inputs are the external input and the outputs of the two functions fed back. This can be represented diagrammatically as follows:

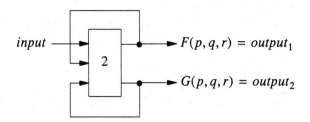

The exact operation of the second output, which has been added purely to make the mechanism work internally, is entirely up to the designer. It does not provide an output which the external world needs. In the analysis below we have chosen a second output which changes state on the trailing edge of the input pulses, where the output provided for the external world changes state at the leading edge of the input pulses. This has the advantage that the two outputs never change at the same instant; if they did, we would not be sure which of them fed back to the corresponding input first.

The sequence of operations is now as follows:

row	input	$feedback_1$	$feedback_2$	$output_1$	$output_2$	event(s)
1	0	0	0	0	0	quiescent, output off
2	1	0	0	1	0	*input* triggers $output_1$
3	1	1	0	1	0	$ouput_1$ feeds back
4	0	1	0	1	1	*input* off, $output_2$ triggered
5	0	1	1	1	1	$output_2$ feeds back
6	1	1	1	0	1	*input* triggers $output_1$ to off
7	1	0	1	0	1	$output_1$ feeds back
8	0	0	1	0	0	*input* off, $output_2$ off
9	0	0	0	0	0	$output_2$ feeds back

The sequence of operations can be described as follows, using the same style as we did with the flip-flop design:

(1) Quiescent situation, input value 0, output values 0, feedback values 0.
(2) [Instantaneous.] The input comes on (1), triggering the first output to 1. The corresponding fed-back input remains briefly at 0.
(3) The input remains at 1. The triggered first output feeds back to its connected input, so that two inputs are now 1. The two outputs remain unchanged at 1 and 0 respectively. The system is now stable.
(4) [Instantaneous.] The input goes back to 0, triggering the second output to change to 1. The second fed-back input remains briefly at 0. The first

output and its feedback remain unchanged at 1.

(5) The input remains at 0. The triggered second output feeds back to the third input, so that both outputs and both fed-back inputs are now 1. The system is now stable.

(6) [Instantaneous.] The input comes on (1) again, switching the first output to 0. The fed-back first input remains briefly at 1.

(7) The input remains at 1. The first output's new value of 0 feeds back to the second input. The system is now stable.

(8) [Instantaneous.] The trigger input goes to 0, setting the second output to 0. The three inputs are now 0, 0 and 1 (the second output has not yet fed back to the third input).

(9) The second output's change to 0 is fed back to the third input, bringing us back to step 1 above.

We now have all possible eight combinations of the three inputs to each mechanism occurring exactly once, so that no inconsistencies arise. This sequence of operations gives the following truth-tables for the two three-input mechanisms:

F	1	1	0	0	$feedback_1$
	1	0	1	0	$feedback_2$
1	0	1	0	1	
0	1	1	0	0	
$input$					

G	1	1	0	0	$feedback_1$
	1	0	1	0	$feedback_2$
1	1	0	1	0	
0	1	1	0	0	
$input$					

These truth-tables give us the formulae:

$$F =_T \overline{input} \cdot feedback_1 + input \cdot \overline{feedback_2};$$

$$G =_T \overline{input} \cdot feedback_1 + input \cdot feedback_2.$$

Note that these contain a common first part, making the total combined circuit surprisingly simple.

3.4.2.3   Scale-of-three circuit

If we wish to change to a scale-of-three circuit, we need two outputs to represent the binary numbers 0, 1 and 2. The combination $(1, 1)$ representing the value 3 will not arise, so will cause *don't care* entries in the truth-table. The logic can be designed either from scratch, as we did for a scale-of-two above, or by using scale-of-two dividers as the basic building blocks.

3.4.2.4   Scale-of-four circuit

A scale-of-four mechanism is most easily created from two scale-of-two mechanisms connected in series.

3.5   Summary

In this chapter we studied Boolean algebra, simplification procedures for obtaining a simple function to represent any truth-table, and universal decision elements. We then looked at a number of applications of the propositional calculus, mainly in the area of computer logic design. We now move on to the predicate calculus, which is an extended calculus much more suited to solving problems in general areas of artificial intelligence and the automatic proof of theorems.

3.6   Worked examples

Example 3.1   Express the function given by the truth-table

		1	1	0	0	r
		1	0	1	0	s
1	1	0	0	0	1	
1	0	1	0	0	0	
0	1	1	0	1	1	
0	0	0	1	1	0	
p	q					

in both full disjunctive normal form and full conjunctive normal form. Use the Karnaugh-map or Quine–McClusky technique to determine a simplified formulae from the truth-table.

Show that the function satisfies the conditions for a universal decision element.

Solution   The FDNF is:

$$(p \cdot q \cdot \bar{r} \cdot \bar{s}) + (p \cdot \bar{q} \cdot r \cdot s) + (\bar{p} \cdot q \cdot r \cdot s)$$

$$+ (\bar{p} \cdot q \cdot \bar{r} \cdot s) + (\bar{p} \cdot q \cdot \bar{r} \cdot \bar{s}) + (\bar{p} \cdot \bar{q} \cdot r \cdot \bar{s}) + (\bar{p} \cdot \bar{q} \cdot \bar{r} \cdot s).$$

The FCNF is:

$$(\bar{p} + \bar{q} + \bar{r} + \bar{s}) \cdot (\bar{p} + \bar{q} + \bar{r} + s) \cdot (\bar{p} + \bar{q} + r + \bar{s})$$

$$\cdot (\bar{p} + q + \bar{r} + s) \cdot (\bar{p} + q + r + \bar{s}) \cdot (\bar{p} + q + \bar{r} + \bar{s})$$

$$\cdot (p + \bar{q} + r + s) \cdot (p + q + \bar{r} + \bar{s}) \cdot (p + q + r + s).$$

Karnaugh form is

		1	1	0	0	r
		1	0	0	1	s
1	1	0	0	1	0	
1	0	1	0	0	0	
0	0	0	1	0	1	
0	1	1	0	1	1	
p	q					

We need

$$(\bar{p}\cdot\bar{q}\cdot r\cdot\bar{s})+(p\cdot\bar{q}\cdot r\cdot s)+(\bar{p}\cdot q\cdot s)+(q\cdot\bar{r}\cdot\bar{s})+(\bar{p}\cdot\bar{r}\cdot s).$$

We do not need

$$\bar{p}\cdot q\cdot\bar{r}.$$

Possible substitutions to show that the function represents a UDE are:

$p\downarrow q =_{df} \Phi(1,1,p,q)$ or $\Phi(p,q,1,0)$;

$p\Rightarrow q =_{df} \Phi(0,1,p,q)$;

$p\Leftrightarrow q =_{df} \Phi(0,0,p,q)$ or $\Phi(p,q,1,1)$ or $\Phi(0,p,q,0)$;

$p\nRightarrow q =_{df} \Phi(q,q,p,p)$ or $\Phi(q,0,0,p)$ or $\Phi(p,1,1,q)$ or $\Phi(1,p,0,q)$;

$p\wedge q =_{df} \Phi(1,0,p,q)$;

$p\Leftrightarrow q =_{df} \Phi(0,p,1,q)$ or $\Phi(p,0,1,q)$ or $\Phi(p,0,q,1)$;

$p\vee q =_{df} \Phi(0,p,0,q)$;

$p/q =_{df} \Phi(p,1,0,q)$ or $\Phi(p,1,q,q)$.

[There are others possible.]

Example 3.2 Prove that a function of three variables cannot be a universal decision element.

Solution Let the three-variable function be $\Phi(x,y,z)$. There are enough possible substitutions of at least one p, at least one q and 1s and 0s. We need eight, there are nine:

$pq1,\quad pq0,\quad p1q,\quad p0q,\quad 1pq,\quad 0pq,\quad ppq,\quad pqp,\quad qpp.$

For the eight two-variable functors we need four substitutions in which $f(1,1)=1$ ($\wedge$, $\vee$, $\Rightarrow$, $\Leftrightarrow$) and four in which $f(1,1)=0$ ($\downarrow$, $/$, $\nRightarrow$, $\Leftrightarrow$). It cannot be done, since in six of the nine substitutions $f(1,1)$ will take the value of $\Phi(1,1,1)$.

Example 3.3 Design a counter with a single input and three outputs to control traffic lights in the sequence 'red', 'red and amber', 'green', 'amber', and back to 'red'. Each pulse on the input should cause the output to move to the next member of the sequence.

Solution   The cycle is of length four. Assume a scale-of-two counter, and use two of them in series. The sequence is

$counter_1$	$counter_2$	red	$amber$	$green$
0	0	1	0	0
1	0	1	1	0
0	1	0	0	1
1	1	0	1	0
0	0	1	0	0

We can then use

$$red =_T \neg counter_1;$$

$$amber =_T counter_1;$$

$$green =_T counter_2 \cdot \overline{counter_1}.$$

Example 3.4   Apply the Quine–McClusky method to the function whose truth-table is given by the table

		1	1	0	0	r
		1	0	1	0	s
1	1	1	1	0	1	
1	0	1	0	1	0	
0	1	1	0	1	0	
0	0	1	1	1	0	
p	q					

Solution   First form the minterms: (give arguments ordered by number of 1s, look for similar pairs …)

row	p	q	r	s	
1	1	1	1	1	four 1s
2	1	1	1	0	
3	1	0	1	1	three 1s
4	0	1	1	1	
5	1	1	0	0	
6	1	0	0	1	
7	0	1	0	1	two 1s
8	0	0	1	1	
9	0	0	1	0	
10	0	0	0	1	one 1
11	1	1	1	*	rows 1 and 2
12	1	*	1	1	rows 1 and 3
13	*	1	1	1	rows 1 and 4
14	1	1	*	0	rows 2 and 5
15	1	0	*	1	rows 3 and 6

row	p	q	r	s	
16	*	0	1	1	rows 3 and 8
17	0	1	*	1	rows 4 and 7
18	0	*	1	1	rows 4 and 8
20	*	0	0	1	rows 6 and 10
21	0	*	0	1	rows 7 and 10
22	0	0	1	*	rows 8 and 9
23	0	0	*	1	rows 8 and 10
24	*	*	1	1	rows 12 and 18; 13 and 16
25	*	0	*	1	rows 15 and 23; 16 and 20
26	0	*	*	1	rows 17 and 23; 18 and 21

Then, to determine disjuncts required,

row	term	1111	1110	1011	0111	1100	1001	0101	0011	0010	0001
11	$p \cdot q \cdot r$	×	×								
14	$p \cdot q \cdot \bar{s}$		×			×					
22	$\bar{p} \cdot \bar{q} \cdot r$								×	×	
24	$r \cdot s$	×		×	×				×		
25	$\bar{q} \cdot s$			×			×		×		×
26	$\bar{p} \cdot s$				×		×	×			×

We need rows 14, 25, 26 and 22 since they all involve a column containing a single ×. We still need to cover the minterm 1111, so we choose row 24 (since it represents a simpler term than row 11). We thus have

$$p \cdot q \cdot \bar{s} + \bar{p} \cdot \bar{q} \cdot r + r \cdot s + \bar{q} \cdot s + \bar{p} \cdot s$$

for the complete formula.

Example 3.5   Show that the formula

$$[p \Rrightarrow q, r, s \Leftrightarrow u]$$

can represent a universal decision element.

Solution   The substitutions for the eight dyadic functors are:

$$p \wedge q =_{df} \Phi(p, 0, q, 1, 0);$$
$$p \vee q =_{df} \Phi(1, 0, p, q, 1);$$
$$p / q =_{df} \Phi(1, p, q, 1, 1);$$
$$p \downarrow q =_{df} \Phi(1, 1, p, q, 0);$$
$$p \Leftrightarrow q =_{df} \Phi(p, 0, q, p, 0);$$
$$p \Lleftarrow q =_{df} \Phi(1, q, p, q, 1)$$
$$p \Leftrightarrow q =_{df} \Phi(1, 0, q, p, 1)$$
$$p \Rrightarrow q =_{df} \Phi(p, q, 1, 1, 1).$$

Example 3.6

(a) Show that the dual of a universal decision element is also a universal decision element.

(b) Show that the function

$$\Phi(U,V,W,X,Y,Z) =_{\text{df}} [U,(V \vee W) \wedge (X/Y),Z]$$

can act as a UDE.

(c) Use the above function to define one of the flip-flop functions.

Solution

(a) Since the two-argument functors we are defining can be put into self-dual pairs, the definition of any one can be used with the dual of the universal decision element to define the other of the pair.

(b) The definitions showing that the function is a UDE are:

$$p \vee q =_{\text{df}} \Phi(1,p,q,0,0,0);$$
$$p \downarrow q =_{\text{df}} \Phi(0,p,q,0,0,1);$$
$$p \wedge q =_{\text{df}} \Phi(0,0,1,p,q,1);$$
$$p/q =_{\text{df}} \Phi(1,0,1,p,q,0);$$
$$p \Rightarrow q =_{\text{df}} \Phi(0,0,p,q,1,1);$$
$$p \nRightarrow q =_{\text{df}} \Phi(1,0,p,q,1,0);$$
$$p \Leftrightarrow q =_{\text{df}} \Phi(0,p,q,p,q,1);$$
$$p \nLeftrightarrow q =_{\text{df}} \Phi(1,p,q,p,q,0).$$

(c) The first of the flipflop formulae is

$$\Phi(1,0,reset,1,feedback,trigger).$$

Example 3.7

(a) Define a UDE.

(b) Is the formula represented by the following truth-table a UDE?

$F(p,q,r,s)$		T	T	F	F	r
		T	F	T	F	s
T	T	F	F	F	T	
T	F	T	T	T	F	
F	T	T	F	T	F	
F	F	F	F	T	T	
p	q					

(c) Minimize the function using the Quine–McClusky method. Comment on the last stage of your method.

Solution

(a) Definition: A logical function is a UDE if, by substitution of variables and logical constants to its arguments, all two-variable functors can be defined.

(b) Substitutions to define eight operators:

$$p \vee q =_{df} F(t,f,p,q);$$
$$p \wedge q =_{df} F(f,p,t,q);$$
$$p \Leftrightarrow q =_{df} F(t,p,f,q);$$
$$p \Leftrightarrow q =_{df} F(p,f,q,f);$$
$$p \downarrow q =_{df} F(t,t,p,q);$$
$$p/q =_{df} F(p,q,f,t);$$
$$p \Rightarrow q =_{df} F(f,p,f,q);$$
$$p \Rightarrow q =_{df} F(p,t,t,q).$$

(c) Quine–McClusky. First form the minterms:

row	p	q	r	s
0	1	1	0	0
1	1	0	1	1
2	1	0	1	0
3	1	0	0	1
4	0	1	1	1
5	0	1	0	1
6	0	0	0	1
7	0	0	0	0

Now combine 1011 and 1010 to give 101*, combine 1011 and 1001 to give 10*1, combine 1001 and 0001 to give *001, combine 0111 and 0101 to give 01*1, combine 0101 and 0001 to give 0*01, combine 0001 and 0000 to give 000* and retain 1100. This gives:

row	p	q	r	s
0	1	0	1	*
1	1	0	*	1
2	*	0	0	1
3	0	1	*	1
4	0	*	0	1
5	0	0	0	*
6	1	1	0	0

Finally, to determine the required disjuncts we have:

term	1100	1011	1010	1001	0111	0101	0001	0000
101*		×	×					
10*1		×		×				
*001				×			×	
01*1					×	×		
0*01						×	×	
000*							×	×
1100	×							

We must include 1100, 101*, 01*1 and 000*, and we make a random choice of 10*1.

The choice of the last term is not explicit, there are two alternatives to cover the 1001 column; we could choose either 10*1 or *001.

The simplified form is:

$$(p \wedge q \wedge \neg r \wedge \neg s) \vee (p \wedge \neg q \wedge r) \vee (p \wedge \neg q \wedge s)$$

$$\vee (\neg p \wedge q \wedge s) \vee (\neg p \wedge \neg q \wedge \neg r).$$

3.7   Exercises

Exercise 3.1   Draw the truth-tables corresponding to the following functions:

(a) $\overline{\overline{p \cdot q} \cdot r \cdot s}$;
(b) $\overline{\overline{p + q} + r + s}$.

Exercise 3.2   Express the functions defined by the following truth-tables in full disjunctive normal form. Simplify them using Karnaugh maps:

x	y	c_{in}	c_{out}	sum
0	0	0	0	0
0	0	1	0	1
0	1	0	0	1
0	1	1	1	0
1	0	0	0	1
1	0	1	1	0
1	1	0	1	0
1	1	1	1	1

Exercise 3.3   Design a simplified circuit to produce the following three outputs from the given three inputs:

Inputs			Outputs		
p	q	r	$F(p,q,r)$	$G(p,q,r)$	$H(p,q,r)$
0	0	0	0	1	1
0	0	1	1	0	0
0	1	0	1	0	1
0	1	1	1	1	0
1	0	0	1	1	1
1	0	1	0	0	0
1	1	0	0	0	1
1	1	1	0	1	0

Exercise 3.4   Use the Quine–McClusky method for minimization of Boolean expressions to simplify the following expression:

$$\bar{p}\cdot q\cdot\bar{r}\cdot\bar{s}+\bar{p}\cdot q\cdot r\cdot s+p\cdot\bar{q}\cdot\bar{r}\cdot s+p\cdot\bar{q}\cdot r\cdot\bar{s}+p\cdot q\cdot\bar{r}+p\cdot q\cdot r.$$

Exercise 3.5   Prove that the universal decision element

$$\Phi(p,q,r,s,t,u) =_T [p,(q\vee r)\wedge(s/t),u]$$

function can also be used to define the functions

$$p\vee q\vee r; \qquad p\wedge q\wedge r.$$

Can it be used to define the triadic functors L_2 and M_2?
Can it be used to define any of the four triadic flip-flop functors?

Exercise 3.6   Devise the logical formulae necessary to provide a scale-of-three counter.

Exercise 3.7   The Karnaugh-map simplification technique can be applied only to functions of up to four variables. Devise a way of using it to produce a simplification of the dual of the formula

$$(p\downarrow(q\wedge(r\vee s))) \Leftrightarrow (q\vee r\vee s) \Leftrightarrow u.$$

Exercise 3.8   Write programs to perform the following operations:

(a) to perform Quine–McClusky minimization, choosing your own notation for the input of the initial truth-table;
(b) to determine whether a given four-variable truth-table represents a UDE;
(c) to determine whether a given four-variable truth-table represents a UDE and can in addition define one of the four flip-flop functions.

Exercise 3.9 Construct the following:

(a) an $\vee$ box using only $/$ boxes;
(b) a half adder from $\downarrow$ decision elements;
(c) a full adder from $\wedge$, $\vee$ and $\neg$ decision elements.

CHAPTER 4

Predicate logic

4.1 Informal introduction

We discuss first the failings of propositional logic and the need for predicates.

As we have seen in the previous chapters, the basic units of propositional logic are logical statements such as 'the Earth is flat', or 'this box is red' or 'that box is red', possibly combined by 'and', 'or', 'implies' or other operators. These propositions are either true or false. We cannot get at the lower-level objects such as 'Earth' or 'box', nor can we have a variable to represent these objects. We cannot extract as a concept the property of 'being red'. To really use logic in most practical applications, we need to be able to talk about these lower-level objects and the properties that they have (or do not have).

In order to introduce this important area of logic the chapter will begin by informally presenting some concepts of predicate logic that will be formally defined in section 2 below.

4.1.1 Background

The statements we wish to express are written in what is known as a *first-order language* which is constructed by considering particular sets of variables, constant symbols, function symbols and predicates (or relation symbols).

When working with a first-order language we (usually) have in our minds the set of objects that the statements of the language are discussing. This is known as our 'universe of discourse'. For each language there are many different universes of discourse that could be considered. A particular statement may say something about one universe and something entirely different about another. Indeed one universe may be of a totally different nature from another. We could have, for example, a set of people as one universe and the set of all positive integers as another.

The variables of the first-order language range over the whole of a universe of discourse. If we are talking about a set of numbers, then the variable x can take any numeric value in that set. If a set of people were under consideration, then x would stand for any person in the set.

The constant symbols each stand for just one distinct member of the universe. For the universe of integers the constant symbol c may stand for the value 0. For a universe of people (including Eric) c may stand for Eric.

A function symbol stands for a function on the universe. For the set of integers the one-place function symbol $f(x)$ may stand for the function $x-1$, so that the integer x is mapped onto a new integer $x-1$. The two-place function symbol $g(x,y)$ could stand for $x+y$. For a set of people the function symbol $f(x)$ could be interpreted as the function which, given a person x, returns the father of that person (as long as the father is in the set under consideration).

A predicate is a symbol which stands for a relation. It can be seen as a function delivering a value of either T or F. Its arguments are terms of the first-order language under consideration. Terms are defined inductively as variables, constant symbols or function symbols applied to 'simpler' terms. In the integer example above, the term $f(g(c,x))$ would represent $(0+x)-1$. Each predicate is assigned (stands for) a relation on the universe of discourse.

Example   A predicate $R(x)$ can be seen by programmers as something similar to a 'Boolean function' (a Boolean function is one which returns just one of two values) in Pascal which delivers a logical (Boolean) result related to some property of its argument x.

Examples of predicates (note the differing number of arguments) are:

Example	Arguments	Meaning
$Equal(i,j)$	i and j are integers	i and j are equal
$Sibling(Eric, Edmund)$	two people's names	they are siblings
$Hcf(f,p,q)$	three integers	f is the hcf of integers p and q

Given a particular first-order language, an interpretation of that language has a domain (or universe of discourse) together with particular assignments of the constant symbols, function symbols and predicates to actual constants, functions and relations in the domain.

Note that, the predicate $Equal(i,j)$ on its own is a symbol standing for a relation. It does not stand for equality unless it is assigned that relation in an interpretation. We could consider the interpretation where the domain of discourse is the set of integers and $Equal(i,j)$ is true if and only if i and j are equal integers. However, there is nothing to stop us considering a different interpretation where we have the same domain of discourse but assign the relation 'i is less than j' to $Equal(i,j)$. The point is that $Equal(i,j)$, $Sibling(a,b)$, $Hcf(f,p,q)$ or any other predicates are just names. When a particular interpretation is considered we assign an actual relation to that name which, when it is given arguments, is either true or false. Of course the truth or falsity of a predicate may therefore differ between interpretations.

A predicate can be assigned any relation regardless of its name. However, generally when we are working in predicate logic, we are thinking about a particular interpretation which we will call the 'intended' interpretation. In the intended interpretation the name of the predicate gives some indication of its 'intended meaning'. So when using a name like $Equal(i, j)$ the intended interpretation is 'equality' and we will have this interpretation in mind.

Each predicate of one argument is a mapping

$$D \to \{T, F\},$$

where D is the universe of discourse (or domain); a predicate of two arguments is a mapping

$$D \times D \to \{T, F\}.$$

The truth-values T and F can be taken to be predicates of zero arguments.

All this is very closely connected with the notion of *sets* since the objects of the universe of discourse must form a set, those satisfying '$Green(x)$' form a subset, those satisfying '$Green(x) \wedge Square(x)$' form the set which is the *intersection* of the sets satisfying '$Green(x)$' and '$Square(x)$'. Those satisfying '$Green(x) \vee Square(x)$' form the set which is the *union* of the sets satisfying '$Green(x)$' and '$Square(x)$'.

Predicates can, therefore, be used to write logical formulae in which the objects are members of some universe of discourse, for example

$Rich(person) \Rightarrow Canbuy(person, object)$;
$(Large(object) \wedge Dense(object)) \Rightarrow Heavy(object)$;
$Even(x) \Rightarrow Factor(2, x)$;
$UK\text{-}passport(x) \Leftrightarrow UK-born(x) \wedge UK\text{-}passport(parent(x))$.

We have thus achieved a notation in which we can talk about objects in our universe, and their properties, instead of our lowest-level variable being complete logical propositions.

4.1.2   Universal and existential quantifiers

So far we can express in logic specific statements such as

A is a liar;
A says that B is ....

But we cannot express more general ideas, such as the famous logical argument:

All men are mortal.
Socrates is a man.
Therefore Socrates is mortal.

If we tried to express this in propositional logic, the following would be obtained:

> *P.*
> *Q.*
> Therefore *R.*

This clearly shows that once the English sentences have been expressed as propositional statements we can no longer say that the argument is valid because we cannot get inside the statements to work with the lower-level objects and concepts (such as 'men', 'Socrates' and 'being mortal').

We need a way to express 'all A's are B', so that the argument becomes

> All A's are B
> > or 'All A's have property B'
> > or 'All objects in set A have property B'.
> C is an A
> > or 'C is in set A'
> > or 'C is a member of set A'.
> Therefore C is B
> > or 'has property B'.

4.1.2.1   Universal quantifier

Follow this sequence of formalizations.

> (a) Every integer has a prime factor.
> (b) For all x,
> > if x is an integer,
> > > then x has a prime factor.
> (c) *For all x, (Is_integer(x) $\Rightarrow$ Has_prime_fac(x)),*

where *Is_integer(x)* is a predicate representing 'x is an integer', and *Has_prime_fac(x)* is a predicate representing 'x has a prime factor'. Our Socratic statement becomes

> *For all x, (Is_a_man(x) $\Rightarrow$ Is_mortal(x)).*

The 'for all' is called the universal quantifier, and is written $\forall$. The above statement becomes

> $\forall x(Is\_integer(x) \Rightarrow Has\_prime\_fac(x)).$

The domain of quantification   When we say 'For all x ...', exactly which values of x do we wish to include? The $\forall x$ we use will mean

> 'For all x in the universe of discourse ....

The 'universe of discourse' is the domain of the interpretation under consideration or, more informally, 'the set of individual objects which we are discussing now'. Thus, when trying to prove things about positive integers, x will range over all positive integer values; we say that the domain of the intended interpretation will be the set of positive integers. Notice that if the domain were the set of positive integers (or the set of all integers) the predicate $Is\_integer(x)$ would be redundant because every x under consideration (all the values of the domain) would already be an integer. If the domain were the set of real numbers or rational numbers, then it would be sensible to have $Is\_integer(x)$ as a predicate.

In the formal specification language Z which is an application of predicate logic to the definition of real-world systems (and which we study in a later chapter) every quantifier is followed by a definition of the particular set of values over which the the variable may range. The notation is

$$\forall x : \langle \text{name of a set} \rangle \cdot \langle \text{Boolean expression} \rangle.$$

In this book we will use this notation only in chapter 6. Elsewhere we will assume, in common with most treatments of mathematical logic, that all variables can have values ranging over the whole universe of discourse.

Scope of quantified variables   The statement

$$\forall x(Is\_integer(x) \Rightarrow Has\_prime\_fac(x))$$

is obviously equivalent exactly to

$$\forall y(Is\_integer(y) \Rightarrow Has\_prime\_fac(y))$$

However, we would not be allowed to replace x by y in the statement

$$\forall x(Is\_integer(x) \wedge Has\_prime\_fac(y))$$

because the independence of the two variables x and y causes the meaning to be changed completely.

The *scope* of the quantified variable is the part of the formula to which it applies. If a variable x falls within the scope of a $\forall x$, then that occurrence of the variable is said to be a *bound* occurrence, and the variable a *bound variable* (this corresponds to the scope of variables in programming, and the naming of procedure arguments in the procedure declaration).

4.1.2.2   Existential quantifier

We also need to be able to translate statements such as

There exists at least one object x such that $Pred(x)$.

We could do it (convince yourself!) by writing

$$\neg\forall x(\neg Pred(x))$$

with the meaning

It is not the case that the property is false for all members.

We introduce a new quantifier *there exists* written $\exists$, as in

$$\exists x(Pred(x)),$$

which is read as

There exists a value of x such that $Pred(x)$.

Note the vital difference between the statements such as

$$\forall x \, \exists y (y = 2 \times x)$$

(which is true in the intended interpretation, for every integer there is another integer equal to twice its value) and

$$\exists y \, \forall x (y = 2 \times x)$$

(which is not true, there is no number which is equal to twice every other number). The correct ordering of quantifiers of different types is vital.

The formal system introduced in this chapter uses only the universal quantifier $\forall$; $\exists$ can always be defined in terms of it.

4.1.3 Translating between first-order languages and the English language

When working with mathematical logic it is important to be able to express natural language statements as logical statements and vice versa. This ability is particularly important when logic is used as a formal specification language (see chapter 6) or as a programming language (see chapter 5). When using first-order logic, quantification is allowed only over the variables. If this restriction were removed we would be dealing with higher-order logics. First-order logic is not as expressive as these higher-order logics but it is expressive enough for most practical uses and indeed for the applications that are looked at in this book. Higher-order logic is beyond our scope.

4.1.3.1 Expressing logical formulae as English sentences

This is, in general, a much easier process than translating from English into logic. Given a logical formula we must first have a meaning for the predicates (or relation symbols) occurring in the formula. Without this no attempt can be made to translate the formula into English. We will see later on in this chapter that different interpretations of formulae (or sets of formulae) can be obtained by considering different meanings for the predicates. However, for the moment, we are concerned with the problem of translating a first-order logical formula into a sentence of the English language, given that the meaning of all the predicates that occur in the formula is known. The process is as follows:

(1) Translate the formula by writing the literal meanings of the logical symbols and predicates as they occur.
(2) Reword the sentence so that it has the same logical meaning (the truth or falsity of the sentence should not change) but is written in more 'acceptable' English. This usually involves avoiding the use of variable names.

Examples   Suppose we have the following predicates:

$Lorry(x)$ x is a lorry;
$Car(x)$ x is a car;
$Bike(x)$ x is a bicycle;
$Expensive(x, y)$ x is more expensive than y;
$Faster(x, y)$ x is faster than y.

(a) Translate the following formula into natural language:

$$\forall x(Bike(x) \Rightarrow \exists y(Car(y) \wedge Expensive(y, x))).$$

Solution   We translate by simply reading the formula from left to right.

'For all x, if x is a bicycle, then there exists a y such that y is a car and y is more expensive than x.'

Rewording this to put it into more acceptable English we have

'For every bicycle there is a car which is more expensive.'

Note the removal of variable names in the final sentence.

(b) Translate the following formula into English:

$$\forall x\, \forall y((Lorry(x) \wedge Bike(y)) \Rightarrow Faster(x, y)).$$

Solution   Literally, the translation is

'For all x, for all y, if x is a lorry and y is a bicycle, then x is faster than y.'

Rewording this we have

'Every lorry is faster than any bicycle.'

(c) Translate the following formula into English:

$$\exists z(Car(z) \wedge \forall x\, \forall y((Lorry(x) \wedge Bike(y)) \Rightarrow$$

$$(Faster(z, x) \wedge Faster(z, y) \wedge Expensive(z, x) \wedge Expensive(z, y)))).$$

Solution   Literally, this says

'There exists z such that z is a car and for all x, for all y if x is a lorry and y is a bicycle, then z is faster than x and z is faster than y and z is more expensive than x and z is more expensive than y.'

Rewording this to put it into more acceptable English we have

'There are some cars which are faster and more expensive than any lorry or bicycle.'

We will now consider the more difficult process of translating from English to first-order logic.

4.1.3.2   Expressing English sentences as first-order logical statements

Suppose we are given a sentence, written in the English language, that we wish to express as a statement of first-order logic. The first thing to do is to identify the predicates required and then rearrange the sentence so that it has a *logical formulation*. (This step can be missed out once proficiency has been gained.) By a logical formulation we mean that the logical connectives and quantifiers should be made explicit. For example, consider the sentence

'Everybody loses money at the horse races.'

Note that we are not (at the moment) concerned with the truth or falsity of this statement. What we are concerned with is expressing it (true or false) as a first-order logical formula. The predicates (or *relations*) can be identified to obtain

'x loses money' (which will be denoted by $Lose(x)$) and
'x is at the horse races' (which will be denoted by $Horse\_race(x)$).

The sentence says that, for all people, being at the races implies losing money so we can deduce that the quantifier is *for all* and there is one logical connective, namely *implication*. The sentence can be rearranged into a logical formulation to obtain

'For all x, if x is at the races then x loses money.'

We can now easily translate the sentence into

$\forall x(Horse\_race(x) \Rightarrow Lose(x))$.

Notice that we have assumed that the universe of discourse is the set of all human beings which, given the sentence, is a reasonable assumption. However, if we took the universe of discourse to be the set of all living creatures on the planet we would have to introduce a new predicate to keep the meaning of the sentence. This is because, as it stands, the $\forall x$ would range over the set of all living creatures and we would be able to derive that if an ant were at the races it would lose money. The predicate $Human(x)$ could be introduced for 'x is a human being'. The formula then becomes

$\forall x((Human(x) \wedge Horse\_race(x)) \Rightarrow Lose(x))$,

which is in literal English

'For all x, if x is a human being and x is at the races then x loses money.'

Ordinarily we would assume that the universe of discourse is that implied by the sentence being translated, so that predicates such as $Human(x)$ above would not be needed.

   To summarize the process (of translating from English to logic), the following steps are performed on a sentence of the English language:

(1) Identify the predicates used in the sentence.

(2) Rearrange the sentence into a logical formulation. By this we mean that the sentence should be reworded so that it has the same meaning but the structure of the sentence should be made up of the relevant predicates, quantifiers and connectives. It is in this step that the quantifiers and connectives are identified.

(3) The sentence should now be in a form that can be easily translated.

Example   Translate the following sentence into a logical formula:

'Some people at the races lose money but there are some astute ones who never lose.'

The predicates required are:

$Horse\_race(x)$ x is at the races;
$Lose(x)$ x loses money;
$Astute(x)$ x is astute.

Notice that we do not need a predicate for 'never losing' because this can be expressed by using $\neg Lose(x)$.

The sentence can be rewritten as

'There exists x such that x is at the races and x loses money, and there exists y such that y is at the races, is astute and does not lose.'

The sentence has been reworded so that it looks more like a logical formula and has the same logical meaning. The word 'but' has been replaced by 'and'. Although it can be argued that this changes the meaning of the sentence, it is a very subtle difference. As mentioned above, the English language is much more expressive than first-order logic. The important point is that replacing 'and' with 'but' and vice versa does not change the truth or falsity of the statement. We can now directly translate into first-order logic to obtain

$$\exists x(Horse\_race(x) \wedge Lose(x)) \wedge \exists y(Horse\_race(y) \wedge Astute(y) \wedge \neg Lose(y)).$$

4.1.4   Hints for translating from English to logic

(a) When using a universal quantifier it is normally followed by the use of an implication (but not always). For example, let us consider the sentence which says that

'All old people have grey hair.'

Let $Old(x)$ stand for 'x is old' and $Grey(x)$ stand for 'x has grey hair'. Rewording the sentence we obtain

'For all x, if x is old then x has grey hair.'

Therefore the translation is

$$\forall x\,(Old(x) \Rightarrow Grey(x)).$$

Notice that the use of an implication follows the use of a $\forall$. It is quite common to make statements of the form

'For every member of the universe of discourse,
if some condition holds then another condition holds.'

The combination

'For every member of the universe of discourse,
if some condition holds then ...'

is really just selecting a subset of our universe. It is less common (but not out of the question) to make statements of the form

'For every member of the universe of discourse
some condition holds and another condition holds.'

For example, if the $\wedge$ symbol were used instead of $\Rightarrow$ in the above statement, we would be saying that

'Everyone is old and has grey hair.'

(b) When using an existential quantifier we usually follow it with a conjunction.

4.1.5 Examples

(a) Translate the following statement into predicate logic.

'Every schoolboy thinks that Robin Hood is a hero.'

The sentence can be reformulated to obtain

'For all x, if x is a schoolboy then x thinks that Robin Hood is a hero.'

Let $Schoolboy(x)$ be 'x is a schoolboy', $Hero(x, y)$ be 'x thinks that y is a hero', and r be 'Robin Hood'.
   Translating the sentence into logic we obtain

$$\forall x(Schoolboy(x) \Rightarrow Hero(x, r)).$$

(b) Consider this statement of the English language:

'Some footballers will never play in the premier league or the first division.'

We will carry out the following operations to this statement:

(i) translate into predicate logic;
(ii) negate the logical formula;
(iii) translate the negation back into English.

The sentence can be reformulated to obtain

'There exists x such that x is a footballer and x will not play in the premier league or in the first division.'

Let *Football*(x) be 'x is a footballer', let *Premier*(x) be 'x will play in the premier league' and let *Div_one*(x) be 'x will play in the first division'.

(i) Translating this to logic we have

$$\exists x(Football(x) \wedge \neg(Premier(x) \vee Div\_one(x))).$$

Note the scope of the $\neg$ connective; the English sentence says

$$\neg(Premier(x) \vee Div\_one(x)),$$

not

$$\neg Premier(x) \vee \neg Div\_one(x).$$

(ii) The negation of this formula is

$$\neg\exists x(Football(x) \wedge \neg(Premier(x) \vee Div\_one(x))),$$

which is equivalent ('$\neg\exists$' becomes '$\forall\neg$') to

$$\forall x(\neg Football(x) \vee Premier(x) \vee Div\_one(x)),$$

which is equivalent to

$$\forall x(Football(x) \Rightarrow (Premier(x) \vee Div\_one(x))).$$

(iii) The literal translation of the negation is

'For all x, if x is a footballer then x plays in the premier league or x plays in the first division.'

Converting this into more acceptable English we have

'Every footballer plays in the premier league or the first division.'

4.1.6   Summary

We now have a way of writing predicate formulae in which logical facts about objects in our universe, and their properties can be expressed. We have seen how first-order predicate formulae can express (some) natural language statements and have discussed methods for translating between first-order predicate logic and English. We have also seen how much more expressive predicate logic is when compared to propositional logic even though it is not as expressive as higher order logic. We will move in the next section to specify more accurately the format of these formulae.

4.1.7   Exercises

Exercise 4.1   For each of the following statements, carry out the operations:

  (a) translate into predicate logic;
  (b) negate the logical formula;
  (c) translate the negation back into English.

   (i) All brave knights are heroes.
  (ii) Some people think that Friar Tuck is a hero.
 (iii) There are some people who think that the Sheriff of Nottingham and King John are both villains.
 (iv) For every hero, there is a villain to be defeated and a heroine to be saved.
  (v) All the Romans are devoted to Gaius Marius but some of them do not like Lucius Cornelius Sulla.
 (vi) Some of those people who are devoted to Gaius Marius are not Romans.
 (vii) Richard III is a good king but some people do not think so.

Exercise 4.2   Given the following predicates:

$Real(x)$	x is a real number;	$Int(x)$	x is an integer;
$Prime(x)$	x is a prime number;	$Pos(x)$	x is positive;
$Odd(x)$	x is odd;	$Even(x)$	x is even;
$Greater(x, y)$	x is greater than y;	$Factor(x, y)$	x is a factor of y;
$Sum(x, y, z)$	$x + y = z$;	$Sub(x, y, z)$	$x - y = z$;
$Mult(x, y, z)$	$x \times y = z$;	$Div(x, y, z)$	$x/y = z$,

rewrite the following propositions which are given in the symbols of predicate logic in English, and indicate which are true and which are false. As far as possible, avoid using identifiers such as x and y in your answers.

(a) $\forall x(\neg Even(x) \Rightarrow Odd(x))$.
(b) $\forall x(\neg Even(x) \Rightarrow Prime(x))$.
(c) $\forall x(Real(x) \Leftrightarrow Int(x))$.
(d) $\forall x((Prime(x) \wedge Greater(x, 2)) \Rightarrow Odd(x))$.
(e) $\exists x(Int(x) \wedge Even(x) \wedge Prime(x))$.
(f) $\forall x \, \forall y \, \exists z((Int(x) \wedge Int(y)) \Rightarrow (Int(z) \wedge Sum(x, y, z)))$.
(g) $\exists z \, \forall x \, \forall y((Int(x) \wedge Int(y)) \Rightarrow (Int(z) \wedge Sum(x, y, z)))$.
(h) $\forall x \forall y((Int(x) \wedge Int(y) \wedge \exists z(Int(z) \wedge Div(x, y, z))) \Rightarrow Mult(y, z, x))$.
(i) $\exists x \, \forall y((Int(x) \wedge Int(y)) \Rightarrow \exists z(Int(z) \wedge Pos(z) \wedge Sub(x, y, z)))$.
(j) $\forall x \, \forall y((Real(x) \wedge Real(y) \wedge Pos(x) \wedge \neg Pos(y)) \Rightarrow Greater(y, x))$.
(k) $\forall x \, \forall y((Real(x) \wedge Real(y) \wedge Pos(x) \wedge \neg Pos(y)) \Rightarrow Factor(x, y))$.

Exercise 4.3   Using the same predicates as those given in the previous question, express the following English sentences using the symbolism of predicate logic.

(a) All prime numbers are positive integers.
(b) Any positive integer that is greater than 1 and is divisible only by 1 and itself is prime.
(c) The set of prime numbers is infinite.
(d) The subtraction function on the real numbers is not commutative (for real numbers, x and y, $y-x$ is not necessarily the same as $y-x$).
(e) On the real numbers, both the multiplication function and the addition function are associative (for real numbers, x, y and z, $x\times(y\times z)$ is always the same as $(x\times y)\times z$ and $x+(y+z)$ is always the same as $(x+y)+z$).
(f) For every positive integer x and every positive integer z there does not exist a positive integer y such that $x-y = z$.

4.2   The semantics of predicate logic

'Semantic' is a Greek word which is concerned with 'meaning'. It has been encountered in chapter 2 when semantic consequences were discussed. When the semantics of predicate logic are discussed we are considering the 'meanings' of the logic. These 'meanings' are given by the interpretations of the first-order languages. In the next section we will be looking at proofs of formulae in axiom systems where (within the system) we are not concerned with the meaning of formulae, just whether or not they can be proved in the system. However, this section is concerned with what formulae mean without any reference to whether or not they can be proved in logical systems. Later on in this chapter we will be looking at axiom systems of predicate logic where every formula which is true is provable and every formula which is provable is true, so that by the conventions of chapter 2 we will be looking at sound and complete systems.

This section will begin by formally defining a first-order language.

4.2.1   First-order languages

Predicate logic will be used to describe statements in a given system. This system will have many different interpretations. The set of all possible statements for a given system is known as a first-order language. These statements about objects and the relations between them are written using an *alphabet*. The statements may or may not be true in any given interpretation. The following definitions are the predicate logic equivalent of the definition of a *wff* in propositional logic. An alphabet consists of the following.

4.2.1.1   Punctuation marks

These include '(', ')' and ','.

4.2.1.2   Variables

These will be written in the general case $x_1, x_2, x_3, \ldots$. In a particular case we may use x, y, u and v. Their values range over the current 'universe of discourse'.

4.2.1.3   Constant symbols

These will be written in the general case $a, a_1, a_2, a_3, \ldots$. In a particular case we might have the constant 0 or *nil*. These will be assigned elements in the domain of an interpretation. Not all values will have a representative constant, so that the value 1 may be referred to as '$succ(0)$'*.

4.2.1.4   Function symbols

Function symbols will have varying numbers of arguments, but the interpretations of both the arguments and the results belong to the domain of any given interpretation. If we want to talk about integer values and squares, it may be desirable to write statements in prefix (functional) notation using identifiers, such as

$$sum(sqr(x), succ(prod(2, x))),$$

(the function *sum* delivers the sum of its two arguments, *prod* delivers the product of its two arguments, *succ* delivers the integer 1 larger than its single argument, and *sqr* delivers the square of its single argument) or we may use symbols for the function names

$$+(sqr(x), succ(\times(2, x))),$$

or even write it in infix form as

$$sqr(x) + 2 \times x + 1.$$

In general, the notation $f(x_1, \ldots, x_n)$ will be used to represent a function f of n arguments.

The function represented by the symbol f in some interpretation is a mapping $D \times D \times D \cdots \to D$ or $D^n \to D$, where D is the domain of the interpretation.

Constant symbols can be regarded as function symbols with no arguments.

4.2.1.5   Predicates

These will be of varying numbers of arguments as demonstrated by the following examples:

Is_mortal(a);
Is_parent_of(a_1, a_2);
Equal(x_1, x_2);
$=(x_1, x_2)$.

A more general notation is $R(x_1, \ldots, x_m)$ for the predicate R of m arguments.

The results of predicates are always either T or F, the arguments are in the domain of the interpretation, so that given an interpretation with domain D the

*The 'successor' function *succ* acts on an integer value and delivers the next integer value.

predicate R represents a mapping $D \times D \times D \cdots \rightarrow \{T, F\}$ or $D^m \rightarrow \{T, F\}$. The arguments of the relation are values in the universe; they are *not* other relations, for example, which would give a higher-order language.

4.2.1.6   Logical operations

The symbols $\neg$ and $\Rightarrow$ will be used as primitives to combine predicates. It will be assumed that any other logical operators we accidentally use have previously been declared in terms of these two! Similarly, we will use only the quantifier $\forall$; the quantifier $\exists$ can be defined in terms of it.

4.2.1.7   Typical statements

Typical logical statements might be

$$\forall x (sqr(x+1) = sqr(x) + 2 \times x + 1)$$

or, in prefix (functional) notation,

$$\forall x \, equals\big(sqr(succ(x)), sum(sqr(x), succ(prod(succ(1), x)))\big),$$

where *equals* is a predicate of two arguments, *sqr*, *sum* and *succ* are function symbols, and 1 is a constant symbol.

The set of logical operations and punctuation marks is the same for every alphabet, whereas a particular alphabet has its own set of variables, constant symbols, function symbols and predicates. The set of constant symbols or function symbols may be empty. The set of predicates should have at least one member, otherwise we would not have a very interesting language.

4.2.1.8   Example of a first-order language

The alphabet of the language consists of the given punctuation marks and logical operations together with

the variables	x, y;
the constant symbol	a;
the one-place function symbol	$s(x)$;
the two-place function symbols	$+(x, y), \times(x, y)$;
the two-place predicate	$=(x, y)$.

The first-order language with this alphabet consists of all the possible first-order statements that can be constructed from the alphabet. Remember that predicates cannot be in the argument places of predicates or function symbols.

Examples of statements in the first-order language are:

(a) $=(+(x, y), \times(x, y))$;
(b) $=((\times(x, y), a) \Rightarrow =(+(\times(x, y), z), z))$.

We could consider the (intended) interpretation where the domain of discourse is the set of positive integers, the constant symbol a is assigned to 0 and the function symbols and predicate take their intended meaning. In this intended interpretation the above first-order statements represent the following assertions about the positive integers:

(a') $(x+y) = (x \times y)$;
(b') if $(x \times y) = 0$ then $(x \times y) + z = z$.

Notice that assertion (a') may be true or false depending upon which positive integers (elements of the domain of interpretation) we assign to the variables x and y, whereas assertion (b') is true for every possible assignment of values to x, y and z.

Statements of the first-order language (such as (a) or (b)) are known as first-order formulae. The arguments of the predicates are known as first-order terms. We will now formally define these concepts. A given first-order language will be denoted by $\mathcal{L}$.

4.2.1.9   Terms in the first-order language $\mathcal{L}$

A term in the language* $\mathcal{L}$ is generated from constant symbols, variables, and function symbols. Terms are the things about which we will make logical assertions later. If the domain of an interpretation of the first-order language is the set of positive integers (as above), then the interpretation of a term will be an integer expression; it will be an expression with integer arguments which can take integer values. The definition of a term is as follows:

(a) variables and constant symbols of $\mathcal{L}$ are terms;
(b) if f is a function symbol in $\mathcal{L}$ of n arguments and $t_1, \ldots t_n$ are terms, then $f(t_1, \ldots, t_n)$ is a term;
(c) nothing is a term except by (a) and (b).

(The function symbol in (b) must have the correct number of arguments.) The function symbols for a particular first-order language must be specified by name and number of arguments. Terms (once interpreted) are in the domain of the universe of discourse. A monadic function is a mapping

$D \to D.$

A dyadic function is a mapping

$D \times D \to D.$

4.2.1.10   Atomic formulae or atoms in $\mathcal{L}$

An atomic formula in $\mathcal{L}$ is a predicate with the appropriate number of terms as arguments. It is the simplest form of logical unit in predicate logic. A monadic predicate (relation symbol) is a mapping

$D \to \{T, F\}.$

*The first-order language $\mathcal{L}$ we are now using should not be confused with the propositional logic system L.

A dyadic predicate is a mapping

$D \times D \rightarrow \{T, F\}$.

4.2.1.11   Well-formed formulae in $\mathscr{L}$

A *wff* in $\mathscr{L}$ is constructed from atomic formulae in the same way as *wff*s were constructed from variables in propositional logic. The same connectives are used but, of course, quantifiers are also available in a first-order language.

(a) Every atomic formula is a *wff*.
(b) If A and B are *wff*s and x is a variable, then $(\neg A)$ and $(A \Rightarrow B)$ and $((\forall x)A)$ are *wff*s.
(c) Nothing is a *wff* except by (a) and (b).

Unnecessary parentheses will be omitted (as in the propositional systems in chapter 2).

4.2.1.12   Some definitions

Scope.   We have already stated informally (in section 4.1) that the *scope* of a quantifier is the formula to which it applies. It will be the smallest unit following the quantifier. In the formula

$\forall x\, A(x) \Rightarrow B(x),$

the scope is just the $A(x)$. In the formula

$\forall x\, (A(x) \Rightarrow B(x)),$

the scope is the $(A(x) \Rightarrow B(x))$.

Bound, free, closed.   A particular occurrence of a variable x is *bound* if it is within the scope of a quantifier $\forall x$. Otherwise it is a *free* occurrence. A *wff* P of $\mathscr{L}$ is said to be closed if no variable occurs free in P.
   The variable y is free in the *wff*

$\forall x\, A(y)$

but is bound in the *wff*

$\forall x\, \forall y((B(x, y) \wedge D(z)) \Rightarrow C(y)) \wedge D(w).$

In the latter *wff*, x is also bound but z and w are free.

Closure.   If $y_1, \ldots, y_n$ are the only free variables in A, then $\forall y_1 \cdots \forall y_n A$ is said to be the *universal closure* of A, and is written A^c.

Free for.   A term t is 'free for a variable x in A' if no free occurrence of x in A is within the scope of a $\forall y$, where y is any variable occurring in t. If this definition is satisfied, then the term t can be substituted for all instances of the free variable x without the variable y becoming bound.

Consider the *wff* A defined by $\forall x(B(x) \Rightarrow C(y))$. The term $t_1 = f(x)$ is not free for y in A because when we substitute $f(x)$ for y, the x in t_1 falls under the scope of the $\forall x$ in A. The term $t_2 = f(z)$ is free for y in A.

Given a *wff* such as $A(x, y)$ we will usually use the notation $A(a, b)$ to represent the same *wff* with all free occurrences of x replaced by a and y replaced by b.

4.2.1.13   Example

Suppose we have a first-order language with the following alphabet (remember the punctuation marks and logical connectives are fixed for every possible first-order alphabet, so we need only present the variables, constant symbols, function symbols and predicates):

variables	$x_1, x_2, x_3, \ldots$;
constant symbols	$nil, a_1, a_2, a_3, \ldots$;
function symbol	$subs(t_1, t_2)$, where t_1 and t_2 are terms;
predicate	$app(t_1, t_2, t_3)$, where t_1, t_2, t_3 are terms.

Typical terms of the language are thus

nil;
x_2;
$subs(nil, a_1)$;
$subs(subs(nil, x_1), a_2)$.

Typical atoms of the language are

$app(nil, subs(nil, a_1), nil)$;
$app(subs(a_1, a_2), nil, nil)$.

Typical *wff*s of the language are

$app(nil, subs(nil, a_1), nil)$;
$\neg(app(subs(a_1, a_2), nil, nil) \Rightarrow app(nil, nil, subs(nil, a_2)))$;
$\forall x_1 \, app(nil, x_1, x_1) \Rightarrow app(nil, a_1, a_2)$.

So far, in this example, we have defined the language of the *wff*s. We have not said anything about the *meaning* of *subs* or *app*. The meanings are given by interpretations of the language.

4.2.2   Interpretations

Throughout this chapter, informal references to interpretations of first-order languages have been made. This concept will now be formally defined. We have at this point reached a stage where statements or formulae can be written in a first-order language. The formulae in the language are simply strings of characters, and have no fixed meaning. If logic is to be used to prove statements about the 'real world', then interpretations of the language must be given.

An *interpretation* $\mathcal{A}$ of a first-order language $\mathcal{L}$ is a quadruple of the form

$$\langle |\mathcal{A}|, Rel^{\mathcal{A}}, Fun^{\mathcal{A}}, Con^{\mathcal{A}} \rangle,$$

where

(a) $|\mathcal{A}|$ is the domain of the interpretation, the non-empty set which the variables of $\mathcal{L}$ range over;*

(b) $Rel^{\mathcal{A}} = \{R^{\mathcal{A}} : R$ is an n-place predicate (relation symbol) of $\mathcal{L}$ and $R^{\mathcal{A}}$ is an n-place relation on $|\mathcal{A}|$ which is *assigned* to $R\}$;

(c) $Fun^{\mathcal{A}} = \{f^{\mathcal{A}} : f$ is an n-place function symbol of $\mathcal{L}$ and $f^{\mathcal{A}}$ is an n-place function on $|\mathcal{A}|$ which is *assigned* to $f\}$.

(d) $Con^{\mathcal{A}} = \{c^{\mathcal{A}} : c$ is a constant symbol of $\mathcal{L}$ and $c^{\mathcal{A}}$ is a distinct element of $|\mathcal{A}|$ *assigned* to $c\}$.

Notice that this is a very different (but analagous) concept to that of an interpretation of a propositional formula. In the propositional case there are only propositional variables and our domain of discourse is only over the set $\{T, F\}$.

4.2.2.1   Example

Suppose we have a first-order language with the following alphabet:

the variables	$x, y, \ldots$;
the constant symbol	c;
the two-place function symbol	$g(x, y)$;
the predicates	$R(x, y), Q(x, y)$.

It has one function and two predicates.

We will consider two very different interpretations of this language.

Interpretation 1.   This interpretation of the language is $\mathcal{A}$, where

(a) $|\mathcal{A}|$ is the set of integers;

(b) $R^{\mathcal{A}}(x, y)$ is the relation '$x = y$' on $|\mathcal{A}|$;
    $Q^{\mathcal{A}}(x, y)$ is the relation '$x < y$' on $|\mathcal{A}|$;

(c) $g^{\mathcal{A}}(x, y) = x \times y$ (the product of x and y);

(d) $c^{\mathcal{A}} = 0$.

Given any particular formula of the first-order language such as

$$\forall x \, \forall y ((Q(y, x) \wedge (Q(x, c) \vee R(x, c))) \Rightarrow (Q(c, g(x, y)) \vee R(c, g(x, y)))),$$

we can describe the *meaning* of the formula in the interpretation. In this case the meaning is

*Do not confuse this notation with numeric modulus.

'For all integers x and y, if y is less than x and x is less than or equal to 0 then $x \times y$ is greater than or equal to 0.'

It is not difficult to see that this formula is true for this interpretation. We will define truth (and satisfaction) more formally later on.

For the moment let us consider a second interpretation.

Interpretation 2. This interpretation of the language (which uses the mod operator*) is $\mathscr{B}$, where

(a) $|\mathscr{B}|$ is the set $\{0, 1, 2\}$;
(b) $R^{\mathscr{B}}(x, y)$ is the relation '$x \equiv y \pmod 3$' on $|\mathscr{B}|$;
    $Q^{\mathscr{B}}(x, y)$ is the relation '$x+1 \equiv y \pmod 3$' on $|\mathscr{B}|$;
(c) $g^{\mathscr{B}}(x, y) = x+y$;
(d) $c^{\mathscr{B}} = 2$.

The formula shown in the first interpretation above now has the following meaning in this interpretation.

'For every x and y in $\{0, 1, 2\}$ if $y+1 \equiv x \pmod 3$ and $(x+1 \equiv 2 \pmod 3$ or $x \equiv 2 \pmod 3))$, then $2+1 \equiv x+y \pmod 3$ or $2 \equiv x+y \pmod 3$.'

It is not difficult to see that the formula is false for this interpretation. Take $x = 1$ and $y = 0$; then $y+1 \equiv x$ is true, $x+1 \equiv 2$ is true and $x \equiv 2$ is false, so the left-hand side of the implication is true. However, $0 \equiv x+y$ is false and $2 \equiv x+y$ is also false, so the right-hand side of the implication is false. This makes the implication false for this assignment of the elements of the domain to the variables x and y.

4.2.2.2   Example: A first-order language with *subs* and *app*

Here we consider the language described earlier with *subs* as its function and *app* as its predicate. Again, at least two easy but completely different interpretations exist. Recall that the set of *wff*s in each case is identical.

Interpretation 1. The domain of discourse is the set of positive integers together with the following interpretations:

(a) the constant symbols: *nil* represents unity, the other constant symbols represent any positive integers;
(b) the function symbol: *subs* represents multiplication (note that this gives results which are positive integers, so that they are within the domain of the universe of discourse as required;
(c) the predicate: $app(t_1, t_2, t_3)$ represents the statement '$t_1 \times t_2 = t_3$'.

Interpretation 2. The domain of discourse is the set of all lists of a given set of objects with the following interpretations:

---

*'$p \equiv q \pmod s$' is true if and only if the integers p and q have the same remainder when divided by s.

(a) the constant symbols: *nil* represents the empty list [ ], each other constant a unique list;
(b) the function symbol: *subs* represents the function which substitutes the first element of the first list for the first element of the second list so that

$$subs([m_1,\ldots,m_n],[o_1,\ldots,o_n]) = [m_1,o_2,\ldots,o_n];$$

(c) the predicate: $app(t_1,t_2,t_3)$ represents the statement 't_3 is the list obtained by appending the list t_2 to the list t_1.'

4.2.3   Satisfaction

The next sequence of definitions leads to a definition of the concept of a *wff* being true in an interpretation. This gives us a formal presentation of the ideas we have already briefly discussed in section 4.2.2.

4.2.3.1   Valuations

An assignment, in an interpretation $\mathcal{A}$, of a first-order language $\mathcal{L}$ is a function u from the set of variables in $\mathcal{L}$ to the set $|\mathcal{A}|$. Any assignment u can be extended to a *valuation* v (which is a function from the set of terms of $\mathcal{L}$ to $|\mathcal{A}|$) in the following way:

(a) $v(x) = u(x)$ for each variable of $\mathcal{L}$;
(b) $v(a) = a^{\mathcal{A}}$ for each constant symbol a of $\mathcal{L}$;
(c) $v(f(t_1,\ldots,t_n)) = f^{\mathcal{A}}(v(t_1),\ldots,v(t_n))$ for each n-place function symbol f of $\mathcal{L}$ (where $t_1,\ldots,t_n$ are terms of $\mathcal{L}$).

A valuation gives a value to each term in $\mathcal{L}$ which is its "meaning" in $\mathcal{A}$. There may be many valuations possible in one interpretation (because there are many possible assignments).

Let I be the finite set $\{1,\ldots,n\}$ or the infinite set $\{1,2,3,\ldots\}$, and let $\{x_i : i \in I\}$ be the (finite or infinite) set of variables of $\mathcal{L}$. Two valuations v and v' are said to be *i-equivalent* to each other if $v(x_j) = v'(x_j)$ for every $j \in I$ such that $j \neq i$. The motivation behind this definition is that the valuations v and v' give exactly the same value to every variable except x_i. We use this definition when considering the satisfaction of quantified formulae (below). An alternative definition would be to say that v and v' are x-equivalent (where x is a variable of $\mathcal{L}$ instead of an indexing integer as in the above definition) if $v(y) = v'(y)$ for every variable except x, thus $v(y) = v'(y)$ for every variable $y \in \{v : v$ is a variable of $\mathcal{L}\} - \{x\}$.

4.2.3.2   Example

Let us consider interpretation 1 of example 4.2.2.1. Let u be a valuation which assigns x to 2 and y to 3 and let v be the valuation derived from u. We can see that $v(x) = 2$, $v(y) = 3$, $v(a) = 0$, $v(g(x,a)) = 2 \times 0 = 0$ and $v(g(x,y)) = 2 \times 3 = 6$.

Now let u' be the same assignment as u, except that u' assigns the variable x to 1, and let v' be the valuation formed from u'. v and v' are x-equivalent. Notice that v and v' may give different valuations of terms involving the variable x. For example, $v(g(x, y)) = 6$ and $v'(g(x, y)) = 3$.

4.2.3.3   Satisfaction

Let A and B be *wff*'s in $\mathscr{L}$. A valuation v in $\mathscr{A}$ is defined to *satisfy* a *wff* by induction on the construction of a *wff*:

(a) v satisfies an atomic formula $R(t_1, \ldots, t_n)$ if and only if $R^{\mathscr{A}}(v(t_1), \ldots, v(t_n))$ is true in $\mathscr{A}$;

(b) v satisfies $\neg A$ if it does not satisfy A;

(c) v satisfies $A \Rightarrow B$ if either v satisfies $\neg A$ or v satisfies B;

(d) v satisfies $\forall x_i\, A$ if every valuation v' which is i-equivalent to v satisfies A.

If a valuation v in $\mathscr{A}$ satisfies a *wff* A we write

$$\mathscr{A} \vDash_v A$$

and if it does not

$$\mathscr{A} \nvDash_v A.$$

One of these two cases will always hold.

4.2.3.4   Truth

Definitions. A *wff* A is *true* in an interpretation $\mathscr{A}$ if and only if every valuation in $\mathscr{A}$ satisfies A. $\mathscr{A}$ is said to be a *model* of A. If S is a set of *wff*s of $\mathscr{L}$, then $\mathscr{A}$ is said to be a *model* of S if and only if $\mathscr{A}$ is a model of every member of S. A is said to be *false* in $\mathscr{A}$ if there is no valuation which satisfies A.

For a *wff* A we will write

$$\mathscr{A} \vDash A$$

if and only if A is true in $\mathscr{A}$ (every valuation satisfies A).

Some *wff*s may be neither true nor false, if some valuations satisfy it and others do not.

We have a similar notation for the truth of a set of *wff*s. For a set of *wff*s S

$$\mathscr{A} \vDash S$$

if and only if for every A in S we have $\mathscr{A} \vDash A$.

A *wff* A of $\mathscr{L}$ is *logically valid* if A is true in every interpretation of $\mathscr{L}$. A is *contradictory* if it is false in every interpretation.

Let S be a set of closed *wff*s. A closed *wff* A is called a *semantic consequence* of S if and only if A is true in every model of S. We write $S \vDash A$.

4.2.3.5   Example

We give an example of an equivalence relation. Consider a first-order language $\mathscr{L}$, where $t_1,\ldots,t_i,\ldots,t_n$ and s are terms of $\mathscr{L}$, f is any n-place function symbol of $\mathscr{L}$ and R is any n-place predicate of $\mathscr{L}$. Assume that $\mathscr{L}$ contains a two-place predicate *equals*.

Consider the set of formulae that contains the universal closures of

(a) $equals(x,x)$;
(b) $equals(s,t_i) \Rightarrow equals(f(t_1,\ldots,t_i,\ldots,t_n), f(t_1,\ldots,s,\ldots,t_n))$;
(c) $equals(s,t_i) \Rightarrow (R(t_1,\ldots,t_i,\ldots,t_n) \Rightarrow R(t_1,\ldots,s,\ldots,t_n))$.

If an interpretation is true for this set of *wffs*, then *equals* must be an equivalence relation on the domain of the interpretation (see exercise 4.9). The predicate *equals* could be interpreted as the equality relation in any model but this is not guaranteed by the formulae.

4.2.3.6   Example

We give an example on commutativity. Consider the following *wff* in a first-order language which contains the predicate *equals* and the two-place function symbol f:

$$\forall x \, \forall y \, equals(f(x,y), f(y,x)).$$

If this formula is included with the above formulae, then we are saying that the function symbol f must be interpreted as a commutative function in any model where *equals* is interpreted as the equality relation. If this were not the case, the formula could not be true.

4.2.3.7   Example

The principle of associativity can be demonstrated by the following example. In the same way as that carried out above, we can ensure that a two-place function symbol f is interpreted as an associative function in any model (where *equals* is interpreted as the equality relation) by taking the following formula:

$$\forall x \, \forall y \, \forall z \, equals(f(x, f(y,z)), f(f(x,y), z)).$$

If these two formulae are combined then we are saying that f must be both commutative and associative.

4.2.4   Truth-tables of interpretations

Suppose we have a set S of *wffs* of a particular first-order language and an interpretation $\mathscr{A}$. Given any formula of S we can draw up a truth-table of the formula for the interpretation $\mathcal{A}$. These are similar to the truth-tables we had for propositional logic. However, it is practical to do this only if the domain of $\mathcal{A}$ is small.

Consider the first-order language with the following alphabet:

the constant symbol	a;
the one-place function symbol	$f(x)$;
the two-place function symbol	$g(x, y)$;
the one-place predicate	$R(x)$;
the two-place predicate	$Q(x, y)$;
the set of variables	$\{x, y, \ldots\}$.

Consider also the interpretation $\mathcal{A}$ of this language defined as follows:

$|\mathcal{A}|$ is $\{0, 1, 2\}$;
$a^{\mathcal{A}}$ is 0;
$f^{\mathcal{A}}(x)$ is $x + 1 \pmod 3$;
$g^{\mathcal{A}}(x, y)$ is $x + y \pmod 3$;
$R^{\mathcal{A}}(x)$ is $x \equiv 0 \pmod 3$;
$Q^{\mathcal{A}}(x, y)$ is $x \equiv y \pmod 3$.

We will now construct the truth-tables of each of the following formulae:

(a) $\forall x \, \exists y (R(x) \Leftrightarrow Q(g(x, y), a))$;
(b) $\forall x \, \forall y ((Q(f(x), y) \wedge R(g(x, y))) \Rightarrow R(y))$;
(c) $\forall y (Q(x, f(y)) \Rightarrow R(g(x, y)))$.

(a) Under our interpretation this becomes

$$\forall x \, \exists y (x \equiv 0 \pmod 3 \Leftrightarrow x + y \equiv 0 \pmod 3).$$

The truth-table is

x	y	$\forall x$	$\exists y($	$x \equiv 0 \pmod 3$	$\Leftrightarrow$	$x + y \equiv 0 \pmod 3)$
0	0		T	T	T	T
	1			T	F	F
	2			T	F	F
1	0	T	T	F	T	F
	1			F	T	F
	2			F	F	T
2	0		T	F	T	F
	1			F	F	T
	2			F	T	F

Note the bracketing for the quantifiers. Note also that an existential quantifier returns T if there is at least one instance returning the value T. A universal quantifier returns F if there is one instance of the formula being F.

(b) Under our interpretation this becomes

$$\forall x\, \forall y((x+1 \equiv y \ (\mathrm{mod}\,3) \land x+y \equiv 0 \ (\mathrm{mod}\,3)) \Rightarrow y \equiv 0 \ (\mathrm{mod}\,3)).$$

The truth-table is

$x\ y$	$\forall x$	$\forall y($	$(x+1 \equiv y\ (\mathrm{mod}\,3)$	$\land$	$x+y \equiv 0\ (\mathrm{mod}\,3))$	$\Rightarrow$	$y \equiv 0\ (\mathrm{mod}\,3))$
0			F	F		T	T
0 1	T		T	F	F	T	F
2			F	F		T	F
0			F	F		T	T
1 1	F	F	F	F		T	T
2			T	T	T	F	F
0							
2 1							
2							

(c) Under our interpretation this becomes

$$\forall y(x \equiv y+1 \ (\mathrm{mod}\,3) \Rightarrow x+y \equiv 0 \ (\mathrm{mod}\,3)).$$

The truth-table is

$x\ \ y$	$\forall y($	$(x \equiv y+1\ (\mathrm{mod}\,3)$	$\Rightarrow$	$x+y \equiv 0\ (\mathrm{mod}\,3))$
0		F	T	
0 1	F	F	T	
2		T	F	F
0		T	F	F
1 1	F	F		
2				
0		F	T	
2 1	T	T	T	T
2		F	T	

Note: Formulae (a) and (b) are closed and the truth-tables have a single truth-value. However, formula (c) has one free variable and the truth-table has a truth-value for every possible assignment of an element of the domain of discourse to that variable. The formula takes the value T when x is assigned the value 2. Otherwise it takes the value F.

4.2.5   Herbrand interpretations

In this section we introduce a special kind of interpretation which is particularly important when considering the semantics of logic programming, and in showing the completeness of the predicate calculus. These results are needed in the next chapter.

Suppose we have a first-order language $\mathcal{L}$. The *ground* terms of $\mathcal{L}$ are all the terms of $\mathcal{L}$ in which no variable appears, so that they are the constant terms of $\mathcal{L}$. Note that this is not just the constants themselves; if 0 stands for the constant zero, and *succ* is the successor function which adds 1 to a value given as argument, then '$succ(0)$' is a constant term, but may not be a specific constant of the language. For example, if a, b and c are constant symbols, x is a variable, and f and g are two-place function symbols, then $f(a, g(b, c))$ is a ground term and $f(x, g(b, c))$ is not a ground term.

The set $U_{\mathcal{L}}$ of all the ground terms of $\mathcal{L}$ is known as its *Herbrand universe*. A ground atomic formula is an atomic formula in which all the function arguments are ground terms. The set $B_{\mathcal{L}}$ of all the ground atomic formulae of $\mathcal{L}$ is known as its *Herbrand base*. This is the set of instances of predicate symbols of $\mathcal{L}$ with the elements of $U_{\mathcal{L}}$ as the arguments.

Examples

(a) Suppose we have a first-order language $\mathcal{L}$ whose alphabet consists of constant symbols a, b and c, no function symbols, one-place relation symbols R and S, and a two-place relation symbol Q. So in this case

$$U_{\mathcal{L}} = \{a, b, c\}$$

and

$$B_{\mathcal{L}} = \{R(a), R(b), R(c), S(a), S(b), S(c), Q(a, a), Q(b, b), Q(c, c),$$

$$Q(a, b), Q(b, a), Q(a, c), Q(c, a), Q(b, c), Q(c, b)\}.$$

(b) Suppose we have a first-order language $\mathcal{L}$ whose alphabet consists of constant symbols a and b, a one-place function symbol f and one-place relation symbols R and S. So

$$U_{\mathcal{L}} = \{a, f(a), f(f(a)), \ldots\} \cup \{b, f(b), f(f(b)), \ldots\};$$

$$B_{\mathcal{L}} = \{R(a), R(f(a)), R(f(f(a))), \ldots\} \cup \{R(b), R(f(b)), R(f(f(b))), \ldots\}$$

$$\cup \{S(a), S(f(a)), \ldots\} \cup \{S(b), S(f(b)), \ldots\}$$

We define a *Herbrand interpretation* $\mathcal{A}$ of $\mathcal{L}$ to be an interpretation such that:

(a) $|\mathcal{A}| = U_{\mathcal{L}}$;
(b) for each constant symbol c of $\mathcal{L}$, $c^{\mathcal{A}} = c$;
(c) for each n-place function symbol f of $\mathcal{L}$, $f^{\mathcal{A}}(t_1, \ldots, t_n) = f(t_1^{\mathcal{A}}, \ldots, t_n^{\mathcal{A}})$, where $t_1, \ldots, t_n$ are ground terms.

Thus for a Herbrand interpretation the meaning of constant and function symbols is fixed. The meanings of relation symbols can vary. Hence we can associate each particular Herbrand interpretation with the particular subset of the

Herbrand base whose members are exactly the ones that are true in the Herbrand interpretation.

Example   In case (a) above a Herbrand interpretation $\mathcal{A} = \{R(a), Q(a,b),$ $Q(a,c)\}$ would be the interpretation where

$$|\mathcal{A}| = \{a, b, c\}; \qquad a^{\mathcal{A}} = a, \qquad b^{\mathcal{A}} = b, \qquad c^{\mathcal{A}} = c$$

and

$$R(a), \qquad Q(a,b), \qquad Q(a,c)$$

are true. All other members of $B_{\mathscr{L}}$ are false.

Another interpretation would be

$$\mathcal{A} = \{R(c), S(a), S(c), Q(c,b)\}$$

where each member of this set is interpreted as true and all other members of the Herbrand base as false.

It is easy to see that there is a Herbrand interpretation associated with each subset of the Herbrand base.

Herbrand model

A Herbrand interpretation which is true for a *wff A* is known as a *Herbrand model* of A. If a Herbrand interpretation is true for each member of a set of *wff*s S, then it is known as a *Herbrand model* of S.

4.2.6   Summary

In this section, the ideas of a first-order language and of a *wff* of any given first-order language were introduced.

We also introduced first-order interpretations and looked at the concepts of satisfaction and truth, and briefly considered truth tables of interpretations with small domains.

Finally, we presented a special type of interpretation known as a Herbrand interpretation. These interpretations will occur in the completeness section of this chapter and in the section on the semantics of logic programming in chapter 5.

In the next section, we will develop a system of proofs in predicate logic to parallel that developed in chapter 2 for propositional logic.

4.2.7   Worked examples

Example 4.1   Suppose we have a first-order language $\mathscr{L}$. Let S be a set of closed formulas of $\mathscr{L}$ and let A be some closed formula of $\mathscr{L}$. Show that A is a semantic consequence of S if and only if $S \cup \{\neg A\}$ is unsatisfiable.

Solution

($\Rightarrow$) Assume that A is a semantic consequence of S and that $\mathscr{A}$ is a model of S. Then $\mathscr{A} \vDash A$ by the first assumption. Therefore $\neg A$ is false in $\mathscr{A}$, so $\mathscr{A}$ is not a model of $S \cup \{\neg A\}$, and therefore $S \cup \{\neg A\}$ is unsatisfiable.

($\Leftarrow$) Assume $S \cup \{\neg A\}$ is unsatisfiable. Suppose $\mathscr{A}$ is a model of S. Then $\neg A$ is false in $\mathscr{A}$ because $S \cup \{\neg A\}$ is unsatisfiable. Therefore $\mathscr{A} \vDash A$ and so A is a semantic consequence of S.

Example 4.2 Suppose we have a first-order language $\mathscr{L}$ whose alphabet consists of the constant symbol a, the one-place function symbol f, the one-place relation symbol R and a two-place relation symbol S. Consider the Herbrand interpretation defined by the following subset of the Herbrand base.

$$\{R(a), R(f(a)), R(f(f(a))), S(a, f(a)), S(a, f(f(a)))\}.$$

Determine whether or not this is a Herbrand model of the following formulae:

(a) $\forall x(R(x) \Rightarrow S(x, f(x)))$;
(b) $\forall x(R(x) \Rightarrow \exists y\, S(x, y))$;
(c) $\exists x(R(x) \wedge S(x, f(x)))$.

Solution The domain of the interpretation is the Herbrand universe, in this case $\{a, f(a), f(f(a)), \dots\}$.

(a) The subformula $R(x) \Rightarrow S(x, f(x))$ will be F only when $R(x)$ is T (from the truth-table of $\Rightarrow$). For the given interpretation this is only when the following members of the Herbrand universe are assigned to x: a, $f(a)$ and $f(f(a))$. So for all other instances of x, $R(x) \Rightarrow S(x, f(x))$ is T.

   We are required to determine whether or not $\forall x(R(x) \Rightarrow S(x, f(x)))$ is T for the given interpretation. It therefore remains to check whether or not $R(x) \Rightarrow S(x, f(x))$ is true for the three instances of x that we do not know about.

   It can be seen that if we let x be $f(a)$ then we have $R(f(a)) \Rightarrow S(f(a), f(f(a)))$ which is F because $S(f(a), f(f(a)))$ is not a member of the subset of the Herbrand base that we were given and so is interpreted to be F. This means that $\forall x(R(x) \Rightarrow S(x, f(x)))$ is F for the given interpretation.

(b) The formula $R(x) \Rightarrow \exists y\, S(x, y)$ can only be F when the following members of the Herbrand universe are assigned to x: a, $f(a)$ and $f(f(a))$ (for the same reasons as in the previous case).

   Let x be assigned the ground term $f(a)$. Then $\exists y\, S(f(a), y)$ has truth-value F because there does not exist a y such that $S(f(a), y)$ is T. So $R(x) \Rightarrow \exists y\, S(x, y)$ is F when x is assigned $f(a)$.

   Thus, the given Herbrand interpretation is not a model of $\forall x(R(x) \Rightarrow \exists y\, S(x, y))$.

(c) Let a be assigned to x and we can see that $R(a) \wedge S(a, f(a))$ is T. So $\exists x(R(x) \wedge S(x, f(x)))$ is T for the given Herbrand interpretation.

4.2.8   Exercises

Exercise 4.4   For each occurrence of a variable in the following expressions, state whether it is a free or bound occurrence:

(a) $\forall x \, A(y) \Rightarrow \neg A(x)$;
(b) $\forall x \, \forall y (A(x, y, z) \Rightarrow (B(y) \Rightarrow \neg C(x)))$;
(c) $\forall x \, \neg \forall y \, A(x) \Rightarrow C(x, y)$;
(d) $\forall x \, \forall y (A(x) \Rightarrow B(x, y)) \Rightarrow \neg \forall y \, C(x, y, z)$.

Exercise 4.5   In the given expressions, is the given term free for the given variable?

	Expression	Term	Variable
(a)	$\forall x \, A(x, y, z) \Rightarrow \forall z \, A(z, x, w)$	$f(x, w)$	y
(b)	ditto	$f(y, z)$	y
(c)	ditto	$f(x, z)$	x
(d)	ditto	$f(x, v)$	y
(e)	ditto	$f(w, v)$	y
(f)	$\forall y \, A(y, f(x, y), z) \Rightarrow (B(x) \Rightarrow C(w))$	z	x
(g)	ditto	$f(x, f(z, w))$	w
(h)	ditto	$f(x, f(y, w))$	x

Exercise 4.6   Let $\mathcal{L}$ be the first-order language which includes the individual constant a, a dyadic function f and a dyadic predicate R. Let A denote the *wff*

$$\forall x \, \forall y (R(f(x, y), a) \Rightarrow R(x, y)).$$

Define an interpretation $\mathcal{A}$ as follows:

$|\mathcal{A}|$ is the set of integers;
a is interpreted as 0;
$f(x, y)$ is interpreted as $x - y$;
$R(x, y)$ is interpreted as $x < y$.

Write down the interpretation of A in $\mathcal{A}$. Find another interpretation with the opposite truth-value.

Exercise 4.7   Suppose we have a term $t(x)$ which contains a variable x. Let $t(s)$ be the term obtained by substituting a new term s for the variable x in $t(x)$. Let v be a valuation of $t(x)$ and let v' be the x-equivalent valuation such that $v'(x) = v(s)$.
    Show by induction on the construction of $t(x)$ that $v'(t(x)) = v(t(s))$.

Exercise 4.8   Let $A(x)$ be a *wff* of a first-order language $\mathcal{L}$, let $\mathcal{A}$ be an interpretation of $\mathcal{L}$ and s be a term free for x in A. Let v and v' be defined as in exercise 4.7.

Show by induction on the construction of $A(x)$ that $\mathcal{A} \vDash_v A(s)$ if and only if $\mathcal{A} \vDash_{v'} A(x)$.

Exercise 4.9   Consider the set of formulae given in example 4.2.3.5. Show that the two-place predicate *equals* must be interpreted as an equivalence relation in any model of the formulae.

Exercise 4.10   Show that the following *wff*s are not logically valid:

(a) $\forall x \, \exists y \, A(x, y) \Rightarrow \exists y \, \forall x \, A(x, y)$;
(b) $\forall x \, \forall y \, \forall z (A(x, y, z) \Leftrightarrow A(y, x, z))$

Exercise 4.11   Suppose that a first-order language has the following alphabet:

the constant symbols: a and b;
the one-place function symbols: $f(x)$ and $g(x)$;
the two-place function symbol: $h(x, y)$;
the one-place predicate: $R(x)$;
the two-place predicate: $Q(x, y)$;
the three-place predicate: $S(x, y, z)$.

Consider the interpretation $\mathcal{A}$ defined by

$|\mathcal{A}|$ is $\{0, 1, 2, 3\}$;
$a^{\mathcal{A}} = 0$;
$b^{\mathcal{A}} = 2$;
$f(x)^{\mathcal{A}} \equiv x + 1 \pmod 4$;
$g(x)^{\mathcal{A}} \equiv x + 3 \pmod 4$;
$h(x, y)^{\mathcal{A}} \equiv x + y \pmod 4$;
$R(x)^{\mathcal{A}}$ is $x + 2 \equiv 0 \pmod 4$;
$Q(x, y)^{\mathcal{A}}$ is $x \equiv y \pmod 4$;
$S(x, y, z)^{\mathcal{A}}$ is $x + y + 2 \equiv z \pmod 4$.

Construct the truth-tables of each of the following formulae:

(a) $\forall x \, \exists y (Q(g(x), h(y, a)))$;
(b) $\exists y \, \forall x (Q(a, h(x, y)) \Rightarrow R(f(x) \vee S(x, y, b)))$;
(c) $S(x, h(x, a), g(b)) \Rightarrow \exists z \, Q(z, h(f(x), g(y)))$;
(d) $R(x) \Rightarrow \forall y (S(x, y, y))$.

Exercise 4.12   Construct the Herbrand universe and base of the first-order language given in the previous exercise.

Exercise 4.13   Construct the Herbrand universe and base of the first-order languages with the following alphabets:

(a) the constant symbols a and b, the one-place predicates $Q(x)$ and $R(x)$, and the two-place predicate $S(x, y)$;

(b) The constant symbols a, b and c, the one-place function symbols $f(x)$ and $g(x)$, and the one-place predicate $R(x)$;

(c) the constant symbol a, the two-place function symbol $f(x, y)$ and the two-place predicate $R(x, y)$.

Exercise 4.14 Consider a first-order language with the following alphabet: the constant symbols a and b, the one-place function symbol $f(x)$ and the two-place predicates $R(x, y)$ and $S(x, y)$. Let $\mathcal{A}$ be a Herbrand interpretation determined by

$$\{R(a, b), R(a, f(b)), R(a, f(f(b))), \ldots\}$$

$$\cup \{S(a, b), S(f(a), b), S(f(f(a)), b), \ldots\}.$$

Determine whether or not $\mathcal{A}$ is a Herbrand model of the following formulae:

(a) $\forall x \, \forall y (S(f(x), x) \wedge R(y, f(y)))$;

(b) $\forall x (R(a, f(x)) \Rightarrow S(f(x), b))$;

(c) $\forall x (R(x, f(b)) \Rightarrow S(f(x), b))$;

(d) $\forall x (R(x, f(b)) \Rightarrow \exists y \, S(x, y))$;

(e) $\forall x (R(x, f(b)) \Rightarrow \forall y \, S(x, y))$.

4.3 Syntactical systems of predicate logic

In this section we develop a formal system for predicate logic similar to the system L developed for propositional logic in chapter 2. The system presented there is expanded by introducing axioms and rules to handle quantifiers. The semantics of first-order formulae and the different interpretations that can be put onto them have been discussed earler in this chapter. However, in this section we are not interested in the meaning of formulae; just whether or not they can be proved in the system. The interplay between proof and meaning will be considered in the following section.

We will begin by introducing the axiom system $K_{\mathcal{L}}$ based on a given first-order language $\mathcal{L}$. It is possible to define different axiom systems by using different languages. Thus, strictly speaking, we should always write $K_{\mathcal{L}}$ for the system K depending on the particular first-order language $\mathcal{L}$. However, in most of our reasoning we do not change the first-order language under consideration and the subscript makes the notation look unnecessarily complicated. It is therefore possible to drop the subscript when it is understood that we are dependent on a particular first-order language and that language is not going to be changed. The subscript will be introduced only when it is required.

In the following definition A, B and C will be taken to be any *wff*s of $\mathcal{L}$. The axioms are axiom schemas which means that any *wff* of $\mathcal{L}$ can be substituted for A, B or C. Although we have just five axiom schemas there is really an infinite number of axioms for each particular schema.

4.3.1   The system *K* of predicate logic

4.3.1.1   Background

Our deduction axioms for the system K are (A, B and C are *wff*s of the first-order language $\mathcal{L}$):

A1 $A \Rightarrow (B \Rightarrow A)$;
A2 $(A \Rightarrow (B \Rightarrow C)) \Rightarrow ((A \Rightarrow B) \Rightarrow (A \Rightarrow C))$;
A3 $(\neg A \Rightarrow \neg B) \Rightarrow (B \Rightarrow A)$;
A4 $\forall x A(x) \Rightarrow A(t)$, if t is a term which is free for x in $A(x)$;
A5 $\forall x (A \Rightarrow B) \Rightarrow (A \Rightarrow \forall x B)$, if x does not occur free in A.

Note that the first three are the same axioms that were used in the propositional case. This means that, intuitively, system L can be thought of as a 'subsystem' of system K, so that any proof in L can be turned into a proof in K by replacing statement variables of L by *wff*s of K. The other axioms relate to the universal quantifier (and hence the existential quantifier). In system K the formula $\exists x A$ is taken to be an abbreviation for the *wff* $\neg \forall x \neg A$. Whenever a *wff* appears in K without quantifiers (or we are not making specific use of the quantifiers if they do appear), then we are essentially using system L. Note carefully the scopes of the quantifiers in the last two axiom schemas.

Recall from chapter 2 the definition of a deduction (of a propositional formula P), in the axiom system L, from a set of propositional formulae Γ.

We will now use the same ideas for defining proofs and deductions as were used for system L, but with the axioms and rules of our new system K.

System K has the following two rules:

R1 $\{A, A \Rightarrow B\} \vdash_K B$;
R2 $A \vdash_K \forall x A$.

The first rule is our old friend MP. The second is called the *generalization rule*. The name of the generalization rule will often be abbreviated by *Gen*. There are many slight variations of this system which amount to the same thing. Often these variations involve different axiom schemas but retain the same two rules. However, it is possible to remove the generalization rule and replace it with additional axiom schemas. This type of system is used in [1]. These systems have the interesting feature of having only one rule of inference. The generalization rule can still be used but it is a *derived* rule of inference rather than a specific part of the system.

4.3.1.2   Definitions

A *deduction* in K of a *wff* A from a set of *wff*s Γ (written $\Gamma \vdash_K A$) is a sequence of *wff*s of $\mathcal{L}$ ending with A such that each *wff* is either an instance of an axiom of K or a member of Γ, or obtainable from earlier *wff*s in the sequence using a finite number of applications of MP or *Gen*.

A *proof* in K is a deduction in K from the empty set.

A *wff* A is a *theorem* in K if it is the last member of a proof sequence. It is written

$$\vdash_K A.$$

A *wff* of $\mathcal{L}$ is said to be in *the form of a propositional tautology* if and only if the *wff* can be obtained from a propositional tautology by substituting *wff*s of $\mathcal{L}$ for statement variables.

Examples

(a) $\forall x A \Rightarrow \neg\neg\forall x A$ is in the form of a propositional tautology since it can be obtained from $P \Rightarrow \neg\neg P$ (which is a propositional tautology; check using truth-tables) by substituting $\forall x A$ for P.

(b) $(\forall x A \Rightarrow \exists x B) \Rightarrow (\neg \exists x B \Rightarrow \neg \forall x A)$ is in the form of a propositional tautology since it can be obtained from $(P \Rightarrow Q) \Rightarrow (\neg Q \Rightarrow \neg P)$ by substituting $\forall x A$ for P and $\exists x B$ for Q.

4.3.2   Discussion of the system K

4.3.2.1   The relationship between system K and system L

In this section we will consider some examples of theorem proving in K and some important results concerned with the system. These results are *derived rules* of inference. As with system L, derived rules of inference are essentially abbreviations for a proof sequence which could be carried out using only the given rules.

At this stage in our study of the system we are not concerned with the truth or falsity of *wff*s; we are simply concerned with whether or not *wff*s are provable in K. It can be shown that $\vdash_K A$ holds if and only if $\vDash A$ holds, so that a *wff* is provable in K if and only if it is logically valid. However, the relationship between first-order syntactical systems and the semantics of predicate logic will be discussed fully below in section 4.4. For the moment we will consider some examples of deductions in K.

Examples

(a) Show that

$$\forall x A(x) \vdash_K A(g(y)),$$

where A is a *wff* of $\mathcal{L}$, g is a function symbol of $\mathcal{L}$ and x and y are variables of $\mathcal{L}$ and $g(y)$ is free for x in $A(x)$.

Solution

1	$\forall x\, A(x)$	assumption;
2	$\forall x\, A(x) \Rightarrow A(g(y))$	A4 with $g(y)$ for term t;
3	$A(g(y))$	MP on 1 and 2.

Note: The proviso that $g(y)$ be free for x in $A(x)$ was required at step 2 to apply axiom schema A4.

(b) Show that

$$A(x) \vdash_K \forall x(B(x) \Rightarrow A(x)),$$

where A and B are *wff*s of $\mathcal{L}$ and x is a variable of $\mathcal{L}$.

Solution

1	$A(x)$	assumption;
2	$A(x) \Rightarrow (B(x) \Rightarrow A(x))$	A1;
3	$B(x) \Rightarrow A(x)$	MP on 1 and 2;
4	$\forall x(B(x) \Rightarrow A(x))$	*Gen* on 3.

We will now consider some techniques to enable us to derive certain theorems of system K easily. We have already informally mentioned that system L of propositional logic is in a certain sense a 'subsystem' of system K. What is meant by this is formalized in the theorem below.

Theorem   If a propositional formula P is provable in L, and a *wff* A can be obtained by substituting *wff*s for the statement variables of P, then A is provable in K.

Proof   Consider the proof in L of the formula P. We can go through the complete proof making the same substitutions of *wff*s for the propositional variables of P that allowed us to obtain A from P. The proof in L uses only axiom schemas A1, A2, A3 and MP. If any derived rules of inference occurred in the proof, then they could be replaced by steps involving only MP.

As A1, A2 and A3 are axiom schemas of K and MP is a rule of K, we now have a proof of A in K.

Example   Suppose we wish to show that for a *wff* W

$$\vdash_K \forall x\, W \Rightarrow \forall x\, W.$$

This can be obtained from the propositional formula $P \Rightarrow P$ by substituting $\forall x\, W$ for P.

We know that $\vdash_L P \Rightarrow P$ (the proof has been given in chapter 2 (section 2.2.2)).

Following the method outlined in the theorem, P could be replaced (in the chapter 2 proof) by $\forall x W$ to obtain the following proof in K:

1 $\forall x W \Rightarrow (\forall x W \Rightarrow \forall x W)$	A1 with $\forall x W$ for A and $\forall x W$ for B;
2 $\forall x W \Rightarrow ((\forall x W \Rightarrow \forall x W) \Rightarrow \forall x W)$	A1 with $\forall x W$ for A and $\forall x W \Rightarrow \forall x W$ for B;
3 $(\forall x W \Rightarrow ((\forall x W \Rightarrow \forall x W) \Rightarrow \forall x W)) \Rightarrow$ $((\forall x W \Rightarrow (\forall x W \Rightarrow \forall x W)) \Rightarrow (\forall x W \Rightarrow \forall x W))$	A2 with $\forall x W$ for A, $\forall x W \Rightarrow \forall x W$ for B and $\forall x W$ for C;
4 $(\forall x W \Rightarrow (\forall x W \Rightarrow \forall x W)) \Rightarrow (\forall x W \Rightarrow \forall x W)$	MP on 2 and 3.
5 $\forall x W \Rightarrow \forall x W$	MP on 1 and 4.

Corollary   If a *wff* A is in the form of a propositional tautology then

$\qquad \vdash_K A.$

Proof   Assume that A is in the form of a propositional tautology, then there is a propositional formula P associated with A (A can be obtained from P by substituting *wff*s for the propositional variables of P). We know that $\vDash P$, and so $\vdash_L P$ by the completeness theorem for L (see chapter 2). The result follows by the above theorem.

As was seen with system L of propositional logic, it is useful to *derive* new rules of inference. We will do the same thing for system K. These new rules are not independent of MP and *Gen*, so they do not need to be explicitly stated as part of the system because it would be possible to replace them with a sequence of steps involving just MP and *Gen*. The sequence of steps would essentially be the justifications of the derived rules that are about to be presented. Some of the derived rules pass straight over from system L to system K (using similar arguments to those employed above) because the proofs (or justifications) of the rules do not involve quantifiers (and hence use rule *Gen*). These rules will be considered first.

4.3.2.2   Hypothetical syllogism for K

Let A B and C be *wff*s of $\mathcal{L}$. The rule

$\qquad (A \Rightarrow B), (B \Rightarrow C) \vdash_K (A \Rightarrow C)$

still holds, the proof being again the same as in L.

4.3.2.3   The inverse deduction theorem for *K*

The inverse deduction theorem still holds in the form

> If *A* and *B* are *wff*s of $\mathcal{L}$,
>   and Γ is a set of *wff*s,
>   and $\Gamma \vdash_K A \Rightarrow B$,
> then $\Gamma \cup \{A\} \vdash_K B$.

The proof is exactly the same as in *L*.

Although the inverse deduction theorem passes over from *L* to *K* without any problem this is not the case for the deduction theorem itself. This rule has to be modified to take into account the use of rule *Gen* under certain conditions. However, if we restrict the class of *wff*s to which it applies, then the theorem can be passed straight over from *L* to *K*.

4.3.2.4   The deduction theorem for *K* (for all *wff*s)

If

$$\Gamma \cup \{A\} \vdash_K B$$

and the deduction contains no application of *Gen* using a variable which occurs free in *A*, then

$$\Gamma \vdash_K A \Rightarrow B.$$

Proof   We use induction on the length of the deduction of *B* from $\Gamma \cup \{A\}$.

For the base case this proof is exactly the same as in *L*.

For the induction step the proof again follows exactly the same method as for *L* when *B* is an axiom, member of Γ or follows from MP. The case that needs to be considered a little more carefully is when *B* follows from an earlier *wff* by generalization.

We need to show that

$$\Gamma \vdash_K A \Rightarrow B.$$

Consider *B* to be of the form $\forall x\, C$. Note that *x* does not occur free in *A*, because of the condition of the deduction theorem for *K*. We know that $\Gamma \cup \{A\} \vdash_K C$, so by the induction hypothesis

$$\Gamma \vdash_K A \Rightarrow C.$$

Gen can be applied to $A \Rightarrow C$ to give us

$$\Gamma \vdash_K \forall x (A \Rightarrow C).$$

Axiom A5 gives us

$$\vdash_K \forall x (A \Rightarrow C) \Rightarrow (A \Rightarrow \forall x\, C),$$

which is a permitted instance since *x* is not free in *A*.

Finally by MP on the preceding two results we have

$$\Gamma \vdash_K A \Rightarrow \forall x\, C,$$

which is equivalent to

$$\Gamma \vdash_K A \Rightarrow B.$$

An alternative, less general form of the deduction theorem which follows immediately from the above proof is given in the next section.

4.3.2.5   The deduction theorem for K (for closed *wffs*)

If A is a closed *wff* and

$$\Gamma \cup \{A\} \vdash_K B,$$

then

$$\Gamma \vdash_K A \Rightarrow B.$$

Note: This proof is exactly the same as the one above except that, at the point where axiom A5 is applied, we know that x does not occur free in A (because A is a closed formula), so it is not necessary to impose it as a condition of the theorem.

Derived rules which are specifically concerned with quantification have not yet been considered. We have rule *Gen* which is intuitively a $\forall$-*introduction* rule; from the result $\vdash_K A$, *Gen* can be used to deduce $\vdash_K \forall x A$. Rules will now be presented which will *eliminate* $\forall$ and $\exists$ together with one which will *introduce* $\exists$.

4.3.2.6   The specification rule ($\forall$-elimination)

If t is a term which is free for x in a *wff* A, then $\forall x\, A(x) \vdash_K A(t)$.

Proof   This is a simple application of MP on axiom schema A4 and the hypothesis.

Note: x can be identical with t, so it is possible to derive $A(x)$ from $\forall x A(x)$ using this rule.

Example   Let A and B be *wffs* such that x is not free in B. Show that

$$\vdash_K \forall x(A \Rightarrow B) \Rightarrow (\exists x A \Rightarrow B).$$

This is equivalent to showing that

$$\vdash_K \forall x(A \Rightarrow B) \Rightarrow (\neg \forall x \neg A \Rightarrow B).$$

We will instead first prove the deduction

$$\forall x(A \Rightarrow B),\ \neg \forall x \neg A \vdash_K B.$$

Solution

1	$\forall x(A \Rightarrow B)$	assumption;
2	$\neg\forall x\,\neg A$	assumption;
3	$A \Rightarrow B$	specification on 1;
4	$(A \Rightarrow B) \Rightarrow (\neg B \Rightarrow \neg A)$	form of a propositional tautology;
5	$\neg B \Rightarrow \neg A$	MP on 3 and 4;
6	$\forall x(\neg B \Rightarrow \neg A)$	*Gen* on 5;
7	$(\forall x(\neg B \Rightarrow \neg A)) \Rightarrow (\neg B \Rightarrow \forall x\,\neg A)$	A5 with $\neg B$ for A and $\neg A$ for B (needs x not to be free in B);
8	$\neg B \Rightarrow \forall x\,\neg A$	MP on 6 and 7;
9	$(\neg B \Rightarrow \forall x\,\neg A)$ $\Rightarrow (\neg\forall x\,\neg A \Rightarrow \neg\neg B)$	form of a propositional tautology;
10	$\neg\forall x\,\neg A \Rightarrow \neg\neg B$	MP on 8 and 9;
11	$\neg\neg B$	MP on 2 and 10;
12	$\neg\neg B \Rightarrow B$	form of a propositional tautology;
13	B	MP on 11 and 12.

The result now follows by two applications of the deduction theorem.

4.3.2.7   The existential rule (∃-introduction)

If t is a term which is free for x in a *wff* A, then $A(t) \vdash_K \exists x\,A(x)$.

Proof   First notice that

$$(\forall x\,\neg A(x) \Rightarrow \neg A(t)) \Rightarrow (A(t) \Rightarrow \neg\forall x\,\neg A(x))$$

is in the form of the propositional tautology

$$(P \Rightarrow \neg Q) \Rightarrow (Q \Rightarrow \neg P),$$

with $\forall x\,\neg A(x)$ for P and $A(t)$ for Q. So by the corollary of section 4.3.2.1 we have

$$\vdash_K (\forall x\,\neg A(x) \Rightarrow \neg A(t)) \Rightarrow (A(t) \Rightarrow \neg\forall x\,\neg A(x)).$$

Secondly, recall that $\exists x\,A(x)$ is an abbreviation for $\neg\forall x\,\neg A(x)$. We have the following deduction in K:

1	$A(t)$	assumption;
2	$\forall x\,\neg A(x) \Rightarrow \neg A(t)$	A4 with $\neg A(x)$ for A (needs t not to be free for x in A);
3	$(\forall x\,\neg A(x) \Rightarrow \neg A(t))$ $\Rightarrow (A(t) \Rightarrow \neg\forall x\,\neg A(x))$	form of a propositional tautology;
4	$A(t) \Rightarrow \neg\forall x\,\neg A(x)$	MP on 2 and 3;
5	$\neg\forall x\,\neg A(x)$	MP on 1 and 4.

4.3.2.8   Rule C (∃-elimination)

Let $A(x)$ and B be two *wffs* and let Γ be a set of *wffs*. If $\Gamma \vdash_K \exists x \, A(x)$ and $\Gamma, A(c) \vdash_K B$, then $\Gamma \vdash_K B$, where c is a new constant symbol that does not occur in A, B or any formula of Γ. We also require that the deduction $\Gamma, A(c) \vdash_K B$ contains no application of *Gen* using a variable which occurs free in $A(c)$.

Proof   Using the deduction theorem on $\Gamma, A(c) \vdash_K B$, we can write $\Gamma \vdash_K A(c) \Rightarrow B$. We will now prove the deduction

$$\exists x \, A(x), \ A(c) \Rightarrow B \vdash_K B.$$

1	$\exists x \, A(x)$	assumption;
2	$A(c) \Rightarrow B$	assumption;
3	$\forall v(A(v) \Rightarrow B)$	*Gen* on 2, where v is a new variable not occurring elsewhere;
4	$\forall v(A(v) \Rightarrow B) \Rightarrow (\exists v \, A(v) \Rightarrow B)$	example in section 4.3.2.6 above;
5	$\exists v \, A(v) \Rightarrow B$	MP on 3 and 4;
6	$\exists v \, A(v)$	replace x by v in 1.
7	B	MP on 1 and 5.

The intuitive idea is that if you have a proof of $\exists x \, A(x)$ then you can choose a value of x (a new constant c) for which $A(c)$ is provable in order to derive a *wff* B in which c does not occur.

Example   Show that $\exists x(A(x) \Rightarrow B(x)) \Rightarrow (\forall A(x) \Rightarrow \exists x \, B(x))$.

Proof

1	$\exists x(A(x) \Rightarrow B(x))$	assumption;
2	$\forall x \, A(x)$	assumption;
3	$A(c) \Rightarrow B(c)$	rule C on 1;
4	$A(c)$	specification on 2;
5	$B(c)$	MP on 3 and 4;
6	$\exists x \, B(x)$	existential rule on 5.

Two applications of the deduction theorem give the result.

Note that at step 3 the existential quantifier is eliminated. What is really happening here is that $A(c) \Rightarrow B(c)$ is being taken as an assumption before we go on to derive the result. However, because it is known that $\vdash_K \exists x(A(x) \Rightarrow B(x))$, then by the statement of rule C the result is provable in K.

4.3.2.9   Provable equivalence in K

Now we have developed some rules and techniques to enable us to prove theorems in K. One concept that has not yet been considered is that of *equivalence of formulae* in K.

The operator $\Leftrightarrow$ (introduced in chapter 1) can be used as our provable equivalence operator. Note that in system K we have only connectives $\{\neg, \Rightarrow\}$, but $A \Leftrightarrow B$ can be written as $(A \Rightarrow B) \wedge (B \Rightarrow A)$ (and $\wedge$ in terms of $\{\neg, \Rightarrow\}$).

Example   Show that $\vdash_K \forall x(A \Leftrightarrow B) \Rightarrow (\forall x A \Leftrightarrow \forall x B)$.

Solution   We will show instead that

$$\forall x(A \Leftrightarrow B), \forall x A \vdash_K \forall x B$$

and

$$\forall x(A \Leftrightarrow B), \forall x B \vdash_K \forall x A.$$

1	$\forall x(A \Leftrightarrow B)$	assumption;
2	$\forall x A$	assumption;
3	$A \Leftrightarrow B$	*Gen* on 1;
4	A	*Gen* on 2;
5	$(A \Leftrightarrow B) \Rightarrow (A \Rightarrow B)$	form of a propositional tautology;
6	$A \Rightarrow B$	MP on 3 and 5;
7	B	MP on 4 and 6;
8	$\forall x B$	*Gen* on 7.

By using a very similar proof we can also show

$$\forall x(A \Leftrightarrow B), \forall x B \vdash_K \forall x A.$$

The required result now follows from exercise 4.19 and applications of the deduction theorem.

We want this concept of provable equivalence to be analogous to what is normally understood by the term *equivalence* in natural language. Thus if two formulae A and B are equivalent, then it should be possible to substitute A for B and vice versa when they occur in derivations in K.

The following result allows us to do this in K using the operator $\Leftrightarrow$ to represent equivalence.

Let A_S be a *wff* which has the *wff* S as a subformula. Let A_T be the *wff* obtained by substituting the *wff* T for S at least once in A_S.

Theorem   We will prove that if two formulae are provably equivalent, then whenever one occurs in another formula we can automatically substitute the other one for it:

$$S \Leftrightarrow T, A_S \vdash_K A_T.$$

Proof

1	$S \Leftrightarrow T$	assumption;
2	A_S	assumption;

3   $(S \Leftrightarrow T)^c$ finite number of applications
                                                     of *Gen* to $S \Leftrightarrow T$;

4   $(S \Leftrightarrow T)^c \Rightarrow (A_S \Leftrightarrow A_T)$ worked example later;

5   $A_S \Leftrightarrow A_T$ MP on 3 and 4;

6   $(A_S \Leftrightarrow A_T) \Rightarrow (A_S \Rightarrow A_T)$ form of a propositional tautology;

7   $(A_S \Rightarrow A_T)$ MP on 5 and 6;

8   A_T MP on 2 and 7.

For an application of this see the prenex-form section of chapter 5.

4.3.3   First-order theories

A system of axioms and rules can be used to form a logical deductive system
(known as a first-order theory) in predicate logic. However, the axioms fall
into two classes:

(1) Deductive (or logical) axioms which are independent of the particular
    first-order alphabet (the axiom schemes of system K described above
    provide an example);
(2) axioms which relate to the particular first-order system that is being con-
    sidered, known as proper axioms or hypotheses.

So far, we have considered a formal system, K (with just two rules of inference) and in exercise 4.21 we consider Lemmon's system (with many rules of
inference). Each system is known as a first-order predicate logic system. The
axioms of a predicate calculus are known as the deductive axioms (or logical
axioms). If extra axioms (the proper axioms) are added to the initial predicate
calculus axioms we obtain a new system known as a *first-order theory*.

The predicate calculus K (our set of logical axioms and rules of inference)
can be thought of (intuitively) as the *general structure* of a first-order theory.
The proper axioms are what define a particular first-order theory.

Examples

(a) Suppose all the axioms given by the *wff*s in section 4.2.3.5 are added to
    system K as proper axioms. The resulting system is called E. We would
    need to make sure that K was using a first-order language which included
    the dyadic predicate *equals*. These new axioms impose a particular mean-
    ing on the predicate *equals*. It must be interpreted as an equivalence rela-
    tion in any model of E (see exercise 4.9).

    Any first-order theory with these axioms is known as a first-order theory
    with equality. Any model where *equals* is interpreted as the equality rela-
    tion is known as a *normal* model. In fact, exercise 4.20 tells us that if a
    first-order theory with equality has a model, then it has a *normal* model.

We can write $equals(x_1, x_2)$ as $x_1 = x_2$ in a first-order theory with equality as long as it is understood that it is a predicate symbol (*not* a relation) which will be interpreted as the equality relation.

(b) The first-order theory of commutativity (the first-order theory which says that the two-place function symbol f is commutative) has the following proper axiom (in addition to the equality axioms):

$$\forall x \, \forall y(f(x, y) = f(y, x)).$$

(c) The first-order theory of associativity has the following proper axiom:

$$\forall x \, \forall y \, \forall z(f(x, f(y, z)) = f(f(x, y), z)),$$

where f is a two-place function symbol.

Note: The models of a theory are interpretations in which all the axioms (and theorems – see definitions below) are true. In example (b) above the axiom imposes a condition on the function symbol f. It cannot be interpreted as subtraction in a normal model because the axiom would not be true. However, it can be interpreted as addition or multiplication (and many others) because both of these functions satisfy the axiom. In example (c) all the normal models of the theory must interpret f to be an associative function. It could be interpreted as addition but not subtraction.

Let T denote a first-order theory. All first-order theories (as we have defined them) have system K as a general 'framework' and vary only in the set of proper axioms. T is simply an extension of a first-order predicate calculus. The same notations for proof and satisfaction that were introduced earlier are used.

Let A be a *wff*. A *deduction* in T from a set of *wffs* Γ, written

$$\Gamma \vdash_T A,$$

is a sequence of *wffs* of $\mathcal{L}$ such that each *wff* is either an instance of an axiom of T (an axiom of K or a proper axiom of T) or a member of Γ, or obtainable from earlier *wffs* in the sequence using a finite number of applications of MP or *Gen*.

A *proof* in T is a deduction in T from the empty set.

A *wff* is a *theorem* in T if it is the last member of a proof sequence. We will write

$$\vdash_T A.$$

Notice that this is the same as $\Gamma \vdash_K A$ if Γ is the set of proper axioms of T.

An interpretation $\mathcal{A}$ is said to be a *model* of a first-order theory T (written $\mathcal{A} \models T$) if all the axioms of T are true for $\mathcal{A}$.

Let A be a *wff* of a first-order language $\mathcal{L}$. Recall that A is said to be logically valid if it is true in all interpretations of $\mathcal{L}$ and we write $\models A$.

We write $\models_T A$ if A is true in all the models of the first-order theory T.

4.3.4   Summary

The formal system K of predicate logic was introduced and some derived rules of inference were discussed. This system is the first-order predicate equivalent of the system L of propositional logic.

We also introduced first-order theories by adding sets of axioms (known as the proper axioms) to the axioms of system K (known as the logical axioms).

To complete our treatment parallel to the formalization of propositional logic, we now move on to the soundness and completeness theorems in predicate logic.

4.3.5   Worked example

Establish the following:

$$\vdash_K (S \Leftrightarrow T)^c \Rightarrow (A_S \Leftrightarrow A_T).$$

Proof   We prove this result by induction on the construction of the *wff* A_S.

Base case.   The base case is when $A_S = S$. Therefore $A_T = T$. So all we have to show, in this case is that

$$\vdash_K (S \Leftrightarrow T)^c \Rightarrow (S \Leftrightarrow T).$$

This follows by assuming $\vdash_K (S \Leftrightarrow T)^c$, using specification and applying the deduction theorem.

Induction step.   Suppose that the result holds for all formulae with n connectives or quantifiers and assume that A_S has $n+1$ connectives or quantifiers. Therefore A_S is of one of the three forms:

(1) $\neg B_S$;   (2) $B_S \Rightarrow C_S$;   (3) $\forall x B_S$.

Case 1. A_S is $\neg B_S$. By the induction hypothesis

$$\vdash_K (S \Leftrightarrow T)^c \Rightarrow (B_S \Leftrightarrow B_T).$$

However,

$$((S \Leftrightarrow T)^c \Rightarrow (B_S \Leftrightarrow B_T)) \Rightarrow ((S \Leftrightarrow T)^c \Rightarrow (\neg B_S \Leftrightarrow \neg B_T))$$

is in the form of the propositional tautology

$$(P \Rightarrow (Q \Leftrightarrow R)) \Rightarrow (P \Rightarrow (\neg Q \Leftrightarrow \neg R)),$$

so by the results of section 4.3.2.1 and MP we have the required result.

Case 2. A_S is $B_S \Rightarrow C_S$. By the induction hypothesis

$$\vdash_K (S \Leftrightarrow T)^c \Rightarrow (B_S \Leftrightarrow B_T)$$

and

$$\vdash_K (S \Leftrightarrow T)^c \Rightarrow (C_S \Leftrightarrow C_T).$$

Using the same method as for case 1, it is not difficult to construct a *wff* in the form of a propositional tautology which, upon using MP, will yield

$$\vdash_K (S \Leftrightarrow T)^c \Rightarrow ((B_S \Rightarrow C_{S)} \Leftrightarrow (B_T \Leftrightarrow C_T)).$$

Case 3. A_S is $\forall x \, B_S$. We show that

$$(S \Leftrightarrow T)^c \Rightarrow (\forall x \, B_S \Leftrightarrow \forall x \, B_T).$$

1	$(S \Leftrightarrow T)^c$	assumption;
2	$(S \Leftrightarrow T)^c \Rightarrow (B_S \Leftrightarrow B_T)$	induction hypothesis;
3	$B_S \Leftrightarrow B_T$	MP on 1 and 2;
4	$\forall x(B_S \Leftrightarrow B_T)$	*Gen* on 3;
5	$\forall x(B_S \Leftrightarrow B_T) \Rightarrow (\forall x \, B_S \Leftrightarrow \forall x \, B_T)$	from example 4.3.2.9 above;
6	$(\forall x \, B_S \Leftrightarrow \forall x \, B_T)$	MP on 4 and 5.

The result now follows by the deduction theorem.

4.3.6   Exercises

Exercise 4.15   Prove that the following are theorems of K:

(a) $\exists x(A \Rightarrow B) \Rightarrow (\forall x A \Rightarrow B)$;
(b) $(\exists x A \Rightarrow B) \Rightarrow \forall x(A \Rightarrow B)$, provided x does not occur free in B;
(c) $\forall x(A \Rightarrow B) \Rightarrow (\forall x A \Rightarrow \forall x B)$;
(d) $\forall x(A \Rightarrow B) \Rightarrow (\exists x A \Rightarrow \exists x B)$;
(e) $\exists x(A \Rightarrow B) \Rightarrow (\forall x \Rightarrow \exists x B)$.

Exercise 4.16   Establish the following deductions in system K:

(a) $\forall x(A \Rightarrow B), \exists x A \vdash \exists x B$;
(b) $\exists y \, \forall x A \vdash \forall x \, \exists y A$.

Exercise 4.17   The following *wff*s are provably equivalent in system K under certain conditions:

(a) $\forall x(A \Rightarrow B)$ and $(A \Rightarrow \forall x B)$;
(b) $\exists x(A \Rightarrow B)$ and $(A \Rightarrow \exists x B)$;
(c) $\forall x(A \Rightarrow B)$ and $(\exists x A \Rightarrow B)$;
(d) $\exists x(A \Rightarrow B)$ and $(\forall x A \Rightarrow B)$.

Determine what the conditions are and construct each of the proofs.

Exercise 4.18   Let A be a *wff* of a first-order theory T and let A be its closure. Let $\mathcal{A}$ be an interpretation of T. Show that

(a) $\vdash_T A \Rightarrow \vdash_T A^c$;

(b) $\mathcal{A} \vDash A \Leftrightarrow \mathcal{A} \vDash A^c$.

Exercise 4.19   Show that

$$\Gamma \vdash_K A \Leftrightarrow B \text{ if and only if } \Gamma \vdash_K A \Rightarrow B \text{ and } \Gamma \vdash_K B \Rightarrow A.$$

Exercise 4.20   Let T be a first-order theory with equality. Show that if T has a model, then it has a normal model.

Exercise 4.21   In the system due to E. J. Lemmon described at the end of chapter 2, additional rules need to be made available for predicate logic. Let F and G be *wff*s in Lemmon's system. Here we allow use of all the standard logical connectives to form the formulae (not just $\neg$ and $\Rightarrow$ as in system K).

His rules relating to quantification are outlined as follows.

Abbrev	Full name	From	We obtain
UE	universal quantifier elimination	$\forall x F(x)$	$F(a)$
UI	universal quantifier introduction	$F(a)$ for arbitrary a	$\forall x F(x)$
EI	existential quantifier introduction	$F(a)$ for a particular a	$\exists x F(x)$
EE	existential quantifier elimination	$\exists x F(x)$ and $F(a) \vdash G$	G

These are similar to the specification rule, generality rule, existential rule and rule C, respectively, for system K. In particular the given existential quantifier elimination rule is used in the same way as the derived rule C in system K.

The rules outlined above require some important provisos. Explain what these provisos are and why they are required.

Are any provisos needed to establish the following proofs in Lemmon's system, and if so, what are they:

(a) $\vdash \forall x(A \Rightarrow B) \Rightarrow (A \Rightarrow \forall x B)$;

(b) $\vdash \exists x(A \Rightarrow B) \Rightarrow (\forall x A \Rightarrow B)$;

(c) $\vdash \forall x(\neg A \vee B) \Rightarrow (\forall x A \Rightarrow \forall x B)$?

Establish the following deductions in Lemmon's system:

(a) $\forall x(A(x) \wedge B(x)), B(a) \Rightarrow C(a) \vdash \exists x C(x)$;

(b) $\forall x(A(x) \Rightarrow \neg B(x)), \exists x B(x) \vdash \exists x \neg A(x)$;

(c) $\forall x(A(x) \Rightarrow B(x)), \exists x(\neg B(x), \forall x(\neg A(x) \Rightarrow C(x)) \vdash \exists x C(x)$.

4.4   Soundness and completeness

4.4.1   Introduction

We are considering the proof system K. Two natural questions which occur when working with any proof system are:

(a) Is every theorem of the system logically valid (true in every possible interpretation)?

(b) Is every logically valid formula provable in the system?

These two questions address the concepts of soundness and completeness which were considered in chapter 2 for propositional logic.

The ideas are very similar for predicate logic. A proof in system K is very similar to a proof in system L (except that we have a system with extra axioms and rules). A *wff* of $\mathscr{L}$ being true in an interpretation of $\mathscr{L}$ is analagous to a propositional formula being true for a single line of the truth-table. So a *wff* being logically valid is analogous to a propositional formula being a tautology. Indeed we use similar terminology.

Definitions

The soundness and completeness of system K can be expressed formally as follows:

Soundness of K:

For any *wff* A, if $\vdash_K A$ holds, then $\vDash A$ follows.

Completeness of K:

For any *wff* A, if $\vDash A$ holds, then $\vdash_K A$ follows.

Recall that the soundness and completeness of system L can be similarly expressed as

For any propositional formula P

$\vDash P$ if and only if $\vdash_L P$.

However, note that in the propositional case $\vDash$ represents an entirely different (though analagous) concept to $\vDash$ in the predicate case. In the propositional case, we always have a finite number of variables ranging over the values T and F. In the predicate case, the variables may range over an infinity of values.

We will first show that system K is sound. Indeed this is quite easy to show. The completeness of system K (which will be considered next) is much more difficult.

4.4.2   The soundness of system K

What we are trying to show here is that any *wff* that we can prove in K is logically valid. This is easily done by showing that all the axioms of K are logically valid and that the two rules preserve logical validity.

4.4.2.1   Notation

Consider a *wff* A in the form of a propositional tautology P. Let $p_1, \ldots, p_n$ be the propositional variables which occur in P and let $A_1, \ldots, A_n$ be the *wffs* which are substituted for them in P to obtain A.

Suppose we have any first-order interpretation $\mathcal{A}$ and any valuation v in $\mathcal{A}$. Consider the following propositional interpretation, I:

(a) p_i takes the value true if v satisfies A_i in $\mathcal{A}$;

(b) p_i takes the value false if v does not satisfy A_i in $\mathcal{A}$.

4.4.2.2   Lemma

With the notation introduced above, P takes the value true under the propositional interpretation I if and only if v satisfies A in $\mathcal{A}$.

Proof   We show this by induction on the construction of P. The lemma holds for the base case (in which case P is a propositional variable) by the definition of I.

For the induction step either

(a) P is of form $\neg P_1$,

or

(b) P is of form $P_1 \Rightarrow P_2$.

(a) If P is of the form $\neg P_1$ then A is of the form $\neg B$, where B is obtained by substituting *wffs* for the statement variables of A.

We know that P_1 is true for I if and only if $\mathcal{A} \models_v B$ by the induction hypothesis, so it follows that

$$P_1 \text{ is not true for } I \text{ if and only if } \mathcal{A} \not\models_v B$$

and hence

$$P_1 \text{ is true for } I \text{ if and only if } \mathcal{A} \models_v A.$$

(b) If P is of the form $P_1 \Rightarrow P_2$, then A is of the form $B \Rightarrow C$, where B and C are obtained by substituting *wffs* for the statement variables of P_1 and P_2, respectively.

Now $\mathcal{A} \models_v A$ if and only if $\mathcal{A} \models_v \neg B$ or $\mathcal{A} \models_v C$, which is so if and only if P_1 is false for I or P_2 is true for I (by the induction hypothesis). But this is so if and only if $P_1 \Rightarrow P_2$ is true for I.

The result follows by induction.

4.4.2.3   Lemma

If a *wff* A is in the form of a propositional tautology P then it is logically valid.

Proof Let $\mathcal{A}$ be any first-order interpretation and v be any valuation in $\mathcal{A}$.

Now P is a tautology and so always takes the value true. More specifically P takes the value true in I (the interpretation introduced above by lemma 4.4.2.2), so that v satisfies A in $\mathcal{A}$. Hence A is logically valid.

4.4.2.4   Validity of the axioms of K

(a) Axioms A1, A2 and A3 are logically valid.

> **Proof** These axioms are in the form of propositional tautologies, so the result follows by lemma 4.4.2.3.

(b) Axiom A4 is logically valid.

> **Proof** We have to show that $\forall x(A(x) \Rightarrow A(t))$ is true in every possible interpretation of $\mathcal{L}$. However, we have the proviso that t must be free for x in A. Indeed, the formula is not logically valid without this proviso.
>
> Suppose we have an interpretation $\mathcal{A}$ of $\mathcal{L}$ and a valuation v in $\mathcal{A}$. We need to show that
>
> $$\mathcal{A} \vDash_v \forall x A(x) \Rightarrow A(t).$$
>
> Now either
>
> (1) $\mathcal{A} \nvDash_v \forall x A(x)$
>
> or
>
> (2) $\mathcal{A} \vDash_v \forall x A(x).$
>
> If (1), then by the definition of satisfaction
>
> $$\mathcal{A} \vDash_v \forall x A(x) \Rightarrow A(t).$$
>
> If (2), then $\mathcal{A} \vDash_{v'} A(x)$ for any valuation v' which is x-equivalent to v. Let v'' be the valuation such that $v''(x) = v(t)$ and $v''(y) = v(y)$ for every variable $y \neq x$. Then v'' is x-equivalent to v and so $\mathcal{A} \vDash_{v''} A(x)$.
>
> Now by exercise 4.8 (the proviso is needed in the proof of this exercise) we have $\mathcal{A} \vDash_v A(t)$, giving
>
> $$\mathcal{A} \vDash_v \forall x A(x) \Rightarrow A(t).$$

Thus axiom A4 is shown to be logically valid.

> **Remark** The necessity of the proviso for this axiom schema can be seen by considering the *wff* $\exists y R(x, y)$ (where R is a two-place predicate symbol). If the proviso were omitted, then an instance of the axiom schema would be $\forall x \exists y R(x, y) \Rightarrow \exists y R(y, y)$ (where $\exists y R(x, y)$ is A and the variable y is the term t). This would not be allowed without omitting the proviso because the term y is not free for x in $\exists y R(x, y)$.

Now consider the interpretation that has as domain the set of positive integers and assigns the relation $x < y$ to $R(x, y)$. It can be seen that our instance of the axiom schema is F for this interpretation.

(c) Axiom A5 is logically valid.

Proof   Suppose we have an interpretation $\mathcal{A}$ of $\mathcal{L}$ and a valuation v in $\mathcal{A}$. The proof follows in a similar manner to the proof of theorem 4.4.2.5.
We have either

   (1) $\mathcal{A} \nvDash_v \forall x(A \Rightarrow B)$

or

   (2) $\mathcal{A} \vDash_v \forall x(A \Rightarrow B)$

If (1), then by the definition of satisfaction we have

$$\mathcal{A} \vDash_v \forall x(A \Rightarrow B) \Rightarrow (A \Rightarrow \forall x B).$$

If (2) holds, then $\mathcal{A} \vDash_{v'} A \Rightarrow B$ for any x-equivalent valuation v', and so by the definition of satisfaction we have either

$$\mathcal{A} \nvDash_{v'} A$$

or

$$\mathcal{A} \vDash_{v'} B.$$

Since x is not free in A and v' is x-equivalent to v,

$$\mathcal{A} \nvDash_{v'} A$$

is the same as

$$\mathcal{A} \nvDash_v A.$$

We therefore have $\mathcal{A} \nvDash_v A$ or $\mathcal{A} \vDash_{v'} B$ for any v' which is x-equivalent to v. From this it follows that $\mathcal{A} \nvDash_v A$ or $\mathcal{A} \vDash_v \forall x B$ by the definition of satisfaction.
   Thus we obtain $\mathcal{A} \vDash_v A \Rightarrow \forall x B$ again by the definition of satisfaction.

Remark   We can see that the proviso for this axiom schema is necessary by omitting the proviso and obtaining the following instance of the schema: $\forall x(R(x) \Rightarrow R(x)) \Rightarrow (R(x) \Rightarrow \forall x R(x))$ (where $R(x)$ is substituted for A and for B).
   Now consider the interpretation whose domain is the set of positive integers and that assigns the relation 'x is prime' to $R(x)$. The instance of the axiom schema is F for this interpretation.

We now state and prove the soundness theorem for system K.

4.4.2.5   The soundness theorem for *K*

Let *A* be any *wff* of $\mathcal{L}$. The soundness theorem states that if $\vdash_K A$ holds, then $\vDash A$ also holds.

Proof   The proof follows by induction on the number *n* of steps in the proof of *A* in *K*.

Base case (n = 0).   If $n = 0$, then *A* is an axiom of *K* and so is logically valid.

Induction step.   Assume that *A* has a proof in *K* of *n* steps, where $n > 0$. Any *wff* appearing in the proof before step *n* is logically valid by the induction hypothesis. Now *A* can follow from earlier formulae either by an application of MP or *Gen*.
It is clear from the definition of satisfaction that

   (a) if $\vDash B$ and $\vDash B \Rightarrow C$ then $\vDash C$;
   (b) if $\vDash A(x)$ then $\vDash \forall x\, A(x)$.

Thus it is clear that both MP and *Gen* preserve logical validity. It can then be deduced that $\vDash A$ since *A* follows from earlier logically valid formulae. Therefore, the system *K* is sound.
Before moving on the the completeness of system *K*, we consider another important property of first-order theories, that of consistency, and see that system *K* is consistent.

4.4.3   Consistency

A first-order theory *T* is *consistent* if for no *wff* *A* do we have both $\vdash_T A$ and $\vdash_T \neg A$.

4.4.3.1   System *K* is consistent

Proof   Assume by way of contradiction that for some *wff* *A*

   $\vdash_K A$ and $\vdash_K \neg A$.

However, system *K* is sound so we know that in any interpretation both *A* and $\neg A$ would then be true. This contradicts the definition of truth, so *K* must be consistent.

4.4.4   The completeness of system *K*

We show here that any logically valid *wff* can be proved in the system *K*. This is quite a complicated proof and we will leave some of the technical (tedious but straightforward) details as exercises. The reader who wishes only to get a rough idea of what is going on can omit the exercises. However, first we must present some definitions concerning first-order theories.

Maximality (or fullness)

A first-order theory T is *maximal* or *full* if for any closed *wff* A either

$\vdash_T A$

or

$\vdash_T \neg A.$

Closed

A first-order theory T is said to be *closed* if and only if for every closed formula A (which can be written in the form $\forall x B(x)$) there exists a constant term k of T such that

$\vdash_T B(k) \Rightarrow A,$

where $B(k)$ is $B(x)$ with the variable x replaced by the constant term k.

Note that this is *not* to be confused with a *closed wff*.

Extension

An *extension* of a first-order theory T is a new first-order theory formed by adding one or more proper axioms to the axioms of T. Thus anything which can be proved in T can also be proved in any extension.

In order to prove completeness we will outline two methods of extending a first-order theory.

1. *The maximality method.* We extend a consistent first-order theory to one that is maximal and still consistent.

2. *The closure method.* Here we show how to extend a consistent first-order theory to one that is closed and still consistent.

It will then be possible to apply both methods (simultaneously) to a consistent first-order theory to obtain a consistent, maximal and closed extension. This extension is used to prove the main result of the section, namely that every consistent first-order theory has a model. The completeness of system K will then follow directly.

4.4.4.1 The maximality method of extending a consistent first-order theory

The set of all *wff*s of any first-order theory T is countable. This means that we can assign a distinct non-negative integer to each *wff* of T and list them in order. The ordered (infinite) list $A_1, A_2, A_3, A_4, \ldots$ is called an *enumeration*. Let $A_1, A_2, A_3, \ldots$ be an enumeration of all the closed *wff*s of T.
T can be extended inductively as follows:

- Let $T_0 = T$.
- We now build up an enumeration of extensions of T.
- If A_n is a theorem of T_n then let $T_{n+1} = T_n$.
- If A_n is not a theorem of T_n, then let T_{n+1} be the extension of T_n formed by adding $\neg A_n$ to the list of proper axioms of T_n.
- Let T_∞ be the first-order theory formed by taking all of the axioms of each T_i.
- It can be shown that

  (a) T_∞ is consistent and (see worked example 4.4);
  (b) T_∞ is maximal (see worked example 4.4).

We have taken a consistent first-order theory T and shown how to extend it to a first-order theory T_∞ which is still consistent but which is also maximal. This was done by taking every possible formula of T and, if each formula could not be proved in the theory, then the negation of that formula was added to the theory.

We now show how to extend a consistent first-order theory T to satisfy the condition of being closed while remaining consistent.

4.4.4.2   The closure-method of extending a consistent first-order theory

In extending a consistent first-order theory to one that is closed, we need to add new constant symbols to the first-order language. In the previous method, extensions of the first-order theory were constructed by adding new axioms. In this method we will not only extend the first-order theory but will also extend the first-order language (in which the first-order theory is expressed) by adding new constant symbols. The formal definition of this is as follows.

Extension of a first-order language

An *extension* of a first-order language $\mathscr{L}$ is obtained by adding new relation symbols, function symbols, constant symbols or variables to those already in $\mathscr{L}$.

So far we have denoted a first-order theory by the symbol T. However, each first-order theory is formed from a first-order language $\mathscr{L}$. Strictly speaking, $T_\mathscr{L}$ should be written for the first-order theory T which is formed from the language $\mathscr{L}$. If the language is not being changed in our reasoning, then this subscript is unnecessary. This is the reason why we have so far written T instead of $T_\mathscr{L}$. However, in the construction of this extension we need to extend the language $\mathscr{L}$, so the subscript becomes necessary to keep track of the argument.

Let $T_\mathscr{L}$ be a consistent first-order theory. First extend the first-order language $\mathscr{L}$ of $T_\mathscr{L}$ by adding to it a countable set of distinct new constant symbols $\{c_i : i \in \mathbb{N}\}$* and call this new first-order language $\mathscr{L}^+$. Note that here we

*The symbol $\mathbb{N}$ is read as 'the natural numbers', and means the integer values 0, 1, 2, 3, ... up to infinity.

are not adding new axiom schemes to $T_{\mathscr{L}}$. We are not (strictly speaking) extending $T_{\mathscr{L}}$ but are extending the language of $T_{\mathscr{L}}$. However, this does mean that new *wffs* can be constructed in $T_{\mathscr{L}^+}$ (namely those that involve the new constant symbols).

Let $\forall x_1 B_1(x_1), \forall x_2 B_2(x_2), \ldots$ be an enumeration of all the *wffs* of $T_{\mathscr{L}^+}$ which are of the form $\forall x B(x)$, where $B(x)$ has x as its only free variable. We now build up a corresponding enumeration of extensions of T.

- Let $T^0 = T_{\mathscr{L}^+}$.
- Let T^{n+1} be formed from T^n by adding the following *wff* as a proper axiom:

$$B(c_{n+1}) \Rightarrow \forall x_{n+1} B_{n+1}(x_{n+1}).$$

  Note that c_{n+1} is distinct from each c_i ($0 \le i \le n$), so c_{n+1} does not occur in any other axiom of T^{n+1}.
- If we let T^∞ be formed by taking all of the axioms of each T^i, it can be shown that

  (a) T^∞ is consistent (see exercise 4.22);
  (b) T^∞ is closed (see exercise 4.22).

4.4.4.3   A closed and maximal extension

We have seen how to extend a consistent first-order theory (T) to one that is closed and still consistent (T^∞) and we have seen a quite different method for extending it to one that is maximal and still consistent (T_∞).

If we have a maximal consistent first-order theory, then the new constants can be added as outlined above to make the first-order theory closed. However, this may make it no longer maximal because there are new formulae which are introduced. The maximal method of extension can be applied to remedy this but may make it no longer closed. A method must be found to overcome this problem.

Given a consistent first-order theory T, the method of extension to form a new first-order theory T^+ that is *both* maximal and closed is as follows:

> Carry out the two methods of extension alternately, each infinitely often and then take, as the set of proper axioms, the union of all the new axioms, together with the proper axioms of T itself.

T^+ is then consistent, closed and maximal (see exercise 4.23).

This extension is now used to establish the main result of this section, that any consistent first-order theory has a model.

4.4.4.4   A first-order theory is consistent if and only if it has a model

Let T be a consistent first-order theory and let T^+ be the consistent, closed and maximal extension defined above, and consider $\mathscr{A}$ to be the Herbrand interpretation of T^+ defined as follows:

For each n-place relation symbol R let $R^{\mathcal{A}}(t_1^{\mathcal{A}},\ldots,t_n^{\mathcal{A}})$ have truth-value T if and only if $\vdash_{T^+} R(t_1,\ldots,t_n)$, where $t_1,\ldots,t_n$ are constant terms. Recall that the domain of a Herbrand interpretation is the set of all constant terms of T^+ (hence $t_i^{\mathcal{A}} = t_i$ ($1 \leqslant i \leqslant n$)) and the interpretation of function symbols and constant symbols is fixed.

For $\mathcal{A}$ to be a model of T^+, it has to be shown that, for each *wff* A of T^+, $\mathcal{A} \vDash A$ if and only if $\vdash_{T^+} A$.

It can be assumed that A is closed (see exercise 4.18) and the result of exercise 4.24 can be applied to verify that $\mathcal{A}$ is a model of T^+ (every *wff* of T^+ is true in $\mathcal{A}$).

Since T^+ is an extension of T every *wff* of T is true in $\mathcal{A}$, so that $\mathcal{A}$ is a model of T.

We are now in a position to show the completeness of first-order theories and hence of K since it is a special case of a first-order theory, namely one without any proper axioms. For this reason K is sometimes known as the empty theory.

We have just shown that if a theory is consistent, then it has a model. We still need to show that if T has a model, then it is consistent.

Assume T has a model $\mathcal{A}$ and assume by way of contradiction that T is not consistent. If T is not consistent, then there is a *wff* A of T such that $\vdash_T A$ and $\vdash_T \neg A$. However, $\mathcal{A}$ is a model of T, so $\mathcal{A} \vDash A$ and $\mathcal{A} \vDash \neg A$. This contradicts the definition of satisfaction. Therefore, T is consistent.

The above results show that a first-order theory being consistent is equivalent to it having a model, so that a first-order theory T is consistent if and only if it has a model.

4.4.4.5   Some consequences

In this section we look at some of the important results which follow from the previous section.

The completeness of a consistent first-order theory   If T is a consistent first-order theory and A is a closed *wff* of T, then

$$\vDash_T A \implies \vdash_T A.$$

Proof   Assume $\vDash_T A$ so that A is true for all the models of T (we know that T has at least one model).

Assume by way of contradiction that A is not a theorem of T. We then form a new consistent first-order theory T' by adding $\neg A$ to the proper axioms of T (this can be done by the result of worked example 4.3). T' must have a model (by section 4.4.4.4), so let $\mathcal{A}$ be a model of T' and we can deduce that $\mathcal{A} \vDash \neg A$. However, $\mathcal{A}$ is a model of T', so it must be a model of T which means that $\mathcal{A} \vDash A$ (because $\vDash_T A$). This is a contradiction, so $\vdash_T A$.

The following theorem is the main result of this section.

The completeness of system K

Let A be a closed *wff* of system K, then

$$\vDash A \Rightarrow \vdash_K A.$$

Proof Assume that $\vDash A$ holds.

It is clear that $\vDash_K A$ holds (if A is true in all interpretations then A is true in the models of K). Therefore we can apply the previous theorem to the first-order theory with no proper axioms (this is system K and we know that it is consistent by theorem 4.4.3.1). This gives us the statement that if $\vDash_K A$ holds then $\vdash_K A$ also holds.

Therefore we have shown that if $\vDash A$ holds then $\vdash_K A$ holds, so that any logically valid *wff* is provable in system K.

The compactness theorem Let T be a first-order theory. If every finite subset of proper axioms of T has a model then T has a model.

Proof Assume by way of contradiction that T does not have a model.

Therefore, T is not consistent (by 4.4.4.4), so we have a *wff* A of T such that $\vdash_T A$ and $\vdash_T \neg A$, giving

$$\vdash_T A \wedge \neg A.$$

Let S be the first-order theory formed by taking as proper axioms just the proper axioms of T used in the proof $A \wedge \neg A$. S has as its set of proper axioms a finite subset of the proper axioms of T and so has a model $\mathcal{A}$, say.

Therefore, $\mathcal{A} \vDash A \wedge \neg A$ which contradicts the definition of satisfaction.

4.4.5   Summary

We have shown that the first-order formal system K of predicate logic is both sound and complete and have completed our treatment of predicate logic parallel to the treatment of propositional logic in chapter 2. We will now move on to applications of predicate logic.

4.4.6   Worked examples

Example 4.3 Let T be a consistent first-order theory and let A be a closed *wff* such that A is not a theorem of T. Let T' be the new first-order theory obtained from T by adding $\neg A$ as a new proper axiom. Show that T' is consistent.

Solution Assume by way of contradiction that T' is not consistent, so that for some *wff* B we have both $\vdash_{T'} B$ and $\vdash_{T'} \neg B$.

Now $\neg B \Rightarrow (B \Rightarrow A)$ is in the form of a propositional tautology and T' is an extension of T (which in turn is an extension of K), so $\vdash_{T'} \neg B \Rightarrow (B \Rightarrow A)$ because anything provable in K must also be provable be in T'.

Two applications of MP yield $\vdash_{T'} A$, which is equivalent to $\neg A \vdash_T A$.

Thus $\vdash_T \neg A \Rightarrow A$ (by the deduction theorem) and since $(\neg A \Rightarrow A) \Rightarrow A$ is in the form of a propositional tautology we have (by MP) that $\vdash_T A$, which contradicts the initial assumption.

Example 4.4   Let T be a consistent first-order theory and let T_∞ be the extension defined in section 4.4.4.1. Show that:

(a) T_∞ is consistent;
(b) T_∞ is maximal.

Solution

(a) Assume by way of contradiction that T_∞ is not consistent. Then we can prove $A \wedge \neg A$ in T_∞ for some *wff* A. All proofs are finite (by definition of proof), so the proof would have to use a finite number of the new axioms (this would be greater than zero because T is consistent). If k was the index of the highest axiom (in the enumeration) used in the proof then we would have a proof of

$$A \wedge \neg A \text{ in } T_k.$$

So T_k is inconsistent.

It is therefore sufficient to show that T_n is consistent for all n (this would give us a contradiction). We do this by induction on n.

Base case $(n = 0)$. $T_0 = T$ which is consistent.

Induction step.   Assume T_n is consistent then $T_{n+1} = T_n$ (in which case there is nothing to prove) or $T_{n+1} = T_n'$ (using the notation of example 4.3). Thus T_{n+1} is consistent by example 4.3, giving us the fact that T_n is consistent for all n and so T_∞ is consistent.

(b) Let A_i be any closed *wff* of T_∞ (the subscript i corresponds to the *wffs* position in the enumeration $A_1, A_2, A_3, \dots$).

Now by the definition of T_∞ we have either $\vdash_{T_i} A_i$ or $\vdash_{T_{i+1}} \neg A_i$.

Every theorem of T_i and T_{i+1} is a theorem of T_∞, so either $T_\infty \vdash A_i$ or $T_\infty \vdash \neg A_i$, and so T_∞ is maximal.

The fact that a consistent first-order theory can be extended to one that is both consistent and maximal is often known as Lindenbaum's lemma.

Example 4.5   Suppose we have a consistent first-order theory T. Let A be a closed *wff* of T which can be expressed in the form $\forall x\, B(x)$, where $B(x)$ has x as its only free variable.

Extend the first-order language under consideration by adding a single constant symbol c which must not occur elsewhere in T.

We can now extend the first-order theory T to obtain a new first-order theory T' by adding the following formula as a proper axiom:

$B(c) \Rightarrow A,$

where $B(c)$ is obtained from $B(x)$ by replacing the variable x by the new constant symbol c.

Show that T' is consistent.

Solution   Assume by way of contradiction that T' is not consistent. Then there must exist a *wff* D such that

$\vdash_{T'} D$ and $\vdash_{T'} \neg D,$

giving us

$\vdash_{T'} D \wedge \neg D.$

The formula $(D \wedge \neg D) \Rightarrow \neg(B(c) \Rightarrow A)$ is in the form of a propositional tautology (because if a propositional formula P is always false then $P \Rightarrow Q$ is always true, regardless of the truth-value of Q).

We then have

$\vdash_{T'} (D \wedge \neg D) \Rightarrow \neg(B(c) \Rightarrow A)$

and by MP

$\vdash_{T'} \neg(B(c) \Rightarrow A).$

It follows that

$B(c) \Rightarrow A \vdash_T \neg(B(c) \Rightarrow A),$

which by the deduction theorem gives us

$\vdash_T (B(c) \Rightarrow A) \Rightarrow \neg(B(c) \Rightarrow A).$

Note that

$((B(c) \Rightarrow A) \Rightarrow \neg(B(c) \Rightarrow A)) \Rightarrow \neg(B(c) \Rightarrow A)$

is in the form of the propositional tautology

$(P \Rightarrow \neg P) \Rightarrow \neg P.$

We can now use MP to derive

$\vdash_T \neg(B(c) \Rightarrow A),$

which is equivalent to

$\vdash_T B(c) \wedge \neg A.$

Thus we have

    (1) $\vdash_T B(c)$

and

    (2) $\vdash_T \neg A$.

In the proof of $B(c)$ in T we can replace the constant c throughout by a variable y not already in the proof, and thus $\vdash_T B(y)$.

An application of *Gen* will yield

    $\vdash_T \forall y\, B(y)$

and an instance of axiom schema A4 is

    $\forall y\, B(y) \Rightarrow B(x)$

(since x is free for y in B). So by MP we can derive

    $\vdash_T B(x)$

and by *Gen* we then have

    $\vdash_T A$,

which contradicts (2) (because T is consistent).

4.4.7   Exercises

Exercise 4.22   Let T be a consistent first-order theory and let T^{∞} be the extension defined in section 4.4.4.3. Show that

(a) T^{∞} is consistent;
(b) T^{∞} is closed.

Hint: This is analagous to worked example 4.4. For part (a), justify the fact that it is sufficient to show that T^n is consistent for all values of n and then show this by induction on n. You will require the use of the result of worked example 4.5. Part (b) is quite straightforward.

Exercise 4.23   Given a consistent first-order theory T, show that the extension T^{+} (defined in section 4.4.4.3) is consistent, closed and maximal.

Hint: The union is taken over infinitely many steps. However, the maximality and closure conditions can be established by considering just a finite number of formulae.

Exercise 4.24   Let T be a consistent first-order theory and let T^{+} be the consistent, closed and maximal extension as defined in section 4.4.4.3. Let $\mathcal{A}$ be the Herbrand interpretation of T^{+} as defined in section 4.4.4.4. Show that, for each *wff* A of T^{+}

    $\mathcal{A} \models A$ if and only if $\vdash_{T^{+}} A$.

Hint: Use induction on the number n of logical connectives and quantifiers used in A.

Exercise 4.25 Write computer programs to emulate some of the processes described in this chapter.

(a) Compute the truth-table of a predicate formula where appropriate, such as in the examples given in section 4.2.4. You will need to restrict the choice of formula considerably.
(b) Read in a proof in system K, and validate it. You may choose your own input conventions. Validating a given proof is easy; to generate a proof would be much harder!
(c) Do the same for Lemmon's predicate logic system.

Reference

1. A. Margaris, *First order Mathematical Logic*, 1990. Dover.

CHAPTER 5

Logic programming

5.1 Introduction

All our proofs in both propositional and predicate logic so far in this book have been generated by inspiration; a human has looked at the proof or deduction required, and has decided on an appropriate sequence of *wffs* which will give the proof. It is easy to check that a given proof is correct, but often very hard to decide how to create a proof.

We wish to be able to automate this process, so that machines can perform deductions and theorem proving. This requires the generation of some mechanized process for obtaining results.

One of the fundamental ideas behind what will be discussed in this chapter is the *resolution* rule. This is a rule of inference just like the other rules that have been looked at. In fact, it is very similar to modus ponens (MP) and is essentially a generalized form of MP. This new rule is important because it lends itself particularly well to automation. It was first introduced by Robinson [1] in 1965 and forms the basis of the computer programming language Prolog, which performs its work by implementing a mechanization for a subset of predicate logic. Before introducing the idea of resolution and predicate logic programming in general we will first consider programming with propositional logic.

5.2 Programming with propositional logic

We must introduce some definitions.

5.2.1 Definitions for propositional logic

A *propositional literal* is a propositional variable or the negation of a propositional variable. A *positive propositional literal* is simply a propositional variable and a *negative propositional literal* is the negation of a propositional variable.

A *propositional clause* is a disjunction of propositional literals; it is a propositional formula where a number of propositional literals are connected together by the $\lor$ operator. We have seen in chapter 1 how any propositional formula can be written in terms of a conjunction of clauses, a number of clauses connected together by the $\land$ operator (this was called conjunctive normal form).

An example of a propositional clause is $p \lor \neg q \lor r \lor \neg s$, where p, q, r and s are propositional variables. The propositional formula $p \lor \neg(q \land r) \lor s$ is not a clause because $\neg(q \land r)$ is not a literal. However, an application of De Morgan's law can turn the formula into the propositional clause $p \lor \neg q \lor \neg r \lor s$.

We now consider a certain type of clause, known as a Horn clause, because this class of clauses is particularly important for logic programming.

A *propositional Horn clause* is a propositional clause with at most one positive literal. A Horn clause is thus in one of the following three forms:

(1) q;
(2) $\neg p_1 \lor \cdots \lor \neg p_n \lor q$;
(3) $\neg p_1 \lor \cdots \lor \neg p_n$,

where $p_1, \ldots, p_n, q$ are propositional variables.

Horn clauses of the forms outlined in (1) and (2) with one positive literal are known as *program clauses* (sometimes these are called *definite clauses*). Horn clauses of the type outlined in (1) are sometimes called *unit clauses*. Notice that the Horn clause given in (2) can be rewritten (using De Morgan's law) as

$$\neg(p_1 \land \cdots \land p_n) \lor q$$

and this in turn can be rewritten as

$$(p_1 \land \cdots \land p_n) \Rightarrow q.$$

This is the form that a program clause usually takes in practical applications. The *tail* of the clause is defined to be $(p_1 \land \cdots \land p_n)$ (empty in a clause of type (1)) and the *head* of the clause to be q (empty in a clause of type (3)).

We define a *propositional logic program* to be a set of propositional program clauses.

Horn clauses of the form outlined in (3) are known as *goal clauses*. Notice that (3) can be rewritten (using De Morgan's law) to obtain

$$\neg(p_1 \land \cdots \land p_n).$$

We are now in a position to consider the rule of resolution for propositional clauses.

5.2.2 Propositional resolution

Suppose we have $C_1 \lor p$ and $C_2 \lor \neg p$, where C_1 and C_2 are clauses and p is a propositional variable.

The rule of *resolution* allows us to obtain an expression for $C_1 \vee C_2$ which does not involve the variable p. We can define resolution as the following inference rule:

$$C_1 \vee p, C_2 \vee \neg p \vdash_{\text{Res}} C_1 \vee C_2,$$

where the symbol $\vdash_{\text{Res}}$ denotes deduction using only the resolution rule.* Now this definition of resolution is perfectly valid for all propositional clauses. However, in this chapter we are interested only in programming with Horn clauses, since this is the basis of the operation of Prolog. The later section on the semantics of logic programming outlines some of the arguments in favour of this approach.

Since we are concerned only with Horn clauses, let us as an example take C_1 to be a Horn clause of type (3) and C_2 to be of type (2). We can write

$$C_1 =_{\text{T}} \neg q_1 \vee \cdots \vee \neg q_n$$

and

$$C_2 =_{\text{T}} \neg r_1 \vee \cdots \vee \neg r_m \vee s,$$

where $q_1, \ldots, q_n, r_1, \ldots, r_m, s$ are propositional variables and n and m are non-negative integers.

If we are given the two clauses

(a) $C_1 \vee p$;
(b) $C_2 \vee \neg p$

(where p is a propositional variable) we can rewrite them as

(a) $(q_1 \wedge \cdots \wedge q_n) \Rightarrow p$;
(b) $(p \wedge r_1 \wedge \cdots \wedge r_m) \Rightarrow s$.

We have taken the $\neg p$ in clause (b) into the first part of the implication. We can express the disjunction of these as

(c) $C_1 \vee C_2 =_{\text{T}} \neg q_1 \vee \cdots \vee \neg q_n \vee \neg r_1 \vee \cdots \vee \neg r_m \vee s$

$$=_{\text{T}} (q_1 \wedge \cdots \wedge q_n \wedge r_1 \wedge \cdots \wedge r_m) \Rightarrow s.$$

The variable p has now vanished.

Resolution can thus be seen in terms of propositional Horn clauses as

$$(q_1 \wedge \cdots \wedge q_n) \Rightarrow p, (p \wedge r_1 \wedge \ldots \wedge r_m) \Rightarrow s$$

$$\vdash_{\text{Res}} (q_1 \wedge \cdots \wedge q_n \wedge r_1 \wedge \cdots \wedge r_m) \Rightarrow s.$$

In English, this becomes:

*If a subformula of the form $p \vee p$ occurs in a clause as the result of resolution, we could replace it by p.

Clause (b) says that to derive s we need to derive $p, r_1, \ldots, r_m$. However, (a) says that to derive p we need to derive $q_1, \ldots, q_n$.

The result is that to derive s we need to derive $q_1, \ldots, q_n, r_1, \ldots, r_m$. This is the idea we must bear in mind when constructing resolution trees (see below).

5.2.3   Refutation and deductions

Resolution is the rule of inference that we use in logic programming to carry out deductions. The logic program consists of a set of program clauses, which can be considered as a set of hypotheses. The resolution rule can be applied to the hypotheses to deduce consequents. However, there is a particular method used in logic programming to carry out these deductions. This method is known as *refutation* and it is the method of contradiction discussed in the last section of chapter 1.

Suppose we have a logic program. The program can be presented with *queries*. These are statements that are conjunctions of propositional variables. The question being asked of the program is

'Does the query follow from the program?'

or

'If the clauses of the program are taken as hypotheses, can the query be deduced from these hypotheses using the resolution rule?'

This is equivalent to

'Given a logic program P (which is a set of program clauses) and a query Q, can we establish the deduction

$P \vdash_{\text{Res}} Q$?'

This parallels the concept of testing argument forms in chapter 1; in that section, the test is whether a given conclusion can be deduced from a set of premises.

Now although the only rule to be used in the deduction is resolution, the method of establishing the deduction is by refutation (contradiction). We will add $\neg Q$ as a hypothesis and use resolution to establish a contradiction in the form of the *empty clause*. (In the section on argument forms, the validity was proved by showing that there was no case when all the premises were T, but the conclusion was F.) Using propositional resolution, the only way to obtain the empty clause is by applying the rule to a propositional variable p and to $\neg p$, in which case we have a contradiction. Our contradiction is thus really established in the step before the empty clause is reached. The empty clause is denoted by $\square$.

In logic programming we are interested in establishing deductions of the form

$$P \vdash_{\text{Res}} Q$$

and the way that we do this is by first establishing a deduction of the form

$$P, \neg Q \square.$$

This method is called *refutation by resolution*. These deductions are established by refutation (contradiction) using resolution as the only rule.

Notice that a query is a conjunction of propositional variables, so will be of the form

$$p_1 \wedge \cdots \wedge p_n.$$

The negation of this will be required and this is in the form of the goal clause (Horn clause type (3))

$$\neg p_1 \vee \cdots \vee \neg p_n.$$

We therefore restrict ourselves so that the only hypotheses that we ever work with are Horn clauses, with a number of program clauses and a single goal clause. Notice also that in our definitions a negative literal cannot be a query. This is far too restrictive and some way of handling negative queries will be needed later on. Negation in logic programming is surprisingly complicated. For the moment, we will restrict ourselves to the consideration of positive queries.

Formal resolution deductions

Suppose we have a set of propositional program clauses and a query. The query, upon negation, becomes a goal clause. Resolution is then applied to the hypotheses in an attempt to derive the empty clause. When constructing these deductions by hand, we can attempt to spot a promising hypothesis with which to apply the resolution rule. However, the whole point of this chapter is not just to look at yet another formal deduction system, but to consider one which can be automated. We would like to be able to construct an algorithm which, given a program and a query, tells us whether or not the query can be deduced from the program. For this reason, each program clause is taken in turn to see if resolution can be applied. We will take the program clauses in the order in which they are listed.

Example 5.1 Suppose we have the program

(a) $\neg p \vee \neg q \vee r$
(b) p
(c) q

Now suppose it is presented with the query r. An additional hypothesis, $\neg r$, is added and the proof is as follows. (The rule referred to as *Res* is an abbreviation for resolution, the only rule we are using.)

1 $\neg p \vee \neg q \vee r$ ⎫
2 p ⎬ hypotheses;
3 q ⎭
4 $\neg r$ added hypothesis;
5 $\neg q \vee r$ *Res* on 1 and 2;
6 r *Res* on 3 and 5;
7 $\square$ *Res* on 4 and 6.

The empty clause has been deduced, so the hypotheses combined with $\neg r$ are unsatisfiable (we cannot have the hypotheses T and the query F) so the query r succeeds.

Example 5.2 Remember that propositional program clauses can be written explicitly as disjunctions of propositional literals or they can be transformed into statements involving $\wedge$ and $\Rightarrow$. Suppose we have the program

(a) $(p \wedge q \wedge r) \Rightarrow s$
(b) $(t \wedge w) \Rightarrow r$
(c) q
(d) $(v \wedge r) \Rightarrow p$
(e) t
(f) v
(g) $v \Rightarrow w$

Now suppose it is presented with the query s which means that $\neg s$ is added as an extra hypothesis.

The program could be rewritten in terms of $\neg$ and $\vee$ and the resolution deduction carried out as follows.

The formal resolution deduction

1 $\neg p \vee \neg q \vee \neg r \vee s$ ⎫
2 $\neg t \vee \neg w \vee r$ ⎪
3 q ⎪
4 $\neg v \vee \neg r \vee p$ ⎬ hypotheses;
5 t ⎪
6 v ⎪
7 $\neg v \vee w$ ⎭
8 $\neg s$ added hypothesis;
9 $\neg p \vee \neg q \vee \neg r$ *Res* on 1 and 8;
10 $\neg p \vee \neg q \vee \neg t \vee \neg w$ *Res* on 2 and 9;
11 $\neg p \vee \neg t \vee \neg w$ *Res* on 3 and 10;

12 $\neg t \vee \neg w \vee \neg v \vee \neg r$	*Res* on 4 and 11;
13 $\neg w \vee \neg v \vee \neg r$	*Res* on 5 and 12;
14 $\neg w \vee \neg r$	*Res* on 6 and 13;
15 $\neg v \vee \neg r$	*Res* on 7 and 14;
16 $\neg t \vee \neg w \vee \neg v$	*Res* on 2 and 15;
17 $\neg w \vee \neg v$	*Res* on 5 and 16;
18 $\neg v$	*Res* on 7 and 17;
19 $\square$	*Res* on 6 and 18.

The (one branch) resolution tree

The same argument can be represented in the form of a *resolution tree*. In this simple case, the 'tree' happens to be linear. The tree representing the above argument is shown in figure 1.

For the resolution tree, the program clauses are considered to be written in terms of $\wedge$ and $\Rightarrow$. Each positive literal of the query is then considered to be a *subgoal,* all of which have to be derived in turn. We see if each subgoal matches the head of one (or more) of the program clauses. If so, the tail of the chosen clause gives us more subgoals to derive (or none at all if it is a unit clause). This process is continued until all the subgoals are derived (or until all possibilities have been exhausted if the subgoals cannot be derived). This method is equivalent to the formal deduction method – they are simply different ways of writing the same deduction. The resolution tree given above only had one branch. This was because, at each stage in the deduction, we never had to make a choice of program clause (to apply resolution to). If there is more than one option, then the tree *branches*. We may, of course, go down several branches before we find a successful one (if we ever do). Most practical examples have huge resolution trees with many branches.

The next example provides a case where there are two branches.

Example 5.3   Suppose we have the program

(a) $(p \wedge q) \Rightarrow r$
(b) $w \Rightarrow r$
(c) $s \Rightarrow w$
(d) p
(e) s

Now suppose this program is presented with the query r. Again we add $\neg r$ as an additional hypothesis. There is a choice of which clauses to combine with it (either (a) or (b), since these are the ones containing the variable r which can be combined with the $\neg r$ using the resolution rule). This choice creates two branches in the resolution tree, as shown in figure 2.

Notice that the first branch fails. When this happens we go back to the point in the deduction where there is an alternative clause and start again with the

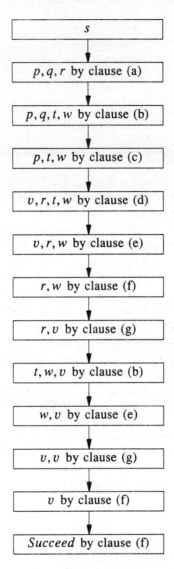

Figure 1

next branch. This procedure is known as *backtracking*. The intuitive idea is that at a certain point in the deduction we have to make a choice of which clause to use. We have decided, at the beginning of this section, that the choice to make will always be the clause which is listed first. If the wrong choice is taken then we ignore what was done from the moment the choice was made and consider the next option.

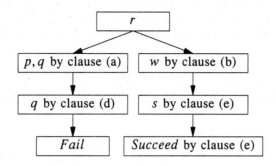

Figure 2

Left-hand side of the tree

The corresponding formal deductions for both sides of the tree are as follows.

$$
\begin{array}{lll}
1 & \neg p \lor \neg q \lor r & \left.\vphantom{\begin{array}{c}1\\2\\3\\4\\5\end{array}}\right\} \text{hypotheses;} \\
2 & \neg w \lor r & \\
3 & \neg s \lor w & \\
4 & p & \\
5 & s & \\
6 & \neg r & \text{added hypothesis;} \\
7 & \neg p \lor \neg q & \textit{Res} \text{ on 1 and 6,} \quad \text{going down the left-hand branch;} \\
8 & \neg q & \textit{Res} \text{ on 4 and 7.}
\end{array}
$$

There is no clause containing q to resolve with $\neg q$, so the derivation of $\square$ has failed.

Right-hand side of the tree

$$
\begin{array}{lll}
1 & \neg p \lor \neg q \lor r & \left.\vphantom{\begin{array}{c}1\\2\\3\\4\\5\end{array}}\right\} \text{hypotheses;} \\
2 & \neg w \lor r & \\
3 & \neg s \lor w & \\
4 & p & \\
5 & s & \\
6 & \neg r & \text{added hypothesis;} \\
7 & \neg w & \textit{Res} \text{ on 2 and 6;} \\
8 & \neg s & \textit{Res} \text{ on 3 and 7;} \\
9 & \square & \textit{Res} \text{ on 5 and 8.}
\end{array}
$$

5.2.4 Negation in logic programming

As we have seen, logic programs express only positive information. It is not possible to show that a negative literal is a consequence of a logic program (in the resolution tree, we would have to look for negative heads and none exist).

The technique most widely used in logic programming considers any query to be false if it cannot be derived from the program. This is known as *negation as failure* or the *closed-world assumption*. This is the technique we will study in this book. Of course, from a strict viewpoint, the closed-world assumption is not ideal; just because you cannot prove a statement, then that statement is not necessarily false. However, using the technique along with Horn clauses does provide the basis of the very useful logic programming language Prolog.

This rule can be expressed as

'If P is a propositional program, q is a query and $P \vdash q$ cannot be established, then we can deduce that $P \vdash \neg q$.'

Example 5.4   Consider the following propositional program:

(a) $n \Rightarrow q$
(b) $(p \wedge r \wedge s) \Rightarrow q$
(c) $w \Rightarrow q$
(d) $u \Rightarrow n$
(e) $t \Rightarrow r$
(f) p
(g) t

To show that $\neg q$ follows from the program we first present it with the query q and consider all the paths of the resolution tree as shown in figure 3. As can be seen from this tree, q cannot be derived from the program. Therefore, by applying the closed-world assumption, we can deduce that $\neg q$ follows from the program.

Notice that up to this point we only had one inference rule (resolution). We now have a second rule, namely the closed-world assumption, although it is important to note that this rule is different in that it contains a meta-statement. From now on, the two rules will be considered together. However, the resolution rule will be slightly modified to make it more amenable to automation.

5.2.5   SLD-resolution

As we have seen, there is a point in most resolution trees where a choice (of which clause to use) must be made. The method we have been using is *top-down*; this means that the clauses are taken in the order in which they are written from the top, working down. This is the same as working in a depth-first manner from left to right in the resolution tree.

So far in our examples we have considered queries that involve only one propositional variable. However, queries can be conjunctions of several variables. A query of more than one variable will become upon negation a goal clause of more than one variable. There will often be more than one variable which matches the head of one of the clauses. In this instance, from the point

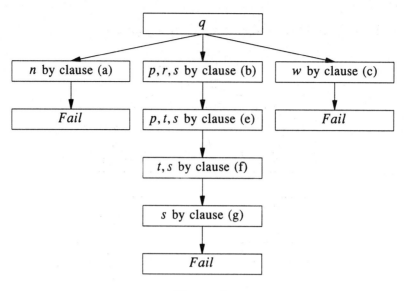

Figure 3

of view of automating the deduction process, it is sensible to introduce a *selection function* which picks out the variable to consider from the goal clause. If this succeeds, then the function picks out the next variable and so on. The use of this selection function with resolution is called SLD-resolution (the SLD stands for selection, linear and definite, respectively).

The selection function used in most Prolog implementations (which are, of course, for predicate logic not propositional logic) is to pick the leftmost subgoal. For the rest of this book we will consider resolution using this selection function and a top-down strategy (together with the closed-world assumption).

Example 5.5   Consider the following logic program:

(a) $(p \wedge r \wedge s) \Rightarrow q$
(b) $p \wedge w \Rightarrow q$
(c) $p \wedge t \Rightarrow n$
(d) $w \Rightarrow n$
(e) $s \Rightarrow w$
(f) $t \Rightarrow r$
(g) p
(h) t
(i) s

Now if the program is presented with the query

$q \wedge n \wedge w,$

then we have the SLD-resolution tree shown in figure 4.

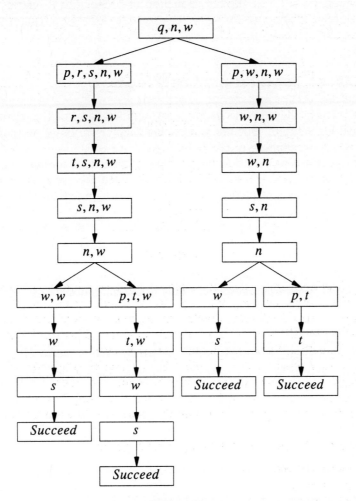

Figure 4

This uses SLD-resolution, in which we have chosen always to take the leftmost variable. This is the *selection function* we have chosen to use. There would be nothing to stop us (and indeed it would be just as sensible) always to pick the rightmost variable. Notice that for this example every branch of the tree succeeds. Thus, in this case, it is not necessary to go down every other branch once we have a success.

Automating deductions in propositional logic

We are now in a position where the techniques outlined above can be applied and a computer used to make the deduction of propositional queries from propositional logic programs for us. See exercise 5.2 for an algorithm which automates this process.

5.3   Clausal form for predicate logic

We have seen, in the previous section, a simplified form of logic programming for propositional logic. For the rest of this chapter we build on these ideas to extend logic programming to predicate logic.

In this section we will see how any closed predicate logic formula can be written in clausal form. Horn clauses will then be defined for predicate logic, and in the next section some arguments will be presented which will support our decision to restrict to Horn clauses.

In the following section (unification) we present a type of *equation-solving* algorithm which is necessary in order to carry out resolution for predicate logic.

Finally, we present an automatic theorem-proving system for predicate logic based on SLD-resolution and the closed-world assumption.

5.3.1   Prenex form

Before a closed predicate logic formula can be put into clausal form we will put it into prenex form. The idea is that *all* of the quantifiers appearing in the formula occur at the front of the formula.

A predicate formula is in prenex form if it is in the form

$$(Q_1 y_1)(Q_2 y_2) \cdots (Q_k y_k)A,$$

where Q_i is either $\forall$ or $\exists$, $y_1, \ldots, y_k$ are variables of A in any order and A is a predicate logic formula with no quantifiers.

An algorithm to convert to prenex normal form

Here we present a simple algorithm which will take a predicate logic formula A (which uses the operators $\neg$, $\Rightarrow$, $\wedge$ and $\vee$) and convert it to an equivalent one which is in prenex form. See exercise 5.5 for a proof that the two formulae are provably equivalent in system K.

The rules for conversion of a predicate logic formula A to prenex form are as follows:

(1) First determine the names of the free variables in the formula. If any bound variables of A are the same as any of the free variables of A, then

replace the bound variables by variables not occurring elsewhere in the formula to make them all different.

For an example, suppose we have the predicate formula

$$\exists x\, A(x) \Rightarrow (B(x) \wedge \neg \forall y\, C(y) \wedge \exists y\, D(y))$$

(where A, B, C and D are predicates and x and y are variables), then x is the only free variable, after step (1) the formula becomes

$$\exists z\, A(z) \Rightarrow (B(x) \wedge \neg \forall y\, C(y) \wedge \exists y\, D(y)).$$

(2) All bound variables should be distinct; if any two are the same, one should be renamed to be distinct from free variables and from other bound variables.

In our example the formula after step (2) would be

$$\exists z\, A(z) \Rightarrow (B(x) \wedge \neg \forall y\, C(y) \wedge \exists w\, D(w)).$$

(3) We wish to move all negation operators inwards, so that eventually they all act directly on predicates. All quantifiers immediately preceded by $\neg$ can be moved to the left of the $\neg$ connective by the following rules:

(a) replace a (sub) formula of the form $\neg \forall x\, A(x)$ by $\exists x\, \neg A(x)$;
(b) replace a (sub) formula of the form $\neg \exists x\, A(x)$ by $\forall x\, \neg A(x)$.

In our example the formula would become

$$\exists z\, A(z) \Rightarrow (B(x) \wedge \exists y\, \neg C(y) \wedge \exists w\, D(w)).$$

(4) We wish to move all quantifiers to the front of the formula. All quantifiers can be moved to the left across dyadic connectives by the following rules:

(a) replace a (sub) formula of the form $A \Rightarrow \forall x\, B$ by $\forall x(A \Rightarrow B)$;
(b) replace a (sub) formula of the form $A \Rightarrow \exists x\, B$ by $\exists x(A \Rightarrow B)$;
(c) replace a (sub) formula of the form $\exists x\, A \Rightarrow B$ by $\forall x(A \Rightarrow B)$;
(d) replace a (sub) formula of the form $\forall x\, A \Rightarrow B$ by $\exists x(A \Rightarrow B)$;
(e) replace a (sub) formula of the form $\forall x\, A \wedge B$ by $\forall x(A \wedge B)$;
(f) replace a (sub) formula of the form $\forall x\, A \vee B$ by $\forall x(A \vee B)$.

Both (a) and (b) require that x does not occur free in A, while (c), (d), (e) and (f) require that x does not occur free in B. This is why we have already substituted alternative identifiers for quantified variables to ensure that

no quantified variable name clashes with a free variable name (step 1);
no two quantified variable names clash (step 2).

In our example we can use rule (e) twice to obtain

$$\exists z\, A(z) \Rightarrow \exists y\, \exists w(B(x) \wedge \neg C(y) \wedge D(w))$$

and can now use rule (c) to obtain

$$\forall z(A(z) \implies \exists y \, \exists w (B(x) \wedge \neg C(y) \wedge D(w)))$$

and rule (b) twice to obtain finally

$$\forall z \, \exists y \, \exists w (A(z) \implies (B(x) \wedge \neg C(y) \wedge D(w))),$$

which is in prenex form.

The order in which the above rules are applied is usually not uniquely defined; there may be several different prenex forms for a given formula.

See exercise 4.17 in chapter 4 for a justification of step 4, rules (a), (b), (c) and (d) in system K. Notice that $\exists$ and $\wedge$ are not formally a part of the language of K; they can, however, both be defined in terms of the language.

5.3.2 Clausal form

We show, in this section, that any closed predicate formula can be reduced to one that is in a particular form (called clausal form). The formula is not exactly equivalent to the reduced version but is satisfiable if and only if the reduced version is satisfiable (this is all that is required for logic programming). We begin this section by considering some definitions.

A *literal* is an atomic formula (a *positive* literal) or the negation of an atomic formula (a *negative* literal).

A *clause* is a formula of the form

$$\forall x_1 \cdots \forall x_n (L_1 \vee \cdots \vee L_m),$$

where each L_i is a literal and $x_1, \ldots, x_n$ are all the variables occurring in $L_1 \vee \cdots \vee L_m$. As every variable occurring in a clause must be universally quantified we usually omit the quantifiers to simplify the notation and simply remember that all variables are universally quantified.

A predicate formula is in *clausal form* if it is a conjunction of clauses. In order to reduce a general predicate formula to clausal form we have to be able to eliminate existential quantifiers. This process is known as *Skolemization*.

Skolemization

The Skolemization process eliminates existential quantifiers. Suppose we have a predicate formula in prenex form and $\exists x$ is the first from the left of the existential quantifiers. Suppose also that $y_1, \ldots, y_n$ are all the universally quantified variables to the left of $\exists x$. The Skolemized form of the formula is obtained by deleting all existential quantifiers as follows:

(a) if $n = 0$ (the $\exists$ is not within the scope of any $\forall$s) the existential quantifier is removed and every occurrence of x is replaced by a new constant symbol distinct from all others;

(b) if $n > 0$, we remove the existential quantifier and replace x everywhere by a new n-place function symbol whose arguments are given by the quantified variables within whose scope the existential quantifier lies.

The above process is repeated for each existential quantifier in the formula.

It is clear that a formula (containing existential quantifiers) is not exactly equivalent to the Skolemized form. However, it can be shown that any predicate formula is satisfiable if and only if the Skolemized form is satisfiable. The proof of this statement is beyond the scope of this book but we can give an intuitive idea of the reasons behind the Skolemization process by considering the following example.

Suppose we have the predicate formula $\exists x\, A(x)$. The Skolemized version of this formula is $A(a)$, where a is a constant symbol of the language.

Consider an interpretation $\mathcal{A}$, where $|\mathcal{A}|$ is the set of non-negative integers and $A^{\mathcal{A}}(x)$ is given by $x = 0$. We can see that $\mathcal{A} \vDash \exists x\, A(x)$ because there does indeed exist a member of the domain which is equal to 0, namely 0 itself. Therefore, the formula is satisfiable.

Let a be a constant symbol of the language and let $a^{\mathcal{A}} = 0$. Then $\mathcal{A} \vDash A(a)$, so the Skolemized version is also satisfiable.

Let us consider another predicate formula $\forall x\, \exists y\, B(x,y)$. A natural question might be:

Why can we not simply replace the y by a constant symbol a?

The answer is obtained by considering the interpretation $\mathcal{A}$ that we have already introduced. Let $B(x, y)^{\mathcal{A}}$ be given by $x < y$.

Now $\mathcal{A} \vDash \forall x\, \exists y\, B(x, y)$ says that 'in the domain of non-negative integers for every integer there does indeed exist one which is larger'. However, if we were to eliminate the existential quantifier by replacing y by a constant symbol b say, then the new formula would be $\forall x\, B(x, b)$ which would not be true in $\mathcal{A}$, because whatever the integer we assign to b it cannot be larger than all non-negative integers.

The Skolemized version of this formula is $\forall x\, B(x, f(x))$ and if we let $f(x)^{\mathcal{A}} = x + 1$ it can be seen that $\mathcal{A} \vDash \forall x\, B(x, f(x))$; the interpretation of this is 'for every x lying in the domain of non-negative integers $x < x + 1$'.

Reduction of a closed predicate logic formula to clausal form

The four steps of an algorithm to reduce a closed formula to clausal form are as follows:

(1) Reduce the formula to prenex form. The quantifiers are now all at the front.
(2) Skolemize the formula. It is in this step that we lose the equivalence but still retain the property that the formula is satisfiable if and only if the clausal form is. There are now no existential quantifiers.

(3) Omit all the universal quantifiers, but remember that any variable appearing is universally quantified.

(4) Apply the manipulation methods of chapter 1, section 1.5 to write the formula in conjunctive normal form. Although we defined CNF only for propositional logic, the same rules apply where the concept of a propositional variable is replaced by a positive literal. The algorithm of chapter 1, exercise 1.4 could be used.

Example 5.6   We consider an example that is already converted to prenex form.

$$\forall z \, \exists y \, \exists w (A(z) \Rightarrow (\neg C(y) \land D(w))).$$

Step 2 of the algorithm for obtaining clausal form tells us to Skolemize. The Skolemized version is

$$\forall z (A(z) \Rightarrow (\neg C(f(z)) \land D(g(z)))).$$

The next step is to omit the quantifier:

$$A(z) \Rightarrow (\neg C(f(z)) \land D(g(z))).$$

To convert to CNF we first convert all other operators into $\land$, $\lor$ and $\neg$:

$$\neg A(z) \lor (\neg C(f(z)) \land D(g(z))).$$

The final step of conversion to CNF now gives us the following clausal form:

$$(\neg A(z) \lor \neg C(f(z))) \land (\neg A(z) \lor D(g(z))).$$

5.3.3   Horn clauses

We have seen how to convert any closed predicate formula into clausal form. This can be thought of as a set of clauses (each member of the set is a clause and each clause is taken in conjunction with the others). Logic programming is usually carried out using *Horn clauses*. We will define Horn clauses for predicate logic and then (in the next section) look at some of the semantic reasons for restricting ourselves to Horn clauses.

A clause is a *Horn clause* if it contains at most one positive literal. It must therefore be in one of the following three forms:

(1) $\forall x_1 \cdots \forall x_n (\neg R_1 \lor \cdots \lor \neg R_s \lor Q)$;
(2) $\forall x_1 \cdots \forall x_n (Q)$;
(3) $\forall x_1 \cdots \forall x_n (\neg R_1 \lor \cdots \lor \neg R_s)$,

where $x_1, \ldots, x_n$ are variables, and $R_1, \ldots, R_s, Q$ are atomic formulae.

Note the similarity of this to the propositional definition earlier in this chapter.

Types (1) and (2) are known as *program clauses* (or *definite* Horn clauses). A set of program clauses is known as a *logic program*. A clause of type (3) is known as a *goal clause*. Remember that we will usually drop the universal quantifiers to simplify the notation.

Equivalent forms of (1)*, (2) and (3) are:

(1′) $(R_1 \wedge \cdots \wedge R_s) \Rightarrow Q$;

(2′) Q;

(3′) $\neg(R_1 \wedge \cdots \wedge R_s)$, which means

$$\forall x_1 \cdots \forall x_n \, \neg(R_1 \wedge \cdots \wedge R_s),$$

which can also be expressed as

$$\neg \exists x_1 \cdots \exists x_n (R_1 \wedge \cdots \wedge R_s).$$

Any query we give to a logic program P is of the form

$$\exists x_1 \cdots \exists x_n (R_1 \wedge \cdots \wedge R_s)$$

and we are asking whether or not this result is derivable from P. As we have seen in the propositional case, the method used is to add the negation of the query as the goal clause

$$\neg R_1 \vee \cdots \vee \neg R_s$$

and to derive a contradiction using the resolution rule modified for predicate logic. The values of the variables $x_1, \ldots, x_n$ in

$$\exists x_1 \cdots \exists x_n (R_1 \wedge \cdots \wedge R_s)$$

are the output of running the program and are known as *answer substitutions*.

Theorem provers of this kind are called *refutation systems*. We have already seen a refutation system for the propositional case.

The restriction to Horn clauses requires some justification. This reduces the expressiveness of the system. The main reason for this restriction is that Horn clauses are particularly well behaved when it comes to automation and even though, in an ideal world, it would be better to have a system that could work with *all* first-order formulae, it is Horn clauses that provide the basis of Prolog. First-order logic itself is far less expressive than higher-order logic, which is not even covered in this book.

5.4   The semantics of logic programming

The basic problem of logic programming can be seen to be that of determining the unsatisfiability of $P \cup \{G\}$ where P is a logic program (a set of program clauses) and G is a goal clause (the negation of a query).

---

*In Prolog this would be written $Q :\text{-} R_1, \ldots, R_s$.

When writing a logic program we naturally argue semantically; the argument is in a particular interpretation of the program rather than in the program itself. This is known as the intended model of the program. We will present a certain model of any given logic program called the *least Herbrand model* which always exists and can be seen to 'stand for' the intended model.

Herbrand interpretations have already been introduced in chapter 4. Recall that the terms Herbrand universe and Herbrand base were also defined there. In this section, the Herbrand universe and base will be considered for particular logic programs. In chapter 4, the notations $U_{\mathscr{L}}$ and $B_{\mathscr{L}}$ were introduced for the Herbrand universe and base respectively of a first-order language $\mathscr{L}$. For a given logic program P the alphabet of the first-order language is taken to consist only of the relation, function and constant symbols occurring in P. We can therefore write U_P and B_P for the Herbrand universe of P and the Herbrand base of P, respectively.

We will begin this section by showing that if there exists a model of a set of Horn clauses H then there is a Herbrand model of H.

Remark   This result is *not* true for an arbitrary set of formulae. This can be shown by considering the set of formulae

$$S = \{R(a), \exists x \, \neg R(x)\}$$

which is not a set of clauses ($\exists x \, \neg R(x)$ is not a clause). Note that

$$U_S = \{a\},$$

$$B_S = \{R(a)\}.$$

There are two Herbrand interpretations:

   (a) { };
   (b) B_S.

(a) Now $R(a)$ is false in { }, so { } is not a model of S.
(b) We have $B_S \vDash R(a)$, so $\neg R(a)$ is false in B_S. This means that $\exists x \, \neg R(x)$ is false in B_S because the only value x can take is a (since the domain of the interpretation is $\{a\}$). It follows that B_S is not a model of S.

Hence we have no Herbrand model, but we can find a model of S as follows.
Let $\mathscr{A}$ be the interpretation where $|\mathscr{A}| = \{Malcolm, Mary\}$ and $a^{\mathscr{A}} = Malcolm$, $R^{\mathscr{A}}(Malcolm) = T$ and $R^{\mathscr{A}}(Mary) = F$.

We can see that $\mathscr{A} \vDash R(a)$ and $\mathscr{A} \vDash \exists x \, \neg R(x)$ because there does now exist an x such that $\neg R(x)$ is T, namely *Mary*. We could give this interpretation more sense by letting $R(x)$ stand for 'x is male'. We would then have that '*Malcolm* is male' (represented by $R(a)$) and there does exist someone (*Mary*) who is not male (represented by $\exists x \, \neg R(x)$).

5.4.1   Horn clauses and their Herbrand models

Let H be a set of Horn clauses and let $\mathcal{B}$ be a model of H. Then $\mathcal{A} = \{R \in B_H : \mathcal{B} \vDash R\}$ is a Herbrand model of H.

Proof   Since $\mathcal{A} \subseteq B_H$, $\mathcal{A}$ is a Herbrand interpretation of H.

Suppose, by way of contradiction, that $\mathcal{A}$ is not a model of H, then there exists a clause of H of one of the forms

(a) $(R_1 \wedge \cdots \wedge R_S) \Rightarrow Q$

or

(b) Q

or

(c) $\neg R_1 \vee \cdots \vee \neg R_S$.

which is false in $\mathcal{A}$. We will prove the theorem for each of these cases.

(a) If $(R_1 \wedge \cdots \wedge R_S) \Rightarrow Q$ is false in $\mathcal{A}$, then $R_1, \ldots, R_S$ must be true in $\mathcal{A}$, and Q is false in $\mathcal{A}$. This means that

$$R_1 \in \mathcal{A}, \ldots, R_S \in \mathcal{A} \text{ and } Q \notin \mathcal{A}.$$

From the condition of membership of $\mathcal{A}$ we know that

$$\mathcal{B} \vDash R_1, \ldots, \mathcal{B} \vDash R_S \text{ and } Q \text{ is false in } \mathcal{B},$$

which can be converted back to an implication so that

$$(R_1 \wedge \cdots \wedge R_S) \Rightarrow Q \text{ is false in } \mathcal{B}.$$

Thus $\mathcal{B}$ is not a model of H, which is a contradiction.

(b) If Q is false in $\mathcal{A}$ then $Q \notin \mathcal{A}$, so that Q is false in $\mathcal{B}$, which is a contradiction.

(c) If $\neg R_1 \vee \cdots \vee \neg R_S$ is false in $\mathcal{A}$ then

$$R_1 \in \mathcal{A}, \ldots, R_S \in \mathcal{A}.$$

From this we get

$$\mathcal{B} \vDash R_1, \mathcal{B} \vDash R_2, \ldots, \mathcal{B} \vDash R_S$$

and so $\neg R_1 \vee \cdots \vee \neg R_S$ is false in $\mathcal{B}$, which is a contradiction.

Remark   It follows that if H does not have a Herbrand model, then H is unsatisfiable.

We now establish a series of results that introduces the least Herbrand model of a logic program and shows that this model presents exactly the facts that can be derived from the program. Thus it can be seen to 'stand for' the intended model. The intended model may contain more information, but it would be information that could not be derived from the program.

5.4.2   Logic programs and their Herbrand models

We show that every logic program has a Herbrand model.

Let P be a logic program; then B_P (the Herbrand base of P) is the required Herbrand model of P.

Proof   Every ground instance of an atomic formula occurring in P is true in the Herbrand interpretation B_P.

So if we have the two program clauses:

$$(R_1 \wedge \cdots \wedge R_S) \Rightarrow Q;$$
$$Q,$$

then the components $R_1, \ldots, R_S, Q$ are all true in B_P, so the clauses themselves are true in B_P.

We now show that there is a unique minimal model, called the least Herbrand model, which is obtained by taking the intersection of all the Herbrand models of the program.

5.4.3   Least Herbrand models

Let

$$\text{Hmod}(P) = \{ \mathcal{A}_i : i \in I \} = \{ \mathcal{A}_1, \mathcal{A}_2, \ldots \}$$

be the set of all Herbrand models of a logic program P.

We first show that the intersection of these

$$\bigcap \text{Hmod}(P) = \mathcal{A}_1 \cap \mathcal{A}_2 \cap \cdots$$

is a Herbrand model of P.

Proof   Assume by way of contradiction that $\bigcap \text{Hmod}(P)$ is not a model of P.

Then there must exist a ground instance of a clause

$$(R_1 \wedge \cdots \wedge R_S) \Rightarrow Q \quad \text{(where } S \geqslant 0),$$

which is not true in $\bigcap \text{Hmod}(P)$, so that

$$\bigcap \text{Hmod}(P) \text{ includes } R_1, \ldots, R_n \text{ but not } Q.$$

So $R_1, \ldots, R_S$ are true in every Herbrand model of P, but there must exist some Herbrand model $\mathcal{A}_i$ such that Q is false in $\mathcal{A}_i$. We then have that

$$(R_1 \wedge \cdots \wedge R_S) \Rightarrow Q \text{ is false in } \mathcal{A}_i,$$

so $\mathcal{A}_i$ is not a model of P. This is a contradiction.

For any given logic program P, $\bigcap \text{Hmod}(P)$ is known as the *least Herbrand model* of P.

We now show that the least Herbrand model of P is actually the set of all ground atomic semantic consequences of P.

Proof   Denote the set of all ground atomic semantic consequences of P by A_P. We show that $\bigcap \text{Hmod}(P) = A_P$.

Clearly, from the definition of a semantic consequence, we have $A_P \subseteq \bigcap \text{Hmod}(P)$. Now let Q be any member of $\bigcap \text{Hmod}(P)$. Q will be true for every Herbrand model of P. We have to show that Q is also true for any non-Herbrand model.

Suppose $\mathcal{B}$ is a non-Herbrand model of P. By our first result we know that $\{R \in B_P : \mathcal{B} \vDash R\}$ is a Herbrand model of P, and since Q is true for every Herbrand model of P we have

$$Q \in \{R \in B_P : \mathcal{B} \vDash R\}.$$

However, if Q is false in $\mathcal{B}$, then

$$Q \notin \{R \in B_P : \mathcal{B} \vDash R\},$$

which is a contradiction, so $\mathcal{B} \vDash Q$ and it follows that $Q \in A_P$. This gives us $\bigcap \text{Hmod}(P) \subseteq A_P$, from which the result $\bigcap \text{Hmod}(P) = A_P$ follows.

5.4.4   Construction of least Herbrand models

The Herbrand universe of a given logic program is the union of the following (infinite list of) sets:

(1) all the constants of P;
(2) all the functions of P with all combinations of objects from (1) as arguments;
(3) all the functions of P with all combinations of objects from (2) as arguments;

... .

These are all the ground terms which can be created from the program P.

Example 5.7   If the only constant of a logic program is a, and the only function f (with one argument), then the Herbrand universe is the infinite set

$$\{a, f(a), f(f(a)), f(f(f(a))), f(f(f(f(a)))), \ldots\}.$$

Example 5.8   If the constants of a program are a and b, and the functions f (with one argument) and g (with two), then the Herbrand universe is the infinite set

$$\{a, b, f(a), f(b), g(a, a), g(a, b), g(b, a), g(b, b), f(f(a)), f(f(b)), f(g(a, a)), \ldots\}.$$

The Herbrand base is the set of all possible predicates of P with all possible combinations of objects from the Herbrand universe as arguments. These are all the ground atomic formulae of P.

Example 5.9 If in the preceding examples we had a logic program which contains as the only predicate E (with one argument), then the Herbrand base in the first case is

$$\{E(a), E(f(a)), E(f(f(a))), E(f(f(f(a)))), E(f(f(f(f(a))))), \ldots\}$$

and in the second case

$$\{E(a), E(b), E(f(a)), E(f(b)), E(g(a, a)), E(g(a, b)), E(g(b, a)),$$

$$E(g(b, b)), E(f(f(a))), \ldots\}.$$

The Herbrand model of a logic program can now be built up from the logic program as follows. We will use the logic program

$$R(x) \Rightarrow R(f(x))$$
$$R(a)$$
$$R(b)$$

as an example.

(1) Include all ground instances of unit clauses in the program. Look at all the unit clauses in the program; if they are already ground (as here), include them; if they contain one or more variables, include them with every member of the Herbrand universe substituted for the variable(s).
    In this case we have

$$R(a),$$
$$R(b).$$

(2) Include all ground instances of atomic formulae Q which occur in ground instances of program clauses of the form

$$(R_1 \wedge \cdots \wedge R_n) \Rightarrow Q,$$

where all the $R_1, \ldots, R_n$ are taken from the step (or steps) above. Our example gives us

$$R(f(a)),$$
$$R(f(b)).$$

This last step can be repeated infinitely many times, giving us additional members

$$R(f(f(a))),$$
$$R(f(f(b))),$$

and so on.

We now give a formal method for constructing the Herbrand model of a logic program. In order to construct $\bigcap \mathrm{Hmod}(P)$ we define the following.

Definitions

Let T_P be a function (called the *semantic consequence operator*) on subsets of the Herbrand base of P which is defined as follows.

For $\mathcal{A} \subseteq B_P$

$$T_P(\mathcal{A}) = \{Q : (R_1 \wedge \cdots \wedge R_S) \Rightarrow Q \text{ is a ground instance of}$$
$$\text{a clause of } P \text{ and } R_1 \in \mathcal{A}, \dots, R_S \in \mathcal{A}\}.$$

We now define ↑ as follows:

$$T_P \uparrow 0 = \varnothing;$$
$$T_P \uparrow (n+1) = T_P(T_P \uparrow n) \quad (n \geqslant 0);$$
$$T_P \uparrow \omega = \bigcup_{n=0}^{\infty} T_P \uparrow n.$$

It can be shown that $T_P \uparrow \omega$ is the least Herbrand model of P. The proof of this statement is beyond the scope of this book.

Intuitively, we set this operator going on the empty set, and we will eventually obtain the set of all the ground atomic formulae that are semantic consequences of the program. This may be (will normally be) infinite.

We will now consider an example of constructing the least Herbrand model using the semantic consequence operator.

Example 5.10 Taking the same logic program as we used above

$$R(x) \Rightarrow R(f(x))$$
$$R(a)$$
$$R(b)$$

the least Herbrand model is obtained by applying the semantic consequence operator as follows:

$$T_P \uparrow 0 = \Phi,$$
$$T_P \uparrow 1 = \{R(a), R(b)\},$$
$$T_P \uparrow 2 = \{R(f(a)), R(f(b))\},$$

$$\vdots$$

The union of all of these is the set

$$\{R(a), R(f(a)), R(f(f(a))), \dots\} \cup \{R(b), R(f(b)), R(f(f(b))), \dots\}.$$

The least Herbrand model is the set of all the possible facts that can follow from the program.

We will now consider the process of programming with predicate logic. This is very similar to the process we have considered for propositional logic. It is, however, more complicated and we have to consider first a concept known as *unification*.

5.5 Unification and answer substitutions

Recall that resolution, as defined for propositional clauses, was the inference rule that allows us to deduce $C_1 \vee C_2$ from $C_1 \vee p$ and $C_2 \vee \neg p$, where C_1 and C_2 are propositional clauses and p is a propositional variable.

A reasonable first attempt at a corresponding rule for predicate logic might be to say that we can deduce $C_1 \vee C_2$ from $C_1 \vee R$ and $C_2 \vee \neg R$, where C_1 and C_2 are predicate clauses and R is an n-place relation symbol. However, the relation symbol has arguments which are terms of the language under consideration.

Suppose we have $C_1 \vee R(a, b)$ and $C_2 \vee \neg R(a, b)$, where C_1 and C_2 are clauses (of predicate logic), R is a two-place relation symbol and a and b are constant symbols. Using resolution we could derive $C_1 \vee C_2$.

However, suppose we had the clauses $C_1 \vee R(x, b)$ and $C_2 \vee \neg R(a, y)$, where x and y are variables. $R(x, b)$ and $R(a, y)$ are not the same atomic formula but can be made the same by variable substitution (substitute a for x and b for y). Remember that the variables are universally quantified, so if we are saying that

$$\forall x (C_1 \vee R(x, b)) \text{ is T,}$$

then $C_1 \vee R(a, b)$ is T because this is just one of the cases (when $x = a$) and the formula is T for all possible values of x (in the domain of interpretation).

After the substitutions have been made, the atomic formulae are the same, so that it is possible to carry out the resolution. This process of substitution is known as *unification,* since we are unifying two apparently different expressions. The process can now be formally defined.

5.5.1 Substitutions

A *substitution* θ is a finite set of the form

$$\{t_1/v_1, \ldots, t_n/v_n\}$$

where each v_i is a variable, each term t_i is a term distinct from v_i, and the variables $v_1, \ldots, v_n$ are all distinct. The / notation can be read as 'for', so that t_1/v_1 reads

'substitute the term t_1 for the variable v_1.'

Each element of the substitution t_i/v_i is called a *binding* of v_i.

A substitution θ is called a *ground substitution* if all the t_i are ground terms. It is called a *variable pure substitution* if all the t_i are variables.

Let N be a set of terms of the language under consideration, and let

$$\theta = \{t_1/v_1,\ldots,t_n/v_n\}$$

be a substitution. Then $N\theta$ is the *instance of N by θ*. This is the set of terms obtained from N by simultaneously replacing all the occurrences of v_i in N by t_i $(i = 1,\ldots,n)$. If $N\theta$ is ground, then it is called a *ground instance* of N.

Let A be a predicate formula. Then $A\theta$ is the 'instance of A by θ', which is the result of replacing all the occurrences of v_i in A by t_i $(i = 1,\ldots,n)$.

The substitution given by the empty set is called the *identity substitution* and is denoted by ε. So for all sets of terms N we have $N\varepsilon = N$.

Example 5.11   A simple substitution.

$$N = \{g(f(x),y,f(a)),g(z,b,f(w))\}$$

(where g is a three-place function symbol, f is a one-place function symbol, a and b are constant symbols and x, y, z and w are variables) and

$$\sigma = \{f(x)/z,b/y\}.$$

Then

$$N\sigma = \{g(f(x),b,f(a)),g(f(x),b,f(w))\}.$$

Composition of substitutions

Let θ and σ be substitutions defined by

$$\theta = \{s_1/u_1,\ldots,s_n/u_n\}; \qquad \sigma = \{t_1/v_1,\ldots,t_m/v_m\},$$

where s_i and t_i are terms and u_i and v_i are variables. Then the *composition* of θ and σ (written $\theta \circ \sigma$) is the substitution arising from performing θ followed by σ, and is obtained from the set

$$\{s_1\sigma/u_1,\ldots,s_m\sigma/u_m,t_1/v_1,\ldots,t_m/v_m\}$$

by deleting any binding

$$s_i\sigma/u_i$$

for which

$$u_i = s_i\sigma$$

and deleting any binding

$$t_j/v_j$$

where $v_j \in \{u_1,\ldots,u_m\}$.

Example 5.12   Suppose we have the substitutions

$$\theta = \{f(x)/y, b/z\}; \qquad \sigma = \{c/x\}.$$

The composition $\theta \circ \sigma$ is the substitution $\{f(c)/y, b/z\}$.

5.5.2   Unification

Suppose we are given a set of terms N and a substitution θ. θ is said to be a *unifier* of N if and only if $N\theta$ is a singleton set. A unifier of a set of terms is a substitution which makes all the terms identical. It is a solution to a set of *term equations*.

Example 5.13   Let us consider the set of terms N given above. If we also consider the substitution

$$\theta = \{f(x)/z, b/y, a/w\},$$

then we see that θ is a unifier of the two terms contained in N.

Now consider once again the example that was looked at at the beginning of this section. We had the clauses $C_1 \vee R(x, b)$ and $C_2 \vee \neg R(a, y)$, where x and y are variables. Let $\theta = \{a/x, b/y\}$. We have

$$\{R(x, b), R(a, y)\}\theta = \{R(a, b)\},$$

so that

$$R(x, b)\theta = R(a, b) = R(a, y)\theta.$$

Thus, although we cannot resolve the original two formulae directly, we can resolve

$$C_1\theta \vee R(x, b)\theta$$

and

$$C_2\theta \vee \neg R(a, y)\theta$$

to obtain

$$C_1\theta \vee C_2\theta.$$

Suppose instead we have the clauses

$$\{C_1 \vee R(x, y), C_2 \vee \neg R(z, b)\}.$$

Then $\theta_1 = \{a/x, a/z, b/y\}$ would act as a unifier. There are other possible unifiers, including $\theta_2 = \{b/x, b/z, b/y\}$ and $\theta_3 = \{f(a)/x, f(a)/z, b/y\}$.

If we consider the substitution $\sigma = \{t/x, t/z, b/y\}$, where t is a variable, we can see that θ_1, θ_2 and θ_3 are all instances of σ. We can see this by letting $\lambda_1 = \{a/t\}$, $\lambda_2 = \{b/t\}$ and $\lambda_3 = \{f(a)/t\}$, then $\sigma \circ \lambda_1 = \theta_1$, $\sigma \circ \lambda_2 = \theta_2$ and $\sigma \circ \lambda_3 = \theta_3$.

σ is said to be more general. Note that σ can still be used in the resolution step. A formal definition of a most general unifier can be provided as follows.

Most general unifier

Let N be a finite set of terms. Let θ and σ be unifiers of N.

θ is called *more general* than σ if there exists a substitution λ such that $\theta \circ \lambda = \sigma$.

θ is called a *most general unifier* (or MGU) for N if for *every* unifier γ of N there exists a substitution λ such that $\theta \circ \lambda = \gamma$.

Disagreement sets

Let N be a finite set of simple expressions. Locate the leftmost symbol position at which not all expressions in N have the same symbol. Extract from each expression the subexpression beginning at that position. The set of all such subexpressions is called the *disagreement set* of N.

Example 5.14 Find the disagreement set of the set of the set of clauses

$$N = \{P(f(x), h(y), a), P(f(x), z, a), P(f(x), h(y), b)\}.$$

The disagreement set in this example is $\{h(y), z\}$.

The unification algorithm

The steps of an algorithm to construct a most-general unifier for a set N of terms are:

(1) put $k = 0$ and $\sigma_0 = \varepsilon$;

(2) if $N\sigma_k$ is a singleton then stop: σ_k is a most general unifier of N, else find the disagreement set D_k of $N\sigma_k$;

(3) if there does not exist a variable and a term in D_k, stop: S is not unifiable:

(4) if there exists a variable v and a term t in D_k, but if v occurs in t, stop: S is not unifiable (this is called an *occurs check*);

(5) choose a variable v and a term t not containing v from D_k, then put $\sigma_{k+1} = \sigma_k \circ \{t/v\}$, increment k and go to step (2).

The algorithm as it is presented is non-deterministic since there may be several choices for v and t in step (5). However the application of any two most general unifiers produced by the algorithm leads to expressions which are variable renamings of one another. A substitution θ is a *variable renaming* of another substitution σ if there exists a variable pure substitution λ such that $\sigma \circ \lambda = \theta$. It is clear that the algorithm terminates since S contains a finite number of variables and step (5) eliminates one variable each time.

The unification theorem

(a) If N is unifiable there is only one most general unifier (up to variable renaming).
(b) The above algorithm will find the most general unifier and terminate if N is unifiable. If not, it will terminate.

The proof of this theorem is beyond the scope of this book.

Example 5.15 Find the most general unifier if it exists (if not report the fact) of the following sets of terms.

(a) $N = \{f(g(a), g(x)), f(y, y)\}$;
(b) $N = \{f(g(a), h(x)), f(y, y)\}$;
(c) $N = \{f(x, x), f(y, g(y))\}$.

Solution

(a) (i) $\theta_0 = \varepsilon$.
  (ii) $D_0 = \{g(a), y\}$, so choose $v = y$ and $t = g(a)$;
    $\theta_1 = \{g(a)/y\}$;
    $N\theta_1 = \{f(g(a), g(x)), f(g(a), g(a))\}$.
  (iii) $D_1 = \{x, a\}$, so choose $v = x, t = a$;
    $\theta_2 = \{g(a)/y, a/x\}$;
    $N\theta_2 = \{f(g(a), g(a))\}$, which is a singleton.
    Therefore θ_2 is the MGU of N.

(b) (i) $\theta_0 = \varepsilon$;
  (ii) $D_0 = \{g(a), y\}$, so choose $v = y$ and $t = g(a)$;
    $\theta_1 = \{g(a)/y\}$. $D_1 = \{h(x), g(a)\}$.
    Therefore N is not unifiable.

(c) (i) $\theta_0 = \varepsilon$;
  (ii) $D_0 = \{x, y\}$, so choose $v = y$ and $t = x$ or the reverse;
    $\theta_1 = \{x/y\}$;
    $N\theta_1 = \{f(x, x), f(x, g(x))\}$.
  (iii) $D_1 = \{x, g(x)\}$.
    Since x occurs in $g(x)$ this is not unifiable.

5.5.3 Practicalities

There are problems with implementing the unification algorithm efficiently. More efficient algorithms are known, but most Prolog implementations do not use them, having a different solution to this efficiency problem. The occurs check is omitted since this is the main cause of the problem. From a practical point of view, this solves an efficiency problem and the occurs check is not often required anyway, but from a theoretical viewpoint this is a disaster since it destroys the soundness of the inference mechanism (it produces wrong answers).

5.6   Programming with predicate logic

We now present the full method for programming with predicate logic.

5.6.1   The resolution rule

Suppose $t_1,\ldots,t_n$ and $t_1',\ldots,t_n'$ are terms such that t_i and t_i' are unifiable with MGU θ for $1 \leqslant i \leqslant n$ and that C_1 and C_2 are clauses.

Resolution says that from $C_1 \vee R(t_1,\ldots,t_n)$ and $C_2 \vee \neg R(t_1',\ldots,t_n')$ we are allowed to derive $C_1\theta \vee C_2\theta$ (where R is an n-place relation symbol).

We can use the same methods as in propositional logic to show that, for Horn clauses, resolution amounts to the following rule:

$$(Q_1 \wedge \cdots \wedge Q_l) \Rightarrow R(t_1,\ldots,t_n),\ (R(t_1',\ldots,t_n') \wedge S_1 \wedge \cdots \wedge S_m) \Rightarrow S_{m+1}$$

$$\vdash_{\mathrm{Res}} (Q_1\theta \wedge \cdots \wedge Q_l\theta \wedge S_1\theta \wedge \cdots \wedge S_m\theta) \Rightarrow S_{m+1}\theta,$$

where θ is the MGU of t_i, t_i' $(1 \leqslant i \leqslant n)$.

If P is a program and G a goal, then an *answer substitution* for $P \cup \{G\}$ is a substitution for variables of G. The substitution does not necessarily contain a binding for every variable of G. If G has no variables, then the only possible answer substitution is the identity substitution.

Let P be a program, G be a goal $\neg A_1 \vee \cdots \vee \neg A_k$ and θ be an answer substitution for $P \cup \{G\}$. θ is a *correct answer substitution* if the closed formula $(A_1 \wedge \cdots \wedge A_n)\theta$ can be derived from P (using resolution).

As we have already indicated, the computer programming language *Prolog* is based on Horn clauses. However, it employs a slightly different notation to the mathematical notation that has been used so far. The Prolog notation is summarized as follows:

:- means 'implied by';
, means 'and'.

In addition, Prolog uses upper-case (capital) letters for variables, and lower-case letters for predicates. Using this convention,

$$(R_1 \wedge \cdots \wedge R_n) \Rightarrow Q$$

is written as

$$\underset{\text{Head}}{q} \ :- \ \underset{\text{Tail}}{r_1, r_2, \ldots, r_n}.$$

For the rest of this section, we will use the Prolog notation.

5.6.2   The proof strategy of Prolog: SLD-resolution

As we have seen in the propositional case there may well be more than one clause in the program that can be used in the resolution process. The Prolog language attempts resolution by working through all the clauses in the program in a top-down manner; it attempts to carry out resolution with the first clause in the program and then with the next one and so on. Prolog also uses the backtracking method outlined in the propositional case. If a branch of the resolution tree fails we go back to the last point in the tree where a decision was made and take an alternative route down the proof tree.

Prolog also uses a selection function to pick out the literal of the goal clause with which it is going to attempt to carry out the resolution process. The selection rule used is to pick out the leftmost literal. This resolution rule is known as SLD-resolution (see section 5.2.5).

We will now consider some examples of resolution proofs with predicate logic.

Example 5.16   Suppose we have the program

(a) $s(X) :- q(Y), r(X, Y)$
(b) $q(X) :- p(X)$
(c) $p(b)$
(d) $r(a, b)$

and suppose we are given the query $s(a)$. The formal resolution proof is as follows:

1   $s(X) \vee \neg q(Y) \vee \neg r(X, Y)$ ⎫
2   $q(X) \vee \neg p(X)$ ⎬ hypotheses;
3   $p(b)$ ⎪
4   $r(a, b)$ ⎭
5   $\neg s(a)$ added hypothesis;
6   $\neg q(Y) \vee \neg r(a, Y)$ *Res* on 1 and 5, (a/X) in 1;
7   $\neg p(Y) \vee \neg r(a, Y)$ *Res* on 2 and 6, (Y/X) in 6;
8   $\neg r(a, b)$ *Res* on 3 and 7, (b/Y) in 7;
9   □   *Res* on 4 and 8.

The resolution tree is shown in figure 5.

Clause (a) tells us that to derive $s(a)$ we need first to derive $q(Y), r(a, Y)$ (for any value of Y). Clause (b) tells us that we can do this by deriving $p(Y), r(a, Y)$. We have $p(b)$ and $r(a, b)$ (clauses (c) and (d)). It follows that $s(a)$ is derivable from the program.

Example 5.17   Suppose we have the program

(a) $s(X) :- q(Y), r(X, Y)$
(b) $s(X) :- l(X)$
(c) $q(X) :- p(X)$
(d) $p(b)$
(e) $l(c)$

and the query $s(X)$.

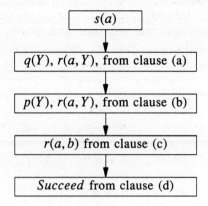

Figure 5

The formal resolution proof is as follows:

1   $s(X) \vee \neg q(Y) \vee \neg r(X, Y)$ ⎫
2   $s(X) \vee \neg l(X)$ ⎪
3   $q(X) \vee \neg p(X)$ ⎬ hypotheses:
4   $p(b)$ ⎪
5   $l(c)$ ⎭
6   $\neg s(X)$ added hypothesis;
7   $\neg l(X)$ *Res* on 2 and 6;
8   $\square$ *Res* on 5 and 7, (c/X).

Note that we have not used 1, 3 or 4.

The substitution $\{(c/X)\}$ is a correct-answer substitution.

In step 7 we used clause (b) and the proof was easy. We could, however, have picked on clause (a), in which case we would have had the following proof:

1   $s(X) \vee \neg q(Y) \vee \neg r(X, Y)$ ⎫
2   $s(X) \vee \neg l(X)$ ⎪
3   $q(X) \vee \neg p(X)$ ⎬ hypotheses;
4   $p(b)$ ⎪
5   $l(c)$ ⎭
6   $\neg s(X)$ added hypothesis;
7   $\neg q(Y) \vee \neg r(X, Y)$ *Res* on 1 and 6, (c/X) in 1;
8   $\neg p(Y) \vee \neg r(X, Y)$ *Res* on 3 and 7 (Y/X) in 3;
9   $\neg r(X, b)$ *Res* on 4 and 8, (b/Y) in 9.

We can get no further because we cannot find $r(X, b)$ (or something which can be made into $r(X, b)$ by unification) and so the proof fails. An algorithm to decide whether or not a query is a consequence of a logic program must take each clause in a specified order and try it out. If we consider an ordering from top to bottom we would try clause (a) first and would fail. We would then try clause (b) and succeed.

The resolution tree is shown in figure 6. Once we fail we go back up the tree to where the failure branch started and try again; we carry out *backtracking*.

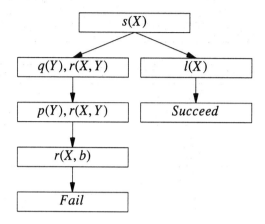

Figure 6

Example 5.18   Suppose we have the program

(a) $m(X)$:- $s(X), n(b)$
(b) $m(X)$:- $s(X), n(X)$
(c) $s(X)$:- $l(X)$
(d) $s(X)$:- $q(Y), r(X, Y)$
(e) $q(X)$:- $p(X)$
(f) $p(b)$
(g) $r(a, b)$
(h) $l(c)$
(i) $n(a)$

Given the query $m(a)$ the complete resolution tree is shown in figure 7.

5.6.3   Negation in logic programming: the closed-world assumption

We have already seen the idea behind the closed-world assumption in the propositional case. The main problem with handling negation is that logic programs express only positive information. A negative literal cannot be a semantic consequence of a logic program since by a proof in section 5.3 we know that the Herbrand base of a logic program is a model and any negative

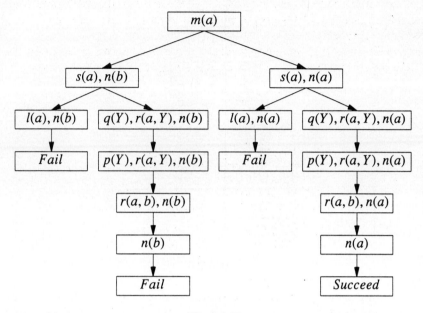

Figure 7

literal is false in this model. Hence, Prolog considers any query to be false if it cannot be derived from the program. This is sometimes called *negation as failure* or the *closed-world assumption*.

5.7   Concluding remarks

The automatic deduction system for predicate logic that we have presented here is sound and complete. It is beyond the scope of this book to present these proofs. There are, however, some problems.

As we have mentioned in the unification section, most Prolog implementations, in an attempt to improve efficiency, omit the occur check. The problem is that, in general, this omission makes Prolog unsound. Another problem is concerned with the proof strategy employed by Prolog.

Consider the following logic program:

    (a) $p(X) :- r(X)$
    (b) $r(X) :- r(f(X))$
    (c) $r(f(a)) :- s(a)$
    (d) $s(a)$

(where p, q and r are predicates and f is a function) and present it with the query $p(f(a))$. The resolution tree will be as shown in figure 8.

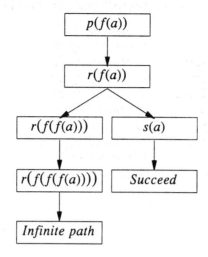

Figure 8

Now, Prolog will go off down an infinite path of the tree. It will never get to the success branch. However, if we used an alternative strategy (such as *bottom-up*) or if we rearranged the clauses, then the success branch could be reached first. Notice that it is not the deduction system that is incomplete (there is a success branch there), it is the method of searching the resolution tree that is incomplete. However, the method of searching is quite efficient.

In summary, Prolog itself is both unsound and incomplete, but these are caused by attempts to make the process efficient. Prolog could be sound and complete but then it would inevitably be very inefficient.

5.8   Worked examples

Example 5.19   Convert the following statements into a propositional logic program:

    If Desmond is hungry then he is eating.
    If Desmond is inebriated then he is content.
    If Desmond is singing and laughing then he is inebriated.
    If Desmond is eating and watching TV then he is content.
    If Desmond is happy and drinking then he is watching TV.
    If Desmond is in the money then he is drinking.
    If Desmond is singing then he is happy.
    If Desmond is happy then he is in the money.
    Desmond is hungry.
    Desmond is singing.

Solution   Assign statements to propositional variables as follows:

'Desmond is hungry'   is denoted by H;
'Desmond is eating'   is denoted by E;
'Desmond is watching TV'   is denoted by W;
'Desmond is laughing'   is denoted by L;
'Desmond is inebriated'   is denoted by I;
'Desmond is content'   is denoted by C;
'Desmond is happy'   is denoted by P;
'Desmond is drinking'   is denoted by D;
'Desmond is in the money'   is denoted by M;
'Desmond is singing'   is denoted by S.

The propositional logic program is

$E :- H$
$C :- I$
$I :- S, L$
$C :- E, W$
$W :- P, D$
$D :- M$
$P :- S$
$M :- P$
H
S

Example 5.20   Determine whether or not the fact that Desmond is content can be derived from the program. Is it possible to derive the fact that Desmond is not inebriated?

Solution   The SLD-resolution tree in figure 9 shows that C can be derived from the program.

It can be seen (from the left-hand branch of the tree) that I cannot be derived. So, by the closed-world assumption, it can be assumed that $\neg I$ can be deduced.

Example 5.21   Consider the following predicate logic program:

$R(x) :- P(x), Q(x)$
$R(x) :- S(x, f(y))$
$R(x) :- T(x)$
$S(f(f(x)), f(y)) :- U(f(f(x)), y)$
$S(x, f(y)) :- U(x, f(y))$
$Q(f(x)) :- V(f(x))$
$V(f(x)) :- V(x)$
$P(f(f(x))) :- P(f(x))$

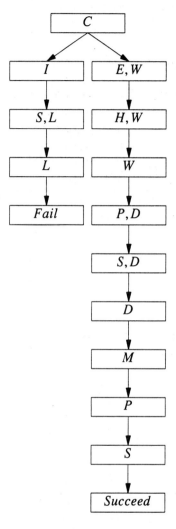

Figure 9

$T(x) :\text{-} W(x)$
$V(b)$
$U(a, a)$
$P(f(a))$
$W(a)$
$U(f(f(a)), f(a))$

Construct SLD-resolution trees for each of the following queries and determine whether or not they can be derived from the program:

(a) $R(a)$;
(b) $R(f(a))$;
(c) $R(f(f(a)))$.

Solution

(a) The SLD-resolution tree for $R(a)$ is shown in figure 10.

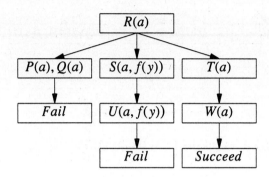

Figure 10

So $R(a)$ can be derived from the program.

(b) The SLD-resolution tree for $R(f(a))$ is shown in figure 11.

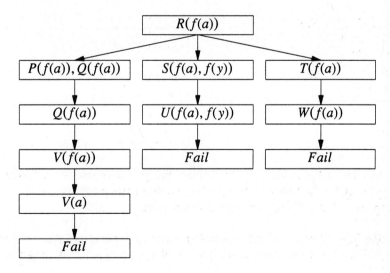

Figure 11

So $R(f(a))$ does not follow from the program. However, $\neg R(f(a))$ does, by the closed-world assumption.

(c) The SLD-resolution tree is shown in figure 12.

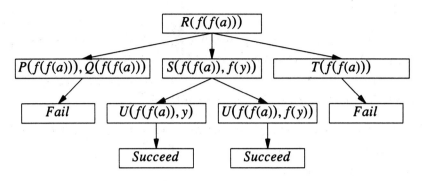

Figure 12

So $R(f(f(a)))$ does follow from the program.

5.9   Exercises

Exercise 5.1   Consider the following propositional logic program using Prolog notation.

$$T :- S, W, P, Q$$
$$U :- P, Q, R, S, T$$
$$U :- V, W$$
$$U :- M$$
$$T :- N$$
$$V :- R$$
$$W :- P, Q$$
$$P$$
$$R$$
$$Q$$

Construct an SLD-resolution tree for the query U and provide a formal resolution proof of the fact that U can be derived from the program.

Show also that $\neg T$ follows from the program.

Exercise 5.2   Give a formal resolution proof and construct the resolution tree to show that P is a semantic consequence of the propositional program:

$$P :- Q, R, S$$
$$Q :- T$$
$$P :- W$$
$$W :- T$$

W :- V, R
T
S

Exercise 5.3 Construct an algorithm which takes any propositional program and a propositional query and always answers the question

'Can we show that $P \vdash Q$, where $\vdash$ is deduction using only SLD-resolution and the closed-world assumption?'

Exercise 5.4 Find formulae in prenex form provably equivalent to the following:

(a) $\forall x \, S(x) \Rightarrow \exists z \, \forall y \, R(z, y)$;
(b) $\forall x (R(x, y) \wedge \neg \forall y \, R(x, y))$;
(c) $\forall x (R(x, y) \Rightarrow \forall y \, S(x)) \Rightarrow (\exists y \, S(y) \Rightarrow \forall z \, R(y, z))$;
(d) $\exists x (R(x, y) \vee \neg \forall y \, S(x)) \Rightarrow (\neg \exists y \, S(y) \wedge \forall z \, S(y))$;
(e) $\exists x \, R(x, y) \vee (S(x) \wedge \neg \exists z \, R(a, z))$;
(f) $\exists x (S(x) \Rightarrow R(x, y)) \Rightarrow (\exists y \, A(y) \Rightarrow \forall z \, B(y, z))$;
(g) $\forall x \, R(x, y) \wedge (\neg S(z) \vee \neg \forall z \, R(x, z))$.

Exercise 5.5 Show that for every *wff* A of system K there is a *wff* A' in prenex form such that $\vdash_K A \Leftrightarrow A'$.

Hint: Use induction on the construction of A.

Exercise 5.6 Extend the algorithm for converting a formula into prenex form to include the connectives $\Leftrightarrow$, $\downarrow$, $\nleftrightarrow$ and $/$.

Use your algorithm to find formulae in prenex form which are provably equivalent to the following:

(a) $\forall x \, S(x) \Leftrightarrow \forall z \, \forall y (R(z, y) \downarrow \exists z \, S(z))$;
(b) $\forall x (R(x, y) \nleftrightarrow \forall y (R(x, y) / \forall z \, R(y, z))$.

Exercise 5.7 Skolemize the formulae given in exercise 5.4 and exercise 5.6.

Exercise 5.8 Convert the formulae given in exercise 5.4 and exercise 5.6 into clausal form.

Exercise 5.9 Find the Herbrand universes, bases and least Herbrand models of the following logic programs:

(a) $S(x)$:- $R(f(x))$
        $S(g(x))$:- $S(f(x))$
        $S(g(a))$:- $S(f(b))$
        $R(f(a))$
        $R(f(b))$

(b) $S(g(x)) :\text{-} R(x, f(x))$
      $S(g(y)) :\text{-} R(y, f(b))$
      $R(a, f(b))$
      $R(b, f(b))$

(c) the program given in example 5.16;
(d) the program given in example 5.17;
(e) the program given in example 5.18.

Exercise 5.10   Show that the following substitution identities hold.
Let θ, σ and γ be substitutions. Then

(a) $\theta \circ \varepsilon = \varepsilon \circ \theta = \theta$;
(b) $(t\theta) \circ \sigma = t(\theta \circ \sigma)$, for all terms t;
(c) $(\theta \circ \sigma) \circ \gamma = \theta \circ (\sigma \circ \gamma)$.

Exercise 5.11   Let θ be an MGU of a set of terms N and let σ be a variable renaming substitution. Show that $\theta \circ \sigma$ is also an MGU of N.

Exercise 5.12   Find the most general unifier if it exists (if not report the fact) of the following sets of terms:

(a) $N = \{f(g(a), g(b)), f(y, y)\}$;
(b) $N = \{f(x, g(b)), f(g(x), y)\}$;
(c) $N = \{h(g(a), e(x), f(a, y)), h(x, e(g(a)), f(y, y))\}$;
(d) $N = \{h(g(x), e(x), f(a, y)), h(y, e(g(a)), f(y, y))\}$;
(e) $N = \{f(g(x), y, h(x)), f(z, b, b), f(y, y, y)\}$.

Exercise 5.13   Construct the SLD-resolution tree when the logic program given in example 5.16 is presented with the queries:

(a) $s(a)$;
(b) $s(b)$;
(c) $s(X)$.

Exercise 5.14   Construct the SLD-resolution tree when the logic program given in example 5.18 is presented with the queries:

(a) $m(b)$;
(b) $\neg m(c)$.

Exercise 5.15   Write computer programs to emulate some of the processes described in this chapter.

(a) Convert a formula in predicate logic to prenex form, and then to clausal form.

(b) State whether or not a formula in clausal form is a Horn clause.
(c) State whether or not a set of formulae forms a logic program.
(d) Given a logic program, offer a user possible pairs of statements which could be combined under the *Res* rule.
(e) Write a program to perform the unification algorithm on a set of terms to find their MGU.

Reference

1. J. A. Robinson, A machine oriented logic based on the resolution principle, *Journal of the Association for Computing Machinery* **12**, 23–41.

CHAPTER 6

Formal system specification

6.1 Introduction

The Z language is a mathematical notation for the description of models of real-world systems. It makes heavy use of both set theory and logic, with the emphasis on the logic of the system rather than the numeric predictions provided by, for example, differential equations. The intention is to be able to specify exactly the workings of a system (such as an oil-tanker terminal, a hotel booking system, or an aircraft control system) and then to be able to use this definition in various ways.

(a) We will be able to prove certain properties of the system directly from the specification, for example that it is consistent (there are no parts giving contradictory statements), and that it is complete (every possible situation is accounted for).
(b) We wish to be able to answer questions about the system, for example 'Can such and such a situation ever arise?'
(c) We would ideally like to be able to produce computer programs directly from the specification, or be able to confirm that an existing program conforms to the specification.

The automated logical proof methods of the preceding chapter will assist in the mechanization of all of these processes.

These objectives have not yet been achieved in full, but many companies are using this (or an equivalent) technique as part of their overall design process.

There remains always, of course, the problem of 'proving' that our mathematics (which we have proved consistent and complete) actually represents the real-world problem that we are trying to represent. This is done informally by 'animating' the specification, so that its behaviour can be compared with what the user expects to happen.

There are several techniques for giving formal specifications. We will describe Z, developed at Oxford University and used by IBM, which is widely accepted and makes extensive use of predicate logic.

We will first introduce the basic ideas of Z by going through a simple example. We will then cover it more formally, and finally define an algebra based on complete units. Appendix A covers the mathematical theory needed for this chapter.

6.1.1   A simple example

Z specifications may be written in a linear form, but appear more frequently in diagrammatic form. The specification is broken down into small units called 'schema', each of which may be thought of as a unit like a programming module. Each schema will have a declaration part and a logical or predicate part. The *declaration part* above the line defines the identifiers to be used in the schema, and the set of objects over which their values may range. In the *predicate part* below the line, we list a number of logical predicates, all of which must be true in the real world that the schema represents. Identifiers followed by a prime indicate the values of objects after the action has taken place. Identifiers followed by a question mark indicate input values (the particular technique for input is immaterial), identifiers followed by an exclamation mark indicate output values.

6.1.2   A state schema

Suppose that we wish to keep a list of people's heights and weights. We decide first that we will maintain a set of the people whose heights and weights we are remembering, and two functions to deliver each person's height and weight, respectively. We may want a particular possible state of our system to be

> $known\text{-}height = \{Pauline, Eric\}$,
>
> $known\text{-}weight = \{Pauline, Eric\}$,
>
> $height = \{(Pauline, 6\ feet\ and\ 3\ inches), (Eric, 5\ feet\ and\ 2\ inches)\}$,
>
> $weight = \{(Pauline, 7\ stones\ and\ 2\ pounds)$,
>
> $\qquad\qquad\qquad\qquad\qquad (Eric, 17\ stones\ and\ 10\ pounds)\}$.

The above statements define the object *known* to be a set of names (two names in this case), *height* to be a function* mapping names to heights and *weight* to be a function mapping names to weights. They could equally well be written

> $height = \{(Pauline \mapsto 6\ feet\ and\ 3\ inches), (Eric \mapsto 5\ feet\ and\ 2\ inches)\}$,
>
> $weight = \{(Pauline \mapsto 7\ stones\ and\ 2\ pounds)$,
>
> $\qquad\qquad\qquad\qquad (Eric \mapsto 17\ stones\ and\ 10\ pounds)\}$.

---

*The word *function* in this chapter refers to finite or infinite functions which map from an argument space (their domain) to a result space (their range). Finite or discrete functions will be considered as sets of pairs of objects, where each pair represents a particular domain value and the corresponding range value onto which it maps.

The symbol $\mapsto$ is read as 'maps on to', so that the height example reads "height is a function which maps 'Pauline' onto '6 feet and 3 inches' and 'Eric' onto '5 feet and 2 inches'". A function is just a set of pairs of values, and can be handled using any set operators. More details of functions appear later in this chapter.

The Z *state-space* definition or *state schema* describes the logic of the overall state of our system, and is written

[*NAME, HEIGHT, WEIGHT*]

```
 ___ Height_and_Weight _____
     known_height : P NAME
     known_weight : P NAME
     height : NAME ↦ HEIGHT
     weight : NAME ↦ WEIGHT
    _____

     known_height = dom height
     known_weight = dom weight
 _____
```

The initial line

[*NAME, HEIGHT, WEIGHT*]

declares that *NAME*, *HEIGHT* and *WEIGHT* are three basic data types which we will not be defining further in this specification. The particular form used will depend on particular implementations, such as the particular measurements to be used. The schema declares that *known_height* and *known_weight* are to be sets of *NAME*s (even though we have not defined exactly what a *NAME* is), that *height* and *weight* are to be partial functions which will act on a *NAME* to give a *HEIGHT* or a *WEIGHT*, respectively, (whatever a *HEIGHT* or *WEIGHT* may turn out to be). *NAME*, *HEIGHT* and *WEIGHT* may well be infinite types. The symbol $\mathbb{P}$ means 'power set of', so that if *known_height* is of type $\mathbb{P}$*NAME*, then it is a set of *NAME*s. A partial function is a function from a subset of its left-hand type, not defined for every possible member of the left-hand type. The fact that *NAME*, *HEIGHT* and *WEIGHT* are not further defined here will not affect the logic of our specification. It will allow us flexibility later when the system implementation stage is envisaged.

The lower part of the schema consists of logical statements which define the system, in this case two lines which declare that:

(a) the set *known_height* is to be exactly equal to the *domain* of the *height* function;

(b) the set *known_weight* is to be exactly equal to the *domain* of the *weight* function.

The domain of a function is the set of names for which the function can provide a mapping. This part of the schema declares logical statements which are always true, and are *invariants* of the system. If there are several statements in the predicate part, their order is immaterial: they all represent conditions which must be true.

Note that *known_height* and *known_weight* are derived objects. They are not strictly necessary, because anywhere they occur, we could write 'dom *height*' or 'dom *weight*' instead. However, it will make definitions more easily readable if we use the identifiers *known_height* and *known_weight*.

Much of Z is based on readability. No definition is sensible unless it can easily be read. A full Z document will also have sections written in English which explain the significance of the Z schema.

6.1.3   Operations or events and their schema

We can declare the action of adding a new height to the list as the schema

$$
\begin{array}{l}
\_\_\ New\_Height \ _____ \\
\hline
\quad \Delta Height\_and\_Weight \\
\quad name?:NAME \\
\quad hgt?:HEIGHT \\
\hline
\quad name? \notin known\_height \\
\quad height' = height \cup \{name? \mapsto hgt?\} \\
\quad weight' = weight \\
\hline
\end{array}
$$

This is known as an *operation schema* since it describes the change to the system brought about by a given operation or event. (Do not confuse the $\mapsto$ symbol with the $\leftrightarrow$ symbol. In this definition we could have used a comma instead of the $\mapsto$.) When we have more than one line in the predicate part, the separate lines are considered to be conjuncted together; the order of lines is immaterial.

In this schema we state on the first line that the schema *Height_and_Weight* (declared elsewhere) will be used, with both its declarations and predicates. The Δ symbol in front of the name indicates that we wish to use this schema in association with a state change. In any state change, a primed identifier indicates the value after the change, the unprimed identifier represents the value before the change. By including the schema $\Delta Height\_and\_Weight$ we are automatically including all of the declarations (from *Height_and_Weight*)

$$known\_height, known\_height' : \mathbb{P}\,NAME$$

$$known\_weight, known\_weight' : \mathbb{P}\,NAME$$

$$height, height' : NAME \leftrightarrow HEIGHT$$

$$weight, weight' : NAME \leftrightarrow WEIGHT$$

in the upper part of the schema, copies of the *Height_and_Weight* schema declarations both without and with primes. The *ΔHeight_and_Weight* also causes the predicates from *Height_and_Weight* to be included in the predicate part, with two versions representing the predicates both before and after the operation. In the predicate part we will thus have the invariants

$known\_height = \mathrm{dom}\, height$

$known\_height' = \mathrm{dom}\, height'$

$known\_weight = \mathrm{dom}\, weight$

$known\_weight' = \mathrm{dom}\, weight'$

from *Height_and_Weight*.

We also declare that there will be an input argument *name?* (the terminating question mark indicates that it is an input value) of type *NAME*, and a second input argument *hgt?* of type *HEIGHT*. From the point of view of Z, we are not interested in just how the value will be input (whether by voice, or using a mouse, or typing at a keyboard in one of a choice of formats), our logic merely wishes to know that it is an input.

Note the predicate

$name? \notin known\_height.$

This predicate is known for obvious reasons as a *pre-condition*, defining conditions which must hold when the operation starts. The second and third predicates are *post-conditions* and describe the conditions after the operation has occurred. We could also describe

$known\_height = \mathrm{dom}\, height$

and

$known\_weight = \mathrm{dom}\, weight$

as pre-conditions, and

$known\_height' = \mathrm{dom}\, height'$

and

$known\_weight' = \mathrm{dom}\, weight'$

as post-conditions.

6.1.3.1   Consistency checks

After the operation has taken place, we would expect that the condition

$known\_height' = known\_height \cup \{name?\}$

would hold. This can now be proved true by straightforward mathematical techniques (which can be mechanized) from the other predicates. One feature of formal techniques is the ability to perform consistency proofs of this type. Alternatively we could add this as an additional predicate, and use the mathematics to check the consistency of the predicates.

6.1.3.2   Observation schema

An *observation schema* is one which provides information about the state of the system, without changing that state. To find a given person's weight, for example, we use the schema*

```
__ Find_Weight _____
      ΞHeight_and_Weight
      name? : NAME
      wgt! : WEIGHT
   _____

      name? ∈ known_weight
      wgt! = weight name?
_____
```

This is a schema delivering information, in which no change to the system occurs. We will refer to it as an *observation schema* or *query schema* or *information schema*. The declaration ΞHeight_and_Weight on the first line is an extension of the ΔHeight_and_Weight idea introduced earlier. It introduces the ΔHeight_and_Weight schema (the declarations and predicates of the Height_and_Weight schema both before and after the operation) and, since we have an observation schema with no change in the system data, it provides the additional predicates

$$known\_height' = known\_height$$

$$known\_weight' = known\_weight$$

$$height' = height$$

$$weight' = weight$$

indicating no change to the system data (the system state). The Ξ version of an included schema introduces similar equality predicates for all identifiers declared in the declaration part of the schema. The exclamation mark in 'wgt!' indicates that this is an output object. As with input items, we do not specify just how it will be output, whether as a computer display, or a flashing light, or as sound.

It is possible to construct a schema which will have as inputs a specific height and weight and will have as output the set of people (that we know about) who have both that height and that weight. This again is an observation schema with no changes to the data in the system.

*Note that some writers use *weight(name?)* instead of *weight name?*, putting the function argument in parentheses. Use whichever notation you find clearest.

```
┌─── Who_is_that_high_and_that_heavy ──────────────────────┐
│    ΞHeight_and_Weight                                     │
│    hgt? : HEIGHT                                          │
│    wgt? : WEIGHT                                          │
│    names! : ℙ NAME                                        │
├──────────────────────────────────────────────────────────┤
│    names! = {n : known_height | heightn = hgt?} ∩         │
│                     {n : known_weight | weight n = wgt?}  │
└──────────────────────────────────────────────────────────┘
```

The set notation used on the last line here is explained in the mathematical material in appendix A.

6.1.3.3   Error messages and the like

We will need in some cases to produce error messages or warnings, perhaps when the input data does not make sense. We do not wish to clutter up our definitions above, since they would then cease to be easily readable. The above schema defines the correct behaviour of our system.

We will first define a new variable type called a *free type definition* as follows:

$$REPORT ::= ok \mid Height\_Already\_Known \mid Height\_Not\_Known$$

$$\mid Weight\_Already\_Known \mid Weight\_Not\_Known$$

This says that any variable of type *REPORT* can take one of five values, referred to by us as *ok*, *Height_Already_Known*, *Height_Not_Known*, *Weight_Already_Known* or *Weight_Not_Known*.

We need one extra schema to define a successful result.

```
┌─── Success ──────────────────────────────────────────────┐
│    report! : REPORT                                       │
├──────────────────────────────────────────────────────────┤
│    report! = ok                                           │
└──────────────────────────────────────────────────────────┘
```

The first line states that five possible reports may arise from operations to do with our height and weight system, represented by the variable *report!*. The Z-schema calculus enables us to combine schema with logical operators, and the schema expression

$$New\_Height \wedge Success$$

gives a schema which combines the declaration parts (the union of the two declaration parts, all the declarations from both schema) and combines the predicate parts of the two schema (combined using the given logical operator, ∧ in this case). The above example will thus effectively add the declaration report! : *REPORT*

to the *New_Height* declaration part, and the condition

report! = ok

to the *New_Height* predicate part.

For each possible error, we can now add a different value with which *report!* is identified, and combine further schema. For the situation where we are adding a new height entry but the height of the person we are adding is already known to the system, we define an extra schema denoting the error condition and the particular state of the *report!* variable we want. This is

```
┌─ Height_Already_Known ──────────────────────────┐
│    ΞHeight_and_Weight                            │
│    name? : NAME                                  │
│    report! : REPORT                              │
│ ────────────────────────                         │
│    name? ∈ known_height                          │
│    report! = height_already_known                │
└──────────────────────────────────────────────────┘
```

The two predicates represent the error condition *name?* ∈ *known_height* and the way we will express it *report!* = *height_already_known*. We can create an 'error handling' version of *New_Height* by using the schema expression

(*New_Height* ∧ *Success*) ∨ *Height_Already_Known*.

This combines the schema *New_Height* and *Success* as described earlier to represent a successful operation, and then performs a logical ∨ with the schema representing an error. We can define this expression to be a new schema by writing (the symbol ≜ is read as 'is defined to be')

Full_New_Height ≜ (*New_Height* ∧ *Success*) ∨ *Height_Already_Known*.

We could instead have added extra parts to the ``ew_Height* schema, but this would have made it less readable.

The combined schema, if written in expanded form in full, would appear as follows:

```
┌─ Full_New_Height ───────────────────────────────┐
│    known_height, known_height' : ℙNAME           │
│    known_weight, known_weight' : ℙNAME           │
│    height, height' : NAME ↦ HEIGHT               │
│    weight, weight' : NAME ↦ WEIGHT               │
│    name? : NAME                                  │
│    hgt? : HEIGHT                                 │
```

$$
\begin{array}{|l}
\hline
\quad report! : REPORT \\
\hline
\quad (name? \notin known\_height \wedge \\
\qquad height' = height \cup \{name? \mapsto hgt?\} \wedge \\
\qquad weight' = weight \wedge \\
\qquad known\_height = \mathrm{dom}\, height \wedge \\
\qquad known\_weight = \mathrm{dom}\, weight \wedge \\
\qquad known\_height' = \mathrm{dom}\, height' \wedge \\
\qquad known\_weight' = \mathrm{dom}\, weight' \wedge \\
\qquad report! = ok) \\
\vee \\
\quad (name? \in known\_height \wedge \\
\qquad height' = height \wedge \\
\qquad weight' = weight \wedge \\
\qquad known\_height = \mathrm{dom}\, height \wedge \\
\qquad known\_weight = \mathrm{dom}\, weight \wedge \\
\qquad known\_height' = \mathrm{dom}\, height' \wedge \\
\qquad known\_weight' = \mathrm{dom}\, weight' \wedge \\
\qquad report! = Height\_Already\_Known) \\
\hline
\end{array}
$$

We now need to improve in a similar way the schema for finding the weight of a named person. The error which can now occur is that the person whose weight is being sought is not known to the system. The additional schema representing the condition that the named person's weight is not known, $name? \notin known\_weight$, and the assertion of the report value, $report! = weight\_not\_known$, is written as

$$
\begin{array}{|l}
\hline
\quad Weight\_Not\_Known \\
\hline
\quad \Xi Height\_and\_Weight \\
\quad name? : NAME \\
\quad report! : REPORT \\
\hline
\quad name? \notin known\_weight \\
\quad report! = weight\_not\_known \\
\hline
\end{array}
$$

For a full version of the *Find_Weight* schema, we can define

$$Full\_Find\_Weight \triangleq (Find\_Weight \wedge Success) \vee Weight\_Not\_Known.$$

If a schema cannot fail, then it is possible to construct a conjunction of that schema with a *Success* schema for consistency and to ensure that every schema includes an assertion about the *report!* variable.

We may similarly have other schema-checking access permissions which are combined with basic retrieval schema in a similar way. This avoids cluttering up the schema which handle the normal working of the system with every possible error condition.

We will probably want to make logical consistency checks to ensure that

(a) every possibility produces a message;
(b) no two messages conflict.

In the above examples, the *New_Height* schema includes the predicate *name?* ∉ *known_height* and is alternated with a schema containing the predicate *name?* ∈ *known_height*. The two schema being combined with the operator ∨ are thus mutually exclusive. The predicate *name?* ∉ *known_weight* and its negation appear in both parts of the second example.

6.1.4   Pre- and post-conditions

The concept of *pre-conditions* and *post-conditions* is very important in descriptions of systems which change with time. The value of a variable after a given operation is indicated by the name having a prime after it. The effect of any operation of a system will be described by logical relationships between the values of variables after the operation and the values before.

Example   The transaction operation will update the value of the global variable *till_state* upon input of one integer parameter *transaction*. If *transaction* is greater than or equal to 1000, then *till_state* is to be set to 2; otherwise *till_state* is to be set to the value 1. The value of *transaction* will be greater than zero on entry and will not be changed by the procedure. The value of *till_state* on entry will be 1 or 2.

The pre-condition is defined to be the conditions which must hold before the operation. In this case it is

$$transaction \geqslant 0 \wedge (till\_state = 1 \vee till\_state = 2).$$

Note the assumption here that the $\geqslant$ and $=$ have highest priority; $\wedge$ and $\vee$ have a lower priority. The post-condition (the conditions that must hold after the operation) is

$$(transaction \geqslant 1000 \Rightarrow till\_state' = 2)$$
$$\wedge (transaction < 1000 \Rightarrow till\_state' = 1)$$
$$\wedge transaction' = transaction.$$

6.2   Notational differences

There are some differences in notation of predicate logic in Z when compared with the preceding chapters. When using quantifiers, we previously had the concept of a 'universe of discourse'. All quantified variables took values ranging over the domain of this universe. If we wish to consider subsets of the universe we will precede all relevant logical predicates by an implication such as

$$\forall x(is\_an\_integer(x) \Rightarrow Pred(x))$$

to restrict a consideration to the set of all integers. The above statement effectively applies the predicate $Pred(x)$ to members of that subset of our universe satisfying the property $is\_an\_integer$.

In practical applications of formal specifications, we may wish to talk of 'For all oil tankers waiting to dock' or of 'For all users currently logged in ...' or of 'There exists a spare part in stock ...'. Z therefore uses a slightly extended notation for quantifiers in which every quantified variable is followed by a specification of the set over which the values range. The statement 'For all values of x in the set S the logical expression $P(x) \wedge Q(x)$ holds' is written

$$\forall x : S \bullet P(x) \wedge Q(x).$$

For sets consisting of all the integers in a given numeric range, we follow Pascal notation and write the set of integers from 1 to 100 inclusive as '1 .. 100'. For the set of natural numbers including zero $(0, 1, 2, ...)$ we write $\mathbb{N}$, for the natural numbers starting at 1 we write $\mathbb{N}_1$, and for all integers (negative, zero and positive) $\mathbb{Z}$.

We also have a notation for multiple variables ranging over the same set, written as, for example,

$$\forall i, j, k : S_1 \bullet \ ...$$

(three variables i, j and k ranging over the set S_1) and variables over different sets as in

$$\forall i, j, k : S_1 ; \ x, y, z : S_2 \bullet \ ...$$

(where i, j and k range over set S_1 and x, y and z over S_2).

The Z language also defines some quantifiers in addition to *for all*, $\forall$, and *there exists*, $\exists$. These are introduced to simplify the notation.

Unique exists.   This is written

$$\exists! x : S \bullet \langle logical \ expr \rangle$$

and has the meaning 'There exists exactly one x in S such that ...'. It can of course be defined in terms of existing quantifiers and is not fundamentally new. The result is logical, either T or F. To express the fact that every natural number has a unique number which follows it (we use the function $succ(n)$ to define the number following n) we could write

$$\forall n : \mathbb{N} \bullet \exists! m : \mathbb{N} \bullet m = succ(n).$$

How many exist?   This is written

$$\Omega x : S \bullet \langle logical\ expr \rangle$$

and gives a numeric (not logical) result which is the number of elements in the given set satisfying the given predicate. Note that

$$\exists x : S \bullet P(x) \Leftrightarrow (\Omega x : S \bullet P(x)) > 0,$$

$$\exists! x : S \bullet P(x) \Leftrightarrow (\Omega x : S \bullet P(x)) = 1.$$

We could perhaps use

$$\Omega account : all\_accounts \bullet balance\ account < 0$$

to express the total number of overdrawn accounts at the bank, where *all_accounts* is the set of all accounts at the bank, and *balance account* is a numeric function which delivers the current value of the account.

Summation.   This is written

$$\Sigma x : S \bullet \langle numeric\ expr \rangle.$$

It sums numeric functions over all the elements in the named set and gives a numeric result. To add together the values of all the accounts at a given bank we could write

$$\Sigma account : all\_accounts \bullet balance\ account.$$

When employing the above quantifiers, be careful that you use logical and numerical expressions ($\forall$, $\exists$ and Ω are followed by a logical expression, Σ uses a numeric expression) and results ($\forall$ and $\exists$ deliver logical results, Ω and Σ deliver numeric results) in their correct places.

Conventions for the empty set (written { }) are that:

$\forall x : \{\ \} \bullet P(x)$ is true;
$\exists x : \{\ \} \bullet P(x)$ is false;
$\exists! x : \{\ \} \bullet P(x)$ is false;
$\Omega x : \{\ \} \bullet P(x)$ is zero;
$\Sigma x : \{\ \} \bullet N(x)$ is zero.

6.3   The Z specification language

A typical Z document will consist of mathematical definitions interspersed with English text. The Z text is written as schema, starting with basic definitions and system constraints (one or more *state schema*), then going on to definitions of systems actions (some of which will change the system, others will be interrogative), and ending with the proofs of various theorems which are necessary for the guaranteed consistency of the definition. Each of the Z units will be supported by appropriate English informal descriptive text.

Z schema are written in pictorial form with the name on the opening line, the declaration(s) in the upper part, and the conjuncted predicates in the lower part. The name of the schema is an identifier, starting with a letter, followed by optional other letters or digits or underscores. The identifiers for the objects used inside the schema are the same as for schema names, but this time can be followed by a terminating decoration. Details are given below.

Schema can be written in either a pictorial or linear form. The pictorial representation of a schema looks like the *Height_and_Weight* examples given earlier. The equivalent non-pictorial or *linear* representation is

$$Height\_and\_Weight \triangleq [known\_height, known\_weight : \mathbb{P}\,NAME;$$

$$height : NAME \nrightarrow HEIGHT; \; weight : NAME \nrightarrow WEIGHT$$

$$|\; known\_height = \mathrm{dom}\,height \wedge known\_weight = \mathrm{dom}\,weight].$$

The declaration part (on separate lines above the short horizontal line, or separated by semi-colons before the vertical bar) consists of definitions of the identifiers and the types of the objects they represent. The predicate part consists of a number of logical predicates (on separate lines or separated by $\wedge$ operators) all of which must be satisfied for the schema to hold. The schema as a whole referred to by name represents the set of declarations plus the conjunction of all of its predicates.

6.3.1   Basic type definitions

Any types which are not defined elsewhere (such as *HEIGHT*, *WEIGHT* and *NAME* in the *Height_and_Weight* example) must be declared before the first schema in the form

[*NAME*, *HEIGHT*, *WEIGHT*]

The correct title for this is a *basic type definition*.

6.3.2   Free type definitions

At the outer level of a specification, we can also have free type definitions. These are typified by

MESSAGE ::= *OK* | *NotKnown* | *AlreadyKnown*.

They define the possible values of types such as messages. This example creates three global objects *OK*, *NotKnown* and *AlreadyKnown* of type *MES-SAGE*. These identifiers cannot be used elsewhere in the specification.

6.3.3   Schema inclusion

We can include in the declaration part of a schema the name of another existing schema. This has the effect of including the other schema's declarations in this schema's declaration part, and of including its predicates in this one's predicate part.

The declaration parts are combined together by union; there must be no declaration clashes (the same identifier defined as two different types). The predicates in both predicate parts are unioned together, which implies that they are ∧-ed together.

6.3.4   Schema types

There are three main and distinct purposes for schema, and we will refer informally to schema in these categories as *state schema*, *operation schema* and *observation schema*.

The *state schema* make overall statements about the system being specified, and may be called *order-schema*, or *state-space schema*. They may include limits set by management (no file bigger than x blocks, no customer has a debt larger than d pounds, no more than q customers in the queue), and fundamental logical constraints (there must be at least one account for every bank customer, there must be a price for every type of object in stock, the value of *total-cash* must always equal the sum of the amounts in all of the cash tills).

Operation schema describe the effect of certain operations which change the state or data in the system, such as, for example, adding a new customer for the bank, or removing a whole queue of vehicles waiting for a ferry. They will involve pre-conditions specifying constraints before the operation, and predicates relating the state of the data after the operation to the state before the operation.

Observation schema correspond to information retrieval commands, in which the system data does not change. However, there will usually be pre-conditions for the information to be available (the name typed must be that of an existing customer) and there may be minor data changes such as the appearance of an output or error message.

6.3.4.1   State schema

State schema describe the overall model. They may specify fundamental relations such as the following:

> We have a set *all_videos* of objects of type *VIDEO*, a subset of them *in_stock* which are held at the video store, and a subset *booked_out* which have been booked out. A video owned by the shop must be in one of the latter two sets.

An appropriate state schema would be

[*VIDEO*]

```
┌─ Video_shop ────────────────────────────────────┐
│    all_videos, in_stock, booked_out : ℙ VIDEO     │
│──────────────────────────────────────────────────│
│    in_stock ∪ booked_out = all_videos             │
└──────────────────────────────────────────────────┘
```

We will also need a similar schema to confirm that these conditions hold after any operation has changed the values of some of the objects.

```
┌─ Video_shop′ ───────────────────────────────────────┐
│    all_videos′, in_stock′, booked_out′ : ℙ VIDEO      │
│──────────────────────────────────────────────────────│
│    in_stock′ ∪ booked_out′ = all_videos′              │
└──────────────────────────────────────────────────────┘
```

From now on, if we declare a schema such as *Video_shop*, then by definition the schema *Video_shop′* will be the same schema with primes added to every identifier. This is called an *ornamentation* of the schema identifier.

There may be other parts of a state schema which are not logical invariants, but which express certain management-defined imposed limits, such as that the number of videos owned by the shop must be less than a given value. In this example, the maximum value would be an integer, declared as

$max\_videos : \mathbb{N}$

and the corresponding predicate would be

$\#all\_videos \leq max\_videos$

to limit the number of videos in the shop. (Remember that the cardinality operator # gives the number of members in a set.)

6.3.4.2 Operation schema

We will then have operation schema which represent operations involving changes to the system. Each of these should be thought of first as a paragraph in an English language document describing what the system is to do. We might have a paragraph as follows:

> *Returning a video.* There is to be an operation representing returning of a video to the shop. The video's name will be given. This video is to be removed from the *booked_out* set and added to the *in_stock* set. The video must not already be in the *in_stock* set.

The schema for this would be

```
┌─ Video_returned ──────────────────────────────────┐
│  ΔVideo_shop                                        │
│  video? : VIDEO                                     │
├─────────────────────────────────────────────────── │
│  video? ∈ booked_out                                │
│  booked_out′ = booked_out − {video?}                │
│  in_stock′ = in_stock ∪ {video?}                    │
│  all_videos′ = all_videos                           │
└─────────────────────────────────────────────────── ┘
```

The first internal line uses *schema inclusion*. We are including in this schema the declarations and predicates of both the schemas *Video_shop* and *Video_shop′*. This gives us the declarations and types of *all_videos*, *in_stock* and *booked_out* and their primed counterparts, and gives the conditions (predicates) that *in_stock* and *booked_out* should combine by union to equal the whole of *all_videos* both before and after the operation.

The next line in the declaration part indicates that we will be given an input value *video?* of type *VIDEO*. A question mark after any identifier indicates that it represents an input argument. The above schema is thus equivalent if written out in full to

```
┌─ Video_returned ──────────────────────────────────┐
│  all_videos, in_stock, booked_out : ℙ VIDEO         │
│  all_videos′, in_stock′, booked_out′ : ℙ VIDEO      │
│  video? : VIDEO                                     │
├─────────────────────────────────────────────────── │
│  in_stock ∪ booked_out = all_videos                 │
│  in_stock′ ∪ booked_out′ = all_videos               │
│  video? ∈ booked_out                                │
│  booked_out′ = booked_out − {video?}                │
│  in_stock′ = in_stock ∪ {video?}                    │
│  all_videos′ = all_videos                           │
└─────────────────────────────────────────────────── ┘
```

For the moment we will assume that every data object must be mentioned, even if it has not changed. Some Z users use a default that data items not mentioned remain unchanged.

Another operation might be described in English as follows:

Removal of a video from the shop's stock. References to the named video must be removed from the *all_videos* list, and from any *in_stock* or *booked_out* lists. The named video must be in the set *all_videos*.

The schema for this would be

```
┌── RemoveVideo ─────────────────────────────────────────┐
│  ΔVideo_shop                                            │
│  video? : VIDEO                                         │
│ ───────────────────────────                            │
│  video? ∈ all_videos                                    │
│  all_videos' = all_videos − {video?}                    │
│  in_stock' = in_stock − {video?}                        │
│  booked_out' = booked_out − {video?}                    │
└─────────────────────────────────────────────────────────┘
```

We do not need to know which of the two subsets of *all_videos* contains the video. We could write the schema

```
┌── RemoveVideo ─────────────────────────────────────────┐
│  ΔVideo_shop                                            │
│  video? : VIDEO                                         │
│ ───────────────────────────                            │
│  video? ∈ all_videos                                    │
│  all_videos' = all_videos − {video?}                    │
│  video? ∈ in_stock ⇒ in_stock' = in_stock − {video?}    │
│  video? ∉ in_stock ⇒ in_stock' = in_stock              │
│  video? ∈ booked_out ⇒ booked_out' = booked_out − {video?} │
│  video? ∉ booked_out ⇒ booked_out' = booked_out        │
└─────────────────────────────────────────────────────────┘
```

We could at this stage prove mathematically the consistency of the above, that if the predicates of the state schema hold before the operation, then they will also hold after the operation. This facility for the mathematical proof of various facts about a Z specification is one of the vital reasons for its use in complex computer systems.

6.3.4.3 Observation or query schema

Observation schema deliver information, but do not affect the state of the model.

We may require a schema to ask whether a named video is in stock or not. We need a new free type to express whether or not the video is in.

$$MESSAGE ::= is\_in\_stock \mid is\_booked\_out$$

and the schema is then

```
┌── FindVideo ───────────────────────────────────────────┐
│  ΞVideo_shop                                            │
│  video? : VIDEO                                         │
│  message! : MESSAGE                                     │
│ ───────────────────────────                            │
│                                                         │
```

$$
\begin{array}{|l}
\hline
video? \in all\_videos \\
video? \in in\_stock \Rightarrow message! = is\_in\_stock \\
video? \notin in\_stock \Rightarrow message! = is\_booked\_out \\
\hline
\end{array}
$$

Notice that output information in the form of messages must be defined in a new type as shown above. This enables consistency proofs to be performed on the Z definition.

There are obviously many equally valid slight variants of the above schema.

The schema name $\Xi SchemaName$ includes the combination of two schema (unprimed and primed) as for $\Delta SchemaName$, and additional predicates for all declared objects that their values are unchanged by the operation (that the primed values equal their unprimed values).

The type $MESSAGE$ above is not further defined as far as the Z specification of the system in concerned. It is enough for us to define that meaning that must be presented somewhere by the message; we are not concerned at the means of presentation.

As a second example of an observation schema, there may be a paragraph in the specification:

> There will be a command which will list the names of all the videos.

Such a schema would have no input argument, and its output would be a set of $VIDEO$s. It would perhaps be written

$$
\begin{array}{|l}
\hline
\quad ListVideos \\
\hline
\Xi Video\_shop \\
list! : \mathbb{P}\, VIDEO \\
\hline
list! = all\_videos \\
\hline
\end{array}
$$

6.3.5   Example: a computer file system

6.3.5.1   State schema

We wish formally to specify certain aspects of a simple computer filing system. This example is similar to one used by Ince [1] and is developed further at the end of the chapter. We assume without further definition the following basic type definitions.

$USERS$	the set of all possible user names;
$FILE\_NAMES$	the set of all possible file names;
$BLOCK\_NOS$	the set of all possible block numbers.

$USERS$ is the set of all the people who may use the system, $FILE\_NAMES$ is the set of all possible names for files (and we will assume for simplicity that all files have distinct names) and *BLOCK_NOS* is the set of the numbers of all the blocks on the disc, areas of a standard size that are available to be used for storing the information in the files. A file may need several blocks.

owns is a function mapping usernames to sets of filenames, which are the files owned by that user. A typical example might be

$$owns = \{(Eric, \{file_1, file_2\}), (Edmund, \{prog_1\})\}.$$

In this example *Eric* owns the two files $file_1$ and $file_2$, and *Edmund* owns the file $prog_1$. We can then write as true logical statements:

$$owns\ Eric = \{file_1, file_2\}; \qquad owns\ Edmund = \{prog_1\}.$$

Further, *occupies* will be a function mapping each filename of an existing file to the set of block numbers which it occupies. In this case it might be

$$occupies = \{(file_1, \{1, 9, 6, 10\}), (file_2, \{2, 3, 4\}), (prog_1, \{5, 7, 8\})\}.$$

The file $file_1$ occupies blocks 1, 9, 6 and 10, $file_2$ occupies blocks 2, 3 and 4, and $prog_1$ occupies blocks 5, 7 and 8. Note that in this case the range of the *occupies* function is a set of sets of block numbers

$$rng\ occupies = \{\{1, 9, 6, 10\}, \{2, 3, 4\}, \{5, 7, 8\}\}.$$

To obtain the set of all occupied blocks as a single set, we need the generalized union operator applied as in

$$\bigcup rng\ occupies = \{1, 2, 3, 4, 5, 6, 7, 8, 9, 10\}.$$

We should perhaps have the range elements of the *occupies* function as sequences rather than sets, since the order of the blocks in a file is vital. We will ignore this feature for this simple example.

We might have as part of the requirements specification written in English:

(a) there will be a set of users *system_users*;
(b) the number of users will be *no_users*;
(c) a list of free (unoccupied) blocks will be maintained;
(d) no block is to be in more than one file;
(e) every block which is not in a file is to be on the free list;
(f) the maximum number of users will be *max_user*.

The general state schema describing this model is

[*USERS, FILE_NAMES, BLOCK_NOS*]

```
_____ FileSystem _____
        owns : USERS ⇸ ℙ FILE_NAMES
        occupies : FILE_NAMES ⇸ ℙ BLOCK_NOS
        file_store : ℙ FILE_NAMES
```

$$all\_blocks : \mathbb{P}\,BLOCK\_NOS$$
$$free\_blocks : \mathbb{P}\,BLOCK\_NOS$$
$$max\_users : \mathbb{N}$$
$$no\_users : \mathbb{N}$$
$$system\_users : \mathbb{P}\,USERS$$

$$\#system\_users \leqslant max\_users$$
$$\#system\_users = no\_users$$
$$\forall file : file\_store \bullet \exists! user : system\_users \bullet file \in owns\ user$$
$$\forall file : file\_store;\ block : all\_blocks \bullet$$
$$\quad block \in occupies\ file \Rightarrow block \notin free\_blocks$$
$$\mathrm{dom}\ owns = system\_users$$
$$file\_store = \bigcup \mathrm{rng}\ owns$$
$$file\_store = \mathrm{dom}\ occupies$$
$$\forall block\_set_1, block\_set_2 : \mathrm{rng}\ occupies \bullet$$
$$\quad block\_set_1 \neq block\_set_2 \Rightarrow block\_set_1 \cap block\_set_2 = \{\ \}$$

A selection of these predicates literally translated to English would read as follows:

(a) the number of elements in the set *system_users* is less than *max_users*;
(b) for all files in the domain of the function *occupies* (meaning 'for all files in the system') there is a unique user who owns that file;
(c) for all files in the system and blocks on the disk, if the block is occupied by a file, it is not on the free list;
(d) every user has an entry in the *owns* function.

To insist that no two files contain a common block, we could give the predicate

$$\forall file_1, file_2 : \mathrm{dom}\ occupies \bullet$$

$$file_1 \neq file_2 \Rightarrow occupies\ file_1 \cap occupies\ file_2 = \{\ \}.$$

To specify that no data block occurs in the free list we could write

$$\forall block\_set : \mathrm{rng}\ occupies \bullet block\_set \cap free\_blocks = \{\ \}$$

or

$$\bigcup \mathrm{rng}\ occupies \cap free\_blocks = \{\ \}.$$

6.3.5.2 Operation schema

To remove a file, the English paragraph in the requirements specification might be:

(a) there is to be a command to remove a file from the system;
(b) the command will be given the name of the file owner, and of the file;
(c) all blocks occupied by the file must be returned to the free list.

In the schema we must therefore delete the file's name from the database and add its blocks to the free-blocks list. The schema of the *RemoveFile* operation might be as follows:

```
┌─── RemoveFile ──────────────────────────────────────┐
│  ΔFileSystem                                         │
│  username? : USERS                                   │
│  file_name? : FILE_NAMES                             │
├──────────────────────────────                        │
│  username? ∈ system_users                            │
│  file_name? ∈ owns username?                         │
│  occupies' = {file_name?} ◁ occupies                 │
│  owns' = owns ⊕                                      │
│              {(username?, (owns username? − {file_name?}))} │
│  free_blocks' = free_blocks ∪ occupies file_name?    │
│  file_store' = file_store − {file_name?}             │
│  no_users' = no_users                                │
│  system_users' = system_users                        │
└──────────────────────────────────────────────────────┘
```

For a schema to add a new file to the system (which must add a directory entry for the new name, but will not allocate any data blocks) we might have

```
┌─── NewFile ─────────────────────────────────────────┐
│  ΔFileSystem                                         │
│  username? : USERS                                   │
│  file_name? : FILE_NAMES                             │
├──────────────────────────────                        │
│  username? ∈ system_users                            │
│  file_name? ∉ file_store                             │
│  owns' = owns ∪                                      │
│              {username? ↦ owns username ∪ {file_name?}} │
│  occupies' = occupies ∪ {file_name? ↦ { }}           │
│  free_blocks' = free_blocks                          │
│  file_store' = file_store ∪ {file_name?}             │
│  no_users' = no_users                                │
│  system_users' = system_users                        │
└──────────────────────────────────────────────────────┘
```

We must remember to mark explicitly as identical all objects of the system state which are left unchanged. This is because later we may be writing mathematical proofs about the effect of a particular combination of operations.

For the operation *RemoveUser* to remove a given user we might have the paragraph:

> The *remove user* command will remove all that user's files, and return their blocks to the free space list. The given user's name will be deleted from the system.

The schema would be

```
__ RemoveUser _____
  ΔFileSystem
  username? : USERS
  _____
  username? ∈ system_users
  owns′ = {username?} ⩤ owns
  occupies′ = owns username? ⩤ occupies
  free_blocks′ = free_blocks ∪
                          ⋃ rng(owns username? ⩤ occupies)
  file_store′ = file_store − owns username?
  no_users′ = no_users − 1
  system_users′ = system_users − {username?}
```

The line defining *free_blocks′* could be written

$$free\_blocks' = free\_blocks \cup \bigcup occupies (|\ owns\ username?\ |).$$

For the operation *AddNewUser* to add a new user to the system (initially owning no files) we might have the schema

```
__ AddNewUser _____
  ΔFileSystem
  username? : USERS
  _____
  username? ∉ system_users
  owns′ = owns ∪ {username? ↦ { }}
  occupies′ = occupies
  free_blocks′ = free_blocks
  file_store′ = file_store
  no_users′ ⩽ max_users
  no_users′ = no_users + 1
  system_users′ = system_users ∪ {username?}
```

The following operation has hidden subtleties. For the operation *NewBlock-ToFile* to add a new block to an existing file (typically required when a file is extended) we might use

```
┌─ NewBlockToFile ──────────────────────────────────────┐
│  ΔFileSystem                                           │
│  file_name? : FILE_NAMES                               │
│  block_no : BLOCK_NOS                                  │
│ ───────────────────────────                            │
│  file_name? ∈ dom occupies                             │
│  block_no ∈ free_blocks                                │
│  owns' = owns                                          │
│  occupies' = occupies ⊕                                │
│              {file_name?, occupies file_name? ∪ {block_no}}│
│  free_blocks' = free_blocks − {block_no}               │
│  file_store' = file_store                              │
│  no_users' = no_users                                  │
│  system_users' = system_users                          │
└────────────────────────────────────────────────────────┘
```

Notice that we do not specify a particular block to add. The above version uses an undefined block number, and gives no explicit way for choosing that block; it merely expresses the requirement that the new block must currently be on the free list. It is not sufficiently explicit to be turned directly into an executable mechanism for adding a block to a file. If we wrote *block_no* as *block_no?* everywhere, this becomes a command which must be supplied with a block number as input, so the choice of block number is moved elsewhere.

6.3.5.3   Observation schema

For output operations involving delivering information from the system, we need to include the schema representing an unchanged system.

For a command specified to list a particular user's filenames and sizes, described perhaps in the paragraph:

> There will be a command *ListFileNames* to list a named user's file names and sizes. The given user must already exist.

the Z schema might be

```
┌─ ListFileNames ──────────────────────────────────────┐
│  ΞFileSystem                                          │
│  username? : USERS                                    │
│  message! : FILE_NAMES ↦ ℕ                            │
│ ───────────────────────────                           │
│  username? ∈ system_users                             │
│  message! = {filename : owns username? •              │
│                      (filename, #occupies filename)}  │
└───────────────────────────────────────────────────────┘
```

For an observation schema to represent a command which accepts a username, and replies with the total number of files owned by that user, we could have

```
┌─ UserFileCount ──────────────────────────────────────────┐
│  ΞFileSystem                                               │
│  username? : USERS                                         │
│  user_file_no! : ℕ                                         │
│ ──────────────────────────                                 │
│  username? ∈ system_users                                  │
│  user_file_no! = #owns username?                           │
└────────────────────────────────────────────────────────────┘
```

For an observation schema to represent a command which accepts a username, and replies with the number of data blocks owned by that user, we could have

```
┌─ UserBlockCount ─────────────────────────────────────────┐
│  ΞFileSystem                                               │
│  username? : USERS                                         │
│  user_blocks! : ℕ                                          │
│ ──────────────────────────                                 │
│  username? ∈ system_users                                  │
│  user_blocks! = #⋃ occupies( owns username? )             │
└────────────────────────────────────────────────────────────┘
```

6.3.6   Axiom schema

It may useful in a specification, as well as commands to display certain information, to have functions which deliver it. These may then be useful in a number of other schema. For example, for the functions to give the number of blocks in a named file, the number of files owned by a named user, and the number of blocks owned by a user, we could have a schema as follows, which merely declares the functions. This is called an *axiom schema,* and must be declared before use. The schema itself has no name; its purpose is purely to make the functions available.

```
│  FileSystem
│  user_file_no : USERS  ↦ ℕ
│  user_blocks : USERS  ↦ ℕ
│  file_blocks : FILE_NAMES  ↦ ℕ
│ ──────────────────────────
│  ∀user : system_users • user_file_no user = #owns user
│  ∀user : system_users • user_blocks user =
│    ( Σ f : owns user • #occupies f)
│  ∀file : file_store • file_blocks file = #occupies file
```

6.4   Schema algebra

A schema can be used to include sets, predicates and functions in the definition of model states, operations and observations. In the previous section we looked at the contents of a schema. We look in this section at some of the operations which can be performed on whole schema.

6.4.1   Linear notation

Instead of using pictorial representation of schema, we can write them in a linear fashion as in

$$Schema \triangleq [declaration_1; declaration_2 \mid predicate_1 \wedge predicate_2]$$

which is equivalent to

```
___ Schema _____
|         declaration₁
|         declaration₂
|      _____
|
|         predicate₁
|         predicate₂
|_____
```

6.4.2   Schema extension

We can define a new schema consisting of an existing one but with additional declarations or predicates using the notation

$$New \triangleq [Old\_schema; new\_declaration \mid new\_predicate]$$

6.4.3   Some other types of definition

6.4.3.1   Basic type definitions

At the outer level of a specification, we can have, as well as Z schema of various types, basic type definitions of our own. These are typified by

$$[NAME, HEIGHT, WEIGHT]$$

They define the names of types which are not to be further defined elsewhere.

6.4.3.2   Free type definitions

At the outer level of a specification, we can also have free type definitions. These are typified by

$$MESSAGE ::= OK \mid NotKnown \mid AlreadyKnown$$

They define the possible values of types such as messages and video account types. This creates three global objects *OK, NotKnown* and *AlreadyKnown* of type *MESSAGE*. The identifiers cannot be used elsewhere in the specification.

6.4.4   Schema inclusion

We have already encountered the concept of schema inclusion in a schema diagram. The effect is to add the included schema's declarations to the declaration part of the current schema (there must be no identifier clashes) and its predicates to the predicate part. There is no theoretical limit to the number of schema which can be included in this way, or to the depth to which such inclusion may be nested. Software implementations may impose limits.

6.4.5   The tuple and pred operators

The monadic operator 'tuple' acts on a schema, and delivers a tuple of all its declarations.

The monadic operator 'pred' acts on a schema, and delivers the conjunction of all its predicates (a logical). It must not be confused with the precondition operator, 'pre', which gives the pre-condition (see below).

6.4.6   Ornamentation of schema names

When a schema is referred to by name, the name may be *ornamented* at the beginning or end in certain ways. If the name has *ornamentation* added at the end, it is assumed that the ornament has also been appended to all identifiers in the schema. The example already encountered is of the use of a prime.

The two accepted ornaments at the start of a schema name are Δ and Ξ, which have already been defined.

6.4.7   Logical operations on schema

All the standard logical operators can be used between schema:

$$\Leftrightarrow, \quad \Rightarrow, \quad \wedge, \quad \vee, \quad \neg.$$

The declarations of the schema being combined must be compatible. The declaration part of the combined schema is always the union of the declaration parts (but the types and identifiers must not clash) of the operand schema, irrespective of the particular logical operator involved.

The new predicate part is the two predicate parts logically combined by the given logical operator. However, remember that the separate lines of a predicate in any one schema are effectively already $\wedge$-ed together. Thus if $schema_1$ has predicate lines $predicate_{11}$ and $predicate_{12}$, and $schema_2$ has predicate lines $predicate_{21}$ and $predicate_{22}$, then the predicate part of

$$schema_1 \land schema_2$$

effectively unions the predicate parts of the two schema, since we have the conjunction of the two sets. It is equal to

$$predicate_{11} \land predicate_{12} \land predicate_{21} \land predicate_{22}$$

or could be written on four lines as

$$predicate_{11}$$

$$predicate_{12}$$

$$predicate_{21}$$

$$predicate_{22}$$

However, the predicate part of

$$schema_1 \lor schema_2$$

is

$$(predicate_{11} \land predicate_{12}) \lor (predicate_{21} \land predicate_{22})$$

which is not the simple union of the predicate parts in the two schema. Similarly

$$\neg schema_1$$

would have the predicate part

$$\neg(predicate_{11} \land predicate_{12})$$

which could also be expressed

$$\neg predicate_{11} \lor \neg predicate_{12}.$$

6.4.8   Schema quantification

Quantifiers can be applied to schema to produce new schema. The form for writing a universal quantification is

$$\forall var : S \bullet SchemaName,$$

where *var* is an object (or list of objects separated by commas) appearing as a declaration inside the schema, and of the same type as the elements in the set. The resulting schema has a declaration part omitting the identifiers declared in the quantification, and a predicate part in which each predicate involving *var* is individually prefaced by

$$\forall var : S \bullet .$$

For instance, if we have

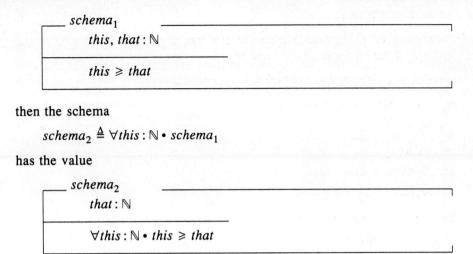

then the schema

$$schema_2 \triangleq \forall this : \mathbb{N} \bullet schema_1$$

has the value

```
___ schema₂ _____
        that : ℕ
    _____
        ∀this : ℕ • this ≥ that
```

Similarly we could define a new schema using the $\exists$ quantifier as

$$schema_3 \triangleq \exists that : \mathbb{N} \bullet schema_1 .$$

6.4.9   Identifier renaming

Individual identifiers can be renamed temporarily using the notation

$$New \triangleq Old[new\_identifier_1/old\_identifier_1,$$
$$new\_identifier_2/old\_identifier_2].$$

This replaces all occurrences of $old\_identifier_1$ and $old\_identifier_2$ by $new\_identifier_1$ and $new\_identifier_2$, respectively, in the new schema.

Renaming is useful when composing one schema from several smaller schema, to avoid clashing identifiers. One schema may be included in another with objects renamed as in

```
___ NewSchema _____
        ChooseNumber[one/out!]
        ChooseNumber[two/out!]
    _____
        one > two
```

6.4.10   Identifier hiding

There is a technique for hiding identifiers within a schema. It is written

$$NewSchema \triangleq OldSchema \backslash identifier_1$$

or to hide more than one

$$NewSchema \triangleq OldSchema \setminus (identifier_1, identifier_2).$$

The effect of hiding is that the named identifiers are removed from the declaration part of the schema, and existentially quantified wherever they occur in the predicate part. Thus if

```
┌─ schema₁ ──────────────────────────────────────────┐
│     this, that : ℕ                                  │
│ ─────────────────────────────                       │
│     this < that                                     │
└─────────────────────────────────────────────────────┘
```

then

$$schema_2 \triangleq schema_1 \setminus this$$

can be defined either as

$$schema_2 \triangleq \exists this : \mathbb{N} \bullet schema_1$$

or can be written in full as

```
┌─ schema₂ ──────────────────────────────────────────┐
│     that : ℕ                                        │
│ ─────────────────────────────                       │
│     ∃this : ℕ • this < that                         │
└─────────────────────────────────────────────────────┘
```

which is true if *that* ≥ 1.

6.4.11   Schema pre-condition

The pre-condition of a schema is the schema obtained by hiding (existentially quantifying) all the primed and output (ornamented with an exclamation mark) components. It is written

pre *schema*

The predicates then have unprimed and input components as their only free (unbound) components.

6.4.12   Schema composition

If one schema represents an operation, we may wish to combine it before or after another operation schema. We wish to define the schema corresponding to the effect of one schema followed by the effect of the other.

We then require two special actions in the composition of the two schema, which may be visualized as follows:

(a) Firstly objects denoted by primed identifiers from the first schema are identified with corresponding objects denoted by unprimed identifiers in the second, where possible. Thus if the second schema has an object *queue* and the first an object *queue'*, then the *queue'* in the first (the value of *queue* after the first operation) is matched with *queue* in the second (the value before the second operation). All identifiers in the second schema which also occur in the first schema have an extra prime added.

(b) Then for any identifiers appearing with double primes, the single primed version is hidden, and the double primed version renamed with a single prime. Thus primed identifiers in the first schema not matched in the second remain unmodified, and primed identifiers arising in the second which do not occur in the first are also preserved.

The schema *ChooseBlock* could be defined to determine the particular block from the free list to be allocated to the next file extension, and remove it from the free list, using a state schema called *FileSystem* defined earlier. We use the definition

```
┌─ ChooseBlock ─────────────────────────────────────┐
│  ΔFileSystem                                       │
│  next_block : BLOCK_NOS                            │
│ ──────────────────────────────                     │
│  next_block' ∈ free_blocks                         │
│  free_blocks' = free_blocks − {next_block'}        │
└────────────────────────────────────────────────────┘
```

The value of *next_block* after this operation is the chosen block, and the block is no longer in the free list. We can now define *AddNamedBlock* to add the block specified by *next_block* to a named file using

```
┌─ AddNamedBlock ───────────────────────────────────┐
│  ΔBase                                             │
│  file? : FILE_NAMES                                │
│ ──────────────────────────────                     │
│  occupies' file? = occupies file? ∪ {next_block}   │
└────────────────────────────────────────────────────┘
```

The composition of these two operations is equivalent to

```
┌─ ChooseAndAdd ────────────────────────────────────┐
│  ΔFileSystem                                       │
│  file? : FILE_NAMES                                │
```

$$
\begin{array}{|l|}
\hline
\;next\_block : BLOCK\_NOS \\
\hline
\;next\_block' \in free\_blocks \\
\;free\_blocks' \; = \; free\_blocks - \{next\_block'\} \\
\;occupies' \; file? \; = \; occupies \; file? \cup \{next\_block'\} \\
\hline
\end{array}
$$

The composition is written with a bold semi-colon, as in

$$ChooseAndAdd \triangleq ChooseBlock \; ; \; AddNamedBlock.$$

6.4.13　Schema piping

Piping between two schema represents the composition of two schema as described earlier, with an additional feature that the output objects of the first schema (those ornamented with an exclamation mark) are identified with the corresponding input objects of the second (those ornamented with a question mark) wherever appropriate declarations exist. In straightforward composition, primed objects in the first schema are identified with unprimed objects in the second schema. It is written

$$u \triangleq s \gg t.$$

The declaration part of the combined schema is the merged declaration parts of the two schema, with those output objects of s which have corresponding input objects in t renamed as the input objects and hidden.

We will demonstrate using another example where one operation chooses a number, and a second one uses the chosen value. In this case, instead of the result of the first operation being left as the value of a (primed) variable, it is an output value. The second operation will pick this up as an input variable. Thus if we have

$$
\begin{array}{|l|}
\hline
\;ChooseValue \\
\hline
\;set : \mathbb{P}\,\mathbb{N} \\
\;value! : \mathbb{N} \\
\hline
\;value! \in set \\
\;\forall i : set \bullet value! \leqslant i \\
\hline
\end{array}
$$

to pick up the smallest value in the set, and

$$
\begin{array}{|l|}
\hline
\;RemoveIt \\
\hline
\;set, set' : \mathbb{P}\,\mathbb{N} \\
\;value? : \mathbb{N} \\
\hline
\end{array}
$$

$$
\begin{array}{|l}
\hline
\quad value? \in set \\
\quad set' = set - \{value?\} \\
\hline
\end{array}
$$

to remove it, then

$$ChooseAndRemove \triangleq ChooseValue \gg RemoveIt$$

has the effect of choosing a value from the set, and removing it.

6.4.14   Axiomatic descriptions

These appear as

$$
\begin{array}{|l}
\quad declarations \\
\hline
\quad predicates \\
\end{array}
$$

Axiomatic description introduces one or more global objects and optionally specifies a constraint on their values. These objects must not have a previous global declaration, and cannot be redeclared elsewhere. The scope of these objects extends from the declaration to the end of the specification. These declarations and their associated predicates become part of global property. An axiom schema has no name. Another example might be

$$
\begin{array}{|l}
\quad Nfiles : NAME \nrightarrow \mathbb{N} \\
\hline
\quad \forall user : system\_users \bullet Nfiles\ user = \#owns\ user \\
\end{array}
$$

declaring the global function *Nfiles* to deliver the number of files owned by any given user.

6.5   Summary

In this chapter we have seen how predicate logic has been applied to the problem of formally specifying computer systems. We introduced the Z language by considering a very simple example before presenting some background mathematics. We then looked at the language in more detail and finally considered the algebra of Z schema. The methods of the previous chapter can be used to automate many aspects of the practical applications of Z.

6.6   Worked examples

6.6.1   Some simple examples

Example 6.1   Write two possible state schema for a video shop similar to the one described earlier, in which the stock is to be distinguished between children's and adult videos.

Solution

(a)

```
┌─ Video_shop1 ──────────────────────────────────┐
│   all_videos, in_stock, booked_out : ℙVIDEO      │
│   children, adult : ℙVIDEO                        │
├──────────────────────────────────────────────────┤
│   children ∪ adult = all_videos                   │
│   children ∩ adult = { }                          │
│   in_stock ∪ booked_out = all_videos              │
└──────────────────────────────────────────────────┘
```

(b)

```
┌─ Video_shop2 ──────────────────────────────────────────┐
│   all_videos : ℙVIDEO                                    │
│   children_in_stock, children_booked_out : ℙVIDEO         │
│   adult_in_stock, adult_booked_out : ℙVIDEO               │
├───────────────────────────────────────────────────────────┤
│   (children_in_stock ∪ children_booked_out) ∩             │
│      (adult_in_stock ∪ adult_booked_out) = { }            │
│   children_in_stock ∪ children_booked_out ∪ adult_in_stock ∪ │
│      adult_booked_out = all_videos                        │
└───────────────────────────────────────────────────────────┘
```

Example 6.2   Write a schema for the operation of adding a new video to the stock defined as follows:

> There is to be a command to add a new video to the stock. The name of the video will be input to the command. It is to be assumed that the new video will go straight into stock. The new video must not already exist.

Solution

```
┌─ NewVideo ─────────────────────────────┐
│   ΔVideo_shop                           │
│   video? : VIDEO                        │
├──────────────────────────────────────────┤
│   video? ∉ all_videos                    │
│   all_videos' = all_videos ∪ {video?}    │
│   booked_out' = booked_out               │
│   in_stock' = in_stock ∪ {video?}        │
└──────────────────────────────────────────┘
```

Example 6.3 Write a schema for the operation *add_video* defined as follows:

There is to be a command to add a new video to the stock. The name of the video will be input to the command, together with a Boolean which will take the value T if the video is to be booked out at the time of registration. The new video must not already be a member of the stock.

Solution We define the type BOOLEAN as

$BOOLEAN ::= T \,|\, F.$

The schema can now be defined either as

```
┌─ NewVideo ──────────────────────────────────────┐
│  ΔVideo_shop                                     │
│  video? : VIDEO                                  │
│  book_out? : BOOLEAN                             │
│ ────────────────────────────                     │
│  video? ∉ all_videos                             │
│  all_videos′ = all_videos ∪ {video?}             │
│  book_out? = T ⟹                                 │
│    (in_stock′ = in_stock ∪ {video?} ∧            │
│      booked_out′ = booked_out)                   │
│  book_out? ≠ T ⟹                                 │
│    (booked_out′ = booked_out ∪ {video?} ∧        │
│      in_stock′ = in_stock)                       │
└──────────────────────────────────────────────────┘
```

or

```
┌─ NewVideo ──────────────────────────────────────┐
│  ΔVideo_shop                                     │
│  video? : VIDEO                                  │
│  book_out? : BOOLEAN                             │
│ ────────────────────────────                     │
│  video? ∉ all_videos                             │
│  all_videos′ = all_videos ∪ {video?}             │
│  (book_out? = T ∧                                │
│    in_stock′ = in_stock ∪ {video?} ∧             │
│      booked_out′ = booked_out) ∨                 │
│        (book_out? ≠ T ∧                          │
│          booked_out′ = booked_out ∪ {video?} ∧   │
│            in_stock′ = in_stock)                 │
└──────────────────────────────────────────────────┘
```

Note that we cannot simplify expressions such as *book_out?* $= T$ since Boolean values are not a built-in part of Z.

Example 6.4   Write a schema to list the videos which are in stock.

Solution

```
___ ListStock _____
|    ΞVideo_shop
|    list! : ℙ VIDEO
|_____
|
|    list! = in_stock
|_____
```

Example 6.5   Design a state schema for a file system with a single level of directories, so that two users may use the same name for a file.

Solution   Instead of a user owning files, we now consider that a user owns a directory, and that all files belonging to a user are stored in that user's directory. The full name for a file is now (*USER_DIR*, *FILE*). Even though two users have files with the same name, the full names for the files are different.

[*DIR, USERS, FILE_NAMES, BLOCK_NOS*]

```
___ FileSystem _____
|    owns : USERS ↦ DIR
|    contains : DIR ↦ ℙ FILE_NAMES
|    occupies : (DIR×FILE_NAMES) ↦ ℙ BLOCK_NOS
|    file_store : ℙ (DIR×FILE_NAMES)
|    free_blocks : ℙ BLOCK_NOS
|    max_users : ℕ
|    no_users : ℕ
|    system_users : ℙ USERS
|_____
|
|    #system_users ⩽ max_users
|    #system_users = no_users
|    ∀dir : dom contains • ∃!user : dom owns • dir = owns user
|    ∀dir : dom contains • ∀file : contains dir •
|      ∀block : occupies(dir, file) • block ∉ free_blocks
|    dom owns = system_users
|    file_store = dom occupies
|    ∀block_set₁, block_set₂ : rng occupies •
|      block_set₁ ≠ block_set₂ ⟹ block_set₁ ∩ block_set₂ = { }
|_____
```

Example 6.6   Write a generalized hierarchical file system.

Solution   In a generalized hierarchical file system, a directory can contain subdirectories or files, and each subdirectory can also contain further subdirectories and files. So the full names for files can be:

USER_DIR/file;

USER_DIR/dir/file;

USER_DIR/dir$_1$/dir$_2$/file.

Instead of a file having a name, it now has a sequence of names:

⟨*USER_DIR, file*⟩;

⟨*USER_DIR, dir, file*⟩;

⟨*USER_DIR, dir$_1$, dir$_2$, file*⟩.

For the system as a whole, a given user's directory *USER_DIR* itself is just a subdirectory of the root, so that the full name for a file is the whole sequence of names from the root.

[*DIR*]

___ *FileSystemHierarchy* _____

    owns : *USERS* ⇸ *DIR*
    contains : *DIR* ⇸ ℙ seq *FILE_NAMES*
    occupies : seq *FILE_NAMES* ⇸ ℙ *BLOCK_NOS*
    free_blocks : ℙ *BLOCK_NOS*
    max_users : ℕ
    no_users : ℕ
    system_users : ℙ *USERS*
_____

    #*system_users* ⩽ *max_users*
    #*system_users* = *no_users*
    ∀*dir* : dom *contains* • ∃!*us* : dom *owns* • *dir* = *owns us*
    ∀*dir* : dom *contains* • ∀*fs* : seq *contains dir* •
      ∀*block* : *occupies*(*dir, file*) • *block* ∉ *free_blocks*
    dom *owns* = *system_users*
    ∀*block_set$_1$*, *block_set$_2$* : rng *occupies* •
      block_set$_1$ ≠ *block_set$_2$* ⇒ *block_set$_1$* ∩ *block_set$_2$* = { }
    ∀*fs* : rng *contains* •
      ∃*ps* : seq *FILE_NAMES* • *fs* = dom *contains⌢ps*

The last statement in the schema above just states that a directory name is also a sequence of *FILE_NAMES*, and it is the front part of a file name.

Example 6.7 Discuss how you would add the UNIX 'ln' command to a system. This command allows for more than one file name (directory entry) to refer to exactly the same file (set of blocks). The block sets occupied by two files will be identical if the two files are linked, and will have an empty intersection otherwise.

Solution   We add a new variable *link* defined as

$$link : FILE\_NAMES \nrightarrow \mathbb{P}\, FILE\_NAMES,$$

which is a function mapping a filename to the set of names of linked files, and add a predicate to say that, if two files are linked, then they must occupy exactly the same blocks.

$$\forall block\_set, block\_set_2 : FILE\_NAMES \mid block\_set_2 = link(block\_set) \bullet$$

$$occupies(block\_set) = occupies(block\_set_2)$$

```
┌─ LinkFileSystem ─────────────────────────────────────────┐
│   FileSystem                                              │
│   link : FILE_NAMES ↛ ℙ FILE_NAMES                       │
└──────────────────────────────────────────────────────────┘
```

When a file $file\_name_2?$ is linked to another file $file\_name_1?$, then $file\_name_1?$ must exist. The original file will occupy the same blocks as the linked file.

```
┌─ CreateLink ─────────────────────────────────────────────┐
│   ΔLinkFileSystem                                         │
│   username? : USERS                                       │
│   file₁? : FILE_NAMES                                     │
│   file₂? : FILE_NAMES                                     │
│ ─────────────────────────────────────────────            │
│   username? ∈ system_users                                │
│   file₁? ∈ file_store                                     │
│   file₂? ∉ file_store                                     │
│   own' = own ⊕ {username? ↦ own(username?) ∪ {file₂?}}    │
│   link'(file₁?) = link(file₁?) ∪ {file₂?}                 │
│   file_store' = file_store ∪ {file₂?}                     │
│   occupies' = occupies ∪ {file₂? ↦ occupies file₁?}      │
│   free_blocks' = free_block                               │
│   no_users' = no_users                                    │
│   system_users' = system_users                           │
└──────────────────────────────────────────────────────────┘
```

Example 6.8   Add a new operation to rename an existing file.

Solution   When renaming occurs, the only thing that will change is the name of the file. The original name will be removed and the new name will be added to the file store and to the list of files that user owns.

```
┌─ RenameFile ─────────────────────────────────────────────┐
│   ΔFileSystem                                             │
│   username? : USER                                        │
```

$$file\_name\_1? : FILE\_NAMES$$
$$file\_name\_2? : FILE\_NAMES$$
___

$username? \in system\_users$
$file\_name\_1? \in file\_store$
$own' = own \oplus$
$\quad\quad\quad\quad \{username? \mapsto own(username?) \cup \{file\_name\_2?\} -$
$\quad\quad\quad\quad\quad\quad\quad\quad\quad\quad\quad\quad\quad\quad\quad\quad\quad \{file\_name\_1?\}\}$
$file\_store' = file\_store \cup \{file\_name\_2?\} - \{file\_name\_1?\}$
$occupies' = occupies \cup$
$\quad\quad\quad\quad\quad\quad \{file\_name\_2? \mapsto occupies\ file\_name\_1?\} -$
$\quad\quad\quad\quad\quad\quad \{file\_name\_1? \mapsto occupies\ file\_name\_1?\}$
$free\_blocks' = free\_block$
$no\_users' = no\_users$
$system\_users' = system\_users$

Example 6.9 Discuss how you would add error handling to some of the file system schema given in the text.

Solution First we define a type to cover all possible error messages:

$MESSAGES ::= ok \mid file\_exists \mid file\_not\_exists \mid user\_exists \mid$

$\quad\quad\quad\quad\quad\quad\quad\quad\quad user\_not\_exists \mid not\_enough\_space.$

Next we define some schemas to identify messages as follows:

___ *Success* _____

$message! : MESSAGES$
___

$message! = ok$

___ *FileDoesntExists* _____

$\Xi FileSystem$
$filename? : FILE\_NAMES$
$message! : MESSAGES$
___

$filename? \notin file\_store$
$message! = file\_not\_exists$

___ *FileAlreadyExists* _____

$\Xi FileSystem$
$filename? : FILE\_NAMES$

$$message!: MESSAGES$$

$$filename? \in file\_store$$
$$message! = file\_exists$$

___ UserDoesntExists _____

$$\Xi FileSystem$$
$$user?: USERS$$
$$message!: MESSAGES$$

$$user? \notin system\_users$$
$$message! = user\_not\_exists$$

___ UserAlreadyExists _____

$$\Xi FileSystem$$
$$user?: USERS$$
$$message!: MESSAGES$$

$$user? \in system\_users$$
$$message! = user\_exists$$

___ NotEnoughSpace _____

$$\Xi FileSystem$$
$$message!: MESSAGES$$

$$free\_blocks = \{\ \}$$
$$message! = not\_enough\_space$$

The full definition for each operation can the be defined by logical operations on schema.

$$FullRemoveFile \triangleq (RemoveFile \wedge Success) \vee FileDoesntExists$$
$$\vee UserDoesntExists;$$

$$FullNewFile \triangleq (NewFile \wedge Success) \vee FileAlreadyExists$$
$$\vee UserDoesntExists \vee NotEnoughSpace;$$

$$FullRemoveUser \triangleq (RemoveUser \wedge Success) \vee UserDoesntExists;$$

$$FullNewUser \triangleq (NewUser \wedge Success) \vee UserAlreadyExists;$$

$$FullNewBlockToFile \triangleq (NewBlockToFile \wedge Success) \vee FileDoesntExists$$
$$\vee NotEnoughSpace.$$

Example 6.10   Write a schema which gives the names of all users with a link to a named file.

Solution   To list all the users with a link to a given file, we have to consider all files which occupies the same blocks as the given file.

```
┌─── ListLinks ────────────────────────────────────────────┐
│   ΞFileSystem                                              │
│   filename? : FILE_NAMES                                   │
│   user_list! : ℙ USERS                                     │
├───────────────────────────────────────                    │
│   filename? ∈ dom occupies                                 │
│   user_list! = {u : USERS; f : FILE_NAMES | f = owns(u) ∧  │
│                    occupies(f) = occupies(filename?) • u}  │
└───────────────────────────────────────────────────────────┘
```

or

```
┌─── ListLinks ────────────────────────────────────────────┐
│   ΞLinkFileSystem                                          │
│   filename? : FILE_NAMES                                   │
│   user_list! : ℙ USERS                                     │
├───────────────────────────────────────                    │
│   filename? ∈ dom link                                     │
│   user_list! = {u : USERS; f : FILE_NAMES |                │
│                   f = link(filename?) ∧ f = owns(u) • u}   │
└───────────────────────────────────────────────────────────┘
```

We will now give one small and one larger case study as examples of the use of Z specifications.

6.6.2   Case study: a video-rental shop

We wish to set up a more detailed formal specification of a video-rental shop to the very simple example presented earlier. The shop rents videos to registered customers whose names, addresses and phone numbers are kept on record. Each video in stock is uniquely identified by reference number; also each customer is allocated his/her own unique reference. Customers can hire videos at a cost of *hire_charge* for the first day and an extra *overdue_fine* for each subsequent day. Customers may also reserve particular videos for a specific day, in which case the reserved video is removed from the shelf on the day of the reservation.

We will use the following types:

customer_name	all possible customer names
customer_address	all possible customer addresses
customer_phone	all possible customer phone numbers
customer_ref	all possible customer references
video_title	all possible video titles

video_ref	all possible video references
date	all possible dates

We will assume the function

$$days\_since : date \nrightarrow \mathbb{N}$$

which gives the number of working days elapsed since the given date and also the constant

$$today : day$$

which is the current day.   We require a state schema, and schema for the operations and observations outlined below and in Exercise 6.3.

name	arguments	result	messages
borrow_video	*video_ref* *customer_ref*	If valid details are given, alter the records to show the customer has taken out the video.	*ok*
reserve_video	*video_ref* *customer_ref*	If valid data are given, alter the records to show the reservation and inform the user if the video is already reserved on that date.	*ok* *already_reserved*
print_reserved_videos		Output list of all videos not on loan that are reserved today.	$\mathbb{P}\,video\_ref$

State schema

[*customer_name, customer_address, customer_phone,*

customer_ref, video_title, video_ref, date]

status_message ::= *ok* | *already_reserved* | *not_reserved* |

reserved_video | *video_not_in*

```
┌─ video_shop ─────────────────────────────────────┐
│   customers : ℙ customer_ref                      
│   cust_name : customer_ref ↦ customer_names       
```

$$cust\_address : customer\_ref \nrightarrow customer\_address$$
$$cust\_phone : customer\_ref \nrightarrow customer\_phone$$
$$videos : \mathbb{P}\, video\_ref$$
$$videos\_in : \mathbb{P}\, video\_ref$$
$$video\_out\_to : video\_ref \nrightarrow customer\_ref$$
$$video\_out\_since : video\_ref \nrightarrow date$$
$$reservations : date \nrightarrow (video\_ref \nrightarrow customer\_ref)$$

$$\mathrm{dom}\, cust\_names = customers$$
$$\mathrm{dom}\, cust\_address = customers$$
$$\mathrm{dom}\, cust\_phone = customers$$
$$videos\_in \cup \mathrm{dom}\, video\_out\_to = videos$$
$$videos\_in \cap \mathrm{dom}\, video\_out\_to = \{\}$$
$$videos\_in \cup \mathrm{dom}\, video\_out\_since = videos$$
$$videos\_in \cap \mathrm{dom}\, video\_out\_since = \{\}$$
$$\forall video : video\_ref \bullet \forall cust : customer\_ref \bullet$$
$$\{video \mapsto cust\} \in \mathrm{rng}\, reservations \Rightarrow$$
$$video \in videos \land cust \in customers$$

Command schema

___ *borrow_video* _____

$$\Delta video\_shop$$
$$video? : video\_ref$$
$$customer? : customer\_ref$$
$$message! : status\_message$$

$$customer? \in customers$$
$$video? \in videos\_in$$
$$videos\_in' = videos\_in - \{video?\}$$
$$video\_out\_to' = video\_out\_to \cup \{video? \mapsto cust?\}$$
$$video\_out\_since' = video\_out\_since \cup \{video? \mapsto today\}$$
$$message! = ok$$

___ *reserve_video_base* _____

$$\Delta video\_shop$$
$$customer? : customer\_ref$$
$$video? : video\_ref$$
$$day? : date$$
$$message! : status\_message$$

```
___ reserve_video_ok _____
|  reserve_video_ok
|  _____
|
|  video ∉ dom reservations day?
|  reservations' day? = reservations day? ∪
|                                   {video? ↦ customer}
|  message! = ok
|_____
```

```
___ reserve_video_already_reserved _____
|  reserve_video_base
|  _____
|
|  video? ∈ dom reservations day?
|  message! = already_reserved
|_____
```

reserve_video ≜ reserve_video_ok ∨ reserve_video_already_reserved

```
___ add_customer _____
|  Δvideo_shop
|  name? : customer_name
|  address? : customer_address
|  phone? : customer_phone
|  customer! : customer_ref
|  _____
|
|  customer! ∉ customers
|  cust_names' = cust_names ∪ {customer! ↦ name?}
|  cust_address' = cust_address ∪ {customer! ↦ address?}
|  cust_phone' = cust_phone ∪ {customer! ↦ phone?}
|_____
```

```
___ print_reserved_videos _____
|  Ξvideo_shop
|  reserved_videos! : ℙ video_ref
|  _____
|
|  reserved_videos! = dom reservations today ∩ videos_in
|_____
```

6.6.3 Case study: a car-ferry terminal

We wish to set up a formal specification of a car-ferry port system.

   The port maintains a set of waiting vehicles for each of the ferries in dock. Cars arrive either booked (in which case they are added to the set of vehicles waiting for that ferry) or unbooked (in which case they are added to the end of a single general queue). When a ferry leaves, any vacancies are filled from the front of the general queue.

There will be certain overall restrictions as follows:

(a) the capacity of each ferry is *ferry_max* vehicles;
(b) the length of the general queue must not exceed *general_max* vehicles.

We will write state and invariant schema. We need sets of ferry references and car references. We will also write operation schema for the following commands:

Ferry_scheduled. The command will have as input a ferry reference. The effect is to add the ferry's reference to the set of currently active ferries. If the ferry already exists, an error should be reported.

Ferry_departs. The command will have as input a ferry reference. Any vacancies should be filled from the front of the general queue of waiting vehicles. The ferry's entry should then be deleted. If the ferry does not exist, an error should be reported.

Booked_car_arrives. The operation will be given as input a ferry reference and a car reference. The car should be added to the set waiting for the given ferry. Error should be reported if the car reference already exists, the ferry reference does not exist, or if there are already *ferry_max* vehicles waiting for that ferry.

Unbooked_car_arrives. The command will have as input a car reference. The car is added at the end of the general queue. An error should be reported if the car reference already exists, or if the general queue is already full.

We will write observation schema for the following commands:

List_ferry. Given a ferry reference, list the references of all vehicles waiting for it. Report an error if the ferry reference is invalid.

List_all. List for each waiting ferry the references of all vehicles waiting for it.

List_total_vacancies. Give the total number of spaces on all waiting ferries combined.

List_general_queue. List the references of cars in the general queue.

List_general_queue_length. Give the length of the general queue.

Can_ferry_take_queue. Given a ferry reference, give the message '*OK*' if that ferry has enough space for the waiting general queue, '*No*' otherwise. Report an error if the ferry reference is invalid.

Can_ferries_take_queue. Give the message '*OK*' if there is enough space on all the waiting ferries combined for the waiting general queue, '*No*' otherwise.

Solution   We assume the undefined objects

$$ferry\_ref \quad \text{all possible ferry references}$$
$$car\_ref \quad \text{all possible car references}$$

State schema

$[\,ferry\_ref,\, car\_ref\,]$

```
┌─── ferries ─────────────────────────────────────────┐
│   ferry_max : ℕ                                      │
│   general_q_max : ℕ                                  │
│   known_ferries : ℙ ferry_ref                        │
│   known_cars : ℙ car_ref                             │
│   general_queue : seq car_ref                        │
│   ferry_load : ferry_ref ↦ ℙ car_ref                 │
├──────────────────────────────────────────────────────┤
│   known_ferries = dom ferry_load                     │
│   known_cars = rng general_queue ∪ ⋃ rng ferry_load  │
│   #general_queue ≤ general_q_max                     │
│   ∀ f : known_ferries • #ferry_load f ≤ ferry_max    │
└──────────────────────────────────────────────────────┘
```

$message ::= unknown\_ferry \mid known\_ferry \mid unknown\_car \mid$

$known\_car \mid unbooked\_arrives\_ok \mid general\_q\_full \mid$

$can\_take\_queue \mid cannot\_take\_all\_queue$

```
┌─── unknown_ferry_ref ────────────────────────────────┐
│   Ξferries                                           │
│   ferry? : ferry_ref                                 │
│   result! : message                                  │
├──────────────────────────────────────────────────────┤
│   ferry? ∉ known_ferries                             │
│   result! = unknown_ferry                            │
└──────────────────────────────────────────────────────┘
```

```
┌─── known_ferry_ref ──────────────────────────────────┐
│   Ξferries                                           │
│   ferry? : ferry_ref                                 │
│   result! : message                                  │
├──────────────────────────────────────────────────────┤
│   ferry? ∈ known_ferries                             │
│   result! = known_ferry                              │
└──────────────────────────────────────────────────────┘
```

```
┌─ unknown_car_ref ──────────────────────────────────────┐
│   Ξferries                                              │
│   car? : car_ref                                        │
│   result! : message                                     │
│ ───────────────────────────                             │
│   car? ∉ known_cars                                     │
│   result! = unknown_car                                 │
└─────────────────────────────────────────────────────────┘
```

```
┌─ known_car_ref ────────────────────────────────────────┐
│   Ξferries                                              │
│   car? : car_ref                                        │
│   result! : message                                     │
│ ───────────────────────────                             │
│   car? ∈ known_cars                                     │
│   result! = known_car                                   │
└─────────────────────────────────────────────────────────┘
```

Operation schema

```
┌─ initialize ───────────────────────────────────────────┐
│   Δferries                                              │
│ ───────────────────────────                             │
│   ferry_load' = { }                                     │
│   known_cars' = { }                                     │
│   known_ferries' = { }                                  │
│   general_queue' = ⟨ ⟩                                  │
└─────────────────────────────────────────────────────────┘
```

```
┌─ ferry_scheduled_ok ───────────────────────────────────┐
│   Δferries                                              │
│   ferry? : ferry_ref                                    │
│ ───────────────────────────                             │
│   ferry? ∉ known_ferries                               │
│   ferries' = ferries ∪ {ferry?}                        │
│   ferry_load' = ferry_load ∪ (ferry? ↦ { })            │
└─────────────────────────────────────────────────────────┘
```

$ferry\_scheduled \triangleq ferry\_scheduled\_ok \lor known\_ferry\_ref$

```
┌─ ferry_departs_full ───────────────────────────────────┐
│   Δferries                                              │
│   ferry? : ferry_ref                                    │
│ ───────────────────────────                             │
│                                                         │
```

$$
\begin{array}{|l}
\hline
\textit{ferry?} \in \textit{known\_ferries} \\
\#\textit{ferry\_load ferry?} = \textit{ferry\_max} \\
\textit{known\_ferries}' = \textit{known\_ferries} - \{\textit{ferry?}\} \\
\textit{ferry\_load}' = \{\textit{ferry?}\} \lhd \textit{ferry\_load} \\
\hline
\end{array}
$$

---

fillferry_from_general_q_1

$\Delta \textit{ferries}$
$\textit{ferry?} : \textit{ferry\_ref}$
$\textit{spare} : \mathbb{N}$

$\textit{ferry?} \in \textit{known\_ferries}$
$\#\textit{ferry\_load ferry?} < \textit{ferry\_max}$
$\textit{spare} = \textit{ferry\_max} - \#\textit{ferry\_load ferry?}$
$\textit{spare} \geq \#\textit{general\_queue}$
$\textit{general\_queue}' = \langle \, \rangle$
$\textit{ferry\_load}' \; \textit{ferry?} = \textit{ferry\_load ferry?} \cup$
$\qquad\qquad\qquad\qquad\qquad\qquad \text{rng } \textit{general\_queue}$

---

fillferry_from_general_q_2

$\Delta \textit{ferries}$
$\textit{spare} : \mathbb{N}$
$\textit{ferry?} : \textit{ferry\_ref}$

$\textit{ferry?} \in \textit{known\_ferries}$
$\#\textit{ferry\_load ferry?} < \textit{ferry\_max}$
$\textit{spare} = \textit{ferry\_max} - \#\textit{ferry\_load ferry?}$
$\textit{spare} < \#\textit{general\_queue}$
$\textit{general\_queue}' = \text{squash}(\{1 \,..\, \textit{spare}\} \lhd \textit{general\_queue})$
$\textit{ferry\_load}' \; \textit{ferry?} = \textit{ferry\_load ferry?} \cup$
$\qquad\qquad\qquad\qquad \text{rng}(\{1 \,..\, \textit{spare}\} \lhd \textit{general\_queue})$

$$\textit{ferry\_departs} \triangleq \textit{ferry\_departs\_full} \lor \textit{fill\_ferry\_from\_general\_q\_1} \lor$$

$$\textit{fill\_ferry\_from\_general\_q\_2} \lor \textit{unknown\_ferry\_ref}$$

$$\textit{full\_or\_not} ::= \textit{is\_full} \mid \textit{not\_full}$$

ferry_full

$\Xi \textit{ferries}$
$\textit{ferry?} : \textit{ferry\_ref}$
$\textit{result!} : \textit{full\_or\_not}$

```
 ┌─────────────────────────────────
 │   #ferry_load ferry? ⩾ ferry_max ⇒ result! = is_full
 │   #ferry_load ferry? < ferry_max ⇒ result! = not_full
 └─────────────────────────────────
```

$$\begin{array}{l}
\text{\_\_ booked\_car\_arrives\_ok _____} \\
\quad \Delta ferries \\
\quad car? : car\_ref \\
\quad ferry? : ferry\_ref \\
\text{_____} \\
\quad car? \notin known\_cars \\
\quad ferry? \in known\_ferries \\
\quad \#ferry\_load\, ferry? < ferry\_max \\
\quad ferry\_load'\ ferry? = ferry\_load\, ferry? \cup \{car?\} \\
\end{array}$$

$booked\_car\_arrives \triangleq booked\_car\_arrives\_ok \vee$

$$unknown\_ferry\_ref \vee known\_car\_ref \vee ferry\_full$$

$$\begin{array}{l}
\text{\_\_ unbooked\_car\_arrives\_ok _____} \\
\quad \Delta ferries \\
\quad car? : known\_cars \\
\quad result! : message \\
\text{_____} \\
\quad car? \notin known\_cars \\
\quad \#general\_queue < general\_q\_max \\
\quad general\_queue' = general\_queue^\frown \{1 \mapsto car?\} \\
\quad result! = unbooked\_arrives\_ok \\
\end{array}$$

$$\begin{array}{l}
\text{\_\_ general\_q\_full _____} \\
\quad \Xi ferries \\
\quad result! : message \\
\text{_____} \\
\quad \#general\_queue \geqslant general\_q\_max \\
\quad result! = general\_q\_full \\
\end{array}$$

$unbooked\_car\_arrives \triangleq unbooked\_car\_arrives\_ok \vee$

$$unknown\_car\_ref \vee general\_q\_full$$

Observation schema

$$\begin{array}{l}
\text{\_\_ list\_ferry\_ok _____} \\
\quad \Xi ferries \\
\quad ferry? : ferry\_ref \\
\end{array}$$

_____
| *result!* : $\mathbb{P}\, car\_ref$
|_____
| *ferry?* $\in$ *known_ferries*
| *result!* = *ferry_load ferry?*
|_____

list_ferry $\triangleq$ *list_ferry_ok* $\vee$ *unknown_ferry_ref*

___ *list_all_by_ferry* _____
| Ξ*ferries*
| *result!* : *ferry_ref* $\nrightarrow$ $\mathbb{P}\, car\_ref$
|_____
| *result!* = *ferry_load*
|_____

___ *list_all_ok* _____
| Ξ*ferries*
| *ferry?* : *ferry_ref*
| *result!* : $\mathbb{N}$
|_____
| *ferry?* $\in$ *known_ferries*
| *result!* = *ferry_max* − #*ferry_load ferry?*
|_____

list_all $\triangleq$ *list_all_ok* $\vee$ *unknown_ferry_ref*

___ *list_general_queue* _____
| Ξ*ferries*
| *result!* : seq *car_ref*
|_____
| *result!* = *general_queue*
|_____

___ *list_general_queue_length* _____
| Ξ*ferries*
| *result!* : $\mathbb{N}$
|_____
| *result!* = #*general_queue*
|_____

___ *list_total_vacancies* _____
| Ξ*ferries*
| *result!* : $\mathbb{N}$
|_____
| *result!* = Σ*ferry* : *known_ferries* •
| (*ferry_max* − *ferry_load ferry*)
|_____

```
┌─ can_ferry_take_queue_ok ─────────────────────────────────┐
│   Ξferries                                                 │
│   ferry? : ferry_ref                                       │
│   result! : message                                        │
│ ──────────────────────────────                            │
│   ferry? ∈ known_ferries                                   │
│   #ferry_load ferry? + #general_queue ⩽ ferry_max          │
│   result! = can_take_queue                                 │
└────────────────────────────────────────────────────────────┘
```

```
┌─ can_ferry_take_queue_fail ───────────────────────────────┐
│   Ξferries                                                 │
│   ferry? : ferry_ref                                       │
│   result! : message                                        │
│ ──────────────────────────────                            │
│   ferry? ∈ known_ferries                                   │
│   #ferry_load ferry? + #general_queue > ferry_max          │
│   result! = cannot_take_all_queue                          │
└────────────────────────────────────────────────────────────┘
```

$$can\_ferry\_take\_queue \triangleq can\_ferry\_take\_queue\_ok \lor$$
$$can\_ferry\_take\_queue\_fail \lor$$
$$unknown\_ferry\_ref$$

```
┌─ can_ferries_take_queue_ok ───────────────────────────────┐
│   Ξferries                                                 │
│   result! : message                                        │
│ ──────────────────────────────                            │
│   (Σferry : known_ferries •                                │
│    (ferry_max − #ferry_load ferry)) ⩽ #general_queue       │
│   result! = can_take_queue                                 │
└────────────────────────────────────────────────────────────┘
```

```
┌─ can_ferries_take_queue_fail ─────────────────────────────┐
│   Ξferries                                                 │
│   result! : message                                        │
│ ──────────────────────────────                            │
│   (Σferry : known_ferries •                                │
│    (ferry_max − #ferry_load ferry)) > #general_queue       │
│   result! = cannot_take_all_queue                          │
└────────────────────────────────────────────────────────────┘
```

$$can\_ferries\_take\_queue \triangleq can\_ferries\_take\_queue\_ok \lor$$
$$can\_ferries\_take\_queue\_fail$$

6.7   Exercises

Exercise 6.1   In the *Height_and_Weight* example at the beginning of the chapter, construct a *Healthy* schema which takes as input a person's name and compares the height with the weight of that person to report overweight, underweight or OK. You should include error-handling schemas.

Exercise 6.2   Amend the *Height_and_Weight* example to take both height and weight as two integers representing the feet and inches, and stones and pounds, respectively, and to check the validity of the given heights and weights.

Exercise 6.3   For the video-shop case study (on page 271), write schema for the following commands:

name	arguments	result	messages
collect_reserved	*video_ref* *customer_ref*	Allow a user to collect a video he/she reserved. Check details and adjust records. Make sure video is not on loan.	*ok* *video_not_in*
return_video	*video_ref*	Customer returns video. Calculate and output charge and inform user whether this video is reserved today (for putting aside).	*not_reserved* *reserved*
print_bad_customers		Output all customers that have had a video on loan for 3 days or more.	$\mathbb{P}$ *customer_ref*
add_video	*video_title*	Allocate a unique reference for the new video and update the records. Output the new video reference.	*video_ref*

Exercise 6.4   For the video-shop example, amend the system so that the shop (more realistically) stocks multiple copies of each video. The number of copies will, of course, depend on the particular video.

Exercise 6.5 Add a schema to the car-ferry system to represent the command *list_ferry_spaces* defined as follows:

> Given a ferry reference, give the number of spaces on it. Report an error if the ferry reference is invalid.

Exercise 6.6 Write an operation schema for the car-ferry system called

> *Add_waiting_vehicles_for_one_named_ferry_to_another_named_ferry*

to operate as follows:

> The command will be given as input two ferry references. The vehicles waiting for the first ferry will be added to those waiting for the second ferry. An error should be reported if either ferry does not exist, or if the combined set is too big for the new ferry.

Exercise 6.7 For the car-ferry system, write a schema called *can_ferries_combine* to operate as follows:

> The input is two ferry references. Give the message 'OK' if there is enough space on the second ferry for the vehicles currently scheduled for the first ferry, or the message 'Not_enough_space' otherwise. Report an error if either of the ferry references is invalid.

Exercise 6.8 For the car-ferry system, consider the Z implications of each of the following enhancements:

(a) Each ferry has a specific capacity defined as an integer in terms of the number of cars it can carry.
(b) Each vehicle has a specified length, and each ferry's capacity is specified in terms of total length of vehicles it can carry.
(c) Each ferry has a specified length of storage available for high vehicles, and a specified length for low vehicles, each arriving vehicle having a specified height as well as length.
(d) Adding an operation 'arrival of high-priority vehicle', permitting an arriving vehicle to jump the queue.
(e) Each ferry has a specified destination, and unbooked cars queue for a specified destination.

Reference

1. D. C. Ince, *An Introduction to Discrete Mathematics and Formal System Specification*, 1988. Oxford.

Mathematical background

The concept of induction proofs described here is vital in all chapters of this book. Most of the other mathematical ideas are used in chapter 6. For this reason we will use the notation of the Z language where appropriate rather than the standard notation of chapter 5.

A1   Induction proofs

Induction is a tool used to prove properties about the non-negative integers. The main idea behind induction is that any non-negative integer can be reached from 0 by adding 1 enough times. Induction proofs can be used when we wish to prove that a given result holds for all positive values of some integer variable, say n, or perhaps for all non-negative values (including zero).

The technique is first to prove the result for some initial value of n, say $n = 0$ or $n = 1$. This is called the *base case* of the proof.

For weak induction, we then assume that the result is true for any particular value of n and show that it must also be true for the value $n+1$. It is equivalent to assume that the result holds for the value $n-1$ and prove that it then holds for the value n. This is called the *induction step*.

If we can prove this, then the informal argument is as follows:

> Prove the result for $n = 1$.
> We proved the result for $n = 1$, so it must hold also for $n = 2$.
> Since it holds for $n = 2$, so it must hold also for $n = 3$.
> Since it holds for $n = 3$, so it must hold also for $n = 4$.

and so on, so that the result holds for all positive values of n.

The proof of the initial value is called the *base* of the proof, and the second part is the *induction step*.

For strong induction, the induction step uses the assumption that the result holds for all values up to and including a particular n to prove that the result will hold for the value $n+1$. An equivalent method is to assume that the

284

theorem holds for all values strictly less than a particular value n, and prove that it then must hold for the value n itself. The argument is now as follows:

> Prove the result for $n = 1$.
> We proved the result for $n = 1$, so it must hold also for $n = 2$.
> Since it holds for $n = 1$ and $n = 2$, so it must hold also for $n = 3$.
> Since it holds for $n = 1$ and $n = 2$ and $n = 3$, so it must hold also for $n = 4$.

and so on, so that the result holds for all positive values of n.

Example   We will show by induction that, for all positive values of n,

$$\sum_{r=1}^{n} r^2 = \tfrac{1}{6}n(n+1)(2n+1).$$

Solution

Base case $(n = 1)$.

$$\sum_{r=1}^{1} r^2 = 1^2 = 1$$

and $\tfrac{1}{6}(1+1)(2 \times 1 + 1) = \tfrac{1}{6}(2) \times (3) = 1$. So the result holds for $n = 1$.

Induction step.   We assume the result holds for a particular value $n = k$, so that we can use the result

$$\sum_{r=1}^{k} r^2 = \tfrac{1}{6}k(k+1)(2k+1).$$

We must show that the result holds for the value $k+1$, that is,

$$\sum_{r=1}^{k+1} r^2 = \tfrac{1}{6}(k+1)(k+2)(2k+3).$$

We have

$$\sum_{r=1}^{k+1} r^2 = \sum_{r=1}^{k} r^2 + (k+1)^2$$

$$= \tfrac{1}{6}k(k+1)(2k+1) + (k+1)^2,$$

by the induction assumption (or hypothesis),

$$= \tfrac{1}{6}(k+1)[k(2k+1) + 6(k+1)],$$

taking $\tfrac{1}{6}(k+1)$ out of the expression,

$$= \tfrac{1}{6}(k+1)(2k^2 + 7k + 6)$$

$$= \tfrac{1}{6}(k+1)(k+2)(2k+3).$$

The result follows for all n by induction.

A2   Set theory

This notation follows the standard mathematical set notation. We will briefly review the main aspects. For a further account see, for example, A. Chetwynd and P. Diggle [1].

A2.1   Comprehensive specification of a set

The comprehensive specification of a set involves three parts, referred to as the *signature* (giving the name and type of the objects to be used), the *formula* and the *term*. A comprehensive specification is written

$$\{\langle identifiers \rangle : \langle superset \rangle \mid \langle formula \rangle \bullet \langle term \rangle\}.$$

For example, the set of positive integers in the range 1 .. 50 is specified as

$$\{n : \mathbb{N}_1 \mid n \leqslant 50 \bullet n\}.$$

Read this as 'For all n in the set of positive natural numbers for which $n \leqslant 50$ we include n in the set.' The set of all positive integers which can be expressed as the sum of three squares could be written

$$\{l, m, n, p : \mathbb{N}_1 \mid p = l^2 + m^2 + n^2 \bullet p\}.$$

The set of pairs of positive integers which can be multiplied together to get 10 is written

$$\{l, m : \mathbb{N}_1 \mid 10 = l \times m \bullet (l, m)\}.$$

Notice that the expression following the $\bullet$ is now a pair of values; the set we are defining is a set of ordered pairs. The set is $\{(1, 10), (10, 1), (2, 5), (5, 2)\}$.

If the list of variables following the initial opening curly bracket is the same as the list following the dot, the latter may be omitted. If no dot appears, insert the initial list of variables there. The first of the above examples would normally appear as

$$\{n : \mathbb{N} \mid n \leqslant 50\}$$

and the third as

$$\{l, m : \mathbb{N} \mid 10 = l \times m\}.$$

It is better to use the longer form for clarity and readability.

Unlike ordinary mathematics, where sets may contain any type of object, sets in Z are all typed by the type of object of which they consist. For example, we will talk of a set of positive integers, or a set of open files, or a set of car ferries. This type will be defined by the superset written after the ':' in the comprehensive specification.

The empty set (written { }) may need special consideration in various contexts.

A2.2   Operations involving sets

The first operators on our list are operators which act on a element and a set of objects of the same type as the object, and deliver a logical result. The two operators are

Meaning	Written
'belongs to' or 'is a member of'	$\in$
'does not belong to' or 'is not a member of'	$\notin$

There are a number of dyadic set-comparison operators delivering logical results. Although mathematically speaking the arguments can be any two sets, in Z they will always be sets of the same type of object. Z is always concerned about the types of objects.

Meaning	Written
subset	$\subseteq$
proper subset	$\subset$
superset	$\supseteq$
proper superset	$\supset$
equality between sets	$=$

These take two sets of the same type of object as arguments and give a logical result.

There is then the monadic operator

Meaning	Written
power set	$\mathbb{P}$

This takes a set as argument. It gives as its result the set of all sets which are subsets of the given set. Thus

$$\mathbb{P}\{1,2,3\} = \{\{\ \}, \{1\}, \{2\}, \{3\}, \{2,3\}, \{1,3\}, \{1,2\}, \{1,2,3\}\}.$$

The empty set will always be included.

We move on to the dyadic operators set union, $\cup$, and intersection, $\cap$. These take two sets as arguments and give a set as their result. When using these operators in Z specifications, the two arguments (and hence the result also) will be sets of the same type of object.

There is a different union operator for combining a number of sets into a single set. We will have a number of sets of the same type of object, and we wish to combine all of their members into one set. This operation is written

$$\bigcup \{S_1, S_2, S_3\}$$

and the result is a single combined set. The sets we wish to combine are expressed as a single set of sets to be given as the single argument to $\bigcup$. The operator is called *generalized union*, and is a monadic operator taking as its single argument a set of sets of the same type.

Similarly, there is a *generalized intersection* operator, written

$$\bigcap \{S_1, S_2, S_3\}.$$

The set difference operator $\langle S_1 \rangle - \langle S_2 \rangle$ takes two sets as arguments. The result is the set of members of S_1 excluding any which also occur in S_2.

The monadic operator 'cardinality of', #, acts upon a set. It delivers the number of elements in the set, $\#\langle set \rangle$, a non-negative integer result. The result is zero for the empty set.

A3 Bags

A *bag* is similar to a set but, whereas a set may contain only one copy of any item, a bag may contain repeated items. There is, however, still no ordering within a bag. The notation for specifying a bag is

$$B_1 = [\![red, red, green, blue]\!]; \qquad B_2 = [\![red, green, pink]\!].$$

The set operator 'is a member of' is replaced by the operator 'in', so that

$$red \text{ in } B_1$$

has the value T. The operator 'in' will have a single object as its left operand and a bag of the same type as its right operand.

The ordinary set union operator is replaced by a *bag union* operator with the obvious result:

$$B_1 \uplus B_2 = [\![red, red, red, green, green, blue, pink]\!].$$

We will also need to be able to find out how many of each type of object exist in a particular bag; bag theory provides a numeric extension of the operator 'is a member of' for sets. This is the function 'count' unique to bags, which takes a bag identifier as argument and delivers as its result a function mapping the items in the bag to the number of occurrences. Thus

$$\text{count } B_1 = \{red \mapsto 2, \; green \mapsto 1, \; blue \mapsto 1\}.$$

A further argument can then be given to this resulting function to find the number of occurrences of a particular given object, so that

$$\text{count } B_1 \, red = 2; \qquad \text{count}(B_1 \uplus B_2) \, red = 3.$$

These could be written with the arguments in parentheses as in

$$\text{count } B_1(red) = 2; \qquad \text{count}(B_1 \uplus B_2)(red) = 3.$$

In a Z schema, an object which is a bag of objects of a given type will be declared as

$$object\_name : \text{bag } type.$$

The empty bag is written

⟦ ⟧.

A4   Relations

If we wish to say that *birthday* is a general relation between objects from the set *NAMES* and objects from the set *DATES*, we will write

   birthday : *NAMES* ↔ *DATES*.

We may also read this as '*birthday* is a relation over *NAMES*×*DATES*'. This is a general relation; it would permit any combination of one-to-one, one-to-many or many-to-one relationships.

A4.1   Domain and range

The monadic operator 'domain of', dom, takes a relation as argument, and delivers the set of 'left-hand' or 'from' elements. The monadic operator 'range of', rng, similarly delivers the set of 'right-hand' or 'into' elements. The results are sets of the appropriate type of elements.

A relation is a set of pairs of objects; relations can therefore be acted upon by any of the set operators above. We can thus have three functions E, J and U defined as sets of pairs of values as

   $E = \{(Eric, 12Mar37)\}$;

   $J = \{(Joy, 10Jun35)\}$;

   $U = \{(Eric, 12Mar37), (Joy, 10Jun35)\}$

and can then use E, J and U as sets as in

   $U = E \cup J$; $U \supseteq E$; $J \subset U$,

or can use them as functions as in

   $U\,Joy = 10Jun35$; $(E \cup J)Eric = 12Mar37$

and so on. Note that some users put parentheses around function arguments, so that the last two examples would become

   $U(Joy) = 10Jun35$; $(E \cup J)(Eric) = 12Mar37$.

In this book we will generally not use the additional parentheses. You may find it clearer to do so.

We then have a group of operators which act on relations and deliver a relation as their result.

A4.2   Composition

The first case if that of 'relation composition'. We can form a new relation by composing two existing relations, where the range of the first will be of the same type as the domain of the second. We write

$$new\_relation = relation_1 \circ relation_2$$

to indicate that *new_relation* is the composition of *relation₁* and *relation₂*. The combined relation has a domain of the same type as the domain of *relation₁* and a range of the same type as the range of *relation₂*. The composition has the effect of applying the first relation, followed by the second one acting on the result.

We can define composition formally as

$$R \circ S = \{x:X, z:Z \mid (\exists y:Y \bullet (x,y) \in R \wedge (y,z) \in S) \bullet (x, z)\}$$

or

$$R \circ S = \{x:X, z:Z \mid (\exists y:Y \bullet Rx = y \wedge Sy = z) \bullet (x,z)\},$$

where R is a relation over $X \times Y$ and S is a relation over $Y \times Z$. Note the similarity between the comprehensive set notation and the quantifier notation; there is a close connection between their meanings.

A relation is said to be *homogeneous* if its domain and range are of the same type. Homogeneous relations can be composed with themselves, and we will write R composed with itself as R^2.

The *identity relation* acting on any element of a given set takes an object into itself. It is usually written id. It must be given a set as its operand and cannot act on elements not in that set.

A4.3   Domain and range operations

There are four dyadic operators: 'domain restrict', $\lhd$, 'range restrict', $\rhd$, and the reverse of these: 'domain exclude', $\overline{\lhd}$, and 'range exclude', $\overline{\rhd}$. Each takes as arguments a relation and a set. The result in each case is a relation of the same type.

Suppose K is the relation

$$K = \{(Angus, \ 6May62), \ (Rory, 27Jan64), \ (Hamish, 24Jul65)\}.$$

Domain restriction takes as its right operand a relation and as its left operand a set of objects of the same type as the domain of the relation. Then domain restriction on the relation such as

$$\{Angus, Hamish\} \lhd K$$

is the relation

{(*Angus*, 6*May*62), (*Hamish*, 24*Jul*65)}.

The domain has been restricted by $\lhd$ to members of the given set. Any item in the relation whose 'left-hand element' is not in the given set has been excluded. Read the expression

{*Angus*, *Hamish*} $\lhd K$

as 'the relation K domain restricted by the set Angus and Hamish'.

The domain exclusion operator works in a similar fashion, but this time the elements in the set given as the left-hand operand are used to exclude certain pairs from the relation. Exactly the same function as we obtained earlier results from using the domain exclusion operator in the expression

{*Rory*} $\ntriangleleft K$

by excluding certain entries from the domain. This is read as 'the relation K domain excluded by the element Rory'.

In these two operators the original relation is the right-hand operand, and the left-hand operand must be a set of objects of the same type as the domain of the relation (usually a proper subset of the domain). The result in both cases is a relation of the same type as that given.

These operators can be defined mathematically as

$$S \lhd R = (\mathrm{id}\, S)\circ R; \qquad S \ntriangleleft R = (\mathrm{dom}\, R - S) \lhd R.$$

Again, if K is the relation defined above, then range restriction works in a similar way on the range of the relation, so that

$K \rhd$ {6*May*62, 24*Jul*65}

is the relation

{(*Angus*, 6*May*62), (*Hamish*, 24*Jul*65)}.

In this case the range has been restricted, the only elements remaining in the function are those whose second part is in the set {6*May*62, 24*Jul*65}. This is read as 'the relation K range restricted by the set Angus and Hamish'. Exactly the same function results from using range exclusion as is

$K \ntriangleright$ {27*Jan*65}

by excluding certain entries from the range. In both of these the original relation appears as the left-hand operand, and the set of objects of the same type as the range of the relation appears as the right-hand operand. The result is a relation of the same type as the original.

These range operators can be defined mathematically as

$$R \rhd S = R\circ(\mathrm{id}\, S); \qquad R \ntriangleright S = R \rhd (\mathrm{rng}\, R - S).$$

A4.4   Override operation

The *override* operator $\oplus$ acts between relations of the same type, and delivers a new relation of the same type. The relation

$$K \oplus \{(Angus, 25Dec\,89)\}$$

is the relation

$$K = \{(Angus, 25Dec\,89), (Rory, 27Jan\,64), (Hamish, 24Jul\,65)\}.$$

Any pairs in the original relation with the same left-hand element as one in the right-hand operand are removed and replaced by the new entry.

   The mathematical definition of this operator could be written as

$$R \oplus S = (\text{dom}\,S \vartriangleleft R) \cup S.$$

A4.5   Set image

The *set image* operator is for viewing a set of objects as transformed by a relation. It is written

$$R(\!|S|\!),$$

where R is a relation and S is a set of objects of the same type as the domain of R. The type of the domain of the relation must be the same as that of the set of objects. The result is a set of objects of the range type of the relation, and consists of the given set of objects after they have been operated upon by the relation. This expression is read as 'the set of objects S viewed through the relation R'. If we have a many-to-one relation, the image may have less elements than the original set, since two or more of the resulting objects may be identical. Thus

$$\{(1,2), (2,2), (3,4), (4,2), (5,3)\}(\!|\{1,2,3\}|\!) = \{2,4\}.$$

Note that

$$R(\!|\text{dom}\,R|\!) = \text{rng}\,R.$$

The *inverse* of a relation is written $\langle relation \rangle^{-1}$, is a relation with its pairs reversed. Note that

$$R^{-1}(\!|\text{rng}\,R|\!) = \text{dom}\,R.$$

The *transitive closure* of a homogeneous operator is the union of all the powers of the operator

$$R \cup (R \circ R) \cup (R \circ R \circ R) \cup \dots .$$

If the relation defines a set of direct interconnections between towns, for example, then

$R \circ R$

gives towns connected using two roads via one intermediate town,

$R \circ R \circ R$

defines those using three roads and going via two intermediate towns, and so on. The transitive closure thus gives the overall connectivity of such a network. This application occurs often in computing. (For example, if a relation specifies for a program the procedures called directly by a given procedure, its closure gives the procedures called directly or indirectly by that procedure. As a second example, we may have two separate networks of interconnected computers. The transitive closure of the connection relation gives the two sets of computers.)

A4.6   Equivalence relations

There is a certain class of relations which are similar to the relation 'equality on numbers' that we are all familiar with. These relations are called 'equivalence relations'.

A relation R on a set A is called an equivalence relation if and only if it satisfies the following three properties:

(a) *Reflexivity*: R is reflexive if and only if for every $a \in A$, $(a, a) \in R$;
(b) *Symmetry*: R is symmetric if and only if $(a, b) \in R \Rightarrow (b, a) \in R$, for example, if aRb then bRa;
(c) *Transitivity*: R is transitive if and only if $((a, b) \in R$ and $(b, c) \in R) \Rightarrow (a, c) \in R$, for example, if aRb and bRc then aRc.

A4.6.1   Examples

Example A1   The most famous equivalence relation is equality on the integers (or reals). It is easy to check that for $n, m, p \in \mathbb{Z}$:

(a) for every $n \in \mathbb{Z}$, $n = n$ (reflexivity);
(b) if $n = m$ then $m = n$ (symmetry);
(c) if $n = m$ and $m = p$ then $n = p$ (transitivity).

Example A2   Consider the relation on the set of integers defined by xRy if and only if x and y leave the same remainder when divided by n, where n is a positive integer. This relation is known as *congruence modulo n* and is usually written $x \equiv y \pmod{n}$. We show that congruence modulo n is an equivalence relation as follows:

(a) Let $x \in \mathbb{Z}$. Then clearly $x \equiv x \pmod{n}$.
(b) Assume that $x \equiv y \pmod{n}$. Then x and y leave the same remainder when they are divided by n. Therefore, y and x leave the same remainder when they are divided by n, i.e. $y \equiv x \pmod{n}$.

(c) Assume that $x \equiv y \pmod{n}$ and $y \equiv z \pmod{n}$. Then x and y leave the same remainder when divided by n and y and z leave the same remainder when divided by n. Therefore, x and z leave the same remainder when divided by n, i.e. $x \equiv z \pmod{n}$.

A5   Functions

A *function* as used in Z is a discrete function, which acts on a discrete element from a particular set (its domain) as its argument, and delivers an corresponding element from the same or another set as its result. For this purpose it is defined to be a relation with its left-hand elements unique. This should not be confused with the term *function* as used in chapter 4 as part of the construction of a term in a first-order language.

The condition for a relation to be a function is that

$$\#R = \#\mathrm{dom}\,R.$$

This therefore excludes one-to-many relations. The function may still be many-to-one, for example the height-and-weight example in the text. We talk of the function *mapping* elements from its domain into elements of its range. The following relations will be functions:

    mapping bank customers to sets of account numbers
        (but not mapping customers to single account numbers,
        since one customer may have several accounts);
    mapping file-names to areas on disk
        (if each file occupies a unique and distinct area);
    mapping car number-plates to model names
        (all number plates should be distinct).

A *partial function* (we will use the symbol $\nrightarrow$ instead of $\leftrightarrow$) is one in which the domain is a proper subset of the possible left-hand elements of the relation. A *total function* (the symbol is $\rightarrow$) is one in which the domain is the complete set. If a relation acts upon the name of a computer and delivers its cost, a total function would have an entry for every known computer, a partial function would have limited information. If a relation acted on bank account numbers and delivered the amount in that account, it would be a partial function from the set of all possible account numbers (perhaps 10-digit numbers), so we would declare it in a Z schema as

   balance : *account_number* $\nrightarrow$ *cash_amount*.

An *injective function* is one whose inverse is also a function. The concepts of partial and total functions still apply. These now give us *partial injective functions* (the symbol is $\rightarrowtail$) and *total injective functions* (with the symbol $\rightarrowtail$). An injective function is a one-to-one relation.

Finally we have *surjective functions* which can be both partial and total. A function is surjective if its range is the total set of possible objects. The adjectives *partial* and *total* still refer to the domain. A function is *bijective* if it is both injective and surjective.

Functions are a particular type of relation. All the operations applicable to relations which were described in the previous section also apply to functions. When writing explicit entries in a function, we shall normally use the $\mapsto$ symbol instead of a comma.

A6   Sequences

The concept of an ordered collection of elements is very important in computing. For example, a *queue* is a collection of objects in which the ordering is important, and will occur in many real-life situations. The order of the disk blocks occupied by a file is important. Sequences are represented in Z by functions whose domain is a continuous range of integers starting at 1, and which maps the number 1 into the first element, 2 to the second element, and so on. In declarations we will use the type seq, as in

> *waiting* : seq *people*;   *file* : seq *blocks*,

where *people* is the type of object in *waiting* and *blocks* is the type of object occupied by a *file*. It is used in a similar context to $\mathbb{P}$, so that

> *family* : $\mathbb{P}$ *people*

gives us an object in which there is no ordering, whereas

> *waiting* : seq *people*

gives an ordered compound object.

If *people* is the set

> {*Fred*, *John*, *Sue*}

we may also, of course, write a sequence explicitly as

> *queue* = {(1, *Fred*), (2, *John*), (3, *Sue*)},

or for more clarity as

> *queue* = {1 $\mapsto$ *Fred*, 2 $\mapsto$ *John*, 3 $\mapsto$ *Sue*}.

To specify a particular sequence directly, the notation can be simplified to

> $\langle$ *Fred*, *John*, *Sue* $\rangle$.

We write the empty sequence as $\langle\ \rangle$.

The concatenation operator $\frown$ acts between sequences, and gives a sequence as a result, with the left-hand operand as the first set of elements in the sequence, followed by the elements from the right-hand operand. All elements are, of course, renumbered to start at 1.

There is a new operator to convert a function to a sequence. This is the monadic operator 'squash' and takes as argument any function whose domain is a subset of $\mathbb{N}_1$. The result is a sequence, in which the range elements of the original function have been ordered by the numeric values in the domain, and the domain elements have been replaced by consecutive integer values starting at 1. Thus

$$\text{squash}\{9 \mapsto e,\, 5 \mapsto f,\, 7 \mapsto r,\, 11 \mapsto d\} = \langle f, r, e, d \rangle.$$

It is often used as in

$$new\_seq = \text{squash}(\{5\} \lhd old\_seq)^\frown another\_seq.$$

There are also the monadic operators 'head' and 'tail' which operate on a sequence. As you would expect, 'head' delivers the first object (a single element), while 'tail' delivers the sequence with the head removed (a sequence which may be empty).

Reference

1. A. Chetwynd and P. Diggle, *Discrete Mathematics*, 1995, Edward Arnold.

APPENDIX B

Other notations

Some books and research papers use other notations for some of the logical operators encountered in this book.

B1 Alternative notations

We will first look at other symbols which are used to represent the common logical operators.

Operation	Our notation	Other notations		
negation	$\neg p$	$\bar{p}$	$\sim p$	p'
conjunction	$p \wedge q$	$p \cdot q$	$p \& q$	
disjunction	$p \vee q$	$p + q$		
equivalence	$p \Leftrightarrow q$	$p \equiv q$	$p \leftrightarrow q$	
non-equivalence	$p \not\Leftrightarrow q$	$p \not\equiv q$	$p \veebar q$	$p \vee_e q$
implication	$p \Rightarrow q$	$p \supset q$	$p \rightarrow q$	

The operators &, $\equiv$ and $\supset$ will be found in older books on logic. The arithmetic operators · and + tend to be used in books geared more towards Boolean algebra than to general logic. In addition, some books replace the $=_{df}$ symbol used earlier on by a $\hat{=}$ symbol.

B2 Polish notation

At times it may be convenient to use the following alternative notations for logical expressions. This is a completely different notation, and was devised by the Polish logician Łukasiewicz. It is therefore sometimes known as Polish or Łukasiewicz or (for reasons which will become apparent) as *parenthesis-free notation* or *prefix notation*. The essence of this notation is that the dyadic operators (operators with two operands) precede their operands instead of

297

appearing between them. This is why the term *prefix notation* is sometimes used. There is also a corresponding *postfix notation*, sometimes called *reverse Polish notation*, in which the operators appear after their operands. The traditional numeric algebraic notation, in which operators appear between their operands, is known as *infix* notation.

In arithmetic formulae, we might have the following examples:

Infix notation	Prefix notation	Postfix notation
$p+q$	$+pq$	$pq+$
$p+q\times r$	$+p\times qr$	$pqr\times+$
$(p+q)\times r$	$\times+pqr$	$pq+r\times$
$(p\times r)+(q\times r)$	$+\times pr\times qr$	$pr\times qr\times+$
$p\times(r+q)\times q$	$\times p\times+rqq$	$prq+\times q\times$
$((p+q)+r)+s$	$+++pqrs$	$pq+r+s+$
$p+(q+(r+s))$	$+p+q+rs$	$qprs+++$

The variables appear in exactly the same order in all variations.

It will be seen from the last two examples that parentheses are never needed in Polish notation. There is no concept of the priority of operators, since the order of evaluation is completely defined by the formula itself. Note also that the variables will consist of single characters, so that sequences of identifiers can be distinguished.

Monadic operators conventionally precede their operands in ordinary infix notation, as in the formulae

$$(p-q)\times-r; \quad -(p\times q/r).$$

This is not fundamental, and certain formalizations are now using monadic operators written after their operand. In prefix notation, monadic operators always precede their operand, and in postfix, they always follow it. For reasons of ambiguity, monadic operators must be distinguishable from dyadic operators in Polish notations. Consider the formula

$$--pq$$

in prefix notation. Since there are two operators and two operands, one of the negations is monadic and one dyadic, but it is not obvious which is which. The two interpretations in infix notation would be

$$-(p-q); \quad ((-p)-q).$$

We therefore use a different symbol for monadic negation, typically θ.

When Łukasiewicz devised his notation for use in logic, he also decided to use upper-case (capital) letters to represent operators instead of symbols. Lower-case letters must be used for variables. The operators are represented by letters as follows:

Infix	Polish
$\neg p$	Np
$p \lor q$	Apq
$p \land q$	Kpq
$p \Rightarrow q$	Cpq
$p \nRightarrow q$	Bpq
$p \Leftrightarrow q$	Epq
$p \nLeftrightarrow q$	Rpq
$p \downarrow q$	Jpq
$p \,/\, q$	Spq

The letters chosen reflect the Polish terms for the operations; think of the 'K' relating to Konjunction, the 'A' to Alternation, and 'C' to Conditional.

Some examples of logical formulae using this notation are the following:

Infix	Prefix
$p \land (q \lor r)$	$KpAqr$
$(p \land q) \lor r$	$AKpqr$
$\neg((\neg p) \lor (\neg q))$	$NANpNq$
$\neg p \lor \neg q \lor r \land \neg p \lor q \lor \neg r$	$ANpANqAKrNpAqNr$
$((p \land q) \land r) \land s$	$KKKpqrs$
$p \land (q \land (r \land s))$	$KpKqKrs$

Again observe that there is no longer any need for parentheses. A significant advantage of this notation is that the major connective can be seen immediately at the beginning of the expression. The absence of parentheses also simplifies any automated searching for common patterns between formulae.

Note that the unbracketed expression

$p \land q \land r \land s$

can be expressed as either

$KKKpqrs$

or

$KpKqKrs$.

Postfix notation is used extensively in computing. The low-level computer operations involved in, for example, multiplying two numbers may typically be

fetch the first number,
fetch the second number,
now multiply,

which can be represented in some way as

$p \; ; \; q \; ; \times \; ;$

In Polish notation, all operators must be distinguishable. Each operator can have as many operands as we wish, providing such details are known in advance, and can deliver more than one result. For conditioned disjunction, we will use the notation $Dqpr$ for $[p, q, r]$; note the change in the order of the operands.

B3   Worked examples

Example B1   Convert the formula

$$p \wedge (p \vee q \Rightarrow (q \Rightarrow r \Rightarrow s))$$

to Polish notation.

Solution

$KpCApqCCqrs$.

Example B2   Translate the following formulae into infix notation:

(a) $AEqNqq$;
(b) $NCCpqNCqp$;
(c) $NCRAqp$;
(d) $CKpKCpqCNrNqEpNRrq$.

Solution

(a) $(p \Leftrightarrow (\neg q)) \vee q$.
(b) $\neg((p \Rightarrow q) \Rightarrow (\neg(q \Rightarrow p)))$.
(c) $\neg(r \Rightarrow (q \vee p))$.
(d) $(p \wedge (p \Rightarrow q) \wedge \neg r \Rightarrow \neg q) \Rightarrow (p \Leftrightarrow \neg(r \Leftrightarrow q))$.

B4   Exercises

Exercise B1   Convert the following infix expressions into Polish notation:

(a) $((p \Leftrightarrow (\neg q)) \vee q)$;
(b) $\neg((p \Rightarrow q) \Rightarrow (\neg(q \Rightarrow p)))$;
(c) $(((\neg p) \wedge (\neg q)) \Rightarrow (\neg r))$;
(d) $(r \Rightarrow (q \vee p))$;
(e) $((q \vee r) \Rightarrow ((\neg r) \Rightarrow q))$.

Exercise B2   Convert the following Polish expressions into infix notation:

(a) *AEpNqq*;
(b) *NCCpqNCqp*;
(c) *NCrAqp*;
(d) *CKpKCpqCNrNqNEpNRrq*;
(e) *AKKApqNSrsqr*.

Symbols used in the book

The following symbols are used in the text.

C1 Truth values

T   the truth-value true
1   the truth-value true (chapter 3)
F   the truth-value false
0   the truth-value false (chapter 3)

C2 Logical operators

$\neg$	$\neg p$	the logical unary negation operator
$\overline{}$	$\bar{p}$	not (chapter 3)
$\wedge$	$p \wedge q$	conjunction, and
$\cdot$	$p \cdot q$	and (chapter 3)
$\vee$	$p \vee q$	disjunction, or
$+$	$p + q$	or (chapter 3)
$\Leftrightarrow$	$p \Leftrightarrow q$	equivalence
$\not\Leftrightarrow$	$p \not\Leftrightarrow q$	non-equivalence, exclusive or
$\Rightarrow$	$p \Rightarrow q$	implication
$:-$	$P :- Q$	implication (chapter 5)
$\Leftarrow$	$p \Leftarrow q$	is implied by
$\not\Rightarrow$	$p \not\Rightarrow q$	non-implication
$/$	p/q	incompatibility, nand
$\downarrow$	$p \downarrow q$	joint denial, nor
$[\,,\,]$	$[p,q,r]$	conditioned disjunction
$\forall x$	$\forall x\, A(x) \Rightarrow B(y)$	for all values of x in the universe of discourse
$\exists x$	$\exists x\, A(x) \Rightarrow B(y)$	there exists at least one value of x in the ...
$\exists! x$	$\exists! x\, A(x) \Rightarrow B(y)$	there exists exactly one value of x in the ...

C3 Metasymbols

P^D		the dual of P
$=_T$	$(p \wedge q)^D =_T p \vee q$	has the same truth-table as
$=_{df}$	$p \Rightarrow q =_{df} \neg p \vee q$	is defined by the function
$\vDash P$		P is a tautology (chapter 1)
$A, B \vDash C$		A, B gives C is a valid argument form
$\vdash P$		P is provable (chapter 2)
$\vdash_L P$		P is provable in system L
$\vdash_K$	$P, (P \Rightarrow Q) \vdash_K Q$	yields in K
$\vdash_{Res}$	$P \vdash_{Res} Q$	yields using only rule Res (chapter 5)
Γ		hypothesis set (chapter 2)
$\Gamma \vdash P$		P is deducible from hypothesis set Γ
$P \dashv\vdash Q$		P and Q are interderivable formulae
$\nvDash_v$	$\mathcal{A} \nvDash_v A$	not satisfied by valuation v (chapter 4)
$T_P \uparrow n$		semantic consequence operator (chapter 5)
p^I		variable p under the interpretation I

C4 Substitutions

$\rightarrow$	$\{y \rightarrow f(a)\}$	a textual substitution
$\circ$	$\theta \circ \sigma$	two substitutions combined

C5 Formal specification using Z

Numbers

$\mathbb{N}$	natural numbers $0, 1, 2, \dots$
$\mathbb{N}_1$	$\mathbb{N}$ (zero excluded) $1, 2, \dots$

Sets

$\mathbb{P}$	$\mathbb{P}\mathbb{N}$	power set operator
$\{\dots\}$	$\{P_1, \dots, P_n\}$	set declaration
$\{ : \mid \bullet \}$	$\{n : \mathbb{N}_1 \mid n \leqslant 50 \bullet n\}$	comprehensive set definition
$\{\ \}$		the empty set
$\in$	$a \in A$	is a member of
$\notin$	$b \notin C$	is not a member of
$\subseteq$	$A \subseteq B$	is a subset of
$\supseteq$	$B \supseteq A$	is a superset of
$\cap$	$A \cap B$	set intersection
$\cup$	$C \cup D$	set union
$\bigcap$	$\bigcap \{S_1, \dots, S_n\}$	generalized intersection
$\bigcup$	$\bigcup^r \; g \; owns$	generalized union
$\#$	$\#A$	cardinality of a set
A^c		universal closure of the set A

Bags

bag		bag type
$[\![\ldots]\!]$	$[\![a_1, \ldots, a_n]\!]$	bag declaration
$[\![\ \ ]\!]$		the empty bag

Sequences

seq		sequence type
$\langle \ldots \rangle$	$\langle a_1, \ldots, a_n \rangle$	sequence declaration
$\langle\ \rangle$		the empty sequence
$\frown$	$\langle a \rangle \frown \langle b, c \rangle$	concatenation of sequences

Relations

$\leftrightarrow$	$A \leftrightarrow B$	general relation type
$\nrightarrow$	$A \nrightarrow B$	partial function type
$\rightarrow$	$A \rightarrow B$	total function type
$\mapsto$	$A \mapsto B$	maps onto
dom	dom $owns$	domain of
rng	rng $owns$	range of
$\vartriangleleft\!\!\!-$	$\{user?\} \vartriangleleft\!\!\!- owns$	domain exclusion operator
$\vartriangleleft$	$\{user?\} \vartriangleleft owns$	domain restriction operator
$\vartriangleright\!\!\!-$	$owns \vartriangleright\!\!\!- \{user?\}$	range exclusion operator
$\vartriangleright$	$owns \vartriangleright \{user?\}$	range restriction operator
$\oplus$	$S \oplus S_1$	override operator
$(\!\!(\ldots)\!\!)$	$R (\!\!(S)\!\!)$	set image operator

Logic

$\forall$	$\forall x : S \bullet P(x)$	universal quantifier
$\exists$	$\exists x : S \bullet P(x)$	existential quantifier
$\exists!$	$\exists! x : S \bullet P(x)$	unique existential quantifier
Ω	$\Omega x : S \bullet P(n)$	counting quantifier
Σ	$\Sigma n : S \bullet N(n)$	summation quantifier

Schema

Δ	$\Delta video\_shop$	incremental inclusion
Ξ	$\Xi video\_shop$	identity inclusion
::=	$MESSAGE ::= yes \,\vert\, no$	free type definition
$\triangleq$	$schema\_2 \triangleq s \wedge t$	schema define
tuple	tuple $video\_shop$	declaration tuple operator
pred	pred $video\_shop$	schema predicate operator
/	new_name / old_name	identifier renaming operator
\	$\backslash old\_name$	identifier hiding operator
pre	pre $video\_shop$	pre-condition operator
;	$Grab \,;\, New$	schema compose
$\gg$	$u \triangleq s \gg t$	schema pipe

Index

absurdity, 13
accordion, 3
adders, 113
addition, 7
adequate set of connectives, 21
algebra, Z schema, 256
algebraic notation, 298
alphabet, 53, 143
alternation, 4
alternative notation, 297
ambiguity in prefix notation, 298
and, 2
answer substitution, 207, 219
argument forms, 32
arithmetic, 298
arrow, 16
artificial intelligence, 6
assertion, 13
assertium, 15
associative, 4
associativity, 172
at least one, two, three, 18
at most one, two, three, 19
atom, 146
axiom, axiom scheme, 54, 61
axioms for predicate logic, 162

backtracking, 197, 222
bag, 288
    empty, 289
    union, 288
base, Herbrand, 156
base case, induction, 284
basic type definition, 234, 244, 256
belongs to a set, 287
biconditional, 7

bijective functions, 295
binary, 2
binding, 8, 214
Boolean algebra, 297
bound, 135, 147
    variable, 135
bracketed, 27
branching tree, 196

capital letters, 12
cardinality of a set, 288
clausal form, 204
clause, propositional logic, 191
closed, 147
    first-order theory, 181
    -world assumption, 199, 223
closure, transitive, 292
    universal, 147
CNF, 26
combination, 3
commutative, 3
commutativity, 172
complete
    adders, 115
    set of connectives, 21
completeness theorem, 74
composition, 215
    of relations, 290
    of schema, 260
comprehensive specification of a set, 286
computable, 75
concatenation operator, 295
conditional proof, 80
conditioned
    disjunction, 17
    incompatibility, 17

congruence modulo n, 293
conjunct, 4
conjunction, 2
conjunctive normal form (CNF), 26
connective, 1
consequent, 34
consistency, 248
consistent
  first-order theory, 180
  substitution, 33
constant, logical, 23
construct a truth-table, 9
contingent, 13
contradiction, 13
contrapositive, 6
correct answer substitution, 219
count operator for bags, 288
counting quantifier in Z, 242
cover, 101
CP rule, 80
CWA, 199

De Morgan's law, 27
decidable, 75
declaration part of a Z schema, 233, 244
deduction
  first-order theory, 172
  in L, 63
  predicate logic, 163
  propositional logic, 55
  rules of, 55
  theorem, 65
    predicate logic, 166
definite clause, 191
degenerate, 15
delta ornamentation, 257
derived
  object in Z, 235
  rules, 163
difference (between sets), 288
disagreement set, 217
disjoin, 24
disjunction, 4
disjunctive normal form (DNF), 25
DN rule, 80
DNF, 25
domain, 289
  exclusion, 290
  of quantification, 134
  of a Z function, 234
  restriction, 290
don't care, 104
double negation rule, 80

dual, 29, 96
dyadic, 2

EE rule, 175
EI rule, 175
elimination of
  $\wedge$, 80
  $\vee$, 80
  quantifiers, 175
empty
  bag, 289
  clause, 193
  sequence, 295
  set, 243, 286
enumeration, 181
equality (between sets), 287
equation solving, 202
equivalence, 7
  relations, 293
error handling in Z, 238
exclamation mark in Z, 233, 237
exclusion
  domain, 290
  range, 291
exclusive or, 4, 7, 16
existential quantifier, 135
exists quantifier in Z, unique, 242
extension, 181
  of a first-order language, 182
  schema, 256

failure, negation as, 199
false, interpretation, 152
falsum, 15, 16
FCNF, 25
FDNF, 24
file-system example, 249
first-order
  language, 131, 143
  theory, 171
flip-flops, 116
for all, 134
formal system specification, 232
formula (in a set specification), 286
free, 147
  for, 147
  type definition, 238, 244, 256
full
  adder, 114
  conjunctive normal form (FCNF), 25
  disjunctive normal form (FDNF), 24
fullness, 181

function, 294
  bijective, 295
  injective, 294
  mapping by a, 234, 294
  partial, 294
  surjective, 295
  total, 294
general structure, 171
generalization rule, 162
generalized
  De Morgan's law, 27
  intersection, 288
  union, 287
goal clause, 191
  predicate logic, 207
ground
  instance, 215
  substitution, 215

half adder, 114
head (of a clause), 19₁
height and weight example, 233
Herbrand
  base, 156
  interpretation, 156
  model, 157
  universe, 156
hiding identifiers in Z, 259
homogeneous, 290
Horn clause, propositional logic, 191, 206
HS, 68
hypothesis, 34, 55
hypothetical syllogism
  predicate logic, 165
  propositional logic, 68

i-equivalent, 151
identical truth-tables, 11
identifier
  hiding in Z, 259
  renaming in Z, 259
identity
  relation, 290
  substitution, 215
if, 6
if-and-only-if, 36
image of a set, 292
implication, 5
in operator for bags, 288
inclusion, schema, 245, 247, 257
inclusive or, 4
incompatibility, 16
independence of axioms, 76

index of symbols, 302
induction
  proof, 284
  step, 284
  strong, 284
  weak, 284
infix notation, 298
information schema in Z, 237
injective function, 294
input value in Z, 233, 236, 247
instance, 215
interderivable, 57, 71
interpretation, 59, 148
  first-order language, 149
  Herbrand, 156
intersection, 133, 287
  generalized, 288
introduction of
  $\wedge$, 80
  $\vee$, 80
  quantifiers, 175
invariant ornamentation, 257
invariants in Z, 235
inverse
  deduction theorem, 67
  of a relation, 292

joint denial, 16

Karnaugh map, 101

L_1 function, 18
L_2 function, 18
L_3 function, 18
leading edge, 119
Lemmon, E. J. 78
Lindenbaum's lemma, 186
linear notation in Z, 256
literal, 204
logic
  operation on schema, 257
  program, predicate logic, 206
logical
  constant, 23
  equivalence, 32
  formulation, 138
  implication, 32
logically
  equivalent, 13
  implies, 13
  valid, 152
lower-case, 12
Łukasiewicz notation, 297

M_i function, 19
majority function, 18
map, Karnaugh, 101
mapping by a function, 234, 294
mathematical background, 284
maximal first-order theory, 181
McClusky–Quine minimization, 105
Meccano, 96
member of a set, 287
minterm, 105
mixed formula, 13
model
  first-order theory, 172
  Herbrand, 157
  interpretation, 152
modus
  ponens (MP), 55
  tollens (MT), 80
monadic, 2, 15
most-general unifier, 217
MP rule, 55, 80
MT rule, 80

nand, 16
negation, 2
  as failure, 199, 223
negative
  literal, 204
  propositional literal, 190
non-equivalence, 16
non-implication, 17
non-membership of a set, 287
nor, 16
normal
  form, 24
    conjunctive, 26
    disjunctive, 25
    full conjunctive, 25
    full disjunctive, 24
  model, 171
not, 2
numeric algebraic notation, 298

observation schema, 254
  in Z, 237, 248
occurs check, 217
operation schema in Z, 235, 246
or, 4
ornamentation
  delta, 257
  invariant, 257
  schema, 246, 257
output value in Z, 233
override, 292

parenthesis-free notation, 297
partial function, 294
Pierce's arrow, 16
piping, schema, 262
Polish notation, 297
positive
  literal, 204
  propositional literal, 190
post-condition in Z, 236, 241
postfix notation, 298, 299
power set, 287
pre-condition
  in Z, 236, 241
  schema, 260
predicate, 131
  operator in Z, 257
  part in Z, 233, 244
prefix notation, 297
premise, 5, 55
prenex form, 202
prime (') in Z, 246
priority of operators, 8
procedure, rules of, 55
program clause, 191
proof
  first-order theory, 172
  induction, 284
  Lemmon style, 80
  predicate logic, 163
  propositional logic, 55
proper
  subset, 287
  superset, 287
propositional
  clause, 191
  Horn clause, 191
  literal, 190
  logic program, 191
  resolution, 192
  tautology, 163
provable equivalence, 170
pseudo-Sheffer function, 23

quantification, domain of, 134
quantifier, 133
  in Z, 242
  existential, 135
  universal, 134
  Z schema, 258
query, 193
  schema in Z, 237
question mark in Z, 233, 236
queue, 295
Quine–McClusky minimization, 105

RAA rule, 80
range, 289
   exclusion, 291
   restriction, 291
reductio ad absurdum, 80
reflexivity, 293
refutation, 193
   by resolution, 194
   system, 207
relation, 138, 289
relations
   composition of, 290
   equivalence, 293
relay, 97
renaming
   identifiers in Z, 259
   variable, 217
resolution, 190
   propositional logic, 192
   refutation by, 194
   rule, 192
   tree, 196
restriction
   domain, 290
   range, 291
reverse Polish notation, 298
rule, resolution, 192
rules
   derived, 163
   for predicate logic, 162
   of deduction, 55
   of procedure, 55

satisfaction, 152
scale-of-two circuit, 118
schema
   algebra in Z, 238
   composition, 260
   extension, 256
   in Z, 233
   inclusion, 245, 247, 257
   observation, 254
   ornamentation, 246, 257
   piping, 262
   pre-condition, 260
   quantifier, Z, 258
scope, 135, 147
selection function, 200, 201
semantic consequence operator, 213
semantics, 131
sequence, 295
   empty, 295
   logic, 115

set, 133
   belongs to a, 287
   cardinality of a, 288
   comprehensive specification of a, 286
   difference, 288
   empty, 286
   image, 292
   member of a, 287
   non-membership of a, 287
   theory, 286
Sheffer function, 23
   stroke, 16
SI rule, 93
signature (in a set specification), 286
simplification, 98
Skolemization, 204
SLD
   selection, linear and definite, 220
   resolution, 199
soundness theorem, 72
specification, formal, 232
squash sequence operator, 296
state
   change in Z, 235
   schema in Z, 234, 245
state-space schema in Z, 234, 245
stroke, 16
strong induction, 284
subgoal, 196
subset, 287
substitution, 54, 214
   answer, 207
   instance, 93
   rule, 33
summation quantifier in Z, 243
superset, 287
surjective function, 295
symbols used in the book, 302
symmetry, 293
system specification, 232

tail (of a clause), 191
tautology
   propositional, 163
   propositional logic, 12
term, 146
   equation, 216
   in a set specification, 286
theorem
   first-order theory, 172
   of L, 62
   predicate logic, 163
there exists, 135
tollens, modus, 80

top-down, 199
total function, 294
transistor, 97
transitive closure, 292
transitivity, 293
true, interpretation, 152
truth, 152
truth-table, 2
truth-value, 1
tuple operator in Z, 257

UDE, 110
UE rule, 175
UI rule, 175
unary, 2
unification, 214
   theorem, 218
unifier, 216
union, 287
   bag, 288
   generalized, 287
unique exists in Z, 242
unit clause, 191

universal
   closure, 147
   decision element, 110
   quantifier, 134
universe, Herbrand, 156
upper-case, 12

valuation, first-order language, 151
variable
   bound, 135
   pure substitution, 215
   renaming, 217
verum, 15, 16

weak induction, 284
well-formed formula, 53
wff, 53
   in $\mathcal{L}$, 147
whenever, 6

Z
   schema, 233
      algebra, 256
   specification language, 232